# Research Methods
## Core Concepts and Skills for Psychology
## Version 2.0

Paul C. Price

978-1-4533-9203-4

Research Methods: Core Concepts and Skills for Psychology
Version 2.0

Paul C. Price

Published by:

FlatWorld
175 Portland Street
Boston, MA 02114

# Brief Contents

# Contents

# About the Author

Paul C. Price received his B.A. in psychology from Washington University and his M.A. and Ph.D. in cognitive psychology from the University of Michigan. Since 1996 he has been a professor of psychology at California State University, Fresno—teaching research methods and statistics, along with courses in judgment and decision making, social cognition, and health psychology. In 2018, he won the Provost's Award for Excellence in Teaching—his university's highest teaching honor. Paul also directs the Judgment and Reasoning Lab at California State University, Fresno. The research that he and his students conduct has been funded by the National Science Foundation and has resulted in numerous journal publications and conference presentations. Paul is also a regular peer reviewer for several professional journals and on the editorial board of the *Journal of Behavioral Decision Making*.

# Acknowledgments

This book would certainly not exist without the support of several organizations and individuals. California State University, Fresno has provided me the space and time to conduct research, to teach about conducting research, and now to write about conducting research. My colleagues in the Department of Psychology have been generous with their advice and encouragement. Karl Oswald, in particular, has been a valued source of ideas related to teaching—especially the teaching of research methods—for many years now. On the publishing side, Michael Boezi, Jenn Yee, and Melissa Yu were instrumental in bringing version 1.0 into existence. The same is true of the incredibly patient Lindsey Kaetzel for version 2.0.

The following external reviewers provided numerous comments and suggestions that improved the book tremendously.

Stan Morse, University of Massachuetts Boston

Gary Starr, Metropolitan State University

Seth Wagerman, California Lutheran University

Harold Stanislaw, California State University, Stanislaus

Laura Edelman, Mulhenberg College

Harvey Ginsburg, Texas State University

Pamela Schuetze, SUNY College at Buffalo

Luis A. Vega, California State University, Bakersfield

Luis A. Cordón, Eastern Connecticut State University

Donald Keller, George Washington University

Di You, Alvernia University

April Fugett Fuller, Marshall University

Kristie Campana, Minnesota State University, Mankato

Carrie Wyland, Tulane University

Matthew Wiediger, MacMurray College

Mark G. Rivardo, Saint Vincent College

Romona F Banks, Ashford University

Khaled Wahba, Algoma University, Ontario, Canada

Mark Chu, Western New Mexico University

Finally, I would like to thank my family—Barb, Joe, and Vera—for all their support over the years. I love you guys.

# Dedication

## Paul C. Price

To all my research methods students—past, present, and future.

# Preface

The research methods course is among the most frequently required in the psychology major—and with good reason. Consider that a cross-cultural psychologist and a cognitive neuroscientist meeting at a professional conference might know next to nothing about the phenomena and theories that are important in each other's work. Yet they would certainly both know about the difference between an experiment and a correlational study, the function of independent and dependent variables, the importance of reliability and validity in psychological measurement, and the need for replication in psychological research. In other words, psychologists' research methods are at the very core of their discipline.

At the same time, most students majoring in psychology do not go on to graduate school. And among those who do, only a fraction become cross-cultural psychologists, cognitive neuroscientists, or researchers of any sort. The rest pursue careers in clinical practice, social services, and a wide variety of fields that may be completely unrelated to psychology. For these students, the study of research methods is important primarily because it prepares them to be effective consumers of psychological research and because it promotes critical thinking skills and attitudes that are applicable in many areas of life.

My goal, then, was to write a book that would present the methodological concepts and skills that are widely shared by researchers across the field of psychology and to do so in a way that would also be accessible to a wide variety of students. Among the features I tried to incorporate to help achieve this goal are the following.

- Straightforward Writing—I have kept the writing simple and clear, avoiding idiosyncratic terminology and concepts that rarely come up in practice.
- Limited References—Instead of including several hundred references (which would be typical), I have limited the references to methodological classics and to sources that serve as specific examples.
- Minimal Digressions—I have tried to minimize technical and philosophical digressions to avoid distracting students from the main points. (The instructor's manual, however, includes ideas for incorporating such digressions into lecture.)
- Diverse Examples—I have used a variety of examples from across the entire range of psychology—including plenty of examples from clinical and counseling psychology, which tend to be underrepresented in research methods textbooks.
- Traditional Structure—By and large I have maintained the overall structure of the typical introductory research methods textbook, which should make it relatively easy for experienced instructors to use.

This book evolved from a series of handouts that I wrote for my own students because I was frustrated by the cost of existing textbooks. This is why I am especially excited to be publishing with FlatWorld. I hope you find that *Research Methods: Core Concepts and Skills* serves your own purposes...and I look forward to hearing about your experiences with it.

Paul C. Price

# What's New in Version 2.0

Based on positive feedback from users of Version 1.0, I have retained the style, structure, and nearly all the content of the original. Among the most important changes are the following:

- I have checked and updated all external links and added several new ones.
- I have added several "callouts" (or sidebars) on a variety of interesting and useful topics, including *Open Access Journals*, *Estimating Pearson's* r, *Online Measurement Resources*, *WEIRD People*, and *Looking Up the* p *Value*.
- I have eliminated the tables of critical values on Chapter 13 and focused on using $p$ value calculators to obtain the exact $p$ value.
- I have added a final chapter titled *The Big Picture* that describes concerns about some traditional research practices and their effect on the reliability of research results (i.e., the "replication crisis"). In this chapter, I also present meta-analysis and the open science movement as ways to address these concerns.

# CHAPTER 1
# Scientific Psychology

Many people believe that women tend to talk more than men—with some even suggesting that this difference has a biological basis. One widely cited estimate is that women speak 20,000 words per day on average and men speak only 7,000. This claim seems plausible, but is it *true*? A group of psychologists led by Matias Mehl decided to find out. They checked to see if anyone had actually tried to count the daily number of words spoken by women and men. No one had. So these researchers conducted a study in which female and male college students (369 in all) wore audio recorders while they went about their lives. The result? The women spoke an average of 16,215 words per day and the men spoke an average of 15,669—an extremely small difference that could easily be explained by chance. In an article in the journal *Science*, these researchers summed up their findings as follows: "We therefore conclude, on the basis of available empirical evidence, that the widespread and highly publicized stereotype about female talkativeness is unfounded" (Mehl, Vazire, Ramirez-Esparza, Slatcher, & Pennebaker, 2007, p. 82).[1]

**FIGURE 1.1**

Although many people believe that women are more talkative than men, scientific research on college students suggests that there is no overall difference.

Source: © Thinkstock

Psychology is usually defined as the scientific study of human behavior and mental processes, and this example illustrates the features that make it scientific. In this chapter, we look closely at these features, introduce a model of scientific research in psychology, and address several basic questions that students often have about it. Who conducts scientific research in psychology? Why? Does scientific psychology tell us anything that common sense does not? Why should I bother to learn the scientific approach—especially if I want to be a clinical psychologist and not a researcher? These are extremely good questions, by the way, and answering them now will provide a solid foundation for learning the rest of the material in this book.

# 1.1 Understanding Science

## Learning Objectives

1. Define science.
2. Describe three fundamental features of science.
3. Explain why psychology is a science.
4. Define pseudoscience and give some examples.
5. Explain the limitations of common sense when it comes to achieving a detailed and accurate understanding of human behavior.

# What Is Science?

Some people are surprised to learn that psychology is a **science**. They generally agree that astronomy, biology, and chemistry are sciences but wonder what psychology has in common with these other fields. Before answering this question, however, it is worth reflecting on what astronomy, biology, and chemistry have in common with *each other*. It is clearly not their subject matter. Astronomers study celestial bodies, biologists study living organisms, and chemists study matter and its properties. It is also not the equipment and techniques that they use. Few biologists would know what to do with a radio telescope, for example, and few chemists would know how to track a moose population in the wild. For these and other reasons, philosophers and scientists who have thought deeply about this question have concluded that what the sciences have in common is a general approach to understanding the natural world. Psychology is a science because it takes this same general approach to understanding one aspect of the natural world: human behavior.

# Features of Science

The general scientific approach can be said to have three fundamental features (Stanovich, 2010).[2] The first is **systematic empiricism**. Empiricism means learning based on observation, so scientists learn about the natural world systematically, by carefully planning, making, recording, and analyzing observations of it. As we will see, logical reasoning and even creativity play important roles in science too, but scientists are unique in their insistence on checking their ideas about the way the world is against their systematic observations. Notice, for example, that Mehl and his colleagues did not trust other people's stereotypes or even their own informal observations. Instead, they systematically recorded, counted, and compared the number of words spoken by a large sample of women and men. Furthermore, when their systematic observations turned out to conflict with the stereotype, they trusted their systematic observations.

The second feature of the scientific approach—which follows in a straightforward way from the first—is that it concerns **empirical questions**. These are questions about the way the world actually is and, therefore, can be answered by systematically observing it. The question of whether women talk more than men is empirical in this way. Either women really do talk more than men or they do not, and this can be determined by systematically observing how much women and men actually talk. There are many interesting and important questions that are not empirically testable and that science cannot answer. Among them are questions about values—whether things are good or bad, just or unjust, or beautiful or ugly—and questions about how things *ought* to be. So, although the question of whether a stereotype is accurate or inaccurate is an empirically testable one that science can answer, the question of whether it is bad for people to hold inaccurate stereotypes is not. Similarly, the question of whether criminal behavior has a genetic component is an empirical question that science can answer, but the question of what should be done with people who commit crimes is not. It is especially important for researchers in psychology to be mindful of this distinction.

The third feature of science is that it creates **public knowledge**. After asking their empirical questions, making their systematic observations, and drawing their conclusions, scientists publish their work. This usually means writing an article for publication in a professional journal, in which they put their research question in the context of previous research, describe in detail the methods they used to answer their question, and clearly present their results and conclusions. Publication is an essential feature of science for two reasons. One is that science is a social process—a large-scale collaboration among many researchers distributed across both time and space. Our current scientific knowledge of most topics is based on many different studies conducted by many different researchers who have shared their work with each other over the years. The second is that publication allows science to be self-correcting. Individual scientists understand that despite their best efforts, their methods can be flawed and their conclusions incorrect. Publication allows others in the scientific community to detect and correct these errors so that, over time, scientific knowledge increasingly reflects the way the world actually is.

# Science Versus Pseudoscience

**Pseudoscience** refers to activities and beliefs that are claimed to be scientific by their proponents—and may *appear* to be scientific at first glance—but are not. Consider the theory of biorhythms (not to be confused with sleep cycles or other biological cycles that do have a scientific basis). The idea is that people's physical, intellectual, and emotional abilities run in cycles that begin when they are born and continue until they die. The physical cycle has a period of 23 days, the intellectual cycle a period of 33 days, and the emotional cycle a period of 28 days. So, for example, if you had the option of when to schedule an exam, you would want to schedule it for a time when your intellectual cycle will be at a high point. The theory of biorhythms has been around for more than 100 years, and you can find numerous popular books and websites about biorhythms, often containing impressive and scientific-sounding terms like *sinusoidal wave* and *bioelectricity*. The problem with biorhythms, however, is that there is no evidence that they exist and plenty of evidence that they do not (Hines, 1998).[3]

A set of beliefs or activities can be said to be pseudoscientific if (a) its adherents claim or imply that it is scientific but (b) it lacks one or more of the three features of science. It might lack systematic empiricism. Either there is no relevant scientific research or, as in the case of biorhythms, there is relevant scientific research but it is ignored. It might also lack public knowledge. People who promote the beliefs or activities might claim to have conducted scientific research but never publish that research in a way that allows others to evaluate it.

A set of beliefs and activities might also be pseudoscientific because it does not address empirical questions. The philosopher Karl Popper was especially concerned with this idea (Popper, 2002).[4] He argued more specifically that any scientific claim must be expressed in such a way that there are observations that would—if they were made—count as evidence against the claim. In other words, scientific claims must be **falsifiable**. The claim that women talk more than men is falsifiable because systematic observations could reveal either that they do talk more than men or that they do not. As an example of an unfalsifiable claim, consider that many people who study extrasensory perception (ESP) and other psychic powers claim that such powers can disappear when they are observed too closely. This makes it so that no possible observation would count as evidence against ESP. If a careful test of a self-proclaimed psychic showed that she predicted the future at better-than-chance levels, this would be consistent with the claim that she had psychic powers. But if she failed to predict the future at better-than-chance levels, this would also be consistent with the claim because her powers can supposedly disappear when they are observed too closely.

Why should we concern ourselves with pseudoscience? There are at least three reasons. One is that learning about pseudoscience helps bring the fundamental features of science—and their importance—into sharper focus. A second is that biorhythms, psychic powers, astrology, and many other pseudoscientific beliefs are widely held and are promoted on the Internet, on television, and in books and magazines. Learning what makes them pseudoscientific can help us to identify and evaluate such beliefs and practices when we encounter them. A third reason is that many pseudosciences purport to explain some aspect of human behavior and mental processes, including biorhythms, astrology, graphology (handwriting analysis), and magnet therapy for pain control. It is important for students of psychology to distinguish their own field clearly from this "pseudopsychology."

**pseudoscience**

A set of beliefs or activities that is claimed to be scientific but lacks one or more of the three features of science.

**falsifiability**

An important property of scientific claims. A claim is falsifiable if there is an observation that would—if it were made—count as evidence against the claim.

## The Skeptic's Dictionary

An excellent source for information on pseudoscience is *The Skeptic's Dictionary* (http://www.skepdic.com). Among the pseudoscientific beliefs and practices you can learn about are the following:

- **Cryptozoology.** The study of "hidden" creatures like Bigfoot, the Loch Ness monster, and the chupacabra.
- **Pseudoscientific psychotherapies.** Past-life regression, rebirthing therapy, and bio-scream therapy, among others.
- **Homeopathy.** The treatment of medical conditions using natural substances that have been diluted in a solution, sometimes to the point of no longer being present.
- **Pyramidology.** Odd theories about the origins and functions of the Egyptian pyramids (e.g., that they were built by extraterrestrials) and the idea that pyramids in general have healing and other special powers.

## Key Takeaways

- Science is a general way of understanding the natural world. Its three fundamental features are systematic empiricism, empirical questions, and public knowledge.
- Psychology is a science because it takes the scientific approach to understanding human behavior.
- Pseudoscience refers to beliefs and activities that are claimed to be scientific but lack one or more of the three features of science. It is important to distinguish the scientific approach to understanding human behavior from the many pseudoscientific approaches.
- People's intuitions about human behavior, also known as folk psychology, often turn out to be wrong. This is one primary reason that psychology is based on scientific research rather than common sense.

## Exercises

1. Discussion: People sometimes suggest that psychology cannot be a science because either (a) human behavior cannot be predicted with perfect accuracy or (b) much of its subject matter (e.g., thoughts and feelings) cannot be observed directly. Do you agree or disagree with each of these ideas? Why?
2. Practice: List three empirical questions about human behavior. List three nonempirical questions about human behavior.
3. Discussion: Consider the following psychological claim. "People's choice of spouse is strongly influenced by their perception of their own parents. Some choose a spouse who is similar in some way to one of their parents. Others choose a spouse who is different from one of their parents." Is this claim falsifiable? If not, how could it be changed so that it is?
4. Practice: For each of the following intuitive beliefs about human behavior, list three reasons that it might be true and three reasons that it might not be true:
    a. You cannot truly love another person unless you love yourself.
    b. People who receive "crisis counseling" immediately after experiencing a traumatic event are better able to cope in the long run.
    c. Studying is most effective when it is always done in the same location.

# 1.2 Scientific Research in Psychology

## Learning Objectives

1. Describe a general model of scientific research in psychology and give specific examples that fit the model.
2. Explain who conducts scientific research in psychology and why they do it.
3. Distinguish between basic research and applied research.

## A Model of Scientific Research in Psychology

Figure 1.2 presents a more specific model of scientific research in psychology. The researcher (who more often than not is really a small group of researchers) formulates a research question, conducts a study designed to answer the question, draws conclusions about the answer to the question, and publishes the results so that they become part of the research literature. Because the research literature is one of the primary sources of new research questions, this process can be thought of as a cycle. New research leads to new questions, which lead to new research, and so on. Figure 1.2 also indicates that research questions can originate outside of this cycle either with informal observations or with practical problems that need to be solved. But even in these cases, the researcher would start by checking the research literature to see if the question had already been answered and to refine it based on what previous research had already found.

**FIGURE 1.2** A Simple Model of Scientific Research in Psychology

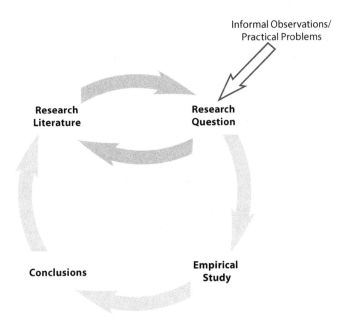

The research by Mehl and his colleagues is described nicely by this model. Their question—whether women are more talkative than men—was suggested to them both by people's stereotypes and by published claims about the relative talkativeness of women and men. When

they checked the research literature, however, they found that this question had not been adequately addressed in scientific studies. They conducted a careful empirical study—finding very little difference between women and men—and published their work so that it became part of the research literature. The publication of their article is not the end of the story, however, because their work suggests many new questions (about the reliability of the result, about potential cultural differences, etc.) that will likely be taken up by them and by other researchers inspired by their work.

**FIGURE 1.3**
Scientific research has confirmed that cell phone use impairs a variety of driving behaviors.

Source: © 2010 Thinkstock

As another example, consider that as cell phones became more widespread during the 1990s, people began to wonder whether, and to what extent, cell phone use had a negative effect on driving. Many psychologists decided to tackle this question scientifically (Collet, Guillot, & Petit, 2010).[5] It was clear from previously published research that engaging in a simple verbal task impairs performance on a perceptual or motor task carried out at the same time, but no one had studied the effect specifically of cell phone use on driving. Under carefully controlled conditions, these researchers compared people's driving performance while using a cell phone with their performance while not using a cell phone, both in the lab and on the road. They found that people's ability to detect road hazards, reaction time, and control of the vehicle were all impaired by cell phone use. Each new study was published and became part of the growing research literature on this topic.

# Who Conducts Scientific Research in Psychology?

**doctor of philosophy [PhD]**

The highest degree in most academic fields, including psychology. Scientific researchers in psychology typically have this degree.

Scientific research in psychology is generally conducted by people with doctoral degrees (usually the **doctor of philosophy [PhD]**) and master's degrees in psychology and related fields, often supported by research assistants with bachelor's degrees or other relevant training. Some of them work for government agencies, for nonprofit organizations, or in the private sector. However, the majority are college and university faculty members, who often collaborate with their graduate and undergraduate students. Although some researchers are trained and licensed as clinicians—especially those who conduct research in clinical psychology—the majority are not. Instead, they have expertise in one or more of the many other subfields of psychology: behavioral neuroscience, cognitive psychology, developmental psychology, personality psychology, social psychology, and so on. Doctoral-level researchers might be employed to conduct research full-time or, like many college and university faculty members, to conduct research in addition to teaching classes and serving their institutions and communities in other ways.

Of course, people also conduct research in psychology because they enjoy the intellectual and technical challenges involved and the satisfaction of contributing to scientific knowledge of human behavior. You might find that you enjoy the process too. If so, your college or university might offer opportunities to get involved in ongoing research as either a research assistant or a participant. Of course, you might find that you do not enjoy the process of conducting scientific research in psychology. But at least you will have a better understanding of where scientific knowledge in psychology comes from, an appreciation of its strengths and limitations, and an awareness of how it can be applied to solve practical problems in psychology and everyday life.

## Scientific Psychology Online

A fun and easy way to learn about current scientific research in psychology is to follow some of the many thought-provoking blogs and Twitter accounts that summarize new studies and discuss their implications. Consider starting with the ones listed below.

- **Blogs**
  - Mind Hacks: http://www.mindhacks.com
  - British Psychological Society's Research Digest: http://digest.bps.org.uk
  - PsyBlog: http://www.spring.org.uk
- **Twitter Accounts**
  - Association for Psychological Science: http://www.twitter.com/PsychScience
  - Dan Ariely: http://www.twitter.com/danariely
  - Psychology Today: http://www.twitter.com/PsychToday
  - Society for a Science of Clinical Psychology: http://www.twitter.com/_SSCP
  - Stanford University Department of Psychology: http://www.twitter.com/StanfordPsych

# The Broader Purposes of Scientific Research in Psychology

People have always been curious about the natural world, including themselves and their behavior. (In fact, this is probably why you are studying psychology in the first place.) Science grew out of this natural curiosity and has become the best way to achieve detailed and accurate knowledge. Keep in mind that most of the phenomena and theories that fill psychology textbooks are the products of scientific research. In a typical introductory psychology textbook, for example, one can learn about specific cortical areas for language and perception, principles of classical and operant conditioning, biases in reasoning and judgment, and people's surprising tendency to obey authority. And scientific research continues because what we know right now only scratches the surface of what we *can* know.

Scientific research is often classified as being either basic or applied. **Basic research** in psychology is conducted primarily for the sake of achieving a more detailed and accurate understanding of human behavior, without necessarily trying to address any particular practical problem. The research of Mehl and his colleagues falls into this category. **Applied research** is conducted primarily to address some practical problem. Research on the effects of cell phone use on driving, for example, was prompted by safety concerns and has led to the enactment of laws to limit this practice. Although the distinction between basic and applied research is convenient, it is not always clear-cut. For example, basic research on sex differences in talkativeness could eventually have an effect on how couples therapy is practiced, and applied research on the effect of cell phone use on driving could produce new insights into basic processes of perception, attention, and action.

**basic research**

Scientific research that is conducted primarily for the sake of learning something new.

**applied research**

Scientific research that is conducted primarily to solve some practical problem.

## Key Takeaways

- Research in psychology can be described by a simple cyclical model. A research question based on the research literature leads to an empirical study, the results of which are published and become part of the research literature.

- Scientific research in psychology is conducted mainly by people with doctoral degrees in psychology and related fields, most of whom are college and university faculty members. They do so for professional and for personal reasons, as well as to contribute to scientific knowledge about human behavior.
- Basic research is conducted to learn about human behavior for its own sake, and applied research is conducted to solve some practical problem. Both are valuable, and the distinction between the two is not always clear-cut.

## Exercises

1. Practice: Find a description of an empirical study in a professional journal or in one of the scientific psychology blogs listed in this section. Then write a brief description of the research in terms of the cyclical model presented here. One or two sentences for each part of the cycle should suffice.
2. Practice: Based on your own experience or on things you have already learned about psychology, list three basic research questions and three applied research questions of interest to you.

# 1.3 Science and Common Sense

## Learning Objectives

1. Explain the limitations of common sense when it comes to achieving a detailed and accurate understanding of human behavior.
2. Give several examples of common sense or folk psychology that are incorrect.
3. Define skepticism and its role in scientific psychology.

## Can We Rely on Common Sense?

**folk psychology**

People's intuitive beliefs about human behavior and mental processes.

Some people wonder whether the scientific approach to psychology is necessary. Can we not reach the same conclusions based on common sense or intuition? Certainly we all have intuitive beliefs about people's behavior, thoughts, and feelings—and these beliefs are collectively referred to as **folk psychology**. Although much of our folk psychology is probably reasonably accurate, it is clear that much of it is not. For example, most people believe that anger can be relieved by "letting it out"—perhaps by punching something or screaming loudly. Scientific research, however, has shown that this approach tends to leave people feeling more angry, not less (Bushman, 2002).[6] Likewise, most people believe that no one would confess to a crime that he or she had not committed, unless perhaps that person was being physically tortured. But again, extensive empirical research has shown that false confessions are surprisingly common and occur for a variety of reasons (Kassin & Gudjonsson, 2004).[7]

## Some Great Myths

In *50 Great Myths of Popular Psychology*, psychologist Scott Lilienfeld and colleagues discuss several widely held commonsense beliefs about human behavior that scientific research has shown to be *incorrect* (Lilienfeld, Lynn, Ruscio, & Beyerstein, 2010).[8] Here is a short list.

- "People use only 10% of their brain power."
- "Most people experience a midlife crisis in their 40's or 50's."
- "Students learn best when teaching styles are matched to their learning styles."
- "Low self-esteem is a major cause of psychological problems."
- "Psychiatric admissions and crimes increase during full moons."

# How Could We Be So Wrong?

How can so many of our intuitive beliefs about human behavior be so wrong? Notice that this is a psychological question, and it just so happens that psychologists have conducted scientific research on it and identified many contributing factors (Gilovich, 1991).[9] One is that forming detailed and accurate beliefs requires powers of observation, memory, and analysis to an extent that we do not naturally possess. It would be nearly impossible to count the number of words spoken by the women and men we happen to encounter, estimate the number of words they spoke per day, average these numbers for both groups, and compare them—all in our heads. This is why we tend to rely on mental shortcuts in forming and maintaining our beliefs. For example, if a belief is widely shared—especially if it is endorsed by "experts"—and it makes intuitive sense, we tend to assume it is true. This is compounded by the fact that we then tend to focus on cases that confirm our intuitive beliefs and not on cases that disconfirm them. This is called **confirmation bias**. For example, once we begin to believe that women are more talkative than men, we tend to notice and remember talkative women and silent men but ignore or forget silent women and talkative men. We also hold incorrect beliefs in part because it would be nice if they *were* true. For example, many people believe that calorie-reducing diets are an effective long-term treatment for obesity, yet a thorough review of the scientific evidence has shown that they are not (Mann et al., 2007).[10] People may continue to believe in the effectiveness of dieting in part because it gives them hope for losing weight if they are obese or makes them feel good about their own "self-control" if they are not.

Scientists—especially psychologists—understand that they are just as susceptible as anyone else to intuitive but incorrect beliefs. This is why they cultivate an attitude of **skepticism**. Being skeptical does not mean being cynical or distrustful, nor does it mean questioning every belief or claim one comes across (which would be impossible anyway). Instead, it means pausing to consider alternatives and to search for evidence—especially systematically collected empirical evidence—when there is enough at stake to justify doing so. Imagine that you read a magazine article that claims that giving children a weekly allowance is a good way to help them develop financial responsibility. This is an interesting and potentially important claim (especially if you have kids). Taking an attitude of skepticism, however, would mean pausing to ask whether it might be instead that receiving an allowance merely teaches children to spend money—perhaps even to be more materialistic. Taking an attitude of skepticism would also mean asking what evidence supports the original claim. Is the author a scientific researcher? Is any scientific evidence cited? If the issue was important enough, it might also mean turning to the research literature to see if anyone else had studied it.

**confirmation bias**

The tendency to notice and remember evidence that is consistent with what we already believe and to ignore evidence that is inconsistent with what we already believe.

**skepticism**

A critical-thinking attitude that involves considering alternatives and searching for evidence before accepting that a belief or claim is true.

**tolerance for uncertainty**

A critical-thinking attitude that involves withholding judgment about whether a belief or claim is true when there is insufficient evidence for it.

Because there is often not enough evidence to fully evaluate a belief or claim, scientists also cultivate **tolerance for uncertainty**. They accept that there are many things that they simply do not know. For example, it turns out that there is no scientific evidence that receiving an allowance causes children to be more financially responsible, nor is there any scientific evidence that it causes them to be materialistic. Although this kind of uncertainty can be problematic from a practical perspective—for example, making it difficult to decide what to do when our children ask for an allowance—it is exciting from a scientific perspective. If we do not know the answer to an interesting and empirically testable question, science may be able to provide the answer.

## Key Takeaways

- People's intuitions about human behavior, also known as folk psychology, often turn out to be wrong. This is one primary reason that psychology relies on science rather than common sense.
- Researchers in psychology cultivate certain critical-thinking attitudes. One is skepticism. They search for evidence and consider alternatives before accepting a claim about human behavior as true. Another is tolerance for uncertainty. They withhold judgment about whether a claim is true or not when there is insufficient evidence to decide.

## Exercise

1. Practice: For each of the following intuitive beliefs about human behavior, list three reasons that it might be true and three reasons that it might not be true:
    a. You cannot truly love another person unless you love yourself.
    b. People who receive "crisis counseling" immediately after experiencing a traumatic event are better able to cope with that trauma in the long term.
    c. Studying is most effective when it is always done in the same location.

# 1.4 Science and Clinical Practice

## Learning Objectives

1. Define the clinical practice of psychology and distinguish it from the science of psychology.
2. Explain how science is relevant to clinical practice.
3. Define the concept of an empirically supported treatment and give some examples.

**clinical practice of psychology**

The diagnosis and treatment of psychological disorders and related problems.

Again, psychology is the scientific study of behavior and mental processes. But it is also the application of scientific research to "benefit society and improve people's lives" (American Psychological Association, 2018).[11] By far the most common and widely known application is the **clinical practice of psychology**—the diagnosis and treatment of psychological disorders and related problems. Let us use the term *clinical practice* broadly to refer to the activities of clinical and counseling psychologists, school psychologists, marriage and family therapists, licensed clinical social workers, and others who work with people individually or in small groups to identify and solve their psychological problems. It is important to consider the relationship between scientific research and clinical practice because many students are especially interested in clinical practice, perhaps even as a career.

The main point here is that psychological disorders and other behavioral problems are part of the natural world. This means that questions about their nature, causes, and consequences are empirically testable and therefore subject to scientific study. As with other questions about human behavior, we cannot rely on our intuition or common sense for detailed and accurate answers. Consider, for example, that dozens of popular books and thousands of websites claim that adult children of alcoholics have a distinct personality profile, including low self-esteem, feelings of powerlessness, and difficulties with intimacy. Although this sounds plausible, scientific research has demonstrated that adult children of alcoholics are no more likely to have these problems than anybody else (Lilienfeld et al., 2010).[12]

Similarly, questions about whether a particular psychotherapy works are empirically testable questions that can be answered by scientific research. If a new psychotherapy is an effective treatment for depression, then systematic observation should reveal that depressed people who receive this psychotherapy improve more than a similar group of depressed people who do not receive this psychotherapy (or who receive some alternative treatment). An **empirically supported treatment** is one that has been studied scientifically and shown to result in greater improvement than no treatment, a placebo, or some alternative treatment. The Society for Clinical Psychology provides a detailed list of empirically supported treatments for psychological disorders at http://www.div12.org/psychological-treatments/. This list is quite extensive and continues to be updated as new research is conducted. Below is a small sample of treatments that are currently considered to have "strong" support.

- Acceptance and Commitment Therapy for Chronic Pain.
- Behavioral Activation for Depression
- Cognitive Behavioral Therapy for Insomnia
- Dialectical Behavior Therapy for Borderline Personality Disorder
- Exposure Therapy for Specific Phobias
- Family Focused Therapy for Bipolar Disorder

At the same time, however, it is also true that many clinical practitioners do not value science as a source of knowledge about psychological disorders or their treatment. In fact, some are outright hostile to it—often claiming that the clinical practice of psychology is an "art" that cannot be evaluated according to scientific criteria (Dawes, 1994).[13] Unfortunately, these attitudes can lead to the creation and spread of pseudoscientific and potentially harmful treatments. One such treatment is "past life regression therapy," which is based on the assumption that people's psychological problems are caused by traumas they experienced in *past* lives. The treatment involves hypnotizing them and encouraging them to recall these traumas so they can cope with them more effectively in the present. Not surprisingly, there is absolutely no scientific evidence for any of these claims.

One of the great challenges of the field of clinical practice is continuing to promote the scientific approach—which has proved immensely fruitful—and discouraging the pseudoscientific and potentially harmful ones.

**FIGURE 1.4**

The effectiveness of various forms of psychotherapy—for example, cognitive behavioral therapy for depression—can be determined by scientific research.

Source: © 2010 Thinkstock

## Key Takeaways

- The clinical practice of psychology—the diagnosis and treatment of psychological problems—is one important application of the scientific discipline of psychology.
- Scientific research is relevant to clinical practice because it provides detailed and accurate knowledge about psychological problems and establishes whether treatments are effective.

## Exercises

1. Discussion: Some clinicians argue that what they do is an "art form" based on intuition and personal experience and therefore cannot be evaluated scientifically. Write a paragraph about how satisfied you would be with such a clinician and why from each of three perspectives:

   a. a potential client of the clinician

   b. a judge who must decide whether to allow the clinician to testify as an expert witness in a child abuse case

   c. an insurance company representative who must decide whether to reimburse the clinician for his or her services

2. Practice: Create a short list of questions that a client could ask a clinician to determine whether he or she pays sufficient attention to scientific research.

# Endnotes

1. Mehl, M. R., Vazire, S., Ramirez-Esparza, N., Slatcher, R. B., & Pennebaker, J. W. (2007). Are women really more talkative than men? *Science, 317*, 82.

2. Stanovich, K. E. (2010). *How to think straight about psychology* (9th ed.). Boston, MA: Allyn & Bacon.

3. Hines, T. M. (1998). Comprehensive review of biorhythm theory. *Psychological Reports, 83*, 19–64.

4. Popper, K. R. (2002). *Conjectures and refutations: The growth of scientific knowledge*. New York, NY: Routledge.

5. Collet, C., Guillot, A., & Petit, C. (2010). Phoning while driving I: A review of epidemiological, psychological, behavioural and physiological studies. *Ergonomics, 53*, 589–601.

6. Bushman, B. J. (2002). Does venting anger feed or extinguish the flame? Catharsis, rumination, distraction, anger, and aggressive responding. *Personality and Social Psychology Bulletin, 28*, 724–731.

7. Kassin, S. M., & Gudjonsson, G. H. (2004). The psychology of confession evidence: A review of the literature and issues. *Psychological Science in the Public Interest, 5*, 33–67.

8. Lilienfeld, S. O., Lynn, S. J., Ruscio, J., & Beyerstein, B. L. (2010). *50 great myths of popular psychology*. Malden, MA: Wiley-Blackwell.

9. Gilovich, T. (1991). *How we know what isn't so: The fallibility of human reason in everyday life*. New York, NY: Free Press.

10. Mann, T., Tomiyama, A. J., Westling, E., Lew, A., Samuels, B., & Chatman, J. (2007). Medicare's search for effective obesity treatments: Diets are not the answer. *American Psychologist, 62*, 220–233.

11. American Psychological Association. (2018). About APA. Retrieved from http://www.apa.org/about.

12. Lilienfeld, S. O., Lynn, S. J., Ruscio, J., & Beyerstein, B. L. (2010). *50 great myths of popular psychology*. Malden, MA: Wiley-Blackwell.

13. Dawes, R. M. (1994). House of cards: Psychology and psychotherapy built on myth. New York, NY: Free Press.

# CHAPTER 2

# Research Basics

Here is the first paragraph of an article by researcher Maggie Bruck published in the *Journal of Experimental Psychology: Applied* (Bruck, 2009).[1]

> *Human figure drawings (HFDs) are commonly used by professionals who interview children about suspected sexual abuse. It is assumed that these drawings will decrease children's linguistic and emotional or motivational limitations, as well as memory problems, and thus will result in the elicitation of more complete and accurate details of abuse. There is, however, little scientific information to support claims of their benefits. This article presents the results of two studies that examined young children's ability to use HFDs to report body touches. (p. 361)*

In this paragraph, the researcher has identified a research question—about the effect of using human figure drawings on the accuracy of children's memories of being touched—and begun to make an argument for why it is interesting. In terms of the general model of scientific research in psychology presented in Figure 1.2, these are activities at the "top" of the cycle. In this chapter, we focus on these activities—finding research ideas, turning them into interesting empirical research questions, and reviewing the research literature. We begin, however, with some more basic concepts that are necessary to understand how research questions in psychology are conceptualized.

## 2.1 Basic Concepts

### Learning Objectives

1. Define the concept of a variable, distinguish quantitative from categorical variables, and give examples of variables that might be of interest to psychologists.
2. Explain the difference between a population and a sample.
3. Describe two basic forms of statistical relationship and give examples of each.
4. Interpret basic statistics and graphs used to describe statistical relationships.
5. Explain why correlation does not imply causation.

Before we address where research questions in psychology come from—and what makes them more or less interesting—it is important to understand the kinds of questions that researchers in psychology typically ask. This requires a quick introduction to several basic concepts, many of which we will return to in more detail later in the book.

**FIGURE 2.1**

Do human figure drawings like this one help children recall accurate information about being touched—for example, in sexual abuse cases? Unfortunately, research suggests they do not.

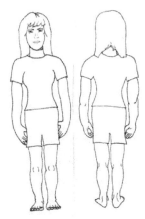

Source: Copyright © 2004 by the American Psychological Association. Reproduced with permission. The official citation that should be used in referencing this material is Aldridge, J., Lamb, M. W., Sternberg, K. J., Orbach, Y., Esplin, P. W., & Bowler, L. (2004). "Using a human figure drawing to elicit information from alleged victims of child sexual abuse." Journal of Consulting and Clinical Psychology, 72, 304–316. The use of APA information does not imply endorsement by the APA.

# Variables

**variable**

A quantity or quality that varies across individuals.

**quantitative variable**

A quantity that varies across individuals and is measured by assigning a number to each individual.

**categorical variable**

A quality that varies across individuals and is measured by assigning a category label to each individual.

**population**

The entire group of individuals that the researcher wants to draw conclusions about.

**sample**

The subset of individuals that the researcher actually studies.

**operational definition**

A definition of a variable or construct in terms of precisely how it will be measured.

Research questions in psychology are about variables. A **variable** is a quantity or quality that varies across people or situations. For example, the height of the students in a psychology class is a variable because it varies from student to student. The sex of the students is also a variable as long as there are both male and female students in the class. A **quantitative variable** is a quantity, such as height, that is typically measured by assigning a number to each individual. Other examples of quantitative variables include people's level of talkativeness, how depressed they are, and the number of siblings they have. A **categorical variable** is a quality, such as sex, and is typically measured by assigning a category label to each individual. Other examples include people's nationality, their occupation, and whether they are receiving psychotherapy.

# Sampling and Measurement

Researchers in psychology are usually interested in drawing conclusions about some very large group of people. This is called the **population**. It could be American teenagers, children with autism, professional athletes, or even just human beings—depending on the interests and goals of the researcher. But they usually study only a small subset or **sample** of the population. For example, a researcher might measure the talkativeness of a few hundred college students with the intention of drawing conclusions about the talkativeness of men and women in general. It is important, therefore, for researchers to use a representative sample—one that is similar to the population in important respects.

One method of obtaining a sample is simple random sampling, in which every member of the population has an equal chance of being selected for the sample. For example, a pollster could start with a list of all the registered voters in a city (the population), randomly select 100 of them from the list (the sample), and ask those 100 whom they intended to vote for. Unfortunately, random sampling is difficult or impossible in most psychological research because the populations are less clearly defined than the registered voters in a city. How could a researcher give all American teenagers or all children with autism an equal chance of being selected for a sample? The most common alternative to random sampling is convenience sampling, in which the sample consists of individuals who happen to be nearby and willing to participate (such as introductory psychology students). The obvious problem with convenience sampling is that the sample might not be representative of the population.

Once the sample is selected, researchers need to measure the variables they are interested in. This requires an **operational definition**—a definition of the variable in terms of precisely how it is to be measured. Most variables can be operationally defined in many different ways. For example, depression can be operationally defined as people's scores on a paper-and-pencil depression scale, the number of depressive symptoms they are experiencing, or whether they have been diagnosed with major depressive disorder. When a variable has been measured for a particular individual, the result is called a score, and a set of scores is called data. Note that *data* is plural—the singular *datum* is rarely used—so it is grammatically correct to say, "Those are interesting data" (and incorrect to say, "That is interesting data").

# Statistical Relationships Between Variables

Some research questions in psychology are about one variable. How accurate are children's memories for being touched? How talkative are American college students? How common is it for people to be diagnosed with major depressive disorder? Answering such questions requires operationally defining the variable, measuring it for a sample, analyzing the results, and drawing conclusions about the population. For a quantitative variable, this would typically involve computing the mean and standard deviation of the scores. For a categorical variable, it would typically involve computing the percentage of scores at each level of the variable.

However, research questions in psychology are more likely to be about statistical relationships between variables. There is a **statistical relationship** between two variables when the average score on one differs systematically across the levels of the other. Studying statistical relationships is important because instead of telling us about behaviors and psychological characteristics in isolation, it tells us about the causes, consequences, development, and organization of those behaviors and characteristics.

There are two basic forms of statistical relationship: differences between groups and correlations between quantitative variables. Although both are consistent with the general definition of a statistical relationship—the average score on one variable differs across levels of the other—they are usually described and analyzed somewhat differently. For this reason it is important to distinguish them clearly.

**statistical relationship**

A difference in the average score on one variable across levels of another variable.

## Differences Between Groups

One basic form of statistical relationship is a difference between the mean scores of two groups on some variable of interest. A wide variety of research questions in psychology take this form. Are women more talkative than men? Do children using human figure drawings recall more touch information than children not using human figure drawings? Do people talking on a cell phone have poorer driving abilities than people not talking on a cell phone? Do people receiving Psychotherapy A tend to have fewer depressive symptoms than people receiving Psychotherapy B? Later we will also see that such relationships can involve more than two groups and that the groups can consist of the very same individuals tested at different times or under different conditions. For now, however, it is easiest to think in terms of two distinct groups.

Differences between groups are usually described by giving the mean score and standard deviation for each group. This information can also be presented in a **bar graph** like that in Figure 2.2, where the heights of the bars represent the group means.

**bar graph**

A graph used to show differences between the mean scores of two or more groups.

**FIGURE 2.2** Bar Graph Showing the Very Small Difference in the Mean Number of Words Spoken per Day by Women and Men in a Large Sample

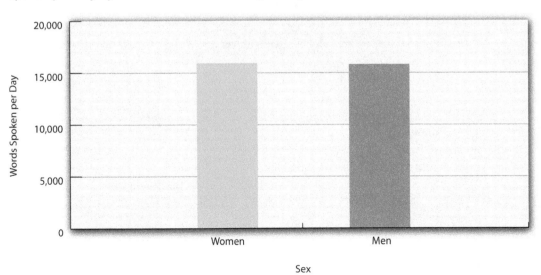

Source: Based on data from Mehl, M. R., Vazire, S., Ramírez-Esparza, N., Slatcher, R. B., & Pennebaker, J. W. (2007). Are women really more talkative than men? Science, 317, 82.

# Correlations Between Quantitative Variables

A second basic form of statistical relationship is a correlation between two quantitative variables, where the average score on one variable differs systematically across the levels of the other. Again, a wide variety of research questions in psychology take this form. Is being a happier person associated with being more talkative? Do children's memories for touch information improve as they get older? Does the effectiveness of psychotherapy depend on how much the patient likes the therapist?

**scatterplot**

A graph used to show the correlation between two quantitative variables.

**positive relationship**

A statistical relationship between two variables in which higher scores on one tend to be associated with higher scores on the other.

**negative relationship**

A statistical relationship between two variables in which higher scores on one tend to be associated with lower scores on the other.

Correlations between quantitative variables are often presented using **scatterplots**. Figure 2.3 shows some hypothetical data on the relationship between the amount of stress people are under and the number of physical symptoms they have. Each point in the scatterplot represents one person's score on both variables. For example, the circled point in Figure 2.3 represents a person whose stress score was 10 and who had three physical symptoms. Taking all the points into account, one can see that people under more stress tend to have more physical symptoms. This is a good example of a **positive relationship**, in which higher scores on one variable tend to be associated with higher scores on the other. A **negative relationship** is one in which higher scores on one variable tend to be associated with lower scores on the other. There is a negative relationship between stress and immune system functioning, for example, because higher stress is associated with lower immune system functioning.

**FIGURE 2.3** Scatterplot Showing a Hypothetical Positive Relationship Between Stress and Number of Physical Symptoms

The circled point represents a person whose stress score was 10 and who had three physical symptoms. Pearson's r for these data is +.51.

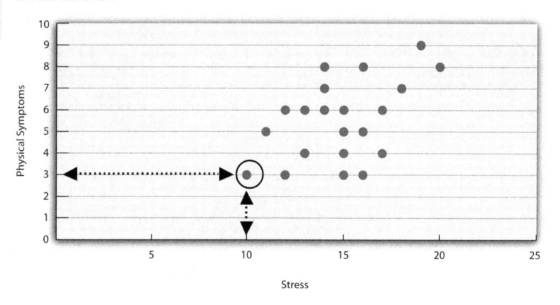

**Pearson's r**

A measure of the strength of the correlation between two quantitative variables.

The strength of a correlation between quantitative variables is typically measured using a statistic called **Pearson's r**. As Figure 2.4 shows, Pearson's r ranges from −1.00 (the strongest possible negative relationship) to +1.00 (the strongest possible positive relationship). A value of 0 means there is no relationship between the two variables. When Pearson's r is 0, the points on a scatterplot form a shapeless "cloud." As its value moves toward −1.00 or +1.00, the points come closer and closer to falling on a single straight line.

**FIGURE 2.4** Range of Pearson's *r*, From –1.00 (Strongest Possible Negative Relationship), Through 0 (No Relationship), to +1.00 (Strongest Possible Positive Relationship)

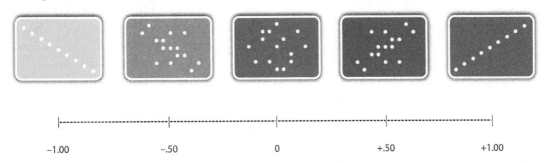

|-----------------------------|-----------------------------|-----------------------------|-----------------------------|

   –1.00            –.50              0              +.50           +1.00

Pearson's *r* is a good measure only for linear relationships, in which the points are best approximated by a straight line. It is not a good measure for nonlinear relationships, in which the points are better approximated by a curved line. Figure 2.5, for example, shows a hypothetical relationship between the amount of sleep people get per night and their level of depression. In this example, the line that best approximates the points is a curve—a kind of upside-down "U"—because people who get about eight hours of sleep tend to be the least depressed. Those who get too little sleep and those who get too much sleep tend to be more depressed. Nonlinear relationships are fairly common in psychology, but measuring their strength is beyond the scope of this book.

**FIGURE 2.5** Hypothetical Nonlinear Relationship Between Sleep and Depression

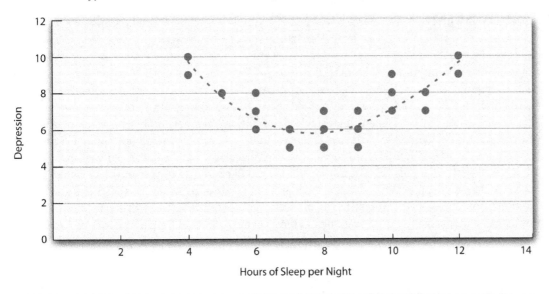

## Estimating Pearson's *r*

A great way to get a feel for Pearson's *r* is to practice estimating it based on data presented in a scatterplot. Below are links to three websites that allow you to do exactly this. Challenge your friends to an *r* estimating contest!

- http://guessthecorrelation.com
- http://www.rossmanchance.com/applets/GuessCorrelation.html
- http://www.istics.net/Correlations/

# Correlation Does Not Imply Causation

**independent variable**

A variable that is thought to be the cause of another variable (called the dependent variable). In an experiment, the independent variable is manipulated by the researcher.

**dependent variable**

A variable that is thought to be the effect of another variable (called the independent variable).

Researchers are often interested in a statistical relationship between two variables because they think that one of the variables causes the other. That is, the statistical relationship reflects a causal relationship. In these situations, the variable that is thought to be the cause is called the **independent variable** (often referred to as $X$ for short), and the variable that is thought to be the effect is called the **dependent variable** (often referred to as $Y$). For example, the statistical relationship between whether or not a depressed person receives psychotherapy and the number of depressive symptoms he or she has reflects the fact that the psychotherapy (the independent variable) *causes* the reduction in symptoms (the dependent variable). Understanding causal relationships is important in part because it allows us to change people's behavior in predictable ways. If we know that psychotherapy causes a reduction in depressive symptoms—and we want people to have fewer depressive symptoms—then we can use psychotherapy to achieve this goal.

But not all statistical relationships reflect causal relationships. This is what psychologists mean when they say, "Correlation does not imply causation." An obvious example comes from a study in Taiwan showing a positive relationship between the number of electrical appliances that people use and the extent to which they use birth control (Stanovich, 2010).[2] It seems clear, however, that this does not mean that owning electrical appliances causes people to use birth control, and it would not make sense to try to increase the use of birth control by giving people toasters and hair dryers.

**directionality problem**

The problem of knowing whether two variables, $X$ and $Y$, are statistically related because $X$ causes $Y$ or because $Y$ causes $X$.

**third-variable problem**

The problem of knowing whether two variables, $X$ and $Y$, are statistically related because one causes the other or because some third variable, $Z$, causes both $X$ and $Y$.

There are two reasons that correlation does not imply causation. The first is called the **directionality problem**. Two variables, $X$ and $Y$, can be statistically related because $X$ causes $Y$ or because $Y$ causes $X$. Consider, for example, a study showing that whether or not people exercise is statistically related to how happy they are—such that people who exercise are happier on average than people who do not. This statistical relationship is consistent with the idea that exercising causes happiness, but it is also consistent with the idea that happiness causes exercise. Perhaps being happy gives people more energy or leads them to seek opportunities to socialize with others by going to the gym. The second reason that correlation does not imply causation is called the **third-variable problem**. Two variables, $X$ and $Y$, can be statistically related not because $X$ causes $Y$, or because $Y$ causes $X$, but because some third variable causes both $X$ and $Y$. For example, the fact that people with more electrical appliances are more likely to use birth control probably reflects the fact that having more education or income causes people to own more appliances *and* causes them to use birth control. Similarly, the statistical relationship between exercise and happiness could mean that some third variable, such as physical health, causes both of the others. Being physically healthy could cause people to exercise and cause them to be happier.

## Does Internet Use "Lead to" Lower Test Scores?

Although researchers in psychology know that correlation does not imply causation, many journalists are unclear on the concept. Researcher and teacher Jon Mueller has a website linking to dozens of media reports about real research where the headline suggests that a causal relationship has been demonstrated even though the research described is clearly correlational.

http://jonathan.mueller.faculty.noctrl.edu/100/correlation_or_causation.htm

One article is about a study showing that introductory psychology students who spent more time browsing the Internet during lecture tended to score worse on their final exam. The headline is, "Internet Use in Class Leads to Lower Test Scores." The expression "leads to" strongly suggests that Internet use *causes* lower test scores. This is certainly one reasonable interpretation of the result but what others can you think of? (Hint: Think about the directionality and third-variable problems.) How could the headline be rewritten so that it does not imply a causal relationship?

As we will see later in the book, there are various ways that researchers address the directionality and third-variable problems. The most effective, however, is to conduct an experiment. An **experiment** is a study in which the researcher manipulates the independent variable. For example, instead of simply measuring how much people exercise, a researcher could make one group of people exercise by running on a treadmill for 20 minutes and a similar group of people not exercise by sitting on a couch for 20 minutes. Now if those who exercised are in more positive moods than those who did not exercise, it makes sense to conclude that the exercise *caused* this difference. Why? First, it cannot be that the people's moods affected whether or not they exercised because it was the *researcher* who determined this. Second, it cannot be that some other variable like physical health affected the people's moods *and* whether or not they exercised because, again, it was the researcher who determined who exercised and who did not. Thus, experiments eliminate the directionality and third variable problems and allow researchers to draw conclusions about causal relationships. We will have much more to say about both experimental and nonexperimental research later in the book.

**experiment**

A type of empirical study in which an independent variable is manipulated and a dependent variable is measured while extraneous variables are controlled.

## Key Takeaways

- Research questions in psychology are about variables and relationships between variables.
- Two basic forms of statistical relationship are differences between group means and correlations between quantitative variables, each of which can be described using a few simple statistical techniques.
- Correlation does not imply causation. A statistical relationship between two variables, $X$ and $Y$, does not necessarily mean that $X$ causes $Y$. It is also possible that $Y$ causes $X$, or that a third variable, $Z$, causes both $X$ and $Y$.

## Exercises

1. Practice: List 10 variables that might be of interest to a researcher in psychology. For each, specify whether it is quantitative or categorical.
2. Practice: Imagine that you categorize people as either introverts (quieter, shyer, more inward looking) or extroverts (louder, more outgoing, more outward looking). Sketch a bar graph showing a hypothetical statistical relationship between this variable and the number of words people speak per day.
3. Practice: Now imagine that you measure people's levels of extroversion as a quantitative variable, with values ranging from 0 (extreme introversion) to 30 (extreme extroversion). Sketch a scatterplot showing a hypothetical statistical relationship between this variable and the number of words people speak per day.
4. Practice: For each of the following statistical relationships, decide whether the directionality problem is present and think of at least one plausible third variable:
   a. People who eat more lobster tend to live longer.
   b. People who exercise more tend to weigh less.
   c. College students who drink more alcohol tend to have poorer grades.

# 2.2 Good Research Questions

### Learning Objectives

1. Describe some common sources of research ideas and generate research ideas using those sources.
2. Describe some techniques for turning research ideas into empirical research questions and use those techniques to generate questions.
3. Explain what makes a research question interesting and evaluate research questions in terms of their interestingness.

Good research must begin with a good research question. Yet coming up with good research questions is something that novice researchers often find surprisingly difficult. This section covers some fairly simple strategies for finding general research ideas, turning those ideas into empirically testable research questions, and finally evaluating those questions in terms of how interesting they are and how feasible they would be to answer.

# Finding Inspiration

Research questions often begin as more general research ideas—usually focusing on some behavior or psychological characteristic: talkativeness, memory for touches, depression, bungee jumping, and so on. Before looking at how to turn such ideas into empirically testable research questions, it is worth looking at where such ideas come from in the first place. Three of the most common sources of inspiration are informal observations, practical problems, and previous research.

Informal observations include direct observations of our own and others' behavior as well as secondhand observations from nonscientific sources, such as newspapers and books. For example, you might notice that you always seem to be in the slowest moving line at the grocery store. Could it be that most people think the same thing? Or you might read in the local newspaper about people donating money and food to a local family whose house has burned down and begin to wonder about who makes such donations and why. Some of the most famous research in psychology has been inspired by informal observations. Stanley Milgram's famous research on obedience, for example, was inspired in part by journalistic reports of the trials of accused Nazi war criminals—many of whom claimed that they were only obeying orders. This led him to wonder about the extent to which ordinary people will commit immoral acts simply because they are ordered to do so by an authority figure (Milgram, 1963).[3]

Practical problems can also inspire research ideas, leading directly to applied research in such domains as law, health, education, and sports. Can human figure drawings help children remember details about being physically or sexually abused? How effective is psychotherapy for depression compared to drug therapy? To what extent do cell phones impair people's driving ability? How can we teach children to read more efficiently? What is the best mental preparation for running a marathon?

Probably the most common inspiration for new research ideas, however, is previous research. Recall that science is a kind of large-scale collaboration in which many different researchers read and evaluate each other's work and conduct new studies to build on it. Of course, experienced researchers are familiar with previous research in their area of expertise and probably have a long list of ideas. This suggests that novice researchers can find inspiration by consulting with a more experienced researcher (e.g., students can consult a faculty member). But they can also find inspiration by picking up a copy of almost any professional journal and reading the titles and abstracts. In one typical issue of *Psychological Science*, for example, you can find articles on the perception of shapes, anti-Semitism, police lineups, the meaning of death, second-language learning, people who seek negative emotional experiences, and many other topics. If you can narrow your interests down to a particular topic (e.g., memory) or domain (e.g., health care), you can also look through more specific journals, such as *Memory & Cognition* or *Health Psychology*.

# Generating Empirically Testable Research Questions

Once you have a research idea, you can use it to generate one or more empirically testable research questions, that is, questions expressed in terms of a single variable or relationship between variables. One way to do this is to look closely at the discussion section in a recent research article on the topic. This is the last major section of the article, in which the researchers summarize their results, interpret them in the context of past research, and suggest directions for future research. These suggestions often take the form of specific research questions, which you could try to answer with additional research.

But you may also want to generate your own research questions. How can you do this? First, if you have a particular behavior or psychological characteristic in mind, you can simply conceptualize it as a variable and ask how frequent or intense it is. How many words on average do people speak per day? How accurate are children's memories of being touched? What percentage of people have sought professional help for depression? If the question has never been studied scientifically—which is something you would learn when you review the research literature—then it might be interesting and worth pursuing.

If scientific research has already answered the question of how frequent or intense the behavior or characteristic is, then you could consider turning it into a question about a statistical relationship between that behavior or characteristic and some other variable. One way to do this is to ask yourself the following series of more general questions and write down all the answers you can think of.

- What are some possible causes of the behavior or characteristic?
- What are some possible effects of the behavior or characteristic?
- What types of people might exhibit more or less of the behavior or characteristic?
- What types of situations might elicit more or less of the behavior or characteristic?

In general, each answer you write down can be conceptualized as a second variable, suggesting a question about a statistical relationship. If you were interested in talkativeness, for example, it might occur to you that a possible cause of this psychological characteristic is family size. Is there a statistical relationship between family size and talkativeness? Or it might occur to you that people seem to be more talkative in same-sex groups than mixed-sex groups. Is there a difference in the average level of talkativeness of people in same-sex groups and people in mixed-sex groups? This approach should allow you to generate many different empirically testable questions about almost any behavior or psychological characteristic.

If through this process you generate a question that has never been studied scientifically—which again is something that you would learn when you review the research literature—then it might be interesting and worth pursuing. But what if you find that it *has* been studied scientifically? Although novice researchers often want to give up and move on to a new question at this point, this is not necessarily a good strategy. For one thing, the fact that the question has been studied scientifically and the research published suggests that it is of interest to the scientific community. For another, the question can almost certainly be refined so that its answer will still contribute something new to the research literature. Again, asking yourself a series of more general questions about the statistical relationship is a good strategy.

- Are there other ways to operationally define the variables?
- Are there types of people for whom the statistical relationship might be stronger or weaker?
- Are there situations in which the statistical relationship might be stronger or weaker—including situations with practical importance?

For example, research has shown that women and men speak about the same number of words per day—but this was when talkativeness was measured in terms of the number of words spoken per day among college students in the United States and Mexico. We can still ask whether other ways of measuring talkativeness—perhaps the number of different people spoken to each day—produce the same result. Or we can ask whether studying elderly people or people from other cultures produces the same result. Again, this approach should help you generate many different research questions about almost any statistical relationship.

# Evaluating Research Questions

Researchers usually generate many more research questions than they ever attempt to answer. This means they must have some way of evaluating the research questions they generate so that they can choose which ones to pursue. In this section, we consider two criteria for evaluating research questions: the interestingness of the question and the feasibility of answering it.

## Interestingness

**interestingness**

A property of research questions that is based in part on the extent to which the answer is in doubt, fills a gap in the research literature, and has important practical implications.

How often do people tie their shoes? Do people feel pain when you punch them in the jaw? Are women more likely to wear makeup than men? Do people prefer vanilla or chocolate ice cream? Although it would be a fairly simple matter to design a study and collect data to answer these questions, you probably would not want to because they are not interesting. We are not talking here about whether a research question is interesting to us personally but whether it is interesting to people more generally and, especially, to the scientific community. But what makes a research question interesting in this sense? Here we look at three factors that affect the **interestingness** of a research question: the answer is in doubt, the answer fills a gap in the research literature, and the answer has important practical implications.

First, a research question is interesting to the extent that its answer is in doubt. Obviously, questions that have been answered by scientific research are no longer interesting as the subject of new empirical research. But the fact that a question has not been answered by scientific research does not necessarily make it interesting. There has to be some reasonable chance that the answer to the question will be something that we did not already know. But how can you assess this before actually collecting data? One approach is to try to think of reasons to expect different answers to the question—especially ones that seem to conflict with common sense. If you can think of reasons to expect at least two different answers, then the question might be interesting. If you can think of reasons to expect only one answer, then it probably is not. The question of whether women are more talkative than men is interesting because there are reasons to expect both answers. The existence of the stereotype itself suggests the answer could be yes, but the fact that women's and men's verbal abilities are fairly similar suggests the answer could be no. The question of whether people feel pain when you punch them in the jaw is not interesting because there is absolutely no reason to think that the answer could be anything other than a resounding yes.

A second important factor to consider when deciding if a research question is interesting is whether answering it will fill a gap in the research literature. Again, this means in part that the question has not already been answered by scientific research. But it also means that the question is in some sense a natural one for people who are familiar with the research literature. For example, the question of whether human figure drawings can help children recall touch information might occur to anyone who was familiar with research on the unreliability of eyewitness memory (especially in children) and the ineffectiveness of some alternative interviewing techniques.

A final factor to consider when deciding whether a research question is interesting is whether its answer has important practical implications. Again, the question of whether human figure drawings help children recall information about being touched has important implications for how children are interviewed in physical and sexual abuse cases. The question of whether cell phone use impairs driving is interesting because it is relevant to the personal safety of everyone who travels by car and to the debate over whether cell phone use should be restricted by law.

## Feasibility

A second important criterion for evaluating research questions is the **feasibility** of successfully answering them. There are many factors that affect feasibility, including time, money, equipment and materials, technical knowledge and skill, and access to research participants. Clearly, researchers need to take these factors into account so that they do not waste time and effort pursuing research that they cannot complete successfully.

**feasibility**

The extent to which a research question can be answered with available resources.

Looking through a sample of professional journals in psychology will reveal many studies that are complicated and difficult to carry out. These include longitudinal designs in which participants are tracked over many years, neuroimaging studies in which participants' brain activity is measured while they carry out various mental tasks, and complex nonexperimental studies involving several variables and complicated statistical analyses. Keep in mind, though, that such research tends to be carried out by teams of highly trained researchers whose work is often supported in part by government and private grants. Keep in mind also that research does not have to be complicated or difficult to produce interesting and important results. Looking through a sample of professional journals will also reveal studies that are relatively simple and easy to carry out—perhaps involving a convenience sample of college students and a paper-and-pencil task.

A final point here is that it is generally good practice to use methods that have already been used successfully by other researchers. For example, if you want to manipulate people's moods to make some of them happy, it would be a good idea to use one of the many approaches that have been used successfully by other researchers (e.g., paying them a compliment). This is good not only for the sake of feasibility—the approach is "tried and true"—but also because it provides greater continuity with previous research. This makes it easier to compare your results with those of other researchers and to understand the implications of their research for yours, and vice versa.

## Key Takeaways

- Research ideas can come from a variety of sources, including informal observations, practical problems, and previous research.
- Research questions expressed in terms of variables and relationships between variables can be suggested by other researchers or generated by asking a series of more general questions about the behavior or psychological characteristic of interest.
- It is important to evaluate how interesting a research question is before designing a study and collecting data to answer it. Factors that affect interestingness are the extent to which the answer is in doubt, whether it fills a gap in the research literature, and whether it has important practical implications.
- It is also important to evaluate how feasible a research question will be to answer. Factors that affect feasibility include time, money, technical knowledge and skill, and access to special equipment and research participants.

## Exercises

1. Practice: Generate five research ideas based on each of the following: informal observations, practical problems, and topics discussed in recent issues of professional journals.
2. Practice: Generate five empirical research questions about each of the following behaviors or psychological characteristics: long-distance running, getting tattooed, social anxiety, online trolling, and memory for early childhood events.
3. Practice: Evaluate each of the research questions you generated in Exercise 2 in terms of its interestingness based on the criteria discussed in this section.
4. Practice: Find an issue of a journal that publishes short empirical research reports (e.g., *Psychological Science*, *Psychonomic Bulletin and Review*, *Personality and Social Psychology Bulletin*). Pick three studies, and rate each one in terms of how feasible it would be for you to replicate it with the resources available to you right now. Use the following rating scale: (1) You could replicate it essentially as reported. (2) You could replicate it with some simplifications. (3) You could not replicate it. Explain each rating.

# 2.3 Reviewing the Research Literature

## Learning Objectives

1. Define the research literature in psychology and give examples of sources that are part of the research literature and sources that are not.
2. Describe and use several methods for finding previous research on a particular research idea or question.

Reviewing the research literature means finding, reading, and summarizing the published research relevant to your question. An empirical research report written in American Psychological Association (APA) style always includes a written literature review, but it is important to review the literature early in the research process for several reasons.

- It can help you turn a research idea into an interesting research question.
- It can tell you if a research question has already been answered.
- It can help you evaluate the interestingness of a research question.
- It can give you ideas for how to conduct your own study.
- It can tell you how your study fits into the research literature.

## What Is the Research Literature?

**research literature**

All the published research in a particular field.

The **research literature** in any field is all the published research in that field. The research literature in psychology is enormous—including millions of scholarly articles and books dating to the beginning of the field—and it continues to grow. Although its boundaries are somewhat fuzzy, the research literature definitely does *not* include self-help and other pop psychology books, dictionary and encyclopedia entries, websites, and similar sources that are intended mainly for the general public. These are considered unreliable because they are not reviewed by other researchers and are often based on little more than common sense or personal experience. Wikipedia contains much valuable information, but the fact that its authors are anonymous and its content continually changes makes it unsuitable as a basis of sound scientific research. For our purposes, it helps to define the research literature as consisting almost entirely of two types of sources: articles in professional journals, and scholarly books in psychology and related fields.

## Professional Journals

**Professional journals** are periodicals that publish original research articles. There are thousands of professional journals that publish research in psychology and related fields. They are usually published monthly or quarterly in individual issues, each of which contains several articles. The issues are organized into volumes, which consist of multiple issues (e.g., all the issues for a particular calendar year). Although many journals continue to publish hard copy versions, it is more common now for researchers to find and read electronic versions on the Internet.

| | |
|---|---|
| | **professional journals**<br><br>Periodicals that publish new research. |

Most articles in professional journals are one of two basic types: empirical research reports and review articles. **Empirical research reports** describe one or more new empirical studies conducted by the authors. They introduce a research question, explain why it is interesting, review previous research, describe their method and results, and draw their conclusions. **Review articles** summarize previously published research on a topic and usually present new ways to organize or explain the results. When a review article is devoted primarily to presenting a new theory, it is often referred to as a **theoretical article**.

| | |
|---|---|
| | **empirical research report**<br><br>A type of journal article in which the author reports on a new empirical research study. |
| | **review article**<br><br>A type of journal article in which the author summarizes previous research on a particular topic. |

Most professional journals in psychology undergo a process of **peer review**. Researchers who want to publish their work in the journal submit a manuscript to the editor—who is generally an established researcher too—who in turn sends it to two or three experts on the topic. Each reviewer reads the manuscript, writes a critical review, and sends the review back to the editor along with his or her recommendations. The editor then decides whether to accept the article for publication, ask the authors to make changes and resubmit it for further consideration, or reject it outright. In any case, the editor forwards the reviewers' written comments to the researchers so that they can revise their manuscript accordingly. Peer review is important because it ensures that the work meets basic standards of the field before it can enter the research literature.

| | |
|---|---|
| | **theoretical article**<br><br>A type of journal article in which the author presents a new theory or evaluates existing theories. |
| | **peer review**<br><br>A process in which new research submitted for publication is reviewed by two or more experts before an editor decides whether to publish it. |

### Open Access Journals in Psychology

In the world of professional journals, "open access" refers to articles that are free for anyone to find and read on the Internet. Many journals now provide some of their articles in an open-access format, while others are entirely open access. Below are links to some of these entirely open access journals in psychology.

- Archives of Scientific Psychology: http://www.apa.org/pubs/journals/arc
- Evolutionary Psychology: http://journals.sagepub.com/home/evp
- Health Psychology Open: http://journals.sagepub.com/home/hpo
- International Journal of Wellbeing: http://internationaljournalofwellbeing.org
- i-Perception: http://journals.sagepub.com/home/ipe
- Journal of Social and Political Psychology: http://jspp.psychopen.eu
- Judgment and Decision Making: http://journal.sjdm.org
- Revista Latinoamercana de Psicologia: http://www.journals.elsevier.com/revista-latinoamericana-de-psicologia

## Scholarly Books

**scholarly books**

A book written by a professional researcher or practitioner primarily for other researchers and practitioners.

**Scholarly books** are books written by researchers and practitioners mainly for use by other researchers and practitioners. They can be written by a single author or a small group of authors and give a coherent presentation of a topic, much like an extended review article. They can also have an editor or a small group of editors who recruit many authors to write separate chapters on different aspects of the same topic. Although these edited volumes can also give a coherent presentation of a topic, it is not unusual for each chapter to take a different perspective or even for the authors of different chapters to openly disagree with each other. In general, scholarly books undergo a peer review process similar to that used by professional journals.

# Literature Search Strategies

## PsycINFO

**PsycINFO**

The primary computer database that catalogs research in psychology.

The primary method for searching the research literature is to use one or more electronic databases. The most important database for our purposes is **PsycINFO**, which is produced by the APA and provided to libraries by vendors such as Ebsco or Proquest. PsycINFO is so comprehensive—covering thousands of professional journals and scholarly books going back more than 100 years—that for most purposes its content is synonymous with the research literature in psychology.

PsycINFO consists of individual records for each article, book chapter, or book in the database. Each record includes basic publication information, an abstract or summary of the work, and a list of other works cited by that work. When using PsycINFO you can enter one or more search terms, and the database returns any records that contain those search terms. Each record also contains lists of keywords that describe the content of the work and a list of index terms. The index terms are especially helpful because they are standardized. Research on differences between women and men, for example, is always indexed under "Human Sex Differences." Research on touching is always indexed under the term "Physical Contact." If you do not know the appropriate index terms, PsycINFO includes a thesaurus that can help you find them.

Given that there are nearly 4.5 million records in PsycINFO, you may have to try a variety of search terms in different combinations and at different levels of specificity before you find what you are looking for. Imagine, for example, that you are interested in the question of whether women and men differ in terms of their ability to recall experiences from when they were very young. If you were to enter "sex differences in childhood memories" as your search term, PsycINFO would return only two records, only one of which is directly relevant to your question. However, if you were to enter the search term "memory," it would return 246,823 records—far too many to look through individually. This is where the thesaurus helps. Entering "memory" into the thesaurus provides several more specific index terms—one of which is "early memories." While searching for "early memories" among the index terms returns 4,423 records—still too many too look through individually—combining it with "human sex differences" as a second search term returns 64 articles, including many that are highly relevant to your topic.

PsycINFO also makes it possible to save, print, or e-mail the relevant records you find. The records might even include links to full-text copies of the works themselves. If not, and you want a copy of the work, you will have to find out if your library carries the journal or has the book, or if it can get what you need from another library.

## Other Search Techniques

Another extremely useful tool is Google Scholar (http://scholar.google.com), which is an Internet search engine that specializes in academic research from all disciplines. The benefits of Google Scholar are that it is freely available to everyone, and it is extremely easy to use. Search results can be sorted by relevance or date and often include links to full-text versions of articles and book chapters. If you create your own profile, you can also save the results of your searches for easy access later. As with PsycINFO, however, you may need to try a variety of search terms in different combinations to find exactly the research you are looking for.

In addition to entering search terms into using PsycINFO or Google Scholar, there are several other techniques you can use to search the research literature. First, if you have one good article or book chapter on your topic—a recent review article is best—you can look through the reference list of that article for other relevant works. And when you find those, you can look through their reference lists for additional relevant works. This is sometimes referred to as "backward chaining." You can also start with a classic article or book chapter on your topic, find it in PsycINFO or Google Scholar, and link from there to a list of later works that have cited that one. And when you find those, you can find other articles that have cited them. This is sometimes referred to as "forward chaining."

It can also be helpful to do a general Internet search using search terms related to your topic or the names of researchers who work on your topic. This might lead you directly to works that are part of the research literature (e.g., articles in open-access journals or posted on researchers' own websites). It might also lead you to websites that are not part of the research literature but that provide references to works that are. Finally, you can talk with people (e.g., your instructor or other faculty members in psychology) who know something about your topic and can suggest relevant articles and book chapters for you to read.

## What to Search For

When you review the research literature, you need to be selective. Not every article, book chapter, and book that relates to your research idea or question will be worth finding, reading, and integrating into your own work. Instead, you want to focus on sources that help you do four basic things: (a) refine your research question, (b) identify appropriate research methods, (c) place your research in the context of previous research, and (d) write an effective research report. Several basic principles can help you find the most useful sources.

First, it is best to focus on recent research, keeping in mind that what counts as recent depends on the topic. For newer topics that are actively being studied, "recent" might mean published in the past year or two. For older topics that are receiving less attention right now, "recent" might mean within the past 10 years. You will get a feel for what counts as recent for your topic when you start your literature search. A good general rule, however, is to start with sources published in the past five years. The main exception to this rule would be classic articles that turn up in the reference list of nearly every other source. If other researchers think that this work is important, even though it is old, then by all means you should include it in your review.

Second, you should look for review articles on your topic because they will provide a useful overview of it—often discussing important definitions, results, theories, trends, and controversies—giving you a good sense of where your own research fits into the literature. You should also look for empirical research reports addressing your question or similar questions, which can give you ideas about how to operationally define your variables and collect your data. As a general rule, it is good to use methods that others have already used successfully unless you have good reasons not to. Finally, you should look for sources that provide information that can help you argue for the interestingness of your research question. For a study on the effects of cell phone use on driving ability, for example, you might look for information about how widespread cell phone use is, how frequent and costly motor vehicle crashes are, and so on.

How many sources are enough for your literature review? This is a difficult question because it depends on how extensively your topic has been studied and also on your own goals. One study found that across a variety of professional journals in psychology, the average number of sources cited per article was about 50 (Adair & Vohra, 2003).[4] This gives a rough idea of what professional researchers consider to be adequate. As a student, you might be assigned a much lower minimum number of references to use, but the principles for selecting the most useful ones remain the same.

## Key Takeaways

- The research literature in psychology is all the published research in psychology, consisting primarily of articles in professional journals and scholarly books.
- Early in the research process, it is important to conduct a review of the research literature on your topic to refine your research question, identify appropriate research methods, place your question in the context of other research, and prepare to write an effective research report.
- There are several strategies for finding previous research on your topic. Among the best is using PsycINFO, a computer database that catalogs millions of articles, books, and book chapters in psychology and related fields.

## Exercise

1. Practice: Use the techniques discussed in this section to find 10 journal articles and book chapters on one of the following research ideas: memory for smells, aggressive driving, the causes of narcissistic personality disorder, the functions of the intraparietal sulcus, or prejudice against the physically handicapped.

# Endnotes

1. Bruck, M. (2009). Human figure drawings and children's recall of touching. *Journal of Experimental Psychology: Applied, 15*, 361–374.
2. Stanovich, K. E. (2010). *How to think straight about psychology* (9th ed.). Boston, MA: Allyn & Bacon.
3. Milgram, S. (1963). Behavioral study of obedience. *Journal of Abnormal and Social Psychology, 67*, 371–378.
4. Adair, J. G., & Vohra, N. (2003). The explosion of knowledge, references, and citations: Psychology's unique response to a crisis. *American Psychologist, 58*, 15–23.

# CHAPTER 3

# Research Ethics

In 1998, a medical journal called *The Lancet* published an article of interest to many psychologists. The researchers claimed to have shown a statistical relationship between receiving the combined measles, mumps, and rubella (MMR) vaccine and the development of autism—suggesting furthermore that the vaccine might even *cause* autism. One result of this report was that many parents decided not to have their children vaccinated, which of course put them at higher risk for measles, mumps, and rubella. However, follow-up studies by other researchers consistently failed to find a statistical relationship between the MMR vaccine and autism—and it is generally accepted now that there is no relationship. In addition, several more serious problems with the original research were uncovered. Among them were that the lead researcher stood to gain financially from his conclusions because he had patented a competing measles vaccine. He had also used biased methods to select and test his research participants and had used unapproved and medically unnecessary procedures on them. In 2010, *The Lancet* retracted the article, and the lead researcher's right to practice medicine was revoked (Burns, 2010).[1]

In this chapter we explore the ethics of scientific research in psychology. We begin with a general framework for thinking about the ethics of scientific research in psychology. Then we look at some specific ethical codes for biomedical and behavioral researchers—focusing on the Ethics Code of the American Psychological Association (APA). Finally, we consider some practical tips for conducting ethical research in psychology.

**FIGURE 3.1**

In 1998, a study linking the MMR vaccine to autism caused vaccination rates to drop and put children at higher risk of measles, mumps, and rubella. Subsequent research failed to find a statistical relationship between the vaccine and autism.

Source: © 2010 Thinkstock

# 3.1 Moral Foundations of Ethical Research

## Learning Objectives

1. Describe a simple framework for thinking about ethical issues in psychological research.
2. Give examples of several ethical issues that arise in psychological research—including ones that affect research participants, the scientific community, and society more generally.

**Ethics** is the branch of philosophy that is concerned with morality—what it means to behave morally and how people can achieve that goal. It can also refer to a set of principles and practices that provide moral guidance in a particular field. There is an ethics of business, medicine, teaching, and of course, scientific research. As the opening example illustrates, many kinds of ethical issues can arise in scientific research, especially when it involves human participants. For this reason, it is useful to begin with a general framework for thinking through these issues.

**ethics**

The branch of philosophy that is concerned with morality. Also a set of principles and practices that provide moral guidance in a particular field.

# A Framework for Thinking About Research Ethics

Table 3.1 presents a framework for thinking through the ethical issues involved in psychological research. The rows of Table 3.1 represent four general moral principles that apply to scientific research: weighing risks against benefits, acting responsibly and with integrity, seeking justice, and respecting people's rights and dignity. (These principles are adapted from those in the American Psychological Association Ethics Code.) The columns of Table 3.1 represent three groups of people that are affected by scientific research: the research participants, the scientific community, and society more generally. The idea is that a thorough consideration of the ethics of any research project must take into account how each of the four moral principles applies to each of the three groups of people.

**TABLE 3.1** A Framework for Thinking About Ethical Issues in Scientific Research

| | Who is affected? | | |
|---|---|---|---|
| Moral principle | Research participants | Scientific community | Society |
| Weighing risks against benefits | | | |
| Acting responsibly and with integrity | | | |
| Seeking justice | | | |
| Respecting people's rights and dignity | | | |

# Moral Principles

Let us look more closely at each of the moral principles and how they can be applied to each of the three groups.

## Weighing Risks Against Benefits

Scientific research in psychology can be ethical only if its risks are outweighed by its benefits. Among the risks to research participants are that a treatment might fail to help or even be harmful, a procedure might result in physical or psychological harm, and their right to privacy might be violated. Among the potential benefits are receiving a helpful treatment, learning about psychology, experiencing the satisfaction of contributing to scientific knowledge, and receiving money or course credit for participating. Scientific research can have risks and benefits to the scientific community and to society too (Rosenthal, 1994).[2] A risk to science is that if a research question is uninteresting or a study is poorly designed, then the time, money, and effort spent on that research could have been spent on more productive research. A risk to society is that research results could be misunderstood or misapplied with harmful consequences. The research that mistakenly linked the measles, mumps, and rubella (MMR) vaccine to autism resulted in both of these kinds of harm. Of course, the benefits of scientific research to science and society are that the research advances scientific knowledge and can contribute to the welfare of society.

It is not necessarily easy to weigh the risks of research against its benefits because the risks and benefits may not be directly comparable. For example, it is common for the risks of a study to be primarily to the research participants but the benefits primarily for science or society. Consider, for example, Stanley Milgram's original study on obedience to authority (Milgram, 1963).[3] The participants were told that they were taking part in a study on the effects of punishment on learning and were instructed to give electric shocks to another participant each time that participant responded incorrectly on a learning task. With each incorrect response, the shock became stronger—eventually causing the other participant (who was in the next room) to protest, complain about his heart, scream in pain, and finally fall silent and stop responding. If the first participant hesitated or expressed concern, the researcher said that he must continue. In reality, the other participant was a **confederate** of the researcher—a helper who pretended to be a real participant—and the protests, complaints, and screams that the real participant heard were an audio recording that was activated when he flipped the switch to administer the "shocks." The surprising result of this study was that most of the real participants continued to administer the shocks right through the confederate's protests, complaints, and screams. Although this is considered one of the most important results in psychology—with implications for understanding events like the Holocaust or the mistreatment of prisoners by US soldiers at Abu Ghraib—it came at the cost of producing severe psychological stress in the research participants.

**confederate**

A researcher who pretends to be someone that he or she is not in the context of an empirical study. Most often, confederates play the role of other participants who interact in scripted ways with the real participants.

### Was It Worth It?

Much of the debate over the ethics of Milgram's obedience study concerns the question of whether the resulting scientific knowledge was worth the harm caused to the research participants. To get a better sense of the harm, consider Milgram's (1963)[4] own description of it.

> *In a large number of cases, the degree of tension reached extremes that are rarely seen in sociopsychological laboratory studies. Subjects were observed to sweat, tremble, stutter, bite their lips, groan, and dig their fingernails into their flesh....Fourteen of the 40 subjects showed definite signs of nervous laughter and smiling. The laughter seemed entirely out of place, even bizarre. Full blown uncontrollable seizures [of laughter] were observed for three subjects. On one occasion we observed a seizure so violently convulsive that it was necessary to call a halt to the experiment (p. 375).*

Milgram also noted that another observer reported that within 20 minutes one participant "was reduced to a twitching, stuttering wreck, who was rapidly approaching the point of nervous collapse" (p. 377).

To Milgram's credit, he went to great lengths to debrief his participants—including returning their mental states to normal—and to show that most of them thought the research was valuable and were glad to have participated. Still, this research would be considered unethical by today's standards.

## Acting Responsibly and With Integrity

Researchers must act responsibly and with integrity. This means carrying out their research in a thorough and competent manner, meeting their professional obligations, and being truthful. Acting with integrity is important because it promotes trust, which is an essential element of all effective human relationships. Participants must be able to trust that researchers are being honest with them (e.g., about what the study involves), will keep their promises (e.g., to maintain confidentiality), and will carry out their research in ways that maximize benefits and minimize risk. An important issue here is the use of deception. Some research questions (such as Milgram's) are difficult or impossible to answer without deceiving research participants. Thus acting with integrity can conflict with doing research that advances scientific knowledge and benefits society. We will consider how psychologists generally deal with this conflict shortly.

The scientific community and society must also be able to trust that researchers have conducted their research thoroughly and competently and that they have reported on it honestly. Again, the example at the beginning of the chapter illustrates what can happen when this trust is violated. In this case, other researchers wasted resources on unnecessary follow-up research and people avoided the MMR vaccine, putting their children at increased risk of measles, mumps, and rubella.

## Seeking Justice

Researchers must conduct their research in a just manner. They should treat their participants fairly, for example, by giving them adequate compensation for their participation and making sure that benefits and risks are distributed across all participants. For example, in a study of a new and potentially beneficial psychotherapy, some participants might receive the psychotherapy while others serve as a control group that receives no treatment. If the psychotherapy turns out to be effective, it would be fair to offer it to participants in the control group when the study ends.

At a broader societal level, members of some groups have historically faced more than their fair share of the risks of scientific research, including people who are institutionalized, are disabled, or belong to racial or ethnic minorities. A particularly tragic example is the Tuskegee syphilis study conducted by the U.S. Public Health Service from 1932 to 1972 (Reverby, 2009).[5] The participants in this study were poor black men in the vicinity of Tuskegee, Alabama, who were told that they were being treated for "bad blood." Although they were given some free medical care, they were not treated for their syphilis. Instead, they were observed to see how the disease developed in untreated patients. Even after the use of penicillin became the standard treatment for syphilis in the 1940s, these men continued to be denied treatment without being given an opportunity to leave the study. The study was eventually discontinued only after details were made known to the general public by journalists and activists. It is now widely recognized that researchers need to consider issues of justice and fairness at the societal level.

### "They Were Betrayed"

In 1997—65 years after the Tuskegee Syphilis Study began and 25 years after it ended—President Bill Clinton formally apologized on behalf of the U.S. government to those who were affected. Here is an excerpt from the apology:

> So today America does remember the hundreds of men used in research without their knowledge and consent. We remember them and their family members. Men who were poor and African American, without resources and with few alternatives, they believed they had found hope when they were offered free medical care by the United States Public Health Service. They were betrayed.

Read the full text of the apology at http://www.cdc.gov/tuskegee/clintonp.htm.

## Respecting People's Rights and Dignity

Researchers must respect people's rights and dignity as human beings. One element of this is respecting their **autonomy**—their right to make their own choices and take their own actions free from coercion. Of fundamental importance here is the concept of **informed consent**. This means that researchers obtain and document people's agreement to participate in a study after having informed them of everything that might reasonably be expected to affect their decision. Consider the participants in the Tuskegee study. Although they agreed to participate in the study, they were not told that they had syphilis but would be denied treatment for it. Had they been told this basic fact about the study, it seems likely that they would not have agreed to participate. Likewise, had participants in Milgram's study been told that they might be "reduced to a twitching, stuttering wreck," it seems likely that many of them would not have agreed to participate. In neither of these studies did participants give true informed consent.

Another element of respecting people's rights and dignity is respecting their **privacy**—their right to decide what information about them is shared with others. This means that researchers must maintain **confidentiality**, which is essentially an agreement not to disclose participants' personal information without their consent or some appropriate legal authorization.

**autonomy**

People's right to make their own decisions and take their own actions free from coercion.

**informed consent**

The process of obtaining and documenting participants' agreement to be in a study, having informed them of everything that might reasonably be expected to affect their decision.

**privacy**

People's right to decide what personal information about them is revealed to others.

**confidentiality**

The researcher's agreement with his or her participants not to reveal personal information about them except with their permission or as required by law.

# Unavoidable Ethical Conflict

It may already be clear that ethical conflict in psychological research is unavoidable. Because there is little, if any, psychological research that is completely risk free, there will almost always be conflict between risks and benefits. Research that is beneficial to one group (e.g., the scientific community) can be harmful to another (e.g., the research participants), creating especially difficult tradeoffs. We have also seen that being completely truthful with research participants can make it difficult or impossible to conduct scientifically valid studies on important questions.

Of course, many ethical conflicts are fairly easy to resolve. Nearly everyone would agree that deceiving research participants and then subjecting them to physical harm would not be justified by filling a small gap in the research literature. But many ethical conflicts are not easy to resolve, and competent and well-meaning researchers can disagree about how to resolve them. Consider, for example, an actual study on "personal space" conducted in a public men's room (Middlemist, Knowles, & Matter, 1976).[6] The researchers secretly observed their participants to see whether it took them longer to begin urinating when there was another man (a confederate of the researchers) at a nearby urinal. While some critics found this to be an unjustified assault on human dignity (Koocher, 1977),[7] the researchers had carefully considered the ethical conflicts, resolved them as best they could, and concluded that the benefits of the research outweighed the risks (Middlemist, Knowles, & Matter, 1977).[8] For example, they had interviewed some preliminary participants and found that none of them was bothered by the fact that they had been observed.

The point here is that although it may not be possible to eliminate ethical conflict completely, it is possible to deal with it in responsible and constructive ways. In general, this means thoroughly and carefully thinking through the ethical issues that are raised, minimizing the risks, and weighing the risks against the benefits. It also means being able to explain one's ethical decisions to others, seeking feedback on them, and ultimately taking responsibility for them.

## Key Takeaways

- A wide variety of ethical issues arise in psychological research. Thinking them through requires considering how each of four moral principles (weighing risks against benefits, acting responsibly and with integrity, seeking justice, and respecting people's rights and dignity) applies to each of three groups of people (research participants, science, and society).

- Ethical conflict in psychological research is unavoidable. Researchers must think through the ethical issues raised by their research, minimize the risks, weigh the risks against the benefits, be able to explain their ethical decisions, seek feedback about these decisions from others, and ultimately take responsibility for them.

## Exercises

1. Practice: Imagine a study testing the effectiveness of a new drug for treating obsessive-compulsive disorder. Give a hypothetical example of an ethical issue from each cell of Table 3.1 that could arise in this research.
2. Discussion: It has been argued that researchers are not ethically responsible for the misinterpretation or misuse of their research by others. Do you agree? Why or why not?

# 3.2 From Moral Principles to Ethics Codes

## Learning Objectives

1. Describe the history of ethics codes for scientific research with human participants.
2. Summarize the American Psychological Association Ethics Code—especially as it relates to informed consent, deception, debriefing, research with nonhuman animals, and scholarly integrity.

The general moral principles of weighing risks against benefits, acting with integrity, seeking justice, and respecting people's rights and dignity provide a useful starting point for thinking about the ethics of psychological research because essentially everyone agrees on them. As we have seen, however, even people who agree on these general principles can disagree about specific ethical issues that arise in the course of conducting research. This is why there also exist more detailed and enforceable ethics codes that provide guidance on important issues that arise frequently. In this section, we begin with a brief historical overview of such ethics codes and then look closely at the one that is most relevant to psychological research—that of the APA.

# Historical Overview

One of the earliest ethics codes was the **Nuremberg Code**—a set of 10 principles written in 1947 in conjunction with the trials of Nazi physicians accused of shockingly cruel research on concentration camp prisoners during World War II. It provided a standard against which to compare the behavior of the men on trial—many of whom were eventually convicted and either imprisoned or sentenced to death. The Nuremberg Code was particularly clear about the importance of carefully weighing risks against benefits and the need for informed consent. The **Declaration of Helsinki** is a similar ethics code that was created by the World Medical Council in 1964. Among the standards that it added to the Nuremberg Code was that research with human participants should be based on a written **protocol**—a detailed description of the research—that is reviewed by an independent committee. The Declaration of Helsinki has been revised several times, most recently in 2004.

In the United States, concerns about the Tuskegee study and others led to the publication in 1978 of a set of federal guidelines called the **Belmont Report**. The Belmont Report explicitly recognized the principle of seeking justice, including the importance of conducting research in a way that distributes risks and benefits fairly across different groups at the societal level. The Belmont Report became the basis for a set of laws—the **Federal Policy for the Protection of Human Subjects** (or the "Common Rule")—that applies to research conducted, supported, or regulated by the federal government. An extremely important part of these regulations is that universities, hospitals, and other institutions that receive support from the federal government must establish an **institutional review board (IRB)**—a committee that is responsible for reviewing research protocols for potential ethical problems. An IRB must consist of at least five people with varying backgrounds, including members of different professions, scientists and nonscientists, men and women, and at least one person not otherwise affiliated with the institution. The IRB helps to make sure that the risks of the proposed research are minimized, the benefits outweigh the risks, the research is carried out in a fair manner, and the informed consent procedure is adequate.

**Nuremberg Code**

An early ethics code for research with human participants that was written in conjunction with the trials of accused Nazi war criminals after World War II.

**Declaration of Helsinki**

An ethics code for biomedical research with human participants written by the World Medical Council in 1964 and last updated in 2004.

**protocol**

A detailed written description of a research project that can be reviewed by an independent committee to evaluate its conformity to ethical standards.

**Belmont Report**

A set of ethical standards for research with human participants published by the U.S. Department of Health and Human Services in 1978.

**Federal Policy for the Protection of Human Subjects**

A set of federal regulations (45 CFR part 46) for research with human participants based in part on the Belmont Report. Also known as the "Common Rule."

**institutional review board (IRB)**

A committee at a university, a hospital, or another institution that reviews research protocols to be sure they conform to ethical standards.

**exempt research**

Extremely low-risk research that is exempt from the Federal Policy for the Protection of Human Subjects.

**minimal risk research**

Research that exposes participants to risks that are no greater than those encountered by healthy people in daily life or during routine physical or psychological examinations.

**at-risk research**

Research that exposes participants to risks that are greater than those encountered by healthy people in daily life or during routine physical or psychological examinations.

The federal regulations also distinguish research that poses three levels of risk. **Exempt research** includes research on the effectiveness of normal educational activities, the use of standard psychological measures and surveys of a nonsensitive nature that are administered in a way that maintains confidentiality, and research using existing data from public sources. It is called exempt because the regulations do not apply to it. **Minimal risk research** exposes participants to risks that are no greater than those encountered by healthy people in daily life or during routine physical or psychological examinations. Minimal risk research can receive an expedited review by one member of the IRB or by a separate committee under the authority of the IRB that can only approve minimal risk research. (Many departments of psychology have such separate committees.) Finally, **at-risk research** poses greater than minimal risk and must be reviewed by the IRB.

## Ethics Codes

The link that follows the list—from the U.S. Department of Health and Human Services—allows you to read the ethics codes discussed in this section in their entirety. They are all highly recommended and, with the exception of the Federal Policy, short and easy to read.

- The Nuremberg Code
- The Declaration of Helsinki
- The Belmont Report
- Federal Policy for the Protection of Human Subjects (Listed as *45 Code of Federal Regulations 46*)

https://www.hhs.gov/ohrp/international/ethical-codes-and-research-standards/index.html

# APA Ethics Code

**APA Ethics Code**

The ethics code of the American Psychological Association, formally titled *Ethical Principles of Psychologists and Code of Conduct*. Standard 8 concerns the ethics of research and publication.

The APA's *Ethical Principles of Psychologists and Code of Conduct* (also known as the **APA Ethics Code**) was first published in 1953 and has been revised several times since then, most recently in 2002 (American Psychological Association, 2017)[9]. It includes about 150 specific ethical standards that psychologists and their students are expected to follow. Much of the APA Ethics Code concerns the clinical practice of psychology—advertising one's services, setting and collecting fees, having personal relationships with clients, and so on. For our purposes, the most relevant part is *Standard 8: Research and Publication*. Although *Standard 8* is reproduced here in its entirety, we should consider some of its most important aspects—informed consent, deception, debriefing, the use of nonhuman animal subjects, and scholarly integrity—in more detail.

### APA Ethics Code

Standard 8: Research and Publication

8.01 Institutional Approval

When institutional approval is required, psychologists provide accurate information about their research proposals and obtain approval prior to conducting the research. They conduct the research in accordance with the approved research protocol.

8.02 Informed Consent to Research

a. When obtaining informed consent as required in Standard 3.10, Informed Consent, psychologists inform participants about (1) the purpose of the research, expected duration, and procedures; (2) their right to decline to participate and to withdraw from the research once participation has begun; (3) the foreseeable consequences of declining or withdrawing; (4) reasonably foreseeable factors that may be expected to influence their willingness to participate such as potential risks, discomfort, or adverse effects; (5) any prospective research benefits; (6) limits of confidentiality; (7) incentives for participation; and (8) whom to contact for questions about the research and research participants' rights. They provide opportunity for the prospective participants to ask questions and receive answers. (See also Standards 8.03, Informed Consent for Recording Voices and Images in Research; 8.05, Dispensing With Informed Consent for Research; and 8.07, Deception in Research.)

b. Psychologists conducting intervention research involving the use of experimental treatments clarify to participants at the outset of the research (1) the experimental nature of the treatment; (2) the services that will or will not be available to the control group(s) if appropriate; (3) the means by which assignment to treatment and control groups will be made; (4) available treatment alternatives if an individual does not wish to participate in the research or wishes to withdraw once a study has begun; and (5) compensation for or monetary costs of participating including, if appropriate, whether reimbursement from the participant or a third-party payor will be sought. (See also Standard 8.02a, Informed Consent to Research.)

8.03 Informed Consent for Recording Voices and Images in Research

Psychologists obtain informed consent from research participants prior to recording their voices or images for data collection unless (1) the research consists solely of naturalistic observations in public places, and it is not anticipated that the recording will be used in a manner that could cause personal identification or harm, or (2) the research design includes deception, and consent for the use of the recording is obtained during debriefing. (See also Standard 8.07, Deception in Research.)

8.04 Client/Patient, Student, and Subordinate Research Participants

a. When psychologists conduct research with clients/patients, students, or subordinates as participants, psychologists take steps to protect the prospective participants from adverse consequences of declining or withdrawing from participation.

b. When research participation is a course requirement or an opportunity for extra credit, the prospective participant is given the choice of equitable alternative activities.

8.05 Dispensing With Informed Consent for Research

Psychologists may dispense with informed consent only (1) where research would not reasonably be assumed to create distress or harm and involves (a) the study of normal educational practices, curricula, or classroom management methods conducted in educational settings; (b) only anonymous questionnaires, naturalistic observations, or archival research for which disclosure of responses would not place participants at risk of criminal or civil liability or damage their financial standing, employability, or reputation, and confidentiality is protected; or (c) the study of factors related to job or organization effectiveness conducted in organizational settings for which there is no risk to participants' employability, and confidentiality is protected or (2) where otherwise permitted by law or federal or institutional regulations.

8.06 Offering Inducements for Research Participation

a. Psychologists make reasonable efforts to avoid offering excessive or inappropriate financial or other inducements for research participation when such inducements are likely to coerce participation.

b. When offering professional services as an inducement for research participation, psychologists clarify the nature of the services, as well as the risks, obligations, and limitations. (See also Standard 6.05, Barter With Clients/Patients.)

8.07 Deception in Research

a. Psychologists do not conduct a study involving deception unless they have determined that the use of deceptive techniques is justified by the study's significant prospective scientific, educational, or applied value and that effective nondeceptive alternative procedures are not feasible.

b. Psychologists do not deceive prospective participants about research that is reasonably expected to cause physical pain or severe emotional distress.

c. Psychologists explain any deception that is an integral feature of the design and conduct of an experiment to participants as early as is feasible, preferably at the conclusion of their participation, but no later than at the conclusion of the data collection, and permit participants to withdraw their data. (See also Standard 8.08, Debriefing.)

8.08 Debriefing

a. Psychologists provide a prompt opportunity for participants to obtain appropriate information about the nature, results, and conclusions of the research, and they take reasonable steps to correct any misconceptions that participants may have of which the psychologists are aware.

b. If scientific or humane values justify delaying or withholding this information, psychologists take reasonable measures to reduce the risk of harm.

c. When psychologists become aware that research procedures have harmed a participant, they take reasonable steps to minimize the harm.

8.09 Humane Care and Use of Animals in Research

a. Psychologists acquire, care for, use, and dispose of animals in compliance with current federal, state, and local laws and regulations, and with professional standards.

b. Psychologists trained in research methods and experienced in the care of laboratory animals supervise all procedures involving animals and are responsible for ensuring appropriate consideration of their comfort, health, and humane treatment.

c. Psychologists ensure that all individuals under their supervision who are using animals have received instruction in research methods and in the care, maintenance, and handling of the species being used, to the extent appropriate to their role. (See also Standard 2.05, Delegation of Work to Others.)

d. Psychologists make reasonable efforts to minimize the discomfort, infection, illness, and pain of animal subjects.

e. Psychologists use a procedure subjecting animals to pain, stress, or privation only when an alternative procedure is unavailable and the goal is justified by its prospective scientific, educational, or applied value.

f. Psychologists perform surgical procedures under appropriate anesthesia and follow techniques to avoid infection and minimize pain during and after surgery.

g. When it is appropriate that an animal's life be terminated, psychologists proceed rapidly, with an effort to minimize pain and in accordance with accepted procedures.

8.10 Reporting Research Results

a. Psychologists do not fabricate data. (See also Standard 5.01a, Avoidance of False or Deceptive Statements.)

b. If psychologists discover significant errors in their published data, they take reasonable steps to correct such errors in a correction, retraction, erratum, or other appropriate publication means.

8.11 Plagiarism

Psychologists do not present portions of another's work or data as their own, even if the other work or data source is cited occasionally.

8.12 Publication Credit

a. Psychologists take responsibility and credit, including authorship credit, only for work they have actually performed or to which they have substantially contributed. (See also Standard 8.12b, Publication Credit.)

b. Principal authorship and other publication credits accurately reflect the relative scientific or professional contributions of the individuals involved, regardless of their relative status. Mere possession of an institutional position, such as department chair, does not justify authorship credit. Minor contributions to the research or to the writing for publications are acknowledged appropriately, such as in footnotes or in an introductory statement.

c. Except under exceptional circumstances, a student is listed as principal author on any multiple-authored article that is substantially based on the student's doctoral dissertation. Faculty advisors discuss publication credit with students as early as feasible and throughout the research and publication process as appropriate. (See also Standard 8.12b, Publication Credit.)

8.13 Duplicate Publication of Data

Psychologists do not publish, as original data, data that have been previously published. This does not preclude republishing data when they are accompanied by proper acknowledgment.

8.14 Sharing Research Data for Verification

a. After research results are published, psychologists do not withhold the data on which their conclusions are based from other competent professionals who seek to verify the substantive claims through reanalysis and who intend to use such data only for that purpose, provided that the confidentiality of the participants can be protected and unless legal rights concerning proprietary data preclude their release. This does not preclude psychologists from requiring that such individuals or groups be responsible for costs associated with the provision of such information.

b. Psychologists who request data from other psychologists to verify the substantive claims through reanalysis may use shared data only for the declared purpose. Requesting psychologists obtain prior written agreement for all other uses of the data.

8.15 Reviewers

Psychologists who review material submitted for presentation, publication, grant, or research proposal review respect the confidentiality of and the proprietary rights in such information of those who submitted it.

*Source: Copyright © 2017 American Psychological Association.Reproduced with permission. The official citation that should be used in referencing this material is American Psychological Association. (2017). Ethical principles of psychologists and code of conduct (2002, Amended June1, 2010 and January 1, 2017). Retrieved from http://www.apa.org/ethics/code/index.aspx. No further reproduction or distribution is permitted without written permission from the American Psychological Association.*

# Informed Consent

Standards 8.02 to 8.05 are about informed consent. Again, informed consent means obtaining and documenting people's agreement to participate in a study, having informed them of everything that might reasonably be expected to affect their decision. This includes details of the procedure, the risks and benefits of the research, the fact that they have the right to decline to participate or to withdraw from the study, the consequences of doing so, and any legal limits to confidentiality. For example, some states require researchers who learn of child abuse or other crimes to report this information to authorities.

Although the process of obtaining informed consent often involves having participants read and sign a **consent form**, it is important to understand that this is not all it is. Although having participants read and sign a consent form might be enough when they are competent adults with the necessary ability and motivation, many participants do not actually read consent forms or they read them but do not understand them. For example, participants often mistake consent forms for legal documents and mistakenly believe that by signing them they give up their right to sue the researcher (Mann, 1994).[10] Even with competent adults, therefore, it is good practice to tell participants about the risks and benefits, demonstrate the procedure, ask them if they have questions, and remind them of their right to withdraw at any time—in addition to having them read and sign a consent form.

Note also that there are situations in which informed consent is not necessary. These include situations in which the research is not expected to cause any harm and the procedure is straightforward or the study is conducted in the context of people's ordinary activities. For example, if you wanted to sit outside a public building and observe whether people hold the door open for people behind them, you would not need to obtain their informed consent. Similarly, if a college instructor wanted to compare two legitimate teaching methods across two sections of his research methods course, he would not need to obtain informed consent from his students.

**consent form**

A form that participants sign as part of the informed consent process. It describes the procedure, the risks and benefits, participants' right to withdraw from the study, and any confidentiality issues.

# Deception

**Deception** of participants in psychological research can take a variety of forms: misinforming participants about the purpose of a study, using confederates, using phony equipment like Milgram's shock generator, and presenting participants with false feedback about their performance (e.g., telling them they did poorly on a test when they actually did well). Deception also includes not informing participants of the full design or true purpose of the research even if they are not actively misinformed (Sieber, Iannuzzo, & Rodriguez, 1995).[11] For example, a study on incidental learning—learning without conscious effort—might involve having participants read through a list of words in preparation for a "memory test" later. Although participants are likely to assume that the memory test will require them to recall the words, it might instead require them to recall the contents of the room or the appearance of the research assistant.

Some researchers have argued that deception of research participants is rarely if ever ethically justified. Among their arguments are that it prevents participants from giving truly informed consent, fails to respect their dignity as human beings, has the potential to upset them, makes them distrustful and therefore less honest in their responding, and damages the reputation of researchers in the field (Baumrind, 1985).[12]

Note, however, that the APA Ethics Code takes a more moderate approach—allowing deception when the benefits of the study outweigh the risks, participants cannot reasonably be expected to be harmed, the research question cannot be answered without the use of deception, and participants are informed about the deception as soon as possible. This approach acknowledges that not all forms of deception are equally bad. Compare, for example, Milgram's study in which he deceived his participants in several significant ways that resulted in their experiencing severe psychological stress with an incidental learning study in which a "memory test" turns out to be slightly different from what participants were expecting. It also acknowledges that some scientifically and socially important research questions can be difficult or impossible to answer without deceiving participants. Knowing that a study concerns the extent to which they obey authority, act aggressively toward a peer, or help a stranger is likely to change the way people behave so that the results no longer generalize beyond the study itself.

# Debriefing

Standard 8.08 is about **debriefing**. This is the process of informing research participants as soon as possible of the purpose of the study, revealing any deception, and correcting any other misconceptions they might have as a result of participating. Debriefing also involves minimizing harm that might have occurred. For example, an experiment on the effects of being in a sad mood on memory might involve inducing a sad mood in participants by having them think sad thoughts, watch a sad video, or listen to sad music. Debriefing would be the time to return participants' moods to normal by having them think happy thoughts, watch a happy video, or listen to happy music.

# Nonhuman Animal Subjects

Standard 8.09 is about the humane treatment and care of nonhuman animal subjects. Although most contemporary research in psychology does not involve nonhuman animal subjects, a significant minority of it does—especially in the study of learning and conditioning, behavioral neuroscience, and the development of drug and surgical therapies for psychological disorders.

The use of nonhuman animal subjects in psychological research is like the use of deception in that there are those who argue that it is rarely, if ever, ethically acceptable (Bowd & Shapiro, 1993).[13] Clearly, nonhuman animals are incapable of giving informed consent. Yet they can be subjected to numerous procedures that are likely to cause them suffering. They can be confined, deprived of food and water, subjected to pain, operated on, and ultimately euthanized. (Of course, they can also be observed benignly in natural or zoolike settings.) Others point out that psychological research on nonhuman animals has resulted in many important benefits to humans, including the development of behavioral therapies for many disorders, more effective pain control methods, and antipsychotic drugs (Miller, 1985).[14] It has also resulted in benefits to nonhuman animals, including alternatives to shooting and poisoning as means of controlling them.

As with deception, the APA acknowledges that the benefits of research on nonhuman animals can outweigh the costs, in which case it is ethically acceptable. However, researchers must use alternative methods when they can. When they cannot, they must acquire and care for their subjects humanely and minimize the harm to them. For more information on the APA's position on nonhuman animal subjects, see the website of the APA's Committee on Animal Research and Ethics (http://www.apa.org/science/leadership/care/index.aspx).

## Scholarly Integrity

Standards 8.10 to 8.15 are about scholarly integrity. These include the obvious points that researchers must not fabricate data or plagiarize. **Plagiarism** means using others' words or ideas without proper acknowledgment. Proper acknowledgment generally means indicating direct quotations with quotation marks *and* providing a citation to the source of any quotation or idea used.

**plagiarism**
Using others' words or ideas without proper acknowledgment.

The remaining standards make some less obvious but equally important points. Researchers should not publish the same data a second time as though it were new, they should share their data with other researchers, and as peer reviewers they should keep the unpublished research they review confidential. Note that the authors' names on published research—and the order in which those names appear—should reflect the importance of each person's contribution to the research. It would be considered unethical, for example, to include as an author someone who had made only minor contributions to the research (e.g., analyzing some of the data) or for a faculty member to make himself or herself the first author on research that was largely conducted by a student.

**FIGURE 3.2**

According to the APA Ethics Code, faculty advisers should discuss publication credit—who will be an author and the order of authors—with their student collaborators as early as possible in the research process.

Source: © 2010 Thinkstock

## Key Takeaways

- There are several written ethics codes for research with human participants that provide specific guidance on the ethical issues that arise most frequently. These codes include the Nuremberg Code, the Declaration of Helsinki, the Belmont Report, and the Federal Policy for the Protection of Human Subjects.

- The APA Ethics Code is the most important ethics code for researchers in psychology. It includes many standards that are relevant mainly to clinical practice, but *Standard 8* concerns informed consent, deception, debriefing, the use of nonhuman animal subjects, and scholarly integrity in research.

- Research conducted at universities, hospitals, and other institutions that receive support from the federal government must be reviewed by an institutional review board (IRB)—a committee at the institution that reviews research protocols to make sure they conform to ethical standards.

- Informed consent is the process of obtaining and documenting people's agreement to participate in a study, having informed them of everything that might reasonably be expected to affect their decision. Although informed consent often involves having participants read and sign a consent form, it is not equivalent to this. A participant who has signed a consent form without reading it or fully understanding it has not really given informed consent.

- Although some researchers argue that deception of research participants is never ethically justified, the APA Ethics Code allows for its use when the benefits of using it outweigh the risks, participants cannot reasonably be expected to be harmed, there is no way to conduct the study without deception, and participants are informed of the deception as soon as possible.

## Exercises

1. Practice: Read the Nuremberg Code, the Belmont Report, and *Standard 8* of the APA Ethics Code. List five specific similarities and five specific differences among them.
2. Discussion: In a study on the effects of disgust on moral judgment, participants were asked to judge the morality of disgusting acts, including people eating a dead pet and passionate kissing between a brother and sister (Haidt, Koller, & Dias, 1993).[15] If you were on the IRB that reviewed this protocol, what concerns would you have with it? Refer to the appropriate sections of the APA Ethics Code.

# 3.3 Putting Ethics Into Practice

## Learning Objectives

1. Describe several strategies for identifying and minimizing risks and deception in psychological research.
2. Create thorough informed consent and debriefing procedures, including a consent form.

In this section, we look at some practical advice for conducting ethical research in psychology. Again, it is important to remember that ethical issues arise well before you begin to collect data and continue to arise through publication and beyond.

# Know and Accept Your Ethical Responsibilities

As the APA Ethics Code notes in its introduction, "Lack of awareness or misunderstanding of an ethical standard is not itself a defense to a charge of unethical conduct" (American Psychological Association, 2017)[16]. This is why the very first thing that you must do as a new researcher is know and accept your ethical responsibilities. At a minimum, this means reading and understanding the relevant standards of the APA Ethics Code, distinguishing minimal risk from at-risk research, and knowing the specific policies and procedures of your institution—including how to prepare and submit a research protocol for institutional review board (IRB) review. If you are conducting research as a course requirement, there may be specific course standards, policies, and procedures. If any standard, policy, or procedure is unclear—or you are unsure what to do about an ethical issue that arises—you must seek clarification. You can do this by reviewing the relevant ethics codes, reading about how similar issues have been resolved by others, or consulting with more experienced researchers, your IRB, or your course instructor. Ultimately, you as the researcher must take responsibility for the ethics of the research you conduct.

# Identify and Minimize Risks

As you design your study, you must identify and minimize risks to participants. Start by listing all the risks, including risks of physical and psychological harm and violations of confidentiality. Remember that it is easy for researchers to see risks as less serious than participants do or even to overlook them completely. For example, one student researcher wanted to test people's sensitivity to violent images by showing them gruesome photographs of crime and accident scenes. Because she was an emergency medical technician, however, she greatly underestimated how disturbing these images were to most people. Remember too that some risks might apply only to some participants. For example, while most people would have no problem completing a survey about their fear of various crimes, those who have been a victim of one of those crimes might become upset. This is why you should seek input from a variety of people, including your research collaborators, more experienced researchers, and even from nonresearchers who might be better able to take the perspective of a participant.

Once you have identified the risks, you can often reduce or eliminate many of them. One way is to modify the research design. For example, you might be able to shorten or simplify the procedure to prevent boredom and frustration. You might be able to replace upsetting or offensive stimulus materials (e.g., graphic accident scene photos) with less upsetting or offensive ones (e.g., milder photos of the sort people are likely to see in the newspaper). A good example of modifying a research design is a 2009 replication of Milgram's study conducted by researcher Jerry Burger. Instead of allowing his participants to continue administering shocks up to the 450-V maximum, the researcher always stopped the procedure when they were about to administer the 150-V shock (Burger, 2009).[17] This made sense because in Milgram's study (a) participants' severe negative reactions occurred after this point and (b) most participants who administered the 150-V shock continued all the way to the 450-V maximum. Thus the researcher was able to compare his results directly with Milgram's at every point up to the 150-V shock and also was able to estimate how many of his participants would have continued to the maximum—but without subjecting them to the severe stress that Milgram did. (The results, by the way, were that these contemporary participants were just as obedient as Milgram's were.)

**prescreening**

Any procedure used to select participants for further study based on demographic or other characteristics. Often used to identify and remove participants who are particularly at high risk of harm.

A second way to minimize risks is to use a **prescreening** procedure to identify and eliminate participants who are at high risk. You can do this in part through the informed consent process. For example, you can warn participants that a survey includes questions about their fear of crime and remind them that they are free to withdraw if they think this might upset them. Prescreening can also involve collecting data to identify and eliminate participants. For example, Burger used an extensive prescreening procedure involving multiple questionnaires and an interview with a clinical psychologist to identify and eliminate participants with physical or psychological problems that put them at high risk.

A third way to minimize risks is to take active steps to maintain confidentiality. You should keep signed consent forms separately from any data that you collect and in such a way that no individual's name can be linked to his or her data. In addition, beyond people's sex and age, you should only collect personal information that you actually need to answer your research question. If people's sexual orientation or ethnicity is not clearly relevant to your research question, for example, then do not ask them about it. Be aware also that certain data collection procedures can lead to unintentional violations of confidentiality. When participants respond to an oral survey in a shopping mall or complete a questionnaire in a classroom setting, it is possible that their responses will be overheard or seen by others. If the responses are personal, it is better to administer the survey or questionnaire individually in private or to use other techniques to prevent the unintentional sharing of personal information.

# Identify and Minimize Deception

Remember that deception can take a variety of forms, not all of which involve actively misleading participants. It is also deceptive to allow participants to make incorrect assumptions (e.g., about what will be on a "memory test") or simply withhold information about the full design or purpose of the study. It is best to identify and minimize *all* forms of deception.

Remember that according to the APA Ethics Code, deception is ethically acceptable only if there is no way to answer your research question without it. Therefore, if your research design includes any form of active deception, you should consider whether it is truly necessary. Imagine, for example, that you want to know whether the age of college professors affects students' expectations about their teaching ability. You could do this by telling participants that you will show them photos of college professors and ask them to rate each one's teaching ability. But if the photos are not really of college professors but of your own family members and friends, then this would be deception. This deception could easily be eliminated, however, by telling participants instead to *imagine* that the photos are of college professors and to rate them *as if* they were.

In general, it is considered acceptable to wait until debriefing before you reveal your research question as long as you describe the procedure, risks, and benefits during the informed consent process. For example, you would not have to tell participants that you wanted to know whether the age of college professors affects people's expectations about them until the study was over. Not only is this information unlikely to affect people's decisions about whether to participate in the study, but it has the potential to invalidate the results. Participants who know that age is the independent variable might rate the older and younger "professors" differently because they think you want them to. Alternatively, they might be careful to rate them the same so that they do not appear prejudiced. But even this extremely mild form of deception can be minimized by informing participants—orally, in writing, or both—that although you have accurately described the procedure, risks, and benefits, you will wait to reveal the research question until afterward. In essence, participants give their consent to be deceived or to have information withheld from them until later.

# Weigh the Risks Against the Benefits

Once the risks of the research have been identified and minimized, you need to weigh them against the benefits. This requires identifying all the benefits. Remember to consider benefits to the research participants, to science, and to society. If you are a student researcher, remember that one of the benefits is the knowledge you will gain about how to conduct scientific research in psychology—knowledge you can then use to complete your studies and succeed in graduate school or in your career.

If the research poses minimal risk—no more than in people's daily lives or routine physical or psychological examinations—then even a small benefit to participants, science, or society is generally considered enough to justify it. If it poses more than minimal risk, then there should be more benefits. If the research has the potential to upset some participants, for example, then it becomes more important that the study be well designed and answer a scientifically interesting research question or have clear practical implications. It would be unethical to subject people to pain, fear, or embarrassment for no better reason than to satisfy one's personal curiosity. In general, psychological research that has the potential to cause harm that is more than minor or lasts for more than a short time is rarely considered justified by its benefits. Consider, for example, that Milgram's study—as interesting and important as the results were—would be considered unethical by today's standards.

# Create Informed Consent and Debriefing Procedures

Once you have settled on a research design, you need to create your informed consent and debriefing procedures. Start by deciding whether informed consent is necessary according to APA Standard 8.05. If informed consent is necessary, there are several things you should do. First, when you recruit participants—whether it is through word of mouth, posted advertisements, or a participant pool—provide them with as much information about the study as you can. This will allow those who might find the study objectionable to avoid it. Second, if you will be testing research participants in person, prepare a script or set of "talking points" to help you explain the study to your participants in simple everyday language. This should include a description of the procedure, the risks and benefits, and their right to withdraw at any time. If you will be testing them online, then of course this will not be possible. Third, create an informed consent form that covers all the points in Standard 8.02a. If you are testing the participants in person, they can read and sign it. If you are testing them online, they can indicate whether they agree to be in the study by their response to a multiple-choice item. Your university, department, or course instructor may have sample consent forms that you can adapt for your own study. You can also see samples from different universities in the list below. Remember that if appropriate, both the oral and written parts of the informed consent process should include the fact that you are keeping some information about the design or purpose of the study from them but that you will reveal it during debriefing.

## Sample Informed Consent Forms

Below are links to sample informed consent forms that are appropriate for most psychological research. Notice that although they come from different institutions they cover essentially the same information because they are all based on the Federal Policy for the Protection of Human Subjects.

- University of Michigan Office of Research: http://research-compliance.umich.edu/sites/default/files/resource-download/irb-hsbs_general_consent_template_4.18.2018.docx
- Rochester Institute of Technology Office of Human Subjects Research: https://www.rit.edu/research/hsro/informed_consent_document_sample_tips
- Smith College Institutional Review Board: https://www.smith.edu/irb/forms/Consent_to_Participate_Form.doc
- Stanford University Research Compliance Office: http://humansubjects.stanford.edu/consents/SampCons_TEM02C07.doc

Debriefing is similar to informed consent in that you cannot necessarily expect participants to read and understand written debriefing materials. So if you are testing participants in person, it is best to write a script or set of talking points with the goal of being able to explain the study to them in simple everyday language. During debriefing, you should reveal the research question and full design of the study. For example, if participants are tested under only one condition, then you should explain what happened in the other conditions. If you deceived your participants, you should reveal this as soon as possible, apologize for the deception, explain why it was necessary, and correct any misconceptions that participants might have as a result. Debriefing is also a good time to provide additional benefits to research participants by giving them relevant practical information or referrals to other sources of help. For example, in a study of attitudes toward domestic abuse, you could provide pamphlets about domestic abuse and referral information to the university counseling center for those who might want it. If you are testing participants online, then your written debriefing materials must be especially clear and include a way to contact you if they have questions. Online debriefing could also include a link to an audio or video explanation of the study or to other online resources.

# Get Approval

The next step is to get institutional approval for your research based on the specific policies and procedures at your institution or for your course. This will generally require writing a protocol that describes the purpose of the study, the research design and procedure, the risks and benefits, the steps taken to minimize risks, and the informed consent and debriefing procedures. Do not think of the institutional approval process as merely an obstacle to overcome but as an opportunity to think through the ethics of your research and to consult with others who are likely to have more experience or different perspectives than you. If the IRB has questions or concerns about your research, address them promptly and in good faith. This might even mean making further modifications to your research design and procedure before resubmitting your protocol.

# Follow Through

Your concern with ethics should not end when your study receives institutional approval. It now becomes important to stick to the protocol you submitted or to seek additional approval for anything other than a minor change. During the research, you should monitor your participants for unanticipated reactions and seek feedback from them during debriefing. One criticism of Milgram's study is that although he did not know ahead of time that his participants would have such severe negative reactions, he certainly knew after he had tested the first several and should have made adjustments at that point (Baumrind, 1985).[18] Be alert also for potential violations of confidentiality. Keep the consent forms and the data safe and separate from each other and make sure that no one, intentionally or unintentionally, has access to any participant's personal information.

Finally, you must maintain your integrity through the publication process and beyond. Address publication credit—who will be authors on the research and the order of authors—with your collaborators early and avoid plagiarism in your writing. Remember that your scientific goal is to learn about the way the world actually is and that your scientific duty is to report on your results honestly and accurately. So do not be tempted to fabricate data or alter your results in any way. Besides, unexpected results are often as interesting, or more so, than expected ones.

## Key Takeaways

- It is your responsibility as a researcher to know and accept your ethical responsibilities.
- You can take several concrete steps to minimize risks and deception in your research. These include making changes to your research design, prescreening to identify and eliminate high-risk participants, and providing participants with as much information as possible during informed consent and debriefing.
- Your ethical responsibilities continue beyond IRB approval. You need to monitor participants' reactions, be alert for potential violations of confidentiality, and maintain scholarly integrity through the publication process.

## Exercises

1. Discussion: How could you conduct a study on the extent to which people obey authority in a way that minimizes risks and deception as much as possible? (Note: Such a study would not have to look at all like Milgram's.)

2. Practice: Find a study in a professional journal and create a consent form for that study. Be sure to include all the information in Standard 8.02.

# Endnotes

1. Burns, J. F. (2010, May 24). British medical council bars doctor who linked vaccine to autism. *The New York Times*. Retrieved from http://www.nytimes.com/2010/05/25/health/policy/25autism.html?ref=andrew_wakefield

2. Rosenthal, R. M. (1994). Science and ethics in conducting, analyzing, and reporting psychological research. *Psychological Science, 5*, 127–133.

3. Milgram, S. (1963). Behavioral study of obedience. *Journal of Abnormal and Social Psychology, 67*, 371–378.

4. Milgram, S. (1963). Behavioral study of obedience. *Journal of Abnormal and Social Psychology, 67*, 371–378.

5. Reverby, S. M. (2009). *Examining Tuskegee: The infamous syphilis study and its legacy*. Chapel Hill, NC: University of North Carolina Press.

6. Middlemist, R. D., Knowles, E. S., & Matter, C. F. (1976). Personal space invasions in the lavatory: Suggestive evidence for arousal. *Journal of Personality and Social Psychology, 33*, 541–546.

7. Koocher, G. P. (1977). Bathroom behavior and human dignity. *Journal of Personality and Social Psychology, 35*, 120–121.

8. Middlemist, R. D., Knowles, E. S., & Matter, C. F. (1977). What to do and what to report: A reply to Koocher. *Journal of Personality and Social Psychology, 35*, 122–125.

9. American Psychological Association (2017). *Ethical principles for psychologists and code of conduct*. Retrieved from http://www.apa.org/ethics/code/.

10. Mann, T. (1994). Informed consent for psychological research: Do subjects comprehend consent forms and understand their legal rights? *Psychological Science, 5*, 140–143.

11. Sieber, J. E., Iannuzzo, R., & Rodriguez, B. (1995). Deception methods in psychology: Have they changed in 23 years? *Ethics & Behavior, 5*, 67–85.

12. Baumrind, D. (1985). Research using intentional deception: Ethical issues revisited. *American Psychologist, 40*, 165–174.

13. Bowd, A. D., & Shapiro, K. J. (1993). The case against animal laboratory research in psychology. *Journal of Social Issues, 49*, 133–142.

14. Miller, N. E. (1985). The value of behavioral research on animals. *American Psychologist, 40*, 423–440.

15. Haidt, J., Koller, S. H., & Dias, M. (1993). Affect, culture, and morality, or is it wrong to eat your dog? *Journal of Personality and Social Psychology, 65*, 613–628.

16. American Psychological Association (2017). *Ethical principles of psychologists and code of conduct*. Retrieved from http://www.apa.org/ethics/code/.

17. Burger, J. M. (2009). Replicating Milgram: Would people still obey today? *American Psychologist, 64*, 1–11.

18. Baumrind, D. (1985). Research using intentional deception: Ethical issues revisited. *American Psychologist, 40*, 165–174.

# CHAPTER 4
# Theories in Psychology

In the following paragraph, researchers Sherlock Campbell and James Pennebaker describe a remarkable statistical relationship.

> *Multiple laboratories have demonstrated that people who are asked to write about traumatic experiences subsequently exhibit better physical health than people who are asked to write about superficial topics. In these studies, individuals are randomly assigned to write about either emotional or nonemotional topics for 15 to 20 min per day for 3 to 5 consecutive days. In the past 15 years, dozens of replications have demonstrated that emotional writing can influence frequency of physician visits, immune function, stress hormones, blood pressure, and a host of social, academic, and cognitive variables. These effects hold up across cultures, ages, and diverse samples. (Campbell & Pennebaker, 2003, p. 60)[1]*

In other words, researchers have answered the interesting and important question of whether engaging in what has come to be called "expressive writing" improves people's health. It does. But there is a second question that is equally interesting and important: Why? What psychological and biological variables, structures, and processes are involved, and how do they connect the act of expressive writing to improved health? Several ideas have been proposed. For example, people who write about traumatic experiences might habituate to them. That is, the more they think about them, the less negatively they react both psychologically and physiologically—leading to improvements in mental and physical health (Lepore, Greenberg, Bruno, & Smyth, 2002).[2]

This example illustrates that, like all scientists, researchers in psychology distinguish between two sorts of knowledge: their systematic observations and their explanations or interpretations of those observations. Typically, the former are called phenomena and the latter are called theories. Up to this point in the book, we have focused on phenomena. In this chapter, however, we focus on the equally important role of theories. We begin by exploring the distinction between phenomena and theories in more detail. We then look at the wide variety of theories that researchers in psychology construct. Finally, we consider how researchers use theories, and we cover some strategies for incorporating theory into your own research.

**FIGURE 4.1**
Scientific research has shown that engaging in expressive writing causes improvements in health. Several theories have been proposed to explain this phenomenon.

Source: © Thinkstock

# 4.1 Phenomena and Theories

2. Explain the purposes of scientific theories.

3. Explain why there are usually many plausible theories for any set of phenomena.

# Phenomena

A **phenomenon** (plural, *phenomena*) is a general result that has been observed reliably in systematic empirical research. In essence, it is an established answer to a research question. Some phenomena we have encountered in this book are that expressive writing improves health, women do not talk more than men, and cell phone usage impairs driving ability. Some others are that dissociative identity disorder (formerly called multiple personality disorder) increased greatly in prevalence during the late 20th century, people perform better on easy tasks when they are being watched by others (and worse on difficult tasks), and people recall items presented at the beginning and end of a list better than items presented in the middle.

## Some Famous Psychological Phenomena

Phenomena are often given names by their discoverers or other researchers, and these names can catch on and become widely known. The following list is a small sample of famous phenomena in psychology.

- **Blindsight.** People with damage to their visual cortex are often able to respond to visual stimuli that they do not consciously see.
- **Bystander effect.** The more people who are present at an emergency situation, the less likely it is that any one of them will help.
- **Dunning-Kruger effect.** People tend to overestimate their skills in a variety of areas—and it is the *least* skilled people who overestimate the *most*.
- **Fundamental attribution error.** People tend to explain others' behavior in terms of their personal characteristics as opposed to the situation they are in.
- **McGurk effect.** When audio of a basic speech sound is combined with video of a person making mouth movements for a different speech sound, people often perceive a sound that is intermediate between the two. For a demonstration, see http://auditoryneuroscience.com/vocalizations-speech/mcgurk-effect.
- **Own-race effect.** People recognize faces of people of their own race more accurately than faces of people of other races. (Also called the other-race effect and the cross-race effect.)
- **Placebo effect.** Placebos (fake psychological or medical treatments) often lead to improvements in people's symptoms and functioning.
- **Mere exposure effect.** The more often people have been exposed to a stimulus, the more they like it—even when the stimulus is presented subliminally.
- **Serial position effect.** Stimuli presented near the beginning and end of a list are remembered better than stimuli presented in the middle. For a demonstration, see http://cat.xula.edu/thinker/memory/working/serial.
- **Spontaneous recovery.** A conditioned response that has been extinguished often returns with no further training after the passage of time.

Although an empirical result might be referred to as a phenomenon after being observed only once, this term is more likely to be used for results that have been replicated. **Replication** means conducting a study again—either exactly as it was originally conducted or with modifications—to be sure that it produces the same results. Individual researchers often replicate their own studies before publishing them. Many empirical research reports include an initial study and then one or more follow-up studies that replicate the initial study with minor modifications. Particularly interesting results come to the attention of other researchers who conduct their own replications. The positive effect of expressive writing on health and the negative effect of cell phone usage on driving ability are examples of phenomena that have been replicated many times by many different researchers.

Sometimes a replication of a study produces results that differ from the results of the initial study. This could mean that the results of the initial study or the results of the replication were a fluke—they occurred by chance and do not reflect something that is generally true. In either case, additional replications would be likely to resolve this. A failure to produce the same results could also mean that the replication differed in some important way from the initial study. For example, early studies showed that people performed a variety of tasks better and faster when they were watched by others than when they were alone. Some later replications, however, showed that people performed worse when they were watched by others. Eventually researcher Robert Zajonc identified a key difference between the two types of studies. People seemed to perform better when being watched on highly practiced tasks but worse when being watched on relatively unpracticed tasks (Zajonc, 1965).[3] These two phenomena have now come to be called social facilitation and social inhibition.

**replication**

The process of conducting an empirical study again—either exactly as it was originally conducted or with modifications—to see if the same results are observed.

# Theories

## What Is a Theory?

A **theory** is a coherent explanation or interpretation of one or more phenomena. Although theories can take a variety of forms, one thing they have in common is that they go beyond the phenomena they explain by including variables, structures, processes, functions, or organizing principles that have not been observed directly. Consider, for example, Zajonc's theory of social facilitation and social inhibition. He proposed that being watched by others while performing a task creates a general state of physiological arousal, which increases the likelihood of the dominant (most likely) response. So for highly practiced tasks, being watched increases the tendency to make correct responses, but for relatively unpracticed tasks, being watched increases the tendency to make incorrect responses. Notice that this theory—which has come to be called drive theory—provides an explanation of both social facilitation and social inhibition that goes beyond the phenomena themselves by including concepts such as "arousal" and "dominant response," along with processes such as the effect of arousal on the dominant response.

**theory**

A coherent explanation or interpretation of one or more phenomena.

Outside of science, referring to an idea as a theory often implies that it is untested—perhaps no more than a wild guess. In science, however, the term *theory* has no such implication. A theory is simply an explanation or interpretation of a set of phenomena. It *can* be untested, but it can also be extensively tested, well supported, and accepted as an accurate description of the world by the scientific community. The theory of evolution by natural selection, for example, is a theory because it is an explanation of the diversity of life on earth—not because it is untested or unsupported by scientific research. On the contrary, the evidence for this theory is overwhelmingly positive and nearly all scientists accept its basic assumptions as accurate. Similarly, the "germ theory" of disease is a theory because it is an explanation of the origin of various diseases, not because there is any doubt that many diseases are caused by microorganisms that infect the body.

**perspective**

A general approach to explaining or interpreting phenomena. Among the broadest perspectives in psychology are the biological, evolutionary, behavioral, cognitive, and sociocultural perspectives.

**model**

An explanation of a specific phenomenon, often expressed in the form of mathematical equations, computer programs, or biological structures and processes.

**hypothesis**

A prediction about a new phenomenon that would be observed if a particular theory were true. Also used to refer to a relatively simple theory that includes only a few key components.

In addition to *theory*, researchers in psychology use several related terms to refer to their explanations and interpretations of phenomena. A **perspective** is a broad approach—more general than a theory—to explaining and interpreting phenomena. For example, researchers who take a biological perspective tend to explain phenomena in terms of genetics or nervous and endocrine system structures and processes, while researchers who take a behavioral perspective tend to explain phenomena in terms of reinforcement, punishment, and other external events. A **model** is a precise explanation or interpretation of a specific phenomenon—often expressed in terms of equations, computer programs, or biological structures and processes. A **hypothesis** can be an explanation that relies on just a few key concepts—although this term more commonly refers to a prediction about a new phenomenon based on a theory (see Section 3). Adding to the confusion is the fact that researchers often use these terms interchangeably. It would not be considered wrong to refer to the drive theory as the drive model or even the drive hypothesis. And the biopsychosocial model of health psychology—the general idea that health is determined by an interaction of biological, psychological, and social factors—is really more like a perspective as defined here. Keep in mind, however, that the most important distinction remains that between observations and interpretations.

## What Are Theories For?

Of course, scientific theories are meant to provide accurate explanations or interpretations of phenomena. But there must be more to it than this. Consider that a theory can be accurate without being very useful. To say that expressive writing helps people "deal with their emotions" might be accurate as far as it goes, but it seems too vague to be of much use. Consider also that a theory can be useful without being entirely accurate. Figure 4.2 is a representation of the classic multistore model of human memory, which is still cited by researchers and discussed in textbooks despite the fact that it is now known to be inaccurate in a number of ways (Izawa, 1999).[4] These two examples suggest that theories have purposes other than simply providing accurate explanations or interpretations. Here we look at three additional purposes of theories: the organization of known phenomena, the prediction of outcomes in new situations, and the generation of new research.

**FIGURE 4.2** Representation of the Multistore Model of Human Memory
In the multistore model of human memory, information from the environment passes through a sensory store on its way to a short-term store, where it can be rehearsed, and then to a long-term store, where it can be stored and retrieved much later. Information can be forgotten from any of these three stores. This theory has been extremely successful at organizing old phenomena and predicting new ones.

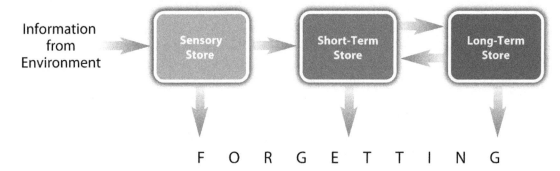

### Organization

One important purpose of scientific theories is to organize phenomena in ways that help people think about them clearly and efficiently. The drive theory of social facilitation and social inhibition, for example, helps to organize and make sense of a large number of seemingly contradictory results. The multistore model of human memory efficiently summarizes many important phenomena: the limited capacity and short retention time of information that is attended to but not rehearsed, the importance of rehearsing information for long-term retention, the serial-position effect, and so on. Or consider a classic theory of intelligence represented by Figure 4.3. According to this theory, intelligence consists of a general mental ability, *g*, plus a small number of more specific abilities that are influenced by *g* (Neisset et al., 1996).[5] Although there are other theories of intelligence, this one does a good job of summarizing a large number of statistical relationships between tests of various mental abilities. This includes the fact that tests of all basic mental abilities tend to be somewhat positively correlated and the fact that certain subsets of mental abilities (e.g., reading comprehension and analogy completion) are more positively correlated than others (e.g., reading comprehension and arithmetic).

**FIGURE 4.3** Representation of One Theory of Intelligence
In this theory of intelligence, a general mental ability (*g*) influences each of three more specific mental abilities: numerical ability, spatial ability, and verbal ability. Theories of this type help to organize a large number of statistical relationships among tests of various mental abilities.

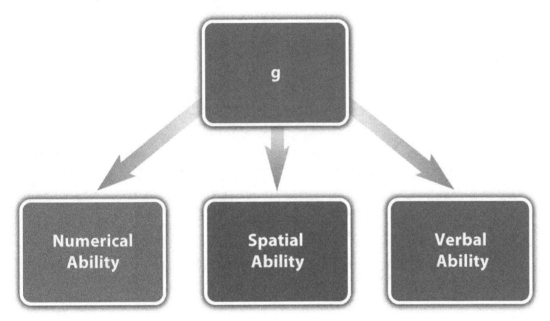

Thus theories are good or useful to the extent that they organize more phenomena with greater clarity and efficiency. Scientists generally follow the principle of **parsimony**, which holds that a theory should include only as many concepts as are necessary to explain or interpret the phenomena of interest. Simpler, more parsimonious theories organize phenomena more efficiently than more complex, less parsimonious theories.

**parsimony**

The extent to which a theory explains or interprets phenomena in as simple a way as possible. A theory that does so is said to be parsimonious.

## Prediction

A second purpose of theories is to allow researchers and others to make predictions about what will happen in new situations. For example, a gymnastics coach might wonder whether a student's performance is likely to be better or worse during a competition than when practicing alone. Even if this particular question has never been studied empirically, Zajonc's drive theory suggests an answer. If the student generally performs with no mistakes, she is likely to perform better during competition. If she generally performs with many mistakes, she is likely to perform worse.

In clinical psychology, treatment decisions are often guided by theories. Consider, for example, dissociative identity disorder (formerly called multiple personality disorder). The prevailing scientific theory of dissociative identity disorder is that people develop multiple personalities (also called alters) because they are familiar with this idea from popular portrayals (e.g., the movie *Sybil*) and because they are unintentionally encouraged to do so by their clinicians (e.g., by asking to "meet" an alter). This theory implies that rather than encouraging patients to act out multiple personalities, treatment should involve discouraging them from doing this (Lilienfeld & Lynn, 2003).[6]

### Generation of New Research

A third purpose of theories is to generate new research by raising new questions. Consider, for example, the theory that people engage in self-injurious behavior such as cutting because it reduces negative emotions such as sadness, anxiety, and anger. This theory immediately suggests several new and interesting questions. Is there, in fact, a statistical relationship between cutting and the amount of negative emotions experienced? Is it causal? If so, what is it about cutting that has this effect? Is it the pain, the sight of the injury, or something else? Does cutting affect all negative emotions equally?

Notice that a theory does not have to be accurate to serve this purpose. Even an inaccurate theory can generate new and interesting research questions. Of course, if the theory is inaccurate, the answers to the new questions will tend to be inconsistent with the theory. This will lead researchers to reevaluate the theory and either revise it or abandon it for a new one. And this is how scientific theories become more detailed and accurate over time.

### What's So Funny?

Researchers Peter McGraw and Caleb Warren (e.g., Warren & McGraw, 2015)[7] have proposed a theory to explain what makes something funny. Specifically, it has to involve a violation of our expectations or norms and simultaneously be perceived as benign (harmless). A particular strength of this *benign violation theory* is its ability to generate interesting new research on humor. For example, McGraw, Warren, Williams, and Leonard (2012)[8] found that joking about a devastating hurricane was not particularly funny while the hurricane was in progress. But this violation gradually became funny as time passed and it began to seem harmless. The peak funniness came about month after the hurricane ended. In the video below you can hear Peter McGraw describe the benign violation theory and some of its implications.

 **Peter McGraw on Benign Violation Theory**

Peter McGraw on Benign Violation Theory

View the video online at: //www.youtube.com/embed/-BxKMgL75as?rel=0

## Multiple Theories

At any point in time, researchers are usually considering multiple theories for any set of phenomena. One reason is that because human behavior is extremely complex, it is always possible to look at it from different perspectives. For example, a biological theory of sexual orientation might focus on the role of sex hormones during critical periods of brain development, while a sociocultural theory might focus on cultural factors that influence how underlying biological tendencies are expressed. A second reason is that—even from the same perspective—there are usually different ways to "go beyond" the phenomena of interest. For example, in addition to the drive theory of social facilitation and social inhibition, there is another theory that explains them in terms of a construct called "evaluation apprehension"—anxiety about being evaluated by the audience. Both theories go beyond the phenomena to be interpreted, but they do so by proposing somewhat different underlying processes.

Different theories of the same set of phenomena can be complementary—with each one supplying one piece of a larger puzzle. A biological theory of sexual orientation and a sociocultural theory of sexual orientation might accurately describe different aspects of the same complex phenomenon. Similarly, social facilitation could be the result of both general physiological arousal *and* evaluation apprehension. But different theories of the same phenomena can also be competing in the sense that if one is accurate, the other is probably not. For example, an alternative theory of dissociative identity disorder—the posttraumatic theory—holds that alters are created unconsciously by the patient as a means of coping with sexual abuse or some other traumatic experience. Because the sociocognitive theory and the posttraumatic theories attribute dissociative identity disorder to fundamentally different processes, it seems unlikely that both can be accurate. See "Where Do Multiple Personalities Come From?", after the following paragraph, for more on these competing theories.

The fact that there are multiple theories for any set of phenomena does not mean that any theory is as good as any other or that it is impossible to know whether a theory provides an accurate explanation or interpretation. On the contrary, scientists are continually comparing theories in terms of their ability to organize phenomena, predict outcomes in new situations, and generate research. Those that fare poorly are assumed to be less accurate and are abandoned, while those that fare well are assumed to be more accurate and are retained and compared with newer—and hopefully better—theories. Although scientists generally do not believe that their theories ever provide perfectly accurate descriptions of the world, they do assume that this process produces theories that come closer and closer to that ideal.

## Where Do Multiple Personalities Come From?

The literature on dissociative identity disorder (DID) features two competing theories. The sociocognitive theory is that DID comes about because patients are aware of the disorder, know its characteristic features, and are encouraged to take on multiple personalities by their therapists. The posttraumatic theory is that multiple personalities develop as a way of coping with sexual abuse or some other trauma. There are now several lines of evidence that support the sociocognitive model over the posttraumatic model (Lilienfeld & Lynn, 2003).[9]

- Diagnosis of DID greatly increased after the release of the book and film *Sybil*—about a woman with DID—in the 1970s.
- DID is extremely rare outside of North America.
- A very small percentage of therapists are responsible for diagnosing the vast majority of cases of DID.
- The literature on treating DID includes many practices that encourage patients to act out multiple personalities (e.g., having a bulletin board on which personalities can leave messages for each other).
- Normal people can easily re-create the symptoms of DID with minimal suggestion in simulated clinical interviews.

## Key Takeaways

- Scientists distinguish between phenomena, which are their systematic observations, and theories, which are their explanations or interpretations of phenomena.
- In addition to providing accurate explanations or interpretations, scientific theories have three basic purposes. They organize phenomena, allow people to predict what will happen in new situations, and help generate new research.
- Researchers generally consider multiple theories for any set of phenomena. Different theories of the same set of phenomena can be complementary or competing.

## Exercises

1. Practice: Think of at least three different theories to explain the fact that married people tend to report greater levels of happiness than unmarried people.
2. Practice: Find a recent article in a professional journal and do two things:
    a. Identify the primary phenomenon of interest.
    b. Identify the theory or theories used to explain or interpret that phenomenon.
3. Discussion: Can a theory be useful even if it is inaccurate? How?

# 4.2 The Variety of Theories in Psychology

## Learning Objectives

1. Describe three dimensions along which theories in psychology vary.
2. Give examples of several different types of theories in psychology.

Researchers in psychology have found that many different types of theories can help them to organize phenomena, predict what will happen in new situations, and generate new research. It is important for beginning researchers to be aware of the different types so that they recognize theories when they see them in the research literature. (They are not always clearly labeled as "theories.") It is also important for them to see that some types of theories are well within their ability to understand, use, and even construct. In this section, we look at the variety of psychological theories in terms of three important dimensions: formality, scope, and theoretical approach.

# Formality

Psychological theories vary widely in their **formality**—the extent to which the components of the theory and the relationships among them are specified clearly and in detail. At the informal end of this dimension are theories that consist of simple verbal descriptions of a few important components and relationships. The habituation theory of expressive-writing effects on health is relatively informal in this sense. So is the drive theory of social facilitation and inhibition. At the more precise, formal end of this dimension are theories that are expressed in terms of mathematical equations or computer programs.

**formality**

The extent to which the components of a theory are specified clearly and lead to precise predictions.

### Formal Theories in Psychology

People who are not familiar with scientific psychology are sometimes surprised to learn that psychological theories can take the form of mathematical equations and computer programs. The following formal theories are among the best known and most successful in the field.

- **ACT-R.** A comprehensive theory of human cognition that is akin to a programming language, within which more specific models can be created. See http://act-r.psy.cmu.edu.
- **Prospect theory.** A formal theory of decision making under uncertainty. Psychologist Daniel Kahneman won the Nobel Prize in economics based in part on prospect theory. Read about Kahneman's Nobel Prize work at https://www.nobelprize.org/prizes/economics/2002/kahneman/auto-biography/.
- **Rescorla-Wagner model.** A theory of classical conditioning that features an equation describing how the strength of the association between unconditioned and conditioned stimuli changes when the two are paired. For more on this formal theory see http://www.scholarpedia.org/article/Rescorla-Wagner_model.

Both informal and formal theories have their place in psychological research. Informal theories tend to be easier to create and to understand but less precise in their predictions, which can make them more difficult to test. They are especially appropriate, however, in the early stages of research when the phenomena of interest have not yet been described in detail. Formal theories tend to be more difficult to create and to understand—sometimes requiring a certain amount of mathematical or computer programming background—but they also tend to be more precise in their predictions and therefore easier to test. They are especially appropriate in the later stages of research when the phenomena of interest have been described in detail.

# Scope

Theories in psychology also vary widely in their **scope**—the number and diversity of the phenomena they explain or interpret. Many early psychological theories were extremely broad in that they attempted to interpret essentially all human behavior. Freud and his followers, for example, applied his theory not only to understanding psychological disorders but also to slips of the tongue and other everyday errors, dreaming, sexuality, art, politics, and even civilization itself (Fine, 1979).[10] Such theories have fallen out of favor in scientific psychology, however, because they tend to be imprecise and difficult to test. In addition, they have not been particularly successful at organizing or predicting the range and complexity of human behavior at the level of detail that scientific researchers usually seek.

**scope**

The number and variety of phenomena explained or interpreted by a theory.

Still, contemporary theories in psychology can vary in their scope. At the broad end of this dimension are theories that apply to many diverse phenomena. Cognitive dissonance theory, for example, assumes that when people hold inconsistent beliefs, this creates mental discomfort that they are motivated to reduce by changing one or both of the beliefs. This theory has been applied to a wide variety of phenomena, including the persistence of irrational beliefs and behaviors (e.g., smoking), the effectiveness of certain persuasion and sales techniques (e.g., asking for a small favor before asking for a big one), and even placebo effects. At the narrow end of this dimension are theories that apply to a small number of closely related phenomena. Consider, for example, a very specific quantitative ability called subitizing. This refers to people's ability to quickly and accurately perceive the number of objects in a scene without counting them—as long as the number is four or fewer. Several theories have been proposed to explain subitizing. Among them is the idea that small numbers of objects are associated with easily recognizable patterns. For example, people know immediately that there are three objects in a scene because the three objects tend to form a "triangle" and it is this pattern that is quickly perceived (Logan & Sbrodoff, 2003).[11]

As with informal and formal theories, both broad and narrow theories have their place in psychological research. Broad theories organize more phenomena but tend to be less formal and less precise in their predictions. Narrow theories organize fewer phenomena but tend to be more formal and more precise in their predictions.

# Theoretical Approach

**theoretical approach**

The kinds of theoretical ideas that a theory is constructed from.

**functional theory**

A theory that explains phenomena in terms of their function or purpose.

In addition to varying in formality and scope, theories in psychology vary widely in the kinds of theoretical ideas they are constructed from. We will refer to this as the **theoretical approach**.

**Functional theories** explain psychological phenomena in terms of their function or purpose. For example, one prominent theory of repeated self-injury (e.g., cutting) is that people do it because it produces a short-term reduction in the intensity of negative emotions that they are feeling (Tantam & Huband, 2009).[12] Note that this theory does not focus on how this happens, but on the function of self-injury for the people who engage in it. Theories from the perspective of evolutionary psychology also tend to be functional—assuming that human behavior has evolved to solve specific adaptive problems faced by our distant ancestors. Consider the phenomenon of sex differences in human mating strategies (Buss & Schmitt, 1993).[13] Men are somewhat more likely than women to seek short-term partners and to value physical attractiveness over material resources in a mate. Women are somewhat more likely than men to seek long-term partners and to value material resources over physical attractiveness in a mate. But why? The standard evolutionary theory holds that because the male investment in becoming a parent is relatively small, men reproduce more successfully by seeking several short-term partners who are young and healthy (which is signaled by physical attractiveness). But because the female investment in becoming a parent is quite large, women reproduce more successfully by seeking a long-term partner who has resources to contribute to raising the child.

**mechanistic theory**

A theory that explains phenomena in terms of underlying variables, structures, and processes, and the interactions among them.

**Mechanistic theories**, on the other hand, focus on specific variables, structures, and processes, and how they interact to produce the phenomena. The drive theory of social facilitation and inhibition and the multistore model of human memory are mechanistic theories in this sense. Figure 4.4 represents another example—a contemporary cognitive theory of hypochondriasis—an extreme form of health anxiety in which people misinterpret ordinary bodily symptoms (e.g., headaches) as signs of a serious illness (e.g., a brain tumor; Williams, 2004).[14] This theory specifies several key variables and the relationships among them. Specifically, people who are high in the personality trait of neuroticism (also called negative emotionality) start to pay excessive attention to negative health information—especially if they have had a significant illness experience as a child (e.g., a seriously ill parent). This attention to negative health information then leads to health anxiety and hypochondriasis, especially among people who are low in effortful control, which is the ability to shift attention away from negative thoughts and feelings.

**FIGURE 4.4** Simplified Representation of One Contemporary Theory of Hypochondriasis
This theory focuses on key variables and the relationships among them.

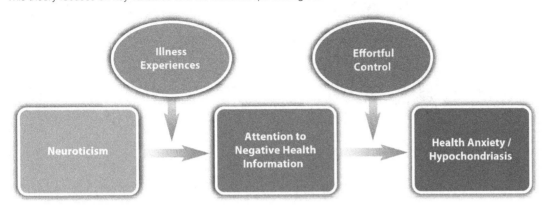

Mechanistic theories can also be expressed in terms of biological structures and processes. With advances in genetics and neuroscience, such theories are becoming increasingly common in psychology. For example, researchers are currently constructing and testing theories that specify the brain structures associated with the storage and rehearsal of information in the short-term store, the transfer of information to the long-term store, and so on. Theories of psychological disorders are also increasingly likely to focus on biological mechanisms. Schizophrenia, for example, has been explained in terms of several biological theories, including theories that focus on genetics, neurotransmitters, brain structures, and even prenatal exposure to infections.

Finally, there are also theoretical approaches that provide organization without necessarily providing a functional or mechanistic explanation. These include **stage theories**, which specify a series of stages that people pass through as they develop or adapt to their environment. Famous stage theories include Abraham Maslow's hierarchy of needs and Jean Piaget's theory of cognitive development. **Typologies** provide organization by categorizing people or behavior into distinct types. These include theories that identify several basic emotions (e.g., happiness, sadness, fear, surprise, anger, and disgust), several distinct types of intelligence (e.g., spatial, linguistic, mathematical, kinesthetic, musical, interpersonal, and intrapersonal), and distinct types of personalities (e.g., Type A vs. Type B).

Researchers in psychology have found that there is a place for all these theoretical approaches. In fact, multiple approaches are probably necessary to provide a complete understanding of any set of phenomena. A complete understanding of emotions, for example, is likely to require identifying the basic emotions that people experience, explaining why we have those emotions, and describing how those emotions work in terms of underlying psychological and biological variables, structures, and processes.

**stage theory**

A theory that specifies a series of stages that people pass through as they develop or adapt to their environment.

**typology**

A theory that categorizes people or behavior into distinct types.

## Key Takeaway

- Theories in psychology vary widely in terms of their formality, scope, and theoretical approach. The different types of theories all play important roles in psychological research.

## Exercises

1. Practice: Find an empirical research report in a professional journal, identify a theory that the researchers present, and then describe the theory in terms of its formality (informal vs. formal), scope (broad vs. narrow), and theoretical approach (functional, mechanistic, etc.).

2. Discussion: Do you think there will ever be a single theory that explains all psychological disorders? Why or why not?

# 4.3 Using Theories in Psychological Research

## Learning Objectives

1. Explain how researchers in psychology test their theories, and give a concrete example.
2. Explain how psychologists reevaluate theories in light of new results, including some of the complications involved.
3. Describe several ways to incorporate theory into your own research.

We have now seen what theories are, what they are for, and the variety of forms that they take in psychological research. In this section, we look more closely at how researchers actually use them. We begin with a general description of how researchers test and revise their theories, and we end with some practical advice for beginning researchers who want to incorporate theory into their research.

## Theory Testing and Revision

### Overview

**hypothetico-deductive method**

The general way that researchers use theories to generate new research and, in the process, test and revise the theories themselves.

The primary way that scientific researchers use theories is sometimes called the **hypothetico-deductive method** (although this term is much more likely to be used by philosophers of science than by scientists themselves). A researcher begins with a set of phenomena and either constructs a theory to explain or interpret them or chooses an existing theory to work with. He or she then makes a prediction about some new phenomenon that should be observed if the theory is correct. Again, this prediction is called a hypothesis. The researcher then conducts an empirical study to test the hypothesis. Finally, he or she reevaluates the theory in light of the new results and revises it if necessary. This process is usually conceptualized as a cycle because the researcher can then derive a new hypothesis from the revised theory, conduct a new empirical study to test the hypothesis, and so on. As Figure 4.5 shows, this approach meshes nicely with the model of scientific research in psychology presented earlier in the book—creating a more detailed model of "theoretically motivated" or "theory-driven" research.

**FIGURE 4.5** A Model of Theoretically Motivated Research

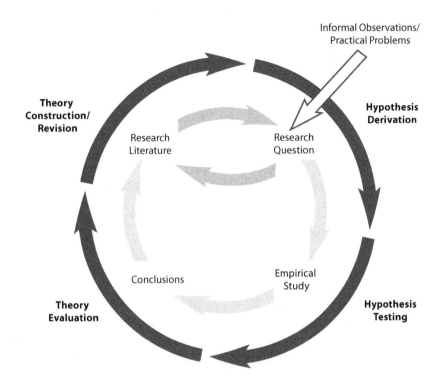

As an example, let us return to Zajonc's research on social facilitation and inhibition. He started with a somewhat contradictory pattern of results from the research literature. He then constructed his drive theory, according to which being watched by others while performing a task causes physiological arousal, which increases an organism's tendency to make the dominant response. This leads to social facilitation for well-learned tasks and social inhibition for poorly learned tasks. He now had a theory that organized previous results in a meaningful way—but he still needed to test it. He hypothesized that if his theory was correct, he should observe that the presence of others improves performance in a simple laboratory task but inhibits performance in a difficult version of the very same laboratory task. To test this hypothesis, one of the studies he conducted used cockroaches as subjects (Zajonc, Heingartner, & Herman, 1969).[15] The cockroaches ran either down a straight runway (an easy task for a cockroach) or through a cross-shaped maze (a difficult task for a cockroach) to escape into a dark chamber when a light was shined on them. They did this either while alone or in the presence of other cockroaches in clear plastic "audience boxes." Zajonc found that cockroaches in the straight runway reached their goal more quickly in the presence of other cockroaches, but cockroaches in the cross-shaped maze reached their goal more slowly when they were in the presence of other cockroaches. Thus he confirmed his hypothesis and provided support for his drive theory.

## Constructing or Choosing a Theory

Along with generating research questions, constructing theories is one of the more creative parts of scientific research. But as with all creative activities, success requires preparation and hard work more than anything else. To construct a good theory, a researcher must know in detail about the phenomena of interest and about any existing theories based on a thorough review of the literature. The new theory must provide a coherent explanation or interpretation of the phenomena of interest and have some advantage over existing theories. It could be more formal and therefore more precise, broader in scope, more parsimonious, or it could take a new perspective or theoretical approach. If there is no existing theory, then almost any theory can be a step in the right direction.

As we have seen, formality, scope, and theoretical approach are determined in part by the nature of the phenomena to be interpreted. But the researcher's interests and abilities play a role too. For example, constructing a theory that specifies the neural structures and processes underlying a set of phenomena requires specialized knowledge and experience in neuroscience (which most professional researchers would acquire in college and then graduate school). But again, many theories in psychology are relatively informal, narrow in scope, and expressed in terms that even a beginning researcher can understand and even use to construct his or her own new theory.

It is probably more common, however, for a researcher to start with a theory that was originally constructed by someone else—giving due credit to the originator of the theory. This is another example of how researchers work collectively to advance scientific knowledge. Once they have identified an existing theory, they might derive a hypothesis from the theory and test it or modify the theory to account for some new phenomenon and then test the modified theory.

## Deriving Hypotheses

Again, a hypothesis is a prediction about a new phenomenon that should be observed if a particular theory is accurate. Theories and hypotheses always have this *if-then* relationship. "*If* drive theory is correct, *then* cockroaches should run through a straight runway faster, and a branching runway more slowly, when other cockroaches are present." Although hypotheses are usually expressed as statements, they can always be rephrased as questions. "Do cockroaches run through a straight runway faster when other cockroaches are present?" Thus deriving hypotheses from theories is an excellent way of generating interesting research questions.

Among the very best hypotheses are those that distinguish between competing theories. For example, Norbert Schwarz and his colleagues considered two theories of how people make judgments about themselves, such as how assertive they are (Schwarz et al., 1991).[16] Both theories held that such judgments are based on relevant examples that people bring to mind. However, one theory was that people base their judgments on the *number* of examples they bring to mind and the other was that people base their judgments on how *easily* they bring those examples to mind. To test these theories, the researchers asked people to recall either six times when they were assertive (which is easy for most people) or 12 times (which is difficult for most people). Then they asked them to judge their own assertiveness. Note that the number-of-examples theory implies that people who recalled 12 examples should judge themselves to be more assertive because they recalled more examples, but the ease-of-examples theory implies that participants who recalled six examples should judge themselves to be more assertive because recalling the examples was easier. Thus the two theories made opposite predictions so that only one of the predictions could be confirmed. The surprising result was that participants who recalled *fewer* examples judged themselves to be *more* assertive—providing particularly convincing evidence in favor of the ease-of-retrieval theory over the number-of-examples theory.

## Evaluating and Revising Theories

If a hypothesis is confirmed in a systematic empirical study, then the theory has been strengthened. Not only did the theory make an accurate prediction, but there is now a new phenomenon that the theory accounts for. If a hypothesis is disconfirmed in a systematic empirical study, then the theory has been weakened. It made an inaccurate prediction, and there is now a new phenomenon that it does not account for.

Although this seems straightforward, there are some complications. First, confirming a hypothesis can strengthen a theory but it can never prove a theory. In fact, scientists tend to avoid the word "prove" when talking and writing about theories. One reason for this is that there may be other plausible theories that imply the same hypothesis, which means that confirming the hypothesis strengthens all those theories equally. A second reason is that it is always possible that another test of the hypothesis or a test of a new hypothesis derived from the theory will be disconfirmed. This is a version of the famous philosophical "problem of induction." One cannot definitively prove a general principle (e.g., "All swans are white.") just by observing confirming cases (e.g., white swans)—no matter how many. It is always possible that a disconfirming case (e.g., a black swan) will eventually come along. For these reasons, scientists tend to think of theories—even highly successful ones—as subject to revision based on new and unexpected observations.

A second complication has to do with what it means when a hypothesis is disconfirmed. According to the strictest version of the hypothetico-deductive method, disconfirming a hypothesis disproves the theory it was derived from. In formal logic, the premises "if *A* then *B*" and "not *B*" necessarily lead to the conclusion "not *A*." If *A* is the theory and *B* is the hypothesis ("if *A* then *B*"), then disconfirming the hypothesis ("not *B*") must mean that the theory is incorrect ("not *A*"). In practice, however, scientists do not give up on their theories so easily. One reason is that one disconfirmed hypothesis could be a fluke or it could be the result of a faulty research design. Perhaps the researcher did not successfully manipulate the independent variable or measure the dependent variable. A disconfirmed hypothesis could also mean that some unstated but relatively minor assumption of the theory was not met. For example, if Zajonc had failed to find social facilitation in cockroaches, he could have concluded that drive theory is still correct but it applies only to animals with sufficiently complex nervous systems.

This does not mean that researchers are free to ignore disconfirmations of their theories. If they cannot improve their research designs or modify their theories to account for repeated disconfirmations, then they eventually abandon their theories and replace them with ones that are more successful.

# Incorporating Theory Into Your Research

It should be clear from this chapter that theories are not just "icing on the cake" of scientific research; they are a basic ingredient. If you can understand and use them, you will be much more successful at reading and understanding the research literature, generating interesting research questions, and writing and conversing about research. Of course, your ability to understand and use theories will improve with practice. But there are several things that you can do to incorporate theory into your research right from the start.

The first thing is to distinguish the phenomena you are interested in from any theories of those phenomena. Beware especially of the tendency to "fuse" a phenomenon to a commonsense theory of it. For example, it might be tempting to describe the negative effect of cell phone usage on driving ability by saying, "Cell phone usage distracts people from driving." Or it might be tempting to describe the positive effect of expressive writing on health by saying, "Dealing with your emotions through writing makes you healthier." In both of these examples, however, a vague commonsense explanation (distraction, "dealing with" emotions) has been fused to the phenomenon itself. The problem is that this gives the impression that the phenomenon has already been adequately explained and closes off further inquiry into precisely why or how it happens.

As another example, researcher Jerry Burger and his colleagues were interested in the phenomenon that people are more willing to comply with a simple request from someone with whom they are familiar (Burger, Soroka, Gonzago, Murphy, & Somervell, 1999).[17] A beginning researcher who is asked to explain why this is the case might be at a complete loss or say something like, "Well, because they are *familiar* with them." But digging just a bit deeper, Burger and his colleagues realized that there are several possible explanations. Among them are that complying with people we know creates positive feelings, that we anticipate needing something from them in the future, and that we like them more and follow an automatic rule that says to help people we like.

The next thing to do is turn to the research literature to identify existing theories of the phenomena you are interested in. Remember that there will usually be more than one plausible theory.

Existing theories may be complementary or competing, but it is essential to know what they are. If there are no existing theories, you should come up with two or three of your own—even if they are informal and limited in scope. Then get in the habit of describing the phenomena you are interested in, followed by the two or three best theories of it. Do this whether you are speaking or writing about your research. When asked what their research was about, for example, Burger and his colleagues could have said something like the following:

> It's about the fact that we're more likely to comply with requests from people we know [the phenomenon]. This is interesting because it could be because it makes us feel good [Theory 1], because we think we might get something in return [Theory 2], or because we like them more and have an automatic tendency to comply with people we like [Theory 3].

At this point, you may be able to derive a hypothesis from one of the theories. At the very least, for each research question you generate, you should ask what each plausible theory implies about the answer to that question. If one of them implies a particular answer, then you may have an interesting hypothesis to test. Burger and colleagues, for example, asked what would happen if a request came from a stranger whom participants had sat next to only briefly, did not interact with, and had no expectation of interacting with in the future. They reasoned that if familiarity created liking, and liking increased people's tendency to comply (Theory 3), then this situation should still result in increased rates of compliance (which it did). If the question is interesting but no theory implies an answer to it, this might suggest that a new theory needs to be constructed or that existing theories need to be modified in some way. These would make excellent points of discussion in the introduction or discussion of an American Psychological Association (APA) style research report or research presentation.

When you do write your research report or plan your presentation, be aware that there are two basic ways that researchers usually include theory. The first is to raise a research question, answer that question by conducting a new study, and then offer one or more theories (usually more) to explain or interpret the results. This format works well for applied research questions and for research questions that existing theories do not address. The second way is to describe one or more existing theories, derive a hypothesis from one of those theories, test the hypothesis in a new study, and finally reevaluate the theory. This format works well when there is an existing theory that addresses the research question—especially if the resulting hypothesis is surprising or conflicts with a hypothesis derived from a different theory.

## Key Takeaways

- Working with theories is not "icing on the cake." It is a basic ingredient of psychological research.
- Like other scientists, psychologists use the hypothetico-deductive method. They construct theories to explain or interpret phenomena (or work with existing theories), derive hypotheses from their theories, test the hypotheses, and then reevaluate the theories in light of the new results.
- There are several things that even beginning researchers can do to incorporate theory into their research. These include clearly distinguishing phenomena from theories, knowing about existing theories, constructing one's own simple theories, using theories to make predictions about the answers to research questions, and incorporating theories into one's writing and speaking.

## Exercise

1. Practice: Find a recent empirical research report in a professional journal. Read the introduction and highlight in different colors descriptions of phenomena, theories, and hypotheses.

# Endnotes

1. Campbell, R. S., & Pennebaker, J. W. (2003). The secret life of pronouns: Flexibility in writing style and physical health. *Psychological Science, 14*, 60–65.

2. Lepore, S. J., Greenberg, M. A., Bruno, M., & Smyth, J. M. (2002). Expressive writing and health: Self-regulation of emotion-related experience, physiology, and behavior. In S. J. Lepore & J. M. Smyth (Eds.), *The writing cure: How expressive writing promotes health and emotional well being* (pp. 99–117). Washington, DC: American Psychological Association.

3. Zajonc, R. B. (1965). Social facilitation. *Science, 149*, 269–274.

4. Izawa, C. (Ed.) (1999). *On human memory: Evolution, progress, and reflections on the 30th anniversary of the Atkinson-Shiffrin model.* Mahwah, NJ: Erlbaum.

5. Neisser, U., Boodoo, G., Bouchard, T. J., Boykin, A. W., Brody, N., Ceci,...Urbina, S. (1996). Intelligence: Knowns and unknowns. *American Psychologist, 51*, 77–101.

6. Lilienfeld, S. O., & Lynn, S. J. (2003). Dissociative identity disorder: Multiplepersonalities, multiple controversies. In S. O. Lilienfeld, S. J. Lynn, & J. M. Lohr (Eds.), *Science and pseudoscience in clinical psychology* (pp. 109–142). New York, NY: Guilford Press.

7. Warren, C., & McGraw, A. P. (2015). What makes things humorous. *Proceedings of the National Academy of Sciences, 112*, 7105-7106.

8. McGraw, A. P., Warren, C., Williams, L., & Leonard, B., (2012). Too close for comfort, or too far to care? Finding humor in distant tragedies and close mishaps. *Psychological Science, 25*, 1215 - 1223.

9. Lilienfeld, S. O., & Lynn, S. J. (2003). Dissociative identity disorder: Multiple personalities, multiple controversies. In S. O. Lilienfeld, S. J. Lynn, & J. M. Lohr (Eds.), *Science and pseudoscience in clinical psychology* (pp. 109–142). New York, NY: Guilford Press.

10. Fine, R. (1979). *A history of psychoanalysis.* New York, NY: Columbia University Press.

11. Logan, G. D., & Sbrodoff, N. J. (2003). Subitizing and similarity: Toward a pattern-matching theory of enumeration. *Psychonomic Bulletin & Review, 10*, 676–682.

12. Tantam, D., & Huband, N. (2009). *Understanding repeated self-injury: A multidisciplinary approach.* New York, NY: Palgrave Macmillan.

13. Buss, D. M., & Schmitt, D. P. (1993). Sexual strategies theory: A contextual evolutionary analysis of human mating. *Psychological Review, 100*, 204–232.

14. Williams, P. G. (2004). The psychopathology of self-assessed health: A cognitive approach to health anxiety and hypochondriasis. *Cognitive Therapy and Research, 28*, 629–644.

15. Zajonc, R. B., Heingartner, A., & Herman, E. M. (1969). Social enhancement and impairment of performance in the cockroach. *Journal of Personality and Social Psychology, 13*, 83–92.

16. Schwarz, N., Bless, H., Strack, F., Klumpp, G., Rittenauer-Schatka, H., & Simons, A. (1991). Ease of retrieval as information: Another look at the availability heuristic. *Journal of Personality and Social Psychology, 61*, 195–202.

17. Burger, J. M., Soroka, S., Gonzago, K., Murphy, E., & Somervell, E. (1999). The effect of fleeting attraction on compliance to requests. *Personality and Social Psychology Bulletin, 27*, 1578–1586.

# CHAPTER 5

# Psychological Measurement

Researchers Tara MacDonald and Alanna Martineau were interested in the effect of female college students' moods on their intentions to have unprotected sexual intercourse (MacDonald & Martineau, 2002).[1] In a carefully designed empirical study, they found that being in a negative mood increased intentions to have unprotected sex—but only for students who were low in self-esteem. Although there are many challenges involved in conducting a study like this, one of the primary ones is the measurement of the relevant variables. In this study, the researchers needed to know whether each of their participants had high or low self-esteem, which of course required measuring their self-esteem. They also needed to be sure that their attempt to put people into a negative mood (by having them think negative thoughts) was successful, which required measuring their moods. Finally, they needed to see whether self-esteem and mood were related to participants' intentions to have unprotected sexual intercourse, which required measuring these intentions.

To students who are just getting started in psychological research, the challenge of measuring such variables might seem insurmountable. Is it really possible to measure things as intangible as self-esteem, mood, or an intention to do something? The answer is a resounding yes, and in this chapter we look closely at the nature of the variables that psychologists study and how they can be measured. We also look at some practical issues in psychological measurement.

## Do You Feel You Are a Person of Worth?

The Rosenberg Self-Esteem Scale (Rosenberg, 1989)[2] is one of the most common measures of self-esteem and the one that MacDonald and Martineau used in their study. Participants respond to each of the 10 items with a rating on a 4-point scale: *Strongly Agree, Agree, Disagree, Strongly Disagree*. Score Items 1, 2, 4, 6, and 7 by assigning 3 points for each *Strongly Agree* response, 2 for each *Agree*, 1 for each *Disagree*, and 0 for each *Strongly Disagree*. Reverse the scoring for Items 3, 5, 8, 9, and 10 by assigning 0 points for each *Strongly Agree*, 1 point for each *Agree*, and so on. A person's overall score, then, is the total number of points.

1. I feel that I'm a person of worth, at least on an equal plane with others.
2. I feel that I have a number of good qualities.
3. All in all, I am inclined to feel that I am a failure.
4. I am able to do things as well as most other people.
5. I feel I do not have much to be proud of.
6. I take a positive attitude toward myself.
7. On the whole, I am satisfied with myself.
8. I wish I could have more respect for myself.
9. I certainly feel useless at times.
10. At times I think I am no good at all.

# 5.1 Understanding Psychological Measurement

## What Is Measurement?

**measurement**

The assignment of scores to individuals so that the scores represent some characteristic of the individuals.

**Measurement** is the assignment of scores to individuals so that the scores represent some characteristic of the individuals. This very general definition is consistent with the kinds of measurement that everyone is familiar with—for example, weighing oneself by stepping onto a bathroom scale, or checking the internal temperature of a roasting turkey by inserting a meat thermometer. It is also consistent with measurement throughout the sciences. In physics, for example, one might measure the potential energy of an object in Earth's gravitational field by finding its mass and height (which of course requires measuring *those* variables) and then multiplying them together along with the gravitational acceleration of Earth ($9.8 \text{ m/s}^2$). The result of this procedure is a score that represents the object's potential energy.

Of course, this general definition of measurement is consistent with measurement in psychology too. (Psychological measurement is often referred to as "psychometrics.") Imagine, for example, that a cognitive psychologist wants to measure a person's working memory capacity—his or her ability to hold in mind and think about several pieces of information all at the same time. To do this, she might use a backward digit span task, where she reads a list of two digits to the person and asks him or her to repeat them in reverse order. She then repeats this several times, increasing the length of the list by one digit each time, until the person makes an error. The length of the longest list for which the person responds correctly is the score and represents his or her working memory capacity. Or imagine a clinical psychologist who is interested in how depressed a person is. He administers the Beck Depression Inventory, which is a 21-item, self-report questionnaire in which the person rates the extent to which he or she has felt sad, lost energy, and experienced other symptoms of depression over the past two weeks. The sum of these 21 ratings is the score and represents his or her current level of depression.

The important point here is that measurement does not require any particular instruments or procedures. It does not require placing individuals or objects on bathroom scales, holding rulers up to them, or inserting thermometers into them. What it *does* require is *some* systematic procedure for assigning scores to individuals or objects so that those scores represent the characteristic of interest.

# Psychological Constructs

Many variables studied by psychologists are straightforward and simple to measure. These include sex, age, height, weight, and birth order. You can almost always tell whether someone is male or female just by looking. You can ask people how old they are and be reasonably sure that they know and will tell you. Although people might not know or want to tell you how much they weigh, you can have them step onto a bathroom scale. Other variables studied by psychologists—perhaps the majority—are not so straightforward or simple to measure. We cannot accurately assess people's level of intelligence by looking at them, and we certainly cannot put their self-esteem on a bathroom scale. These kinds of variables are called **constructs** (pronounced *CON-structs*) and include personality traits (e.g., extroversion), emotional states (e.g., fear), attitudes (e.g., toward taxes), and abilities (e.g., athleticism).

Psychological constructs cannot be observed directly. One reason is that they often represent *tendencies* to think, feel, or act in certain ways. For example, to say that a particular college student is highly extroverted (see "The Big Five") does not necessarily mean that she is behaving in an extroverted way right now. In fact, she might be sitting quietly by herself, reading a book. Instead, it means that she has a general tendency to behave in extroverted ways (talking, laughing, etc.) across a variety of situations. Another reason psychological constructs cannot be observed directly is that they often involve internal processes. Fear, for example, involves the activation of certain central and peripheral nervous system structures, along with certain kinds of thoughts, feelings, and behaviors—none of which is necessarily obvious to an outside observer. Notice also that neither extroversion nor fear "reduces to" any particular thought, feeling, act, or physiological structure or process. Instead, each is a kind of summary of a complex set of behaviors and internal processes.

**construct**

A variable that cannot be observed directly because it represents a tendency to behave in certain ways or a complex pattern of behavior and internal processes. These include personality traits, emotional states, attitudes, and abilities.

## The Big Five

The Big Five is a set of five constructs that capture much of the variation in human personality. Each of the Big Five can even be defined in terms of six more specific constructs called "facets" (Costa & McCrae, 1992).[3]

**TABLE 5.1** The Big Five Personality Dimensions

| Big Five Dimension | Facets | | | | | |
|---|---|---|---|---|---|---|
| **Openness to Experience** | Fantasy | Aesthetics | Feelings | Actions | Ideas | Values |
| **Conscientiousness** | Competence | Order | Dutifulness | Achievement Striving | Self-Discipline | Deliberation |
| **Extraversion** | Warmth | Gregariousness | Assertiveness | Activity | Excitement Seeking | Positive Emotions |
| **Agreeableness** | Trust | Straightforwardness | Altruism | Compliance | Modesty | Tender-Mindedness |
| **Neuroticism** | Worry | Anger | Discouragement | Self-Consciousness | Implusivity | Vulnerability |

One useful measure is the Big Five Inventory.[4] You can take an online version and receive immediate feedback at http://www.outofservice.com/bigfive/.

**conceptual definition**

A description of a variable or construct in terms of the behaviors and internal processes that are involved, along with how that construct relates to other variables.

The **conceptual definition** of a psychological construct describes the behaviors and internal processes that make up that construct, along with how it relates to other variables. For example, a conceptual definition of neuroticism (another one of the Big Five) would be that it is people's tendency to experience negative emotions such as anxiety, anger, and sadness across a variety of situations. This definition might also include that it has a strong genetic component, remains fairly stable over time, and is positively correlated with the tendency to experience pain and other physical symptoms.

Students sometimes wonder why, when researchers want to understand a construct like self-esteem or neuroticism, they do not simply look it up in the dictionary. One reason is that many scientific constructs do not have counterparts in everyday language (e.g., working memory capacity). More important, researchers are in the business of developing definitions that are more detailed and precise—and that more accurately describe the way the world is—than the informal definitions in the dictionary. As we will see, they do this by proposing conceptual definitions, testing them empirically, and revising them as necessary. Sometimes they throw them out altogether. This is why the research literature often includes different conceptual definitions of the same construct. In some cases, an older conceptual definition has been replaced by a newer one that works better. In others, researchers are still in the process of deciding which of various conceptual definitions is the best.

## Operational Definitions

**operational definition**

How a variable or construct is to be measured in a particular context.

**self-report measures**

A measure in which participants report on their own thoughts, feelings, and behaviors. Compare with behavioral measure and physiological measure.

**behavioral measures**

A measure in which the researcher observes and records some aspect of participants' behavior. Compare with self-report measure and physiological measure.

**physiological measures**

A measure that involves recording a physiological variable. Compare with self-report measure and behavioral measure.

While the conceptual definition of a construct tells us essentially what that construct *is*, the **operational definition** of a variable tells us how that construct is to be *measured* in a particular context. Operational definitions generally fall into one of three broad categories. **Self-report measures** are those in which participants report on their own thoughts, feelings, and actions, as with the Rosenberg Self-Esteem Scale. **Behavioral measures** are those in which some other aspect of participants' behavior is observed and recorded. This is an extremely broad category that includes the observation of people's behavior both in highly structured laboratory tasks and in more natural settings. A good example of the former would be measuring working memory capacity using the backward digit span task. A good example of the latter is a famous operational definition of physical aggression from researcher Albert Bandura and his colleagues (Bandura, Ross, & Ross, 1961).[5] They let each of several children play for 20 minutes in a room that contained a clown-shaped punching bag called a Bobo doll. They filmed each child and counted the number of acts of physical aggression he or she committed. These included hitting the doll with a mallet, punching it, and kicking it. Their operational definition, then, was the number of these specifically defined acts that the child committed in the 20-minute period. Finally, **physiological measures** are those that involve recording any of a wide variety of physiological processes, including heart rate and blood pressure, galvanic skin response, hormone levels, and electrical activity and blood flow in the brain.

For any given variable or construct, there will be multiple operational definitions. Stress is a good example. A rough conceptual definition is that stress is an adaptive response to a perceived danger or threat that involves physiological, cognitive, affective, and behavioral components. But researchers have operationally defined it in several ways. The Social Readjustment Rating Scale is a self-report questionnaire on which people identify stressful events that they have experienced in the past year and assigns points for each one depending on its severity. For example, a man who has been divorced (73 points), changed jobs (36 points), and had a change in sleeping habits (16 points) in the past year would have a total score of 125. The Daily Hassles and Uplifts Scale is similar but focuses on everyday stressors like misplacing things and being concerned about one's weight. The Perceived Stress Scale is another self-report measure that focuses on people's feelings of stress (e.g., "How often have you felt nervous and stressed?"). Researchers have also operationally defined stress in terms of several physiological variables including blood pressure and levels of the stress hormone cortisol.

When psychologists use multiple operational definitions of the same construct—either within a study or across studies—they are using **converging operations**. The idea is that the various operational definitions are "converging" on the same construct. When scores based on several different operational definitions are closely related to each other and produce similar patterns of results, this constitutes good evidence that the construct exists as defined and is being measured effectively. The various measures of stress, for example, are all correlated with each other and have all been shown to be correlated with other variables such as immune system functioning (also measured in a variety of ways) (Segerstrom & Miller, 2004).[6] This is what allows researchers eventually to draw useful general conclusions, such as "stress is negatively correlated with immune system functioning," as opposed to more specific and less useful ones, such as "people's scores on the Perceived Stress Scale are negatively correlated with their white blood counts."

**FIGURE 5.1** Preparing to Use an Electroencephalograph (EEG) to Measure Brain Activity
In addition to self-report and behavioral measures, researchers in psychology use physiological measures. An electroencephalograph (EEG) records electrical activity from the brain.

Source: Photo courtesy of James McCue

**converging operations**

Multiple operational definitions of the same construct. When multiple operational definitions are closely related to each other and produce the same pattern of results, this constitutes evidence that the construct is being measured effectively and is a useful one.

**levels of measurement**

Four different ways of assigning scores to individuals that provide increasing amounts of quantitative information about the characteristic being measured. The four levels are nominal, ordinal, interval, and ratio.

# Levels of Measurement

The psychologist S. S. Stevens suggested that scores can be assigned to individuals so that they communicate more or less quantitative information about the variable of interest (Stevens, 1946).[7] For example, the officials at a 100-m race could simply rank order the runners as they crossed the finish line (first, second, etc.), or they could time each runner to the nearest tenth of a second using a stopwatch (11.5 s, 12.1 s, etc.). In either case, they would be measuring the runners' times by systematically assigning scores to represent those times. But while the rank ordering procedure communicates the fact that the second-place runner took longer to finish than the first-place finisher, the stopwatch procedure also communicates *how much* longer the second-place finisher took. Stevens actually suggested four different **levels of measurement** (which he called "scales of measurement") that correspond to four different levels of quantitative information that can be communicated by a set of scores.

**nominal level**

The level of measurement that involves assigning names or category labels to individuals. Scores at the nominal level indicate whether or not one individual is in the same category as another. They do not communicate any quantitative information.

**ordinal level**

The level of measurement that involves rank ordering individuals. Scores at the ordinal level indicate whether one individual has more or less of the characteristic of interest, but they do not indicate how much more or less.

**interval level**

The level of measurement that involves assigning numerical scores so that a given difference between two scores always represents the same difference in the characteristic of interest but a score of zero does not literally represent none of the characteristic. Scores at the interval level indicate how much more or less of the characteristic one individual has than another. Ratios of one score to another are not meaningful at this level.

**ratio level**

The level of measurement that involves assigning numerical scores so that a given difference between two scores always represents the same difference in the characteristic and a score of zero represents none of the characteristic. Ratios of one score to another are meaningful only at this level.

The **nominal level** of measurement is used for categorical variables and involves assigning scores that are category labels. Category labels communicate whether any two individuals are the same or different in terms of the variable being measured. For example, if you look at your research participants as they enter the room, decide whether each one is male or female, and type this information into a spreadsheet, you are engaged in nominal-level measurement. Or if you ask your participants to indicate which of several ethnicities they identify themselves with, you are again engaged in nominal-level measurement.

The remaining three levels of measurement are used for quantitative variables. The **ordinal level** of measurement involves assigning scores so that they represent the rank order of the individuals. Ranks communicate not only whether any two individuals are the same or different in terms of the variable being measured but also whether one individual is higher or lower on that variable. The **interval level** of measurement involves assigning scores so that they represent the precise magnitude of the difference between individuals, but a score of zero does not actually represent the complete absence of the characteristic. A classic example is the measurement of heat using the Celsius or Fahrenheit scale. The difference between temperatures of 20°C and 25°C is precisely 5°, but a temperature of 0°C does not mean that there is a complete absence of heat. In psychology, the intelligence quotient (IQ) is often considered to be measured at the interval level. Finally, the **ratio level** of measurement involves assigning scores in such a way that there is a true zero point that represents the complete absence of the quantity. Height measured in meters and weight measured in kilograms are good examples. So are counts of discrete objects or events such as the number of siblings one has or the number of questions a student answers correctly on an exam.

Stevens's levels of measurement are important for at least two reasons. First, they emphasize the generality of the concept of measurement. Although people do not normally think of categorizing or ranking individuals as measurement, in fact they are as long as they are done so that they represent some characteristic of the individuals. Second, the levels of measurement can serve as a rough guide to the statistical procedures that can be used with the data and the conclusions that can be drawn from them. With nominal-level measurement, for example, the only available measure of central tendency is the mode. Also, ratio-level measurement is the only level that allows meaningful statements about ratios of scores. One cannot say that someone with an IQ of 140 is twice as intelligent as someone with an IQ of 70 because IQ is measured at the interval level, but one can say that someone with six siblings has twice as many as someone with three because number of siblings is measured at the ratio level.

## Key Takeaways

- Measurement is the assignment of scores to individuals so that the scores represent some characteristic of the individuals. Psychological measurement can be achieved in a wide variety of ways, including self-report, behavioral, and physiological measures.

- Psychological constructs such as intelligence, self-esteem, and depression are variables that are not directly observable because they represent behavioral tendencies or complex patterns of behavior and internal processes. An important goal of scientific research is to conceptually define psychological constructs in ways that accurately describe them.

- For any conceptual definition of a construct, there will be many different operational definitions or ways of measuring it. The use of multiple operational definitions, or converging operations, is a common strategy in psychological research.

- Variables can be measured at four different levels—nominal, ordinal, interval, and ratio—that communicate increasing amounts of quantitative information. The level of measurement affects the kinds of statistics you can use and conclusions you can draw from your data.

## Exercises

1. Practice: Complete the Rosenberg Self-Esteem Scale and compute your overall score.
2. Practice: Think of three operational definitions for sexual jealousy, decisiveness, and social anxiety. Consider the possibility of self-report, behavioral, and physiological measures. Be as precise as you can.
3. Practice: For each of the following variables, decide which level of measurement is being used.
    a. A college instructor measures the time it takes his students to finish an exam by looking through the stack of exams at the end. He assigns the one on the bottom a score of 1, the one on top of that a 2, and so on.
    b. A researcher accesses her participants' medical records and counts the number of times they have seen a doctor in the past year.
    c. Participants in a research study are asked whether they are right-handed or left-handed.

# 5.2 Reliability and Validity of Measurement

## Learning Objectives

1. Define reliability, including the different types and how they are assessed.
2. Define validity, including the different types and how they are assessed.
3. Describe the kinds of evidence that would be relevant to assessing the reliability and validity of a particular measure.

Again, measurement involves assigning scores to individuals so that they represent some characteristic of the individuals. But how do researchers know that the scores actually represent the characteristic, especially when it is a construct like intelligence, self-esteem, depression, or working memory capacity? The answer is that they conduct research using the measure to confirm that the scores make sense based on their understanding of the construct being measured. This is an extremely important point. Psychologists do not simply *assume* that their measures work. Instead, they collect data to *demonstrate* that they work. If their research does not demonstrate that a measure works, they stop using it.

As an informal example, imagine that you have been dieting for a month. Your clothes seem to be fitting more loosely, and several friends have asked if you have lost weight. If at this point your bathroom scale indicated that you had lost 10 pounds, this would make sense and you would continue to use the scale. But if it indicated that you had gained 10 pounds, you would rightly conclude that it was broken and either fix it or get rid of it. In evaluating a measurement method, psychologists consider two general dimensions: reliability and validity.

# Reliability

**reliability**

The extent to which the scores on a measure are consistent across time, across multiple items on the same measure, and across researchers when a measure has an element of subjective judgment.

**test-retest reliability**

The extent to which scores on a measure are consistent across time for the same individuals.

**test-retest correlation**

The correlation between individuals' scores on a measure used at two different times.

**Reliability** refers to the consistency of a measure. Psychologists consider three types of consistency: over time (test-retest reliability), across items (internal consistency), and across different researchers (interrater reliability).

## Test-Retest Reliability

When researchers measure a construct that they assume to be consistent across time, then the scores they obtain should also be consistent across time. **Test-retest reliability** is the extent to which this is actually the case. For example, intelligence is generally thought to be consistent across time. A person who is highly intelligent today will be highly intelligent next week. This means that any good measure of intelligence should produce roughly the same scores for this individual next week as it does today. Clearly, a measure that produces highly inconsistent scores over time cannot be a very good measure of a construct that is supposed to be consistent.

Assessing test-retest reliability requires using the measure on a group of people at one time, using it again on the *same* group of people at a later time, and then looking at **test-retest correlation** between the two sets of scores. This is typically done by graphing the data in a scatterplot and computing Pearson's *r*. Figure 5.2 shows the correlation between two sets of scores of several college students on the Rosenberg Self-Esteem Scale, given two times a week apart. Pearson's *r* for these data is +.95. In general, a test-retest correlation of +.80 or greater is considered to indicate good reliability.

**FIGURE 5.2** Test-Retest Correlation Between Two Sets of Scores of Several College Students on the Rosenberg Self-Esteem Scale, Given Two Times a Week Apart

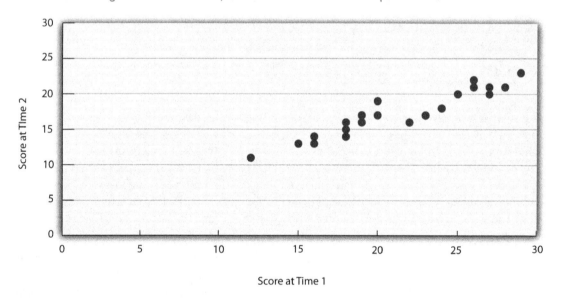

Again, high test-retest correlations make sense when the construct being measured is assumed to be consistent over time, which is the case for intelligence, self-esteem, and the Big Five personality dimensions. But other constructs are not assumed to be stable over time. The very nature of mood, for example, is that it changes. So a measure of mood that produced a low test-retest correlation over a period of a month would not be a cause for concern.

# Internal Consistency

A second kind of reliability is **internal consistency**, which is the consistency of people's responses across the items on a multiple-item measure. In general, all the items on such measures are supposed to reflect the same underlying construct, so people's scores on those items should be correlated with each other. On the Rosenberg Self-Esteem Scale, people who agree that they are a person of worth should tend to agree that that they have a number of good qualities. If people's responses to the different items are not correlated with each other, then it would no longer make sense to claim that they are all measuring the same underlying construct. This is as true for behavioral and physiological measures as for self-report measures. For example, people might make a series of bets in a simulated game of roulette as a measure of their level of risk seeking. This measure would be internally consistent to the extent that individual participants' bets were consistently high or low across trials.

**internal consistency**

The extent to which the items on a multiple-item measure are consistent with each other.

Like test-retest reliability, internal consistency can only be assessed by collecting and analyzing data. One approach is to look at a **split-half correlation**. This involves splitting the items into two sets, such as the first and second halves of the items or the even- and odd-numbered items. Then a score is computed for each set of items, and the relationship between the two sets of scores is examined. For example, Figure 5.3 shows the split-half correlation between several college students' scores on the even-numbered items and their scores on the odd-numbered items of the Rosenberg Self-Esteem Scale. Pearson's *r* for these data is +.88. A split-half correlation of +.80 or greater is generally considered good internal consistency.

**split-half correlation**

The correlation between scores based on one half of the items on a multiple-item measure and scores based on the other half of the items.

**FIGURE 5.3** Split-Half Correlation Between Several College Students' Scores on the Even-Numbered Items and Their Scores on the Odd-Numbered Items of the Rosenberg Self-Esteem Scale

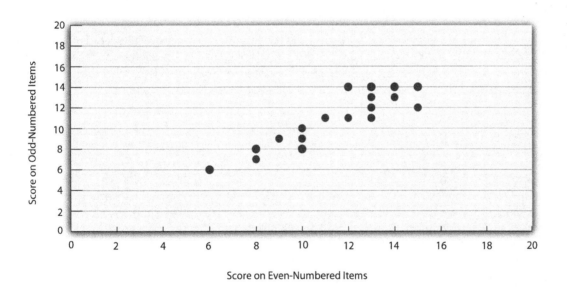

Perhaps the most common measure of internal consistency used by researchers in psychology is a statistic called **Cronbach's α** (the Greek letter alpha). Conceptually, α is the mean of all possible split-half correlations for a set of items. For example, there are 252 ways to split a set of 10 items into two sets of five. Cronbach's α would be the mean of the 252 split-half correlations. Note that this is not how α is actually computed, but it is a correct way of interpreting the meaning of this statistic. Again, a value of +.80 or greater is generally taken to indicate good internal consistency.

**Cronbach's α (alpha)**

A statistic used to assess the internal consistency of a multiple-item measure. It is conceptually equivalent to the mean of all possible split-half correlations.

## Interrater Reliability

**interrater reliability**

When a measure involves human judgment, the extent to which different observers are consistent in their judgments.

**Cohen's κ (kappa)**

A statistic used to assess interrater reliability when the observer judgments are categorical.

Many behavioral measures involve significant judgment on the part of an observer or a rater. **Interrater reliability** is the extent to which different observers are consistent in their judgments. For example, if you were interested in measuring college students' social skills, you could make video recordings of them as they interacted with another student whom they are meeting for the first time. Then you could have two or more observers watch the videos and rate each student's level of social skills. To the extent that each participant does in fact have some level of social skills that can be detected by an attentive observer, different observers' ratings should be highly correlated with each other. If they were not, then those ratings could not be an accurate representation of participants' social skills. Interrater reliability is often assessed using Cronbach's α when the judgments are quantitative or an analogous statistic called **Cohen's κ** (the Greek letter kappa) when they are categorical.

# Validity

**validity**

The extent to which scores on a measure represent the variable or construct they are intended to. Validity is a judgment based on the available evidence.

**Validity** is the extent to which the scores from a measure represent the variable they are intended to. But how do researchers make this judgment? We have already considered one factor that they take into account—reliability. When a measure is consistent—across time, across items, and across raters—researchers should be more confident that the scores represent what they are supposed to. There has to be more to it, however, because a measure can be extremely reliable but have no validity whatsoever. As an absurd example, imagine someone who believes that people's index finger length reflects their self-esteem and therefore tries to measure self-esteem by holding a ruler up to people's index fingers. Although this measure would have extremely good test-retest reliability, it would have absolutely no validity. The fact that one person's index finger is a centimeter longer than another's would indicate nothing about which one had higher self-esteem.

Textbook presentations of validity usually divide it into several distinct "types." But a good way to interpret these types is that they are other kinds of evidence—in addition to reliability—that should be taken into account when judging the validity of a measure. Here we consider four basic kinds: face validity, content validity, criterion validity, and discriminant validity.

## Face Validity

**face validity**

The extent to which a measure appears "on its face" to measure the variable or construct it is supposed to.

**Face validity** is the extent to which a measurement method appears "on its face" to measure the construct of interest. Most people would expect a self-esteem questionnaire to include items about whether they see themselves as a person of worth and whether they think they have good qualities. So a questionnaire that included these kinds of items would have good face validity. The finger-length method of measuring self-esteem, on the other hand, seems to have nothing to do with self-esteem and therefore has poor face validity. Although face validity can be assessed quantitatively—for example, by having a large sample of people rate a measure in terms of whether it appears to measure what it is intended to—it is usually assessed informally.

Face validity is, at best, very weak evidence that a measurement method is measuring what is intended. One reason is that it is based on people's intuitions about human behavior, which are frequently wrong. It is also the case that many established measures in psychology work quite well despite lacking face validity. The Minnesota Multiphasic Personality Inventory (MMPI) measures many personality characteristics and disorders by having people decide whether each of over 567 different statements applies to them—where many of the statements do not have any obvious relationship to the construct that they measure. Another example is the Implicit Association Test, which measures prejudice in a way that is nonintuitive to most people (see "How Biased Are You?").

### How Biased Are You?

The Implicit Association Test (IAT) requires you to quickly sort words and images representing two contrasting social groups (e.g., white people and black people), along with other positive and negative words and images. For example, for one block of trials you might have to press the "a" key whenever a stimulus representing white people or something negative (e.g., the word "dreadful") appears on the screen, and the "I" key any time a stimulus representing black people or something positive (e.g., the word "wonderful") appears on the screen. But then for another block of trials, you would have to press the "a" key for stimuli representing white people or something positive and the "I" key for stimuli representing black people or something negative. The idea is that if you have an implicit bias in favor of one group over the other, you will respond faster when categorizing that group with positive stimuli than with negative stimuli. The IAT is a behavioral measure that may reveal negative attitudes that people are unaware of or unwilling to admit to on conventional self-report measures. You can learn more about the IAT and take several of them at https://implicit.harvard.edu/implicit/.

## Content Validity

**Content validity** is the extent to which a measure "covers" the construct of interest. For example, if a researcher conceptually defines test anxiety as involving both sympathetic nervous system activation (leading to nervous feelings) and negative thoughts, then his measure of test anxiety should include items about both nervous feelings and negative thoughts. Or consider that attitudes are usually defined as involving thoughts, feelings, and actions toward something. By this conceptual definition, a person has a positive attitude toward exercise to the extent that he or she thinks positive thoughts about exercising, feels good about exercising, and actually exercises. So to have good content validity, a measure of people's attitudes toward exercise would have to reflect all three of these aspects. Like face validity, content validity is not usually assessed quantitatively. Instead, it is assessed by carefully checking the measurement method against the conceptual definition of the construct.

**content validity**

The extent to which a measure covers all aspects of the construct it is supposed to measure.

## Criterion Validity

**Criterion validity** is the extent to which people's scores on a measure are correlated with other variables (known as **criteria**) that one would expect them to be correlated with. For example, people's scores on a new measure of test anxiety should be negatively correlated with their performance on an important school exam. If it were found that people's scores were in fact negatively correlated with their exam performance, then this would be a piece of evidence that these scores really represent people's test anxiety. But if it were found that people scored equally well on the exam regardless of their test anxiety scores, then this would cast doubt on the measure's validity.

A criterion can be any variable that one has reason to think should be correlated with the construct being measured, and there will usually be many of them. For example, one would expect test anxiety scores to be negatively correlated with exam performance and course grades and positively correlated with general anxiety and with blood pressure during an exam. Or imagine that a researcher develops a new measure of physical risk taking. People's scores on this measure should be correlated with their participation in "extreme" activities such as snowboarding and rock climbing, the number of speeding tickets they have received, and even the number of broken bones they have had over the years. Criteria can also include other measures of the same construct. For example, one would expect new measures of test anxiety or physical risk taking to be positively correlated with existing measures of the same constructs. So the use of converging operations is one way to examine criterion validity.

**criterion validity**

The extent to which scores on a measure are correlated with other variables and constructs that they are expected to be correlated with, given the conceptual definition of the construct being measured.

**criterion**

A variable or construct expected to be correlated with scores on a measure that is being evaluated. The plural is *criteria*.

Assessing criterion validity requires collecting data using the measure. Researchers John Cacioppo and Richard Petty did this when they created their self-report Need for Cognition Scale to measure how much people value and engage in thinking (Cacioppo & Petty, 1982).[8] In a series of studies, they showed that college faculty scored higher than assembly-line workers, that people's scores were positively correlated with their scores on a standardized academic achievement test, and that their scores were negatively correlated with their scores on a measure of dogmatism (which represents a tendency toward obedience). In the years since it was created, the Need for Cognition Scale has been used in literally hundreds of studies and has been shown to be correlated with a wide variety of other variables, including the effectiveness of an advertisement, interest in politics, and juror decisions (Petty, Briñol, Loersch, & McCaslin, 2009).[9]

## Discriminant Validity

**discriminant validity**

The extent to which scores on a measure are not correlated with other variables and constructs that are conceptually distinct.

**Discriminant validity** is the extent to which scores on a measure are not correlated with measures of variables that are conceptually distinct. For example, self-esteem is a general attitude toward the self that is fairly stable over time. It is not the same as mood, which is how positive or negative one happens to be feeling right now. So people's scores on a new measure of self-esteem should not be very highly correlated with their moods. If the new measure of self-esteem were highly correlated with a measure of mood, it could be argued that the new measure is not really measuring self-esteem; it is measuring mood instead.

When they created the Need for Cognition Scale, Cacioppo and Petty also provided evidence of discriminant validity by showing that people's scores were not correlated with certain other variables. For example, they found only a weak correlation between people's need for cognition and a measure of their cognitive style—the extent to which they tend to think analytically by breaking ideas into smaller parts or holistically in terms of "the big picture." They also found no correlation between people's need for cognition and measures of their test anxiety and their tendency to respond in socially desirable ways. All these low correlations provide evidence that the measure is reflecting a conceptually distinct construct.

## Key Takeaways

- Psychological researchers do not simply assume that their measures work. Instead, they conduct research to show that they work. If they cannot show that they work, they stop using them.
- There are two distinct criteria by which researchers evaluate their measures: reliability and validity. Reliability is consistency across time (test-retest reliability), across items (internal consistency), and across researchers (interrater reliability). Validity is the extent to which the scores actually represent the variable they are intended to.
- Validity is a judgment based on various types of evidence. The relevant evidence includes the measure's reliability, whether it covers the construct of interest, and whether the scores it produces are correlated with other variables they are expected to be correlated with and not correlated with variables that are conceptually distinct.
- The reliability and validity of a measure is not established by any single study but by the pattern of results across multiple studies. The assessment of reliability and validity is an ongoing process.

## Exercises

1. Practice: Ask several friends to complete the Rosenberg Self-Esteem Scale. Then assess its internal consistency by making a scatterplot to show the split-half correlation (even- vs. odd-numbered items). Compute Pearson's *r* too if you know how.
2. Discussion: Think back to the last college exam you took and think of the exam as a psychological measure. What construct do you think it was intended to measure? Comment on its face and content validity. What data could you collect to assess its reliability, criterion validity, and discriminant validity?
3. Practice: Take an Implicit Association Test and then list as many ways to assess its criterion validity as you can.

# 5.3 Practical Strategies for Psychological Measurement

## Learning Objectives

1. Specify the four broad steps in the measurement process.
2. Explain how you would decide whether to use an existing measure or create your own.
3. Describe multiple strategies to identify and locate existing measures of psychological constructs.
4. Describe several general principles for creating new measures and for implementing existing and new measures.
5. Create a simple plan for assessing the reliability and validity of an existing or new measure.

So far in this chapter, we have considered several basic ideas about the nature of psychological constructs and their measurement. But now imagine that you are in the position of actually having to measure a psychological construct for a research project. How should you proceed? Broadly speaking, there are four steps in the measurement process: (a) conceptually defining the construct, (b) operationally defining the construct, (c) implementing the measure, and (d) evaluating the measure. In this section, we will look at each of these steps in turn.

## Conceptually Defining the Construct

Having a clear and complete conceptual definition of a construct is a prerequisite for good measurement. For one thing, it allows you to make sound decisions about exactly how to measure the construct. If you had only a vague idea that you wanted to measure people's "memory," for example, you would have no way to choose whether you should have them remember a list of vocabulary words, a set of photographs, a newly learned skill, or an experience from long ago. Because psychologists now conceptualize memory as a set of semi-independent systems, you would have to be more precise about what you mean by "memory." If you are interested in long-term declarative memory (memory for facts), then having participants remember a list of words that they learned last week would make sense, but having them remember and execute a newly learned skill would not. In general, there is no substitute for reading the research literature on a construct and paying close attention to how others have defined it.

# Deciding on an Operational Definition

## Using an Existing Measure

It is usually a good idea to use an existing measure that has been used successfully in previous research. Among the advantages are that (a) you save the time and trouble of creating your own, (b) there is already some evidence that the measure is valid (if it has been used successfully), and (c) your results can more easily be compared with and combined with previous results. In fact, if there already exists a reliable and valid measure of a construct, other researchers might expect you to use it unless you have a good and clearly stated reason for not doing so.

If you choose to use an existing measure, you may still have to choose among several alternatives. You might choose the most common one, the one with the best evidence of reliability and validity, the one that best measures a particular aspect of a construct that you are interested in (e.g., a physiological measure of stress if you are most interested in its underlying physiology), or even the one that would be easiest to use. For example, the Ten-Item Personality Inventory (TIPI) is a self-report questionnaire that measures all the Big Five personality dimensions with just 10 items (Gosling, Rentfrow, & Swann, 2003).[10] It is not as reliable or valid as longer and more comprehensive measures, but a researcher might choose to use it when testing time is severely limited.

### Online Measurement Resources

Many existing self-report measures are available free on the Internet for those doing research. These include reliable and valid measures of ambition, forgiveness, disgust, meaning in life, sexism, shyness, and many other constructs. Researcher and teacher Alan Reifman has gathered many of the links together into his Questionnaire Instrument Compendium at http://www.webpages.ttu.edu/areifman/qic.htm.

When an existing measure was created primarily for use in scientific research, it is usually described in detail in a published research article and is free to use in your own research—with a proper citation. You might find that later researchers who use the same measure describe it only briefly but provide a reference to the original article, in which case you would have to get the details from the original article. The American Psychological Association (APA) also has a database called PsycTESTS, which works very much like PsycINFO and may be available through your university library. It catalogs over 50,000 psychological measures that have appeared in the research literature—providing links to relevant articles and additional information about its development and evaluation. In many cases, you can download a copy of the measure itself. A similar resource that may be available online through your university library is *Mental Measurements Yearbook with Tests in Print* produced by the Buros Center for Testing at the University of Nebraska.

Keep in mind, though, that many existing measures—especially those that have applications in clinical psychology—are proprietary. This means that a publisher owns the rights to them and that you would have to purchase them. These include many standard intelligence tests, the Beck Depression Inventory, and the Minnesota Multiphasic Personality Inventory (MMPI). Information about how to obtain them is provided in the online databases.

## Creating Your Own Measure

Instead of using an existing measure, you might want to create your own. Perhaps there is no existing measure of the construct you are interested in or existing ones are too difficult or time-consuming to use. Or perhaps you want to use a new measure specifically to see whether it works in the same way as existing measures—that is, to demonstrate converging operations. In this section, we consider some general issues in creating new measures that apply equally to self-report, behavioral, and physiological measures. More detailed guidelines for creating self-report measures are presented in Chapter 9.

First, be aware that most new measures in psychology are really variations of existing measures, so you should still look to the research literature for ideas. Perhaps you can modify an existing questionnaire, create a paper-and-pencil version of a measure that is normally computerized (or vice versa), or adapt a measure that has traditionally been used for another purpose. For example, the famous Stroop task (Stroop, 1935)[11]—in which people quickly name the colors that various color words are printed in—has been adapted for the study of social anxiety. Socially anxious people are slower at color naming when the words have negative social connotations such as "stupid" (Amir, Freshman, & Foa, 2002).[12]

When you create a new measure, you should strive for simplicity. Remember that your participants are not as interested in your research as you are and that they will vary widely in their ability to understand and carry out whatever task you give them. You should create a set of clear instructions using simple language that you can present in writing or read aloud (or both). It is also a good idea to include one or more practice items so participants can become familiar with the task, and to build in an opportunity for them to ask questions before continuing. It is also best to keep the measure brief to avoid boring or frustrating your participants to the point that their responses start to become less reliable and valid.

The need for brevity, however, needs to be weighed against the fact that it is nearly always better for a measure to include multiple items rather than a single item. There are two reasons for this. One is a matter of content validity. Multiple items are often required to cover a construct adequately. The other is a matter of reliability. People's responses to single items can be influenced by all sorts of irrelevant factors—misunderstanding the particular item, a momentary distraction, or a simple error such as checking the wrong response option. But when several responses are summed or averaged, the effects of these irrelevant factors tend to cancel each other out to produce more reliable scores. Remember, however, that multiple items must be structured in a way that allows them to be combined into a single overall score by summing or averaging. To measure "financial responsibility," a student might ask people about their annual income, obtain their credit score, and have them rate how "thrifty" they are—but there is no obvious way to combine these responses into an overall score. To create a true multiple-item measure, the student might instead ask people to rate the degree to which 10 statements about financial responsibility describe them on the same five-point scale.

Finally, the very best way to assure yourself that your measure has clear instructions, includes sufficient practice, and is an appropriate length is to test several people. (Family and friends often serve this purpose nicely). Observe them as they complete the task, time them, and ask them afterward to comment on how easy or difficult it was, whether the instructions were clear, and anything else you might be wondering about. Obviously, it is better to discover problems with a measure before beginning any large-scale data collection.

## Implementing the Measure

You will want to implement any measure in a way that maximizes its reliability and validity. In most cases, it is best to test everyone under similar conditions that, ideally, are quiet and free of distractions. Testing participants in groups is often done because it is efficient, but be aware that it can create distractions that reduce the reliability and validity of the measure. As always, it is good to use previous research as a guide. If others have successfully tested people in groups using a particular measure, then you should consider doing it too.

**reactivity**

Participants' reactions to the fact that they are being measured.

**socially desirable responding**

Participants' responding in ways they believe to be socially appropriate rather than in ways that reflect their actual thoughts, feelings, and behavior.

**demand characteristics**

Features of a study that cue participants as to how the researcher expects them to behave.

Be aware also that people can react in a variety of ways to being measured that reduce the reliability and validity of the scores. Although some disagreeable participants might intentionally respond in ways meant to "mess up" a study, participant **reactivity** is more likely to take the opposite form. Agreeable participants might respond in ways they believe they are expected to. They might engage in **socially desirable responding**. For example, people with low self-esteem agree that they feel they are a person of worth not because they really feel this way but because they believe this is the socially appropriate response and do not want to look bad in the eyes of the researcher. Additionally, research studies can have built-in **demand characteristics**: cues to how the researcher expects participants to behave. For example, a participant whose attitude toward exercise is measured immediately after she is asked to read a passage about the dangers of heart disease might reasonably conclude that the passage was meant to improve her attitude. As a result, she might respond more favorably because she believes she is expected to by the researcher. Finally, your own expectations can bias participants' behaviors in unintended ways.

There are several precautions you can take to minimize these kinds of reactivity. One is to make the procedure as clear and brief as possible so that participants are not tempted to take out their frustrations on your results. Another is to guarantee participants' anonymity and make clear to them that you are doing so. If you are testing them in groups, be sure that they are seated far enough apart that they cannot see each other's responses. Give them all the same type of writing implement so that they cannot be identified by, for example, the pink glitter pen that they used. You can even allow them to seal completed questionnaires into individual envelopes or put them into a drop box where they immediately become mixed with others' questionnaires. Although informed consent requires telling participants what they will be doing, it does not require revealing your hypothesis or other information that might suggest to participants how you expect them to respond. A questionnaire designed to measure financial responsibility need not be titled "Are You Financially Responsible?" It could be titled "Money Questionnaire" or have no title at all. Finally, the effects of your expectations can be minimized by arranging to have the measure administered by a helper who is unaware of its intent or of any hypothesis being tested. Regardless of whether this is possible, you should standardize all interactions between researchers and participants—for example, by always reading the same set of instructions word for word.

## "How Often Do You Smoke Marijuana?"

Researchers Lauren Durant and colleagues asked college students to complete questionnaires that included items about their illegal drug use and sexual activity (Durant, Carey, & Shroder, 2002).[13] In one condition, participants wrote down their names and birth dates on their questionnaires but were assured that the data would remain confidential. In the other condition, participants instead wrote down a "rule generated pseudonym" based on the first letters of their middle names, birth months, and mother's and father's first names. Participants who did not provide their actual names were more likely to agree to their responses being used by the researchers, less likely to skip individual items, and reported more illegal drug use and sexual activity. Reports of marijuana use, for example, were five to ten times higher in the anonymous condition.

**FIGURE 5.4**

Source: © Shutterstock, Inc.

## Evaluating the Measure

Once you have used your measure on a sample of people and have a set of scores, you are in a position to evaluate it more thoroughly in terms of reliability and validity. Even if the measure has been used extensively by other researchers and has already shown evidence of reliability and validity, you should not assume that it worked as expected for your particular sample and under your particular testing conditions. Regardless, you now have additional evidence bearing on the reliability and validity of the measure, and it would make sense to add that evidence to the research literature.

In most research designs, it is not possible to assess test-retest reliability because participants are tested at only one time. For a new measure, you might design a study specifically to assess its test-retest reliability by testing the same set of participants at two times. In other cases, a study designed to answer a different question still allows for the assessment of test-retest reliability. For example, a psychology instructor might measure his students' attitude toward critical thinking using the same measure at the beginning and end of the semester to see if there is any change. Even if there is no change, he could still look at the correlation between students' scores at the two times to assess the measure's test-retest reliability. It is also customary to assess internal consistency for any multiple-item measure—usually by looking at a split-half correlation or Cronbach's $\alpha$.

Criterion and discriminant validity can be assessed in various ways. For example, if your study included more than one measure of the same construct or measures of conceptually distinct constructs, then you should look at the correlations among these measures to be sure that they fit your expectations. Note also that a successful experimental manipulation also provides evidence of criterion validity. Recall that MacDonald and Martineau manipulated participant's moods by having them think either positive or negative thoughts, and after the manipulation their mood measure showed a distinct difference between the two groups. This simultaneously provided evidence that their mood manipulation worked *and* that their mood measure was valid.

But what if your newly collected data cast doubt on the reliability or validity of your measure? The short answer is that you have to ask why. It could be that there is something wrong with your measure or how you administered it. It could be that there is something wrong with your conceptual definition. It could be that your experimental manipulation failed. For example, if a mood measure showed no difference between people whom you instructed to think positive versus negative thoughts, maybe it is because the participants did not actually think the thoughts they were supposed to or that the thoughts did not actually affect their moods. In short, it is "back to the drawing board" to revise the measure, revise the conceptual definition, or try a new manipulation.

## Key Takeaways

- Good measurement begins with a clear conceptual definition of the construct to be measured. This is accomplished both by clear and detailed thinking and by a review of the research literature.
- You often have the option of using an existing measure or creating a new measure. You should make this decision based on the availability of existing measures and their adequacy for your purposes.
- Several simple steps can be taken in creating new measures and in implementing both existing and new measures that can help maximize reliability and validity.
- Once you have used a measure, you should reevaluate its reliability and validity based on your new data. Remember that the assessment of reliability and validity is an ongoing process.

## Exercises

1. Practice: Write your own conceptual definition of self-confidence, irritability, and athleticism.
2. Practice: Choose a construct (sexual jealousy, self-confidence, etc.) and find two measures of that construct in the research literature. If you were conducting your own study, which one (if either) would you use and why?

# Endnotes

1. MacDonald, T. K., & Martineau, A. M. (2002). Self-esteem, mood, and intentions to use condoms: When does low self-esteem lead to risky health behaviors? *Journal of Experimental Social Psychology, 38,* 299–306.
2. Rosenberg, M. (1989). *Society and the adolescent self-image* (rev. ed.). Middletown, CT: Wesleyan University Press.
3. Costa, P. T., Jr., & McCrae, R. R. (1992). Normal personality assessment in clinical practice: The NEO Personality Inventory. *Psychological Assessment, 4,* 5–13.
4. John, O. P., Naumann, L. P., Soto, C. J. (2008). *Paradigm shift to the integrated Big Five taxonomy: History, measurement, and conceptual issues.* In O. P. John, L. W. Robin, and L. A. Pervin (Eds.), *Handbook of personality: Theory and research* (pp. 114-158). New York, NY: Guilford Press.
5. Bandura, A., Ross, D., & Ross, S. A. (1961). Transmission of aggression through imitation of aggressive models. *Journal of Abnormal and Social Psychology, 63,* 575–582.
6. Segerstrom, S. E., & Miller, G. E. (2004). Psychological stress and the human immune system: A meta-analytic study of 30 years of inquiry. *Psychological Bulletin, 130,* 601–630.

7.  Stevens, S. S. (1946). On the theory of scales of measurement. *Science, 103*, 677–680.

8.  Cacioppo, J. T., & Petty, R. E. (1982). The need for cognition. *Journal of Personality and Social Psychology, 42*, 116–131.

9.  Petty, R. E, Briñol, P., Loersch, C., & McCaslin, M. J. (2009). The need for cognition. In M. R. Leary & R. H. Hoyle (Eds.), *Handbook of individual differences in social behavior* (pp. 318–329). New York, NY: Guilford Press.

10. Gosling, S. D., Rentfrow, P. J., & Swann, W. B., Jr. (2003). A very brief measure of the Big Five personality domains. *Journal of Research in Personality, 37*, 504–528.

11. Stroop, J. R. (1935). Studies of interference in serial verbal reactions. *Journal of Experimental Psychology, 18*, 643–662.

12. Amir, N., Freshman, M., & Foa, E. (2002). Enhanced Stroop interference for threat in social phobia. *Journal of Anxiety Disorders, 16*, 1–9.

13. Durant, L., Carey, M. P., & Shroder, K. E. E. (2002). Effects of anonymity, gender, and erotophilia on the quality of data obtained from self-reports of socially sensitive behaviors. *Journal of Behavioral Medicine, 25*, 439-467.

# CHAPTER 6

# Experimental Research

In the late 1960s, social psychologists John Darley and Bibb Latané proposed a counterintuitive hypothesis. The more witnesses there are to an accident or a crime, the less likely any of them is to help the victim (Darley & Latané, 1968).[1] They also suggested the theory that this happens because each witness feels less responsible for helping—a process referred to as the "diffusion of responsibility." Darley and Latané noted that their ideas were consistent with many real-world cases. For example, a New York woman named Kitty Genovese was assaulted and murdered while several witnesses failed to help. But Darley and Latané also understood that such isolated cases did not provide convincing evidence for their hypothesized "bystander effect." There was no way to know, for example, whether any of the witnesses to Kitty Genovese's murder would have helped had there been fewer of them.

So to test their hypothesis, Darley and Latané created a simulated emergency situation in a laboratory. Each of their college student participants was isolated in a small room and told that he or she would be having a discussion about college life with other students via an intercom system. Early in the discussion, however, one of the students began having what seemed to be an epileptic seizure. Over the intercom came the following: "I could really-er-use some help so if somebody would-er-give me a little h-help-uh-er-er-er-er-er c-could somebody-er-er-help-er-uh-uh-uh (choking sounds)…I'm gonna die-er-er-I'm…gonna die-er-help-er-er-seizure-er- [chokes, then quiet]" (Darley & Latané, 1968, p. 379).[2]

In actuality, there were no other students. These comments had been prerecorded and were played back to create the appearance of a real emergency. The key to the study was that some participants were told that the discussion involved only one other student (the victim), others were told that it involved two other students, and still others were told that it included five other students. Because this was the only difference between these three groups of participants, any difference in their tendency to help the victim would have to have been caused by it. And sure enough, the likelihood that the participant left the room to seek help for the "victim" decreased from 85% to 62% to 31% as the number of "witnesses" increased.

### The Parable of the 38 Witnesses

The story of Kitty Genovese has been told and retold in numerous psychology textbooks. The standard version is that there were 38 witnesses to the crime, that all of them watched (or listened) for an extended period of time, and that none of them did anything to help. However, recent scholarship suggests that the standard story is inaccurate in many ways (Manning, Levine, & Collins, 2007).[3] For example, only six eyewitnesses testified at the trial, none of them was aware that he or she was witnessing a lethal assault, and there have been several reports of witnesses calling the police or even coming to the aid of Kitty Genovese. Although the standard story inspired a long line of research on the bystander effect and the diffusion of responsibility, it may also have directed researchers' and students' attention away from other equally interesting and important issues in the psychology of helping—including the conditions in which people do in fact respond collectively to emergency situations.

The study that Darley and Latané conducted was a particular kind of study called an experiment. Experiments are used to determine not only whether there is a statistical relationship between two variables but also whether the relationship is a causal one. For this reason, experiments are one of the most common and useful tools in the psychological researcher's toolbox. In this chapter, we look at experiments in detail. We consider first what sets experiments apart from other kinds of studies and why they support causal conclusions while other kinds of studies do not. We then look at two basic ways of designing an experiment—between-subjects designs and within-subjects designs—and discuss their pros and cons. Finally, we consider several important practical issues that arise when conducting experiments.

# 6.1 Experiment Basics

## Learning Objectives

1. Explain what an experiment is and recognize examples of studies that are experiments and studies that are not experiments.
2. Explain what internal validity is and why experiments are considered to be high in internal validity.
3. Explain what external validity is and evaluate studies in terms of their external validity.
4. Distinguish between the manipulation of the independent variable and control of extraneous variables and explain the importance of each.
5. Recognize examples of confounding variables and explain how they affect the internal validity of a study.

## What Is an Experiment?

**experiment**

A type of empirical study in which an independent variable is manipulated and a dependent variable is measured while extraneous variables are controlled.

As we saw earlier in the book, an **experiment** is a type of study designed specifically to answer the question of whether there is a causal relationship between two variables. Do changes in an independent variable *cause* changes in a dependent variable? Experiments have two fundamental features. The first is that the researchers manipulate, or systematically vary, the level of the independent variable. The different levels of the independent variable are called conditions. For example, in Darley and Latané's experiment, the independent variable was the number of witnesses that participants believed to be present. The researchers manipulated this independent variable by telling participants that there were either one, two, or five other students involved in the discussion, thereby creating three conditions. The second fundamental feature of an experiment is that the researchers control, or minimize variability in, variables other than the independent and dependent variable. Darley and Latané did this by testing all their participants in the same room, exposing them to the same emergency situation, and so on. They also randomly assigned their participants to conditions so that the three groups would be similar to each other to begin with. Notice that although the words *manipulation* and *control* have similar meanings in everyday language, researchers make a clear distinction between them. They *manipulate* the independent variable by systematically changing its levels and *control* other variables by holding them constant.

Another example comes from the research of Pam Mueller and Daniel Oppenheimer.[4] They were interested in whether the way college students take notes—by hand or on a laptop—affects how well they learn lecture material. To study this, they brought college students to a classroom, showed them videos of lectures, and then tested them on their memory for the lecture material. They randomly assigned half the participants to take notes during the lectures by hand using paper and pencils they provided. And they randomly assigned the other half to take notes using laptops they provided (and which were *not* connected to the Internet). In other words, these researchers manipulated the way the students took notes (the independent variable) to observe the effect on their memory for the lecture material (the dependent variable). They also controlled extraneous variables by testing all participants in the same rooms, on the same video lectures, using the same tests, and so on. The result was that the students who took notes by hand recalled considerably more of the lecture material.

# Internal and External Validity

## Internal Validity

Recall that the fact that two variables are statistically related does not necessarily mean that one causes the other. "Correlation does not imply causation." For example, if it were the case that people who exercise regularly are happier than people who do not exercise regularly, this would not necessarily mean that exercising increases people's happiness. It could mean instead that greater happiness causes people to exercise (the directionality problem) or that something like better physical health causes people to exercise *and* be happier (the third-variable problem).

The purpose of an experiment, however, is to determine whether two variables are statistically related *and* to do so in a way that supports the conclusion that the independent variable caused any observed differences in the dependent variable. The basic logic is this: If the researcher creates two or more highly similar conditions and then manipulates the independent variable to produce just *one* difference between them, then any later difference between the conditions must have been caused by the independent variable. For example, because the only difference between Darley and Latané's conditions was the number of students that participants believed to be involved in the discussion, this must have been responsible for differences in helping between the conditions. Similarly, because the way Mueller and Oppenheimer's conditions was the way the students took notes, this must have been responsible for the difference in memory for the lecture material between the conditions.

An empirical study is said to be have good **internal validity** if the way it was conducted supports the conclusion that the independent variable caused any observed differences in the dependent variable. Thus experiments have good internal validity because the way they are conducted—with the manipulation of the independent variable and the control of extraneous variables—provides strong support for causal conclusions.

**internal validity**

The extent to which the design of a study supports the conclusion that differences in the independent variable caused any observed differences in the dependent variable.

## External Validity

At the same time, the way that experiments are conducted sometimes leads to a different kind of criticism. Specifically, the need to manipulate the independent variable and control extraneous variables means that experiments are often conducted under conditions that seem artificial or unlike "real life" (Stanovich, 2010).[5] In many psychology experiments, the participants are all college undergraduates and come to a classroom or laboratory to fill out a series of paper-and-pencil questionnaires or to perform a carefully designed computerized task. Consider, for example, an experiment in which researcher Barbara Fredrickson and her colleagues had college students come to a laboratory on campus and complete a math test while wearing a swimsuit (Fredrickson, Roberts, Noll, Quinn, & Twenge, 1998).[6] At first, this might seem silly. When will college students ever have to complete math tests in their swimsuits outside of this experiment?

**external validity**

The extent to which the results of a study can be generalized to people and situations beyond those actually studied.

The issue we are confronting is that of external validity. An empirical study is high in **external validity** if the way it was conducted supports generalizing the results to people and situations beyond those actually studied. As a general rule, studies are higher in external validity when the participants and the situation studied are similar to those that the researchers want to generalize to. Imagine, for example, that a group of researchers is interested in how shoppers in large grocery stores are affected by whether breakfast cereal is packaged in yellow or purple boxes. Their study would be high in external validity if they studied the decisions of ordinary people doing their weekly shopping in a real grocery store. If the shoppers bought much more cereal in purple boxes, the researchers would be fairly confident that this would be true for other shoppers in other stores. Their study would be relatively low in external validity, however, if they studied a sample of college students in a laboratory at a selective college who merely judged the appeal of various colors presented on a computer screen. If the students judged purple to be more appealing than yellow, the researchers would not be very confident that this is relevant to grocery shoppers' cereal-buying decisions.

**field experiment**

An experiment that is conducted outside the laboratory.

We should be careful, however, not to draw the blanket conclusion that experiments are low in external validity. One reason is that experiments need not seem artificial. Consider that Darley and Latané's experiment provided a reasonably good simulation of a real emergency situation. Or consider **field experiments** that are conducted entirely outside the laboratory. In one such experiment, Robert Cialdini and his colleagues studied whether hotel guests choose to reuse their towels for a second day as opposed to having them washed as a way of conserving water and energy (Cialdini, 2005).[7] These researchers manipulated the message on a card left in a large sample of hotel rooms. One version of the message emphasized showing respect for the environment, another emphasized that the hotel would donate a portion of their savings to an environmental cause, and a third emphasized that most hotel guests choose to reuse their towels. The result was that guests who received the message that most hotel guests choose to reuse their towels reused their own towels substantially more often than guests receiving either of the other two messages. Given the way they conducted their study, it seems very likely that their result would hold true for other guests in other hotels.

A second reason not to draw the blanket conclusion that experiments are low in external validity is that they are often conducted to learn about psychological *processes* that are likely to operate in a variety of people and situations. Let us return to the experiment by Fredrickson and colleagues. They found that the women in their study, but not the men, performed worse on the math test when they were wearing swimsuits. They argued that this was due to women's greater tendency to objectify themselves—to think about themselves from the perspective of an outside observer—which diverts their attention away from other tasks. They argued, furthermore, that this process of self-objectification and its effect on attention is likely to operate in a variety of women and situations—even if none of them ever finds herself taking a math test in her swimsuit.

## WEIRD People

Researchers Joseph Henrich, Steven Heine, and Ara Norenzayan[8] have recently called attention to the fact that the vast majority or research participants are "WEIRD." That is, they are from cultures that are **W**estern, **E**ducated, **I**ndustrialized, **R**ich, and **D**emocratic, even though the vast majority of the world's population are not. This raises the question of whether most research results in psychology can be said to be true of people in general ... or just true of these WEIRD people.

These researchers show that on the rare occasions when researchers *do* compare across cultures, they often find surprising differences. In the Müller-Lyer illusion below, the two horizontal lines are exactly the same. The only difference between them is that the top one has inward pointing arrows at either end and the bottom one has outward pointing arrows at either end. This causes many people to perceive the top one to be longer. But this effect, which is especially strong among American college students, is almost nonexistent among San foragers of the Kalahari.

**FIGURE 6.1**
The Müller-Lyer Illusion

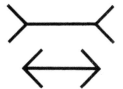

# Manipulation of the Independent Variable

Again, to **manipulate** an independent variable means to change its level systematically so that different groups of participants are exposed to different levels of that variable, or the same group of participants is exposed to different levels at different times. For example, to see whether expressive writing affects people's health, a researcher might instruct some participants to write about traumatic experiences and others to write about neutral experiences. The different levels of the independent variable are referred to as **conditions**, and researchers often give the conditions short descriptive names to make it easy to talk and write about them. In this case, the conditions might be called the "traumatic condition" and the "neutral condition." Mueller and Oppenheimer referred to their conditions as the "longhand condition" and the "laptop condition."

The manipulation of an independent variable must always involve the active intervention of the researcher. Comparing groups of people who differ on the independent variable before the study begins is not the same as manipulating that variable. For example, a researcher who compares the health of people who already keep a journal with the health of people who do not keep a journal has not manipulated this variable and therefore not conducted an experiment. This is important because groups that already differ in one way at the beginning of a study are likely to differ in other ways too. For example, people who choose to keep journals might also be more conscientious, more introverted, or less stressed than people who do not. Therefore, any observed difference between the two groups in terms of their health might have been caused by whether or not they keep a journal, or it might have been caused by any of these other differences.

Of course, there are many situations in which the independent variable cannot be manipulated for practical or ethical reasons and therefore an experiment is not possible. For example, whether or not people have a significant early illness experience cannot be manipulated, making it impossible to do an experiment on the effect of early illness experiences on the development of hypochondriasis. Similarly, the number of concussions people have had cannot be manipulated, making it impossible to do an experiment on the effect of concussions on intellectual functioning. This does not mean it is impossible to study the relationships—only that it must be done using nonexperimental approaches. We will discuss this in detail later in the book.

In many experiments, the independent variable is a construct that can only be manipulated indirectly. For example, a researcher might try to manipulate participants' stress levels indirectly by telling some of them that they have five minutes to prepare a short speech that they will then have to give to an audience of other participants. In such situations, researchers often include a manipulation check in their procedure. A **manipulation check** is a separate measure of the construct the researcher is trying to manipulate. For example, researchers trying to manipulate participants' stress levels might give them a paper-and-pencil stress questionnaire or take their blood pressure—perhaps right after the manipulation or at the end of the procedure—to verify that they successfully manipulated this variable.

**manipulate**

Systematically changing the level of the independent variable across groups or situations.

**conditions**

One level of the independent variable in an experiment.

**manipulation check**

A measure of a manipulated independent variable—usually done at the end of the procedure—to confirm that the independent variable was successfully manipulated.

# Control of Extraneous Variables

**extraneous variable**

Any variable in the context of an experiment other than the independent and dependent variables.

**control**

Holding extraneous variables constant.

An **extraneous variable** is anything that varies in the context of a study other than the independent and dependent variables. In an experiment on the effect of expressive writing on health, for example, extraneous variables would include participant variables (individual differences) such as their writing ability, their diet, and their shoe size. They would also include situation or task variables such as the time of day when participants write, whether they write by hand or on a computer, and the weather. Extraneous variables pose a problem because many of them are likely to have some effect on the dependent variable. For example, participants' health will be affected by many things other than whether or not they engage in expressive writing. This can make it difficult to separate the effect of the independent variable from the effects of the extraneous variables, which is why it is important to **control** extraneous variables by holding them constant.

## Extraneous Variables as "Noise"

Extraneous variables make it difficult to detect the effect of the independent variable in two ways. One is by adding variability or "noise" to the data. Imagine a simple experiment on the effect of mood (happy vs. sad) on the number of happy childhood events people are able to recall. Participants are put into a negative or positive mood (by showing them a happy or sad video clip) and then asked to recall as many happy childhood events as they can. The two leftmost columns of Table 6.1 show what the data might look like if there were no extraneous variables and the number of happy childhood events participants recalled was affected only by their moods. Every participant in the happy mood condition recalled exactly four happy childhood events, and every participant in the sad mood condition recalled exactly three. The effect of mood here is quite obvious. In reality, however, the data would probably look more like those in the two rightmost columns of Table 6.1. Even in the happy mood condition, some participants would recall fewer happy memories because they have fewer to draw on, use less effective strategies, or are less motivated. And even in the sad mood condition, some participants would recall more happy childhood memories because they have more happy memories to draw on, they use more effective recall strategies, or they are more motivated. Although the mean difference between the two groups is the same as in the idealized data (4 vs. 3), this difference is much less obvious in the context of the greater variability in the data. Thus one reason researchers try to control extraneous variables is so their data look more like the idealized data in Table 6.1, which makes the effect of the independent variable easier to detect (although real data never look *that* good).

**TABLE 6.1** Hypothetical Noiseless Data and Realistic Noisy Data

| Idealized "noiseless" data | | Realistic "noisy" data | |
|---|---|---|---|
| **Happy mood** | **Sad mood** | **Happy mood** | **Sad mood** |
| 4 | 3 | 3 | 1 |
| 4 | 3 | 6 | 3 |
| 4 | 3 | 2 | 4 |
| 4 | 3 | 4 | 0 |
| 4 | 3 | 5 | 5 |
| 4 | 3 | 2 | 7 |
| 4 | 3 | 3 | 2 |
| 4 | 3 | 1 | 5 |
| 4 | 3 | 6 | 1 |

| Idealized "noiseless" data | | Realistic "noisy" data | |
| --- | --- | --- | --- |
| 4 | 3 | 8 | 2 |
| M = 4 | M = 3 | M = 4 | M = 3 |

One way to control extraneous variables is to hold them constant. This can mean holding situation or task variables constant by testing all participants in the same location, giving them identical instructions, treating them in the same way, and so on. It can also mean holding participant variables constant. For example, many studies of language limit participants to right-handed people, who generally have their language areas isolated in their left cerebral hemispheres. Left-handed people are more likely to have their language areas isolated in their right cerebral hemispheres or distributed across both hemispheres, which can change the way they process language and thereby add noise to the data.

In principle, researchers can control extraneous variables by limiting participants to one very specific category of person, such as 20-year-old, straight, female, right-handed, sophomore psychology majors. The obvious downside to this approach is that it would lower the external validity of the study—in particular, the extent to which the results can be generalized beyond the people actually studied. For example, it might be unclear whether results obtained with a sample of younger straight women would apply to older gay men. In many situations, the advantages of a diverse sample outweigh the reduction in noise achieved by a homogeneous one.

## Extraneous Variables as Confounding Variables

The second way that extraneous variables can make it difficult to detect the effect of the independent variable is by becoming confounding variables. A **confounding variable** is an extraneous variable that differs on average *across* levels of the independent variable. For example, in almost all experiments, participants' IQs will be an extraneous variable. But as long as their average IQs are roughly equal across conditions, then this is not a problem. What would be problem, however, would be for participants in one condition to have substantially higher or lower IQs on average than participants in another condition. In this case, IQ would be a confounding variable.

**confounding variable**

An extraneous variable that differs across the levels of the independent variable.

To confound means to confuse, and this is exactly what confounding variables do. Because they differ across conditions—just like the independent variable—they provide an alternative explanation for any observed difference in the dependent variable. Figure 6.2 shows the results of a hypothetical study, in which participants in a positive mood condition scored higher on a memory task than participants in a negative mood condition. But if IQ is a confounding variable—with participants in the positive mood condition having higher IQs on average than participants in the negative mood condition—then it is unclear whether it was the positive moods or the higher IQs that caused participants in the first condition to score higher.

**FIGURE 6.2** Hypothetical Results From a Study on the Effect of Mood on Memory

Because IQ also differs across conditions, it is a confounding variable.

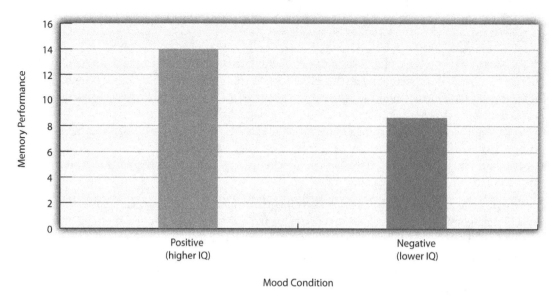

One way to avoid confounding variables is by holding extraneous variables constant. For example, one could prevent IQ from becoming a confounding variable by limiting participants to those with IQs of exactly 100. But this approach is not always desirable for reasons we have already discussed. Two more general approaches to this problem—random assignment to conditions and within-subjects designs—will be discussed in detail shortly.

## Key Takeaways

- An experiment is a type of empirical study that features the manipulation of an independent variable, the measurement of a dependent variable, and control of extraneous variables.
- Studies are high in internal validity to the extent that the way they are conducted supports the conclusion that the independent variable caused any observed differences in the dependent variable. Experiments are generally high in internal validity because of the manipulation of the independent variable and control of extraneous variables.
- Studies are high in external validity to the extent that the result can be generalized to people and situations beyond those actually studied. Although experiments can seem "artificial"—and low in external validity—it is important to consider whether the psychological processes under study are likely to operate in other people and situations.

## Exercises

1. Practice: List five variables that can be manipulated by the researcher in an experiment. List five variables that cannot be manipulated by the researcher in an experiment.
2. Practice: For each of the following topics, decide whether that topic could be studied using an experimental research design and explain why or why not.
   a. Effect of parietal lobe damage on people's ability to do basic arithmetic.
   b. Effect of being clinically depressed on the number of close friendships people have.
   c. Effect of group training on the social skills of teenagers with Asperger's syndrome.
   d. Effect of paying people to take an IQ test on their performance on that test.

# 6.2 Experimental Design

## Learning Objectives

1. Explain the difference between between-subjects and within-subjects experiments, list some of the pros and cons of each approach, and decide which approach to use to answer a particular research question.
2. Define random assignment, distinguish it from random sampling, explain its purpose in experimental research, and use some simple strategies to implement it.
3. Define what a control condition is, explain its purpose in research on treatment effectiveness, and describe some alternative types of control conditions.
4. Define several types of carryover effect, give examples of each, and explain how counterbalancing helps to deal with them.

In this section, we look at some different ways to design an experiment. The primary distinction we will make is between approaches in which each participant experiences one level of the independent variable and approaches in which each participant experiences all levels of the independent variable. The former are called between-subjects experiments and the latter are called within-subjects experiments.

## Between-Subjects Experiments

In a **between-subjects experiment**, each participant is tested in only one condition. Imagine an experiment in which the researchers want to see if people's moods affect their levels of creativity. Figure 6.3 represents a between-subjects design in which each participant is assigned to *either* a happy condition *or* to sad condition before taking a creativity test. Thus the comparison is between the creativity levels of two different groups of people—one happy and one sad. The study by Darley and Latané also involved a between-subjects design because participants believed that there were *either* one, three, or five other students present. The study by Mueller and Oppenheimer also involved a between-subjects design because participants took notes *either* by hand or on a laptop.

**between-subjects experiment**

An experiment in which each participant is tested in one condition.

FIGURE 6.3 Between-Subjects Design
A between-subjects design in which participants are tested in either a happy condition or a sad condition. The condition is determined by random assignment.

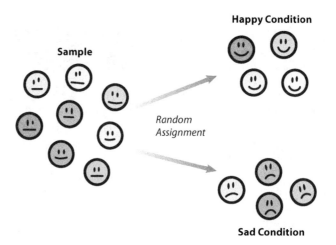

## Random Assignment

It is important in a between-subjects experiment for the researcher to assign participants to conditions so that the different groups are, on average, as similar as possible. Participants writing about a traumatic event and participants writing about a neutral event, for example, should include a similar proportion of men and women, and they should have similar average IQs, similar average levels of motivation, similar average numbers of health problems, and so on. This is a matter of controlling these extraneous participant variables across conditions so that they do not become confounding variables.

The primary way that researchers accomplish this kind of control of extraneous variables across conditions is called **random assignment**, which means using a random process to decide which participants are tested in which conditions. Do not confuse random assignment with random sampling. Random sampling is a method for selecting a sample from a population, and it is rarely used in psychological research. Random assignment is a method for assigning participants in a sample to the different conditions, and it is an important element of all experimental research in psychology and other fields too.

In its strictest sense, random assignment should meet two criteria. One is that each participant has an equal chance of being assigned to each condition (e.g., a 50% chance of being assigned to each of two conditions). The second is that each participant is assigned to a condition independently of other participants. Thus one way to assign participants to two conditions would be to flip a coin for each one. If the coin lands heads, the participant is assigned to Condition A, and if it lands tails, the participant is assigned to Condition B. For three conditions, one could use a computer to generate a random integer from 1 to 3 for each participant. If the integer is 1, the participant is assigned to Condition A; if it is 2, the participant is assigned to Condition B; and if it is 3, the participant is assigned to Condition C. In practice, a full sequence of conditions—one for each participant expected to be in the experiment—is usually created ahead of time, and each new participant is assigned to the next condition in the sequence as he or she is tested. When the procedure is computerized, the computer program often handles the random assignment.

**random assignment**

The assignment of participants to different conditions according to a random procedure, such as flipping a coin, rolling a die, or using a random number generator.

## That's Not Random!

It can help to clarify the concept of random assignment by considering some ways of assigning participants to conditions that are decidedly NOT random.

- **The groups already existed before the study began.** *Students in the morning section of the course were in the daily-quiz condition and students in the afternoon section were in the weekly-quiz condition.*
- **The groups were tested at different times.** *Participants in the happy condition were tested during the fall semester while participants in the sad condition were tested during the spring semester.*
- **The researcher "created" the groups based on participant characteristics.** *Participants who scored high on an anxiety questionnaire were in the anxious condition and participants who scored low were in the non-anxious condition.*
- **Participants sorted themselves into groups.** *Participants decided whether they preferred to be in the handwritten notes condition or the laptop notes condition.*
- **The researcher assigned participants using a nonrandom process.** *The researcher assigned participants who looked to be in good shape to the exercise condition and assigned participants who looked to be in poor shape to the no-exercise condition.*

One problem with coin flipping and other strict procedures for random assignment is that they are likely to result in unequal sample sizes in the different conditions. Unequal sample sizes are generally not a serious problem, and you should never throw away data you have already collected to achieve equal sample sizes. However, for a fixed number of participants, it is statistically most efficient to divide them into equal-sized groups. It is standard practice, therefore, to use a kind of modified random assignment that keeps the number of participants in each group as similar as possible. One approach is **block randomization**. In block randomization, all the conditions occur once in the sequence before any of them is repeated. Then they all occur again before any of them is repeated again. Within each of these "blocks," the conditions occur in a random order. Again, the sequence of conditions is usually generated before any participants are tested, and each new participant is assigned to the next condition in the sequence. Table 6.2 shows such a sequence for assigning nine participants to three conditions. The Research Randomizer website (http://www.randomizer.org) will generate block randomization sequences for any number of participants and conditions. Again, when the procedure is computerized, the computer program often handles the block randomization.

**block randomization**

A method of randomly assigning participants that guarantees that the condition sample sizes are equal or almost equal. A random procedure is used to assign the first $k$ participants into the $k$ conditions, and then to assign the next $k$ participants into the $k$ conditions, and so on until all the participants have been assigned.

**TABLE 6.2** Block Randomization Sequence for Assigning Nine Participants to Three Conditions

| Participant | Condition |
| --- | --- |
| 1 | A |
| 2 | C |
| 3 | B |
| 4 | B |
| 5 | C |
| 6 | A |
| 7 | C |
| 8 | B |
| 9 | A |

Random assignment is not guaranteed to control all extraneous variables across conditions. It is always possible that, just by chance, the participants in one condition might still turn out to be substantially older, less tired, more motivated, or less depressed on average than the participants in another condition. However, there are some reasons that this is not a major concern. One is that random assignment works better than one might expect, especially for large samples. Another is that the inferential statistics that researchers use to decide whether a difference between groups reflects a difference in the population takes the "fallibility" of random assignment into account. Yet another reason is that even if random assignment does result in a confounding variable and therefore produces misleading results, this is likely to be detected when the experiment is replicated. The upshot is that random assignment to conditions—although not infallible in terms of controlling extraneous variables—is always considered a strength of a research design.

## Treatment and Control Conditions

**treatment**

An intervention intended to change people's behavior for the better.

**treatment condition**

A condition in a study in which participants receive some treatment of interest.

**control condition**

A condition in a study in which participants do not receive the treatment of interest.

**randomized clinical trial**

An experiment designed to test the effectiveness of a psychological or medical treatment.

**no-treatment control condition**

A control condition in which participants receive no treatment whatsoever—not even a placebo.

**placebo**

A treatment that lacks any active ingredient or element that should make it effective.

**placebo effect**

The positive effect of a placebo.

Between-subjects experiments are often used to determine whether a treatment works. In psychological research, a **treatment** is any intervention meant to change people's behavior for the better. This includes psychotherapies and medical treatments for psychological disorders but also interventions designed to improve learning, promote conservation, reduce prejudice, and so on. To determine whether a treatment works, participants are randomly assigned to either a **treatment condition**, in which they receive the treatment, or a **control condition**, in which they do not receive the treatment. If participants in the treatment condition end up better off than participants in the control condition—for example, they are less depressed, learn faster, conserve more, express less prejudice—then the researcher can conclude that the treatment works. In research on the effectiveness of psychotherapies and medical treatments, this type of experiment is often called a **randomized clinical trial**. It is common to hear randomized clinical trials referred to as the "gold standard"—the best existing approach—for research on treatment effectiveness.

There are different types of control conditions. In a **no-treatment control condition**, participants receive no treatment whatsoever. One problem with this approach, however, is the existence of placebo effects. A **placebo** is a simulated treatment that lacks any active ingredient or element that should make it effective, and a **placebo effect** is a positive effect of such a treatment. Many folk remedies that seem to work—such as eating chicken soup for a cold or placing soap under the bedsheets to stop nighttime leg cramps—are probably nothing more than placebos. Although placebo effects are not well understood, they are probably driven primarily by people's expectations that they will improve. Having the expectation to improve can result in reduced stress, anxiety, and depression, which can alter perceptions and even improve immune system functioning (Price, Finniss, & Benedetti, 2008).[9]

Placebo effects are interesting in their own right (see "The Powerful Placebo"), but they also pose a serious problem for researchers who want to determine whether a treatment works. Figure 6.4 shows some hypothetical results in which participants in a treatment condition improved more on average than participants in a no-treatment control condition. If these conditions (the two left-most bars in Figure 6.4) were the only conditions in this experiment, however, one could not conclude that the treatment worked. It could be instead that participants in the treatment group improved more because they expected to improve, while those in the no-treatment control condition did not.

**FIGURE 6.4** Hypothetical Results From a Study Including Treatment, No-Treatment, and Placebo Conditions

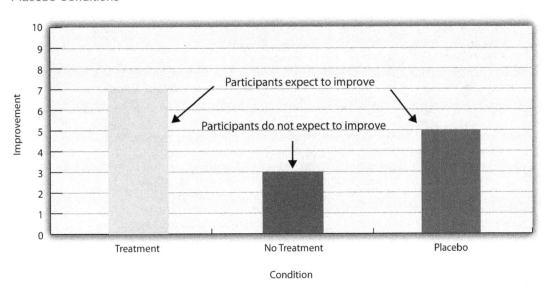

Fortunately, there are several solutions to this problem. One is to include a **placebo control condition**, in which participants receive a placebo that looks much like the treatment but lacks the active ingredient or element thought to be responsible for the treatment's effectiveness. When participants in a treatment condition take a pill, for example, then those in a placebo control condition would take an identical-looking pill that lacks the active ingredient in the treatment (a "sugar pill"). In research on psychotherapy effectiveness, the placebo might involve going to a psychotherapist and talking in an unstructured way about one's problems. The idea is that if participants in both the treatment and the placebo control groups expect to improve, then any improvement in the treatment group over and above that in the placebo control group must have been caused by the treatment and not by participants' expectations. This is what is shown by a comparison of the two outer bars in Figure 6.4.

Of course, the principle of informed consent requires that participants be told that they will be assigned to either a treatment or a placebo control condition—even though they cannot be told which until the experiment ends. In many cases the participants who had been in the control condition are then offered an opportunity to have the real treatment. An alternative approach is to use a **waitlist control condition**, in which participants are told that they will receive the treatment but must wait until the participants in the treatment condition have already received it. This allows researchers to compare participants who have received the treatment with participants who are not currently receiving it but who still expect to improve (eventually). A final solution to the problem of placebo effects is to leave out the control condition completely and compare any new treatment with the best available alternative treatment. For example, a new treatment for simple phobia could be compared with standard exposure therapy. Because participants in both conditions receive a treatment, their expectations about improvement should be similar. This approach also makes sense because once there is an effective treatment, the interesting question about a new treatment is not simply "Does it work?" but "Does it work better than what is already available?"

**placebo control condition**

A control condition in which participants receive a placebo.

**waitlist control condition**

A control condition in which participants are put on a waitlist to receive the treatment after the study is completed.

## The Powerful Placebo

Many people are not surprised that placebos can have a positive effect on disorders that seem fundamentally psychological, including depression, anxiety, and insomnia. However, placebos can also have a positive effect on disorders that most people think of as fundamentally physiological. These include asthma, ulcers, and warts (Shapiro & Shapiro, 1999).[10] There is even evidence that placebo surgery—also called "sham surgery"—can be as effective as actual surgery.

Medical researcher J. Bruce Moseley and his colleagues conducted a study on the effectiveness of two arthroscopic surgery procedures for osteoarthritis of the knee (Moseley et al., 2002).[11] The control participants in this study were prepped for surgery, received a tranquilizer, and even received three small incisions in their knees. But they did not receive the actual arthroscopic surgical procedure. The surprising result was that all participants improved in terms of both knee pain and function, and the sham surgery group improved just as much as the treatment groups. According to the researchers, "This study provides strong evidence that arthroscopic lavage with or without débridement [the surgical procedures used] is not better than and appears to be equivalent to a placebo procedure in improving knee pain and self-reported function" (p. 85).

**FIGURE 6.5**
Research has shown that patients with osteoarthritis of the knee who receive a "sham surgery" experience reductions in pain and improvement in knee function similar to those of patients who receive a real surgery.

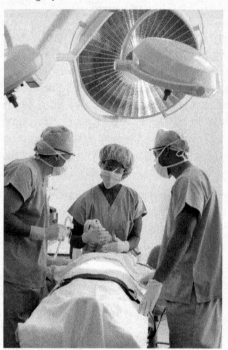

Source: © Thinkstock

# Within-Subjects Experiments

**within-subjects experiment**

An experiment in which each participant is tested in all conditions.

In a **within-subjects experiment**, each participant is tested in all conditions. Figure 6.6 represents a within-subjects design in which each participant's creativity level is tested twice—once in the happy condition and once in the sad condition. Thus the comparison between between the very same people under those different conditions. (Figure 6.6 also shows that participants are randomly assigned to one of the two possible *orders* of conditions. More on this shortly.)

**FIGURE 6.6** Within-Subjects Design

A within-subjects design in which participants are tested in both a happy condition and a sad condition. The order of the conditions is counterbalanced, with some tested in the happy condition followed by the sad condition, and others tested in the sad condition followed by the happy condition. The order of conditions is determined by random assignment.

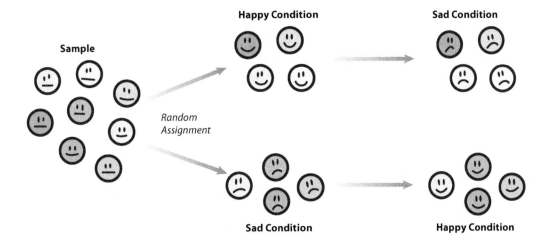

The primary advantage of this approach is that it provides maximum control of extraneous participant variables. Participants in all conditions have the same mean IQ, same socioeconomic status, same number of siblings, and so on—because they are the very same people. Within-subjects experiments also make it possible to use statistical procedures that remove the effect of these extraneous participant variables on the dependent variable and therefore make the data less "noisy" and the effect of the independent variable easier to detect. We will look more closely at this idea later in the book.

# Carryover Effects and Counterbalancing

**carryover effect**

An effect of being tested in one condition on participants' behavior in later conditions.

**practice effect**

A carryover effect in which participants perform better on a task in later conditions because they have had a chance to practice.

**fatigue effect**

A carryover effect in which participants perform worse on a task in later conditions because they have become tired or bored.

**context effect**

An unintended effect of the context in which a response is made. In within-subjects experiments, this can be an effect of being tested in one condition on how participants perceive stimuli or interpret their task and therefore how they respond in later conditions. In survey research, this can be an effect of the surrounding items or the response scale on responses to a particular item.

**counterbalancing**

Systematically varying the order of conditions across participants.

The primary disadvantage of within-subjects designs is that they can result in carryover effects. A **carryover effect** is an effect of being tested in one condition on participants' behavior in later conditions. One type of carryover effect is a **practice effect**, where participants perform a task better in later conditions because they have had a chance to practice it. Another type is a **fatigue effect**, where participants perform a task worse in later conditions because they become tired or bored. Being tested in one condition can also change how participants perceive stimuli or interpret their task in later conditions. This is called a **context effect**. Imagine, for example, a within-subjects experiment on the effect of a criminal defendant's attractiveness on judgments of his guilt. It is possible that an unattractive defendant would be judged especially harshly if he were presented immediately after an attractive one. Likewise, it is possible that an attractive defendant would be judged especially leniently if he were presented after an unattractive one. Within-subjects experiments also make it easier for participants to guess the hypothesis. For example, a participant who is asked to judge the guilt of an attractive defendant and then is asked to judge the guilt of an unattractive defendant is likely to guess that the hypothesis is that defendant attractiveness affects judgments of guilt. This could lead the participant to judge the unattractive defendant more harshly because he thinks this is what he is expected to do. Or it could make participants judge the two defendants similarly in an effort to be "fair."

Carryover effects can be interesting in their own right. (Does the attractiveness of one person depend on the attractiveness of other people that we have seen recently?) But when they are not the focus of the research, carryover effects can be problematic. Imagine, for example, that participants judge the guilt of an attractive defendant and then judge the guilt of an unattractive defendant. If they judge the unattractive defendant more harshly, this might be because of his unattractiveness. But it could be instead that they judge him more harshly because they are becoming bored or tired. In other words, the order of the conditions is a confounding variable. The attractive condition is always the first condition and the unattractive condition the second. Thus any difference between the conditions in terms of the dependent variable could be caused by the order of the conditions and not the independent variable itself.

There is a solution to the problem of order effects, however, that can be used in many situations. It is **counterbalancing**, which means testing different participants in different orders. For example, some participants would be tested in the attractive defendant condition followed by the unattractive defendant condition, and others would be tested in the unattractive condition followed by the attractive condition. Or as Figure 6.3 shows, some participants can be tested in a happy-mood condition followed by a sad-mood condition, and others can be tested in a sad-mood condition followed by a happy-mood condition. With three conditions (A, B, and C), there would be six different orders (ABC, ACB, BAC, BCA, CAB, and CBA), so some participants would be tested in each of the six orders. With counterbalancing, participants are assigned to orders randomly, using the techniques we have already discussed. Thus random assignment plays an important role in within-subjects designs just as in between-subjects designs. Here, instead of randomly assigning to conditions, they are randomly assigned to different orders of conditions. In fact, it can safely be said that if a study does not involve random assignment in one form or another, it is not an experiment.

There are two ways to think about what counterbalancing accomplishes. One is that it controls the order of conditions so that it is no longer a confounding variable. Instead of the attractive condition always being first and the unattractive condition always being second, the attractive condition comes first for some participants and second for others. Likewise, the unattractive condition comes first for some participants and second for others. Thus any overall difference in the dependent variable between the two conditions cannot have been caused by the order of conditions. A second way to think about what counterbalancing accomplishes is that if there are carryover effects, it makes it possible to detect them. One can analyze the data separately for each order to see whether it had an effect.

### When 9 Is "Larger" Than 221

Researcher Michael Birnbaum has argued that the *lack* of context provided by between-subjects designs is often a bigger problem than the context effects created by within-subjects designs. To demonstrate this, he asked one group of participants to rate how large the number 9 was on a 1-to-10 rating scale and another group to rate how large the number 221 was on the same 1-to-10 rating scale (Birnbaum, 1999).[12] Participants in this between-subjects design gave the number 9 a mean rating of 5.13 and the number 221 a mean rating of 3.10. In other words, they rated 9 as larger than 221! According to Birnbaum, this is because participants spontaneously compared 9 with other one-digit numbers (in which case it is *relatively* large) and compared 221 with other three-digit numbers (in which case it is *relatively* small).

## Simultaneous Within-Subjects Designs

So far, we have discussed an approach to within-subjects designs in which participants are tested in one condition at a time. There is another approach, however, that is often used when participants make multiple responses in each condition. Imagine, for example, that participants judge the guilt of 10 attractive defendants and 10 unattractive defendants. Instead of having people make judgments about all 10 defendants of one type followed by all 10 defendants of the other type, the researcher could present all 20 defendants in a sequence that mixed the two types. The researcher could then compute each participant's mean rating for each type of defendant. Or imagine an experiment designed to see whether people with social anxiety disorder remember negative adjectives (e.g., "stupid," "incompetent") better than positive ones (e.g., "happy," "productive"). The researcher could have participants study a single list that includes both kinds of words and then have them try to recall as many words as possible. The researcher could then count the number of each type of word that was recalled. There are many ways to determine the order in which the stimuli are presented, but one common way is to generate a different random order for each participant.

# Between-Subjects or Within-Subjects?

Almost every experiment can be conducted using either a between-subjects design or a within-subjects design. This means that researchers must choose between the two approaches based on their relative merits for the particular situation.

Between-subjects experiments have the advantage of being conceptually simpler and requiring less testing time per participant. They also avoid carryover effects without the need for counterbalancing. Within-subjects experiments have the advantage of controlling extraneous participant variables, which generally reduces noise in the data and makes it easier to detect a relationship between the independent and dependent variables.

A good rule of thumb, then, is that if it is possible to conduct a within-subjects experiment (with proper counterbalancing) in the time that is available per participant—and you have no serious concerns about carryover effects—this is probably the best option. If a within-subjects design would be difficult or impossible to carry out, then you should consider a between-subjects design instead. For example, if you were testing participants in a doctor's waiting room or shoppers in line at a grocery store, you might not have enough time to test each participant in all conditions and therefore would opt for a between-subjects design. Or imagine you were trying to reduce people's level of prejudice by having them interact with someone of another race. A within-subjects design with counterbalancing would require testing some participants in the treatment condition first and then in a control condition. But if the treatment works and reduces people's level of prejudice, then they would no longer be suitable for testing in the control condition. This is true for many designs that involve a treatment meant to produce long-term change in participants' behavior (e.g., studies testing the effectiveness of psychotherapy). Clearly, a between-subjects design would be necessary here.

Remember also that using one type of design does not preclude using the other type in a different study. There is no reason that a researcher could not use both a between-subjects design and a within-subjects design to answer the same research question. In fact, professional researchers often do exactly this.

## Key Takeaways

- Experiments can be conducted using either between-subjects or within-subjects designs. Deciding which to use in a particular situation requires careful consideration of the pros and cons of each approach.
- Random assignment to conditions in between-subjects experiments or to orders of conditions in within-subjects experiments is a fundamental element of experimental research. Its purpose is to control extraneous variables so that they do not become confounding variables.
- Experimental research on the effectiveness of a treatment requires both a treatment condition and a control condition, which can be a no-treatment control condition, a placebo control condition, or a waitlist control condition. Experimental treatments can also be compared with the best available alternative.

## Exercises

1. Discussion: For each of the following topics, list the pros and cons of a between-subjects and within-subjects design and decide which would be better.

   a. You want to test the relative effectiveness of two training programs for running a marathon.

   b. Using photographs of people as stimuli, you want to see if smiling people are perceived as more intelligent than people who are not smiling.

   c. In a field experiment, you want to see if the way a panhandler is dressed (neatly vs. sloppily) affects whether or not passersby give him any money.

   d. You want to see if concrete nouns (e.g., *dog*) are recalled better than abstract nouns (e.g., *truth*).

2. Discussion: Imagine that an experiment shows that participants who receive psychodynamic therapy for a dog phobia improve more than participants in a no-treatment control group. Explain a fundamental problem with this research design and at least two ways that it might be corrected.

# 6.3 Conducting Experiments

## Learning Objectives

1. Describe several strategies for recruiting participants for an experiment.

2. Explain why it is important to standardize the procedure of an experiment and several ways to do this.
3. Explain what pilot testing is and why it is important.

The information presented so far in this chapter is enough to design a basic experiment. When it comes time to conduct that experiment, however, several additional practical issues arise. In this section, we consider some of these issues and how to deal with them. Much of this information applies to nonexperimental studies as well as experimental ones.

# Recruiting Participants

Of course, you should be thinking about how you will obtain your participants from the beginning of any research project. Unless you have access to people with schizophrenia or incarcerated juvenile offenders, for example, then there is no point designing a study that focuses on these populations. But even if you plan to use a convenience sample, you will have to recruit participants for your study.

There are several approaches to recruiting participants. One is to use participants from a formal **subject pool**—an established group of people who have agreed to be contacted about participating in research studies. For example, at many colleges and universities, there is a subject pool consisting of students enrolled in introductory psychology courses who must participate in a certain number of studies to meet a course requirement. Researchers post descriptions of their studies and students sign up to participate, usually via an online system. Participants can also be recruited by posting or publishing advertisements or making personal appeals to groups that represent the population of interest. For example, a researcher interested in studying older adults could arrange to speak at a meeting of the residents at a retirement community to explain the study and ask for volunteers.

**subject pool**

A group of people who have agreed to be contacted about opportunities to be research participants. Many universities have subject pools that consist of introductory psychology students who participate to meet a course requirement.

## The Volunteer Subject

Even if the participants in a study receive compensation in the form of course credit, a small amount of money, or a chance at being treated for a psychological problem, they are still essentially volunteers. This is worth considering because people who volunteer to participate in psychological research have been shown to differ in predictable ways from those who do not volunteer. Specifically, there is good evidence that on average, volunteers have the following characteristics compared with nonvolunteers (Rosenthal & Rosnow, 1976):[13]

- They are more interested in the topic of the research.
- They are more educated.
- They have a greater need for approval.
- They have higher intelligence quotients (IQs).
- They are more sociable.
- They are higher in social class.

This can be an issue of external validity if there is reason to believe that participants with these characteristics are likely to behave differently than the general population. For example, in testing different methods of persuading people, a rational argument might work better on volunteers than it does on the general population because of their generally higher educational level and IQ.

In many field experiments, the task is not recruiting participants but selecting them. For example, researchers Nicolas Guéguen and Marie-Agnès de Gail conducted a field experiment on the effect of being smiled at on helping, in which the participants were shoppers at a supermarket.[14]

A confederate walking down a stairway gazed directly at a shopper walking up the stairway and either smiled or did not smile. Shortly afterward, the shopper encountered another confederate, who dropped some computer diskettes on the ground. The dependent variable was whether or not the shopper stopped to help pick up the diskettes (Guéguen & de Gail, 2003). Notice that these participants were not "recruited," but the researchers still had to select them from among all the shoppers taking the stairs that day. It is extremely important that this kind of selection be done according to a well-defined set of rules that is established before the data collection begins and can be explained clearly afterward. In this case, with each trip down the stairs, the confederate was instructed to gaze at the first person he encountered who appeared to be between the ages of 20 and 50. Only if the person gazed back did he or she become a participant in the study. The point of having a well-defined selection rule is to avoid bias in the selection of participants. For example, if the confederate was free to choose which shoppers he would gaze at, he might choose friendly-looking shoppers when he was set to smile and unfriendly-looking ones when he was not set to smile. As we will see shortly, such biases can be entirely unintentional.

# Standardizing the Procedure

It is surprisingly easy to introduce extraneous variables during an experimental procedure. For example, the same experimenter might give clear instructions to one participant but vague instructions to another. Or one experimenter might greet participants warmly while another barely makes eye contact with them. To the extent that such variables affect participants' behavior, they add noise to the data and make the effect of the independent variable more difficult to detect. If they vary across conditions, they become confounding variables and provide alternative explanations for the results. For example, if participants in a treatment group are tested by a warm and friendly experimenter and participants in a control group are tested by a cold and unfriendly one, then what appears to be an effect of the treatment might actually be an effect of experimenter demeanor.

### Experimenter's Sex as an Extraneous Variable

It is well known that whether research participants are male or female can affect the results of a study. But what about whether the *experimenter* is male or female? There is plenty of evidence that this matters too. Male and female experimenters have slightly different ways of interacting with their participants, and of course participants also respond differently to male and female experimenters (Rosenthal, 1976).[15] For example, in a study on pain perception, participants immersed their hands in icy water for as long as they could (Ibolya, Brake, & Voss, 2004).[16] Male participants tolerated the pain longer when the experimenter was a woman, and female participants tolerated it longer when the experimenter was a man.

**experimenter expectancy effect**

The effect of the researcher's expectations on participants' behavior.

Researcher Robert Rosenthal has spent much of his career showing that this kind of unintended variation in the procedure does, in fact, affect participants' behavior. Furthermore, one important source of such variation is the experimenter's expectations about how participants "should" behave in the experiment. This is referred to as an **experimenter expectancy effect** (Rosenthal, 1976).[17] For example, if an experimenter expects participants in a treatment group to perform better on a task than participants in a control group, then he or she might unintentionally give the treatment group participants clearer instructions or more encouragement or allow them more time to complete the task. In a striking example, Rosenthal and Kermit Fode had several students in a laboratory course in psychology train rats to run through a maze. Although the rats were genetically similar, some of the students were told that they were working with "maze-bright" rats that had been bred to be good learners, and other students were told that they were working with "maze-dull" rats that had been bred to be poor learners. Sure enough, over five days of training, the "maze-bright" rats made more correct responses, made the correct response more quickly, and improved more steadily than the "maze-dull" rats (Rosenthal & Fode, 1963).[18] Clearly it had to have been the students' expectations about how the rats would perform that made the difference. But how? Some clues come from data gathered at the end of the study, which showed that students who expected their rats to learn quickly felt more positively about their animals and reported behaving toward them in a more friendly manner (e.g., handling them more).

The way to minimize unintended variation in the procedure is to standardize it as much as possible so that it is carried out in the same way for all participants regardless of the condition they are in. Here are several ways to do this:

- Create a written protocol that specifies everything that the experimenters are to do and say from the time they greet participants to the time they dismiss them.
- Create standard instructions that participants read themselves or that are read to them word for word by the experimenter.
- Automate the rest of the procedure as much as possible by using software packages for this purpose or even simple computer slide shows.
- Anticipate participants' questions and either raise and answer them in the instructions or develop standard answers for them.
- Train multiple experimenters on the protocol together and have them practice on each other.
- Be sure that each experimenter tests participants in all conditions.

Another good practice is to arrange for the experimenters to be "blind" to the research question or to the condition that each participant is tested in. The idea is to minimize experimenter expectancy effects by minimizing the experimenters' expectations. For example, in a drug study in which each participant receives the drug or a placebo, it is often the case that neither the participants nor the experimenter who interacts with the participants know which condition he or she has been assigned to. Because both the participants and the experimenters are blind to the condition, this is referred to as a **double-blind** study. (A single-blind study is one in which the participant, but not the experimenter, is blind to the condition.) Of course, there are many times this is not possible. For example, if you are both the investigator and the only experimenter, it is not possible for you to remain blind to the research question. Also, in many studies the experimenter *must* know the condition because he or she must carry out the procedure in a different way in the different conditions, such as by handing out paper and pencils in one condition and laptops in another.

**double-blind**

An experimental research design in which both the participants and the experimenters are unaware of which condition the participant has been assigned to.

# Record Keeping

It is essential to keep good records when you conduct an experiment. As discussed earlier, it is typical for experimenters to generate a written sequence of conditions before the study begins and then to test each new participant in the next condition in the sequence. As you test them, it is a good idea to add to this list basic demographic information; the date, time, and place of testing; and the name of the experimenter who did the testing. It is also a good idea to have a place for the experimenter to write down comments about unusual occurrences (e.g., a confused or uncooperative participant) or questions that come up. This kind of information can be useful later if you decide to analyze sex differences or effects of different experimenters, or if a question arises about a particular participant or testing session.

It can also be useful to assign an identification number to each participant as you test them. Simply numbering them consecutively beginning with 1 is usually sufficient. This number can then also be written on any response sheets or questionnaires that participants generate, making it easier to keep them together.

# Pilot Testing

It is always a good idea to conduct a **pilot test** of your experiment. A pilot test is a small-scale study conducted to make sure that a new procedure works as planned. In a pilot test, you can recruit participants formally (e.g., from an established participant pool) or you can recruit them informally from among family, friends, classmates, and so on. The number of participants can be small, but it should be enough to give you confidence that your procedure works as planned. There are several important questions that you can answer by conducting a pilot test:

- Do participants understand the instructions?
- What kind of misunderstandings do participants have, what kind of mistakes do they make, and what kind of questions do they ask?
- Do participants become bored or frustrated?
- Is an indirect manipulation effective? (You will need to include a manipulation check.)
- Can participants guess the research question or hypothesis?
- How long does the procedure take?
- Are computer programs or other automated procedures working properly?
- Are data being recorded correctly?

Of course, to answer some of these questions you will need to observe participants carefully during the procedure and talk with them about it afterward. Participants are often hesitant to criticize a study in front of the researcher, so be sure they understand that this is a pilot test and you are genuinely interested in feedback that will help you improve the procedure. If the procedure works as planned, then you can proceed with the actual study. If there are problems to be solved, you can solve them, pilot test the new procedure, and continue with this process until you are ready to proceed.

## Key Takeaways

- There are several effective methods you can use to recruit research participants for your experiment, including through formal subject pools, advertisements, and personal appeals. Field experiments require well-defined participant selection procedures.
- It is important to standardize experimental procedures to minimize extraneous variables, including experimenter expectancy effects.
- It is important to conduct one or more small-scale pilot tests of an experiment to be sure that the procedure works as planned.

## Exercises

1. Practice: List two ways that you might recruit participants from each of the following populations: (a) elderly adults, (b) unemployed people, (c) regular exercisers, and (d) math majors.
2. Discussion: Imagine a study in which you will visually present participants with a list of 20 words, one at a time, wait for a short time, and then ask them to recall as many of the words as they can. In the stressed condition, they are told that they might also be chosen to give a short speech in front of a small audience. In the unstressed condition, they are not told that they might have to give a speech. What are several specific things that you could do to standardize the procedure?

# Endnotes

1. Darley, J. M., & Latané, B. (1968). Bystander intervention in emergencies: Diffusion of responsibility. *Journal of Personality and Social Psychology, 4*, 377–383.

2. Darley, J. M., & Latané, B. (1968). Bystander intervention in emergencies: Diffusion of responsibility. *Journal of Personality and Social Psychology, 4*, 377–383.

3. Manning, R., Levine, M., & Collins, A. (2007). The Kitty Genovese murder and the social psychology of helping: The parable of the 38 witnesses. *American Psychologist, 62*, 555–562.

4. Mueller, P. A., & Oppenheimer, D. M. (2014). The pen is mightier than the keyboard: Advantages of longhand over laptop note taking. *Psychological Science, 25*, 1159-1168.

5. Stanovich, K. E. (2010). *How to think straight about psychology* (9th ed.). Boston, MA: Allyn & Bacon.

6. Fredrickson, B. L., Roberts, T.-A., Noll, S. M., Quinn, D. M., & Twenge, J. M. (1998). The swimsuit becomes you: Sex differences in self-objectification, restrained eating, and math performance. *Journal of Personality and Social Psychology, 75*, 269–284.

7. Cialdini, R. (2005, April). Don't throw in the towel: Use social influence research. *APS Observer.* Retrieved from http://www.psychologicalscience.org/observer/getArticle.cfm?id=1762

8. Henrich, J., Heine, S. J., & Norenzayan, A. (2010). The weirdest people in the world? *Behavioral and Brain Sciences, 33*, 61-93.

9. Price, D. D., Finniss, D. G., & Benedetti, F. (2008). A comprehensive review of the placebo effect: Recent advances and current thought. *Annual Review of Psychology, 59*, 565–590.

10. Shapiro, A. K., & Shapiro, E. (1999). *The powerful placebo: From ancient priest to modern physician*. Baltimore, MD: Johns Hopkins University Press.

11. Moseley, J. B., O'Malley, K., Petersen, N. J., Menke, T. J., Brody, B. A., Kuykendall, D. H., … Wray, N. P. (2002). A controlled trial of arthroscopic surgery for osteoarthritis of the knee. *The New England Journal of Medicine, 347*, 81–88.

12. Birnbaum, M. H. (1999). How to show that 9 > 221: Collect judgments in a between-subjects design. *Psychological Methods, 4*, 243–249.

13. Rosenthal, R., & Rosnow, R. L. (1976). *The volunteer subject*. New York, NY: Wiley.

14. Guéguen, N., & de Gail, Marie-Agnès. (2003). The effect of smiling on helping behavior: Smiling and good Samaritan behavior. *Communication Reports*, 16, 133–140.

15. Rosenthal, R. (1976). *Experimenter effects in behavioral research* (enlarged ed.). New York, NY: Wiley.

16. Ibolya, K., Brake, A., & Voss, U. (2004). The effect of experimenter characteristics on pain reports in women and men. *Pain, 112*, 142–147.

17. Rosenthal, R. (1976). *Experimenter effects in behavioral research* (enlarged ed.). New York, NY: Wiley.

18. Rosenthal, R., & Fode, K. (1963). The effect of experimenter bias on performance of the albino rat. *Behavioral Science, 8*, 183-189.

CHAPTER 7
# Nonexperimental Research

What do the following classic studies have in common?

- Stanley Milgram found that about two thirds of his research participants were willing to administer dangerous shocks to another person just because they were told to by an authority figure (Milgram, 1963).[1]
- Elizabeth Loftus and Jacqueline Pickrell showed that it is relatively easy to "implant" false memories in people by repeatedly asking them about childhood events that did not actually happen to them (Loftus & Pickrell, 1995).[2]
- John Cacioppo and Richard Petty evaluated the validity of their Need for Cognition Scale—a measure of the extent to which people like and value thinking—by comparing the scores of college professors with those of factory workers (Cacioppo & Petty, 1982).[3]
- David Rosenhan found that confederates who went to psychiatric hospitals claiming to have heard voices saying things like "empty" and "thud" were labeled as schizophrenic by the hospital staff and kept there even though they behaved normally in all other ways (Rosenhan, 1973).[4]

The answer for purposes of this chapter is that they are not experiments. In this chapter we look more closely at nonexperimental research. We begin with a general definition of nonexperimental research, along with a discussion of when and why nonexperimental research is more appropriate than experimental research. We then look separately at three important types of nonexperimental research: correlational research, quasi-experimental research, and qualitative research.

# 7.1 Overview of Nonexperimental Research

## Learning Objectives

1. Define nonexperimental research, distinguish it clearly from experimental research, and give several examples.
2. Explain when a researcher might choose to conduct nonexperimental research as opposed to experimental research.

# What Is Nonexperimental Research?

**nonexperimental research**

Research that lacks the manipulation of an independent variable or the random assignment of participants to conditions or orders of conditions.

**Nonexperimental research** is research that lacks the manipulation of an independent variable, random assignment of participants to conditions or orders of conditions, or both.

In a sense, it is unfair to define this large and diverse set of approaches collectively by what they are *not*. But doing so reflects the fact that most researchers in psychology consider the distinction between experimental and nonexperimental research to be an extremely important one. This is because while experimental research can provide strong evidence that changes in an independent variable cause differences in a dependent variable, nonexperimental research generally cannot. As we will see, however, this does not mean that nonexperimental research is less important than experimental research or inferior to it in any general sense.

# When to Use Nonexperimental Research

As we saw in Chapter 6, experimental research is appropriate when the researcher has a specific research question or hypothesis about a causal relationship between two variables—and it is possible, feasible, and ethical to manipulate the independent variable and randomly assign participants to conditions or to orders of conditions. It stands to reason, therefore, that nonexperimental research is appropriate—even necessary—when these conditions are not met. There are many ways in which this can be the case.

- The research question or hypothesis can be about a single variable rather than a statistical relationship between two variables (e.g., How accurate are people's first impressions?).
- The research question can be about a noncausal statistical relationship between variables (e.g., Is there a correlation between verbal intelligence and mathematical intelligence?).
- The research question can be about a causal relationship, but the independent variable cannot be manipulated or participants cannot be randomly assigned to conditions or orders of conditions (e.g., Does damage to a person's hippocampus impair the formation of long-term memory traces?).
- The research question can be broad and exploratory, or it can be about what it is like to have a particular experience (e.g., What is it like to be a working mother diagnosed with depression?).

Again, the choice between the experimental and nonexperimental approaches is generally dictated by the nature of the research question. If it is about a causal relationship and involves an independent variable that can be manipulated, the experimental approach is typically preferred. Otherwise, the nonexperimental approach is preferred. But the two approaches can also be used to address the same research question in complementary ways. For example, nonexperimental studies establishing that there is a relationship between watching violent television and aggressive behavior have been complemented by experimental studies confirming that the relationship is a causal one (Bushman & Huesmann, 2001).[5] Similarly, after his original study, Milgram conducted experiments to explore the factors that affect obedience. He manipulated several independent variables, such as the distance between the experimenter and the participant, the distance between the participant and the confederate, and the location of the study (Milgram, 1974).[6]

# Types of Nonexperimental Research

Nonexperimental research falls into three broad categories: single-variable research, correlational and quasi-experimental research, and qualitative research. First, research can be nonexperimental because it focuses on a single variable rather than a statistical relationship between two variables. Although there is no widely shared term for this kind of research, we will call it **single-variable research**. Milgram's original obedience study was nonexperimental in this way. He was primarily interested in one variable—the extent to which participants obeyed the researcher when he told them to shock the confederate—and he observed all participants performing the same task under the same conditions. The study by Loftus and Pickrell described at the beginning of this chapter is also a good example of single-variable research. The variable was whether participants "remembered" having experienced mildly traumatic childhood events (e.g., getting lost in a shopping mall) that they had not actually experienced but that the researcher asked them about repeatedly. In this particular study, nearly a third of the participants "remembered" at least one event. (As with Milgram's original study, this study inspired several later experiments on the factors that affect false memories.)

Research can also be nonexperimental because it focuses on a statistical relationship between two variables but does not include the manipulation of an independent variable, random assignment of participants to conditions or orders of conditions, or both. This kind of research takes two basic forms: correlational research and quasi-experimental research. In **correlational research**, the researcher measures the two variables of interest with little or no attempt to control extraneous variables and then assesses the relationship between them. A research methods student who finds out whether each of several middle-school students has been bullied and then measures each student's self-esteem is conducting correlational research. In **quasi-experimental research**, the researcher manipulates an independent variable but does not randomly assign participants to conditions or orders of conditions. For example, a researcher might start an antibullying program (a kind of treatment) at one school and compare the incidence of bullying at that school with the incidence at a similar school that has no antibullying program.

The final way in which research can be nonexperimental is that it can be qualitative. The types of research we have discussed so far are all quantitative, referring to the fact that the data consist of numbers that are analyzed using statistical techniques. In **qualitative research**, the data are usually nonnumerical and are analyzed using nonstatistical techniques. Rosenhan's study of the experience of people in a psychiatric ward was primarily qualitative. The data were the notes taken by the "pseudopatients"—the people pretending to have heard voices—along with their hospital records. Rosenhan's analysis consists mainly of a written description of the experiences of the pseudopatients, supported by several concrete examples. To illustrate the hospital staff's tendency to "depersonalize" their patients, he noted, "Upon being admitted, I and other pseudopatients took the initial physical examinations in a semipublic room, where staff members went about their own business as if we were not there" (Rosenhan, 1973, p. 256).[7]

**single-variable research**

Research that focuses on a single variable rather than on a statistical relationship between variables.

**correlational research**

Research in which two or more variables are measured and the statistical relationships among them are assessed. There is no manipulated independent variable and usually very little attempt to control extraneous variables.

**quasi-experimental research**

Research that involves the manipulation of an independent variable but lacks the random assignment of participants to conditions or orders of conditions. It is generally used in field settings to test the effectiveness of a treatment.

**qualitative research**

Research that typically involves formulating broad research questions, collecting large amounts of data from a small number of participants, and summarizing the data using nonstatistical techniques.

# Internal Validity Revisited

Recall that internal validity is the extent to which the design of a study supports the conclusion that changes in the independent variable caused any observed differences in the dependent variable. Figure 7.1 shows how experimental, quasi-experimental, and correlational research vary in terms of internal validity. Experimental research tends to be highest because it addresses the directionality and third-variable problems with the manipulation of the independent variable and the control of extraneous variables. If the average score on the dependent variable in an experiment differs across conditions, it is quite likely that the independent variable is responsible for that difference. Correlational research is lowest because it fails to address either problem. If the average score on the dependent variable differs across levels of the independent variable, it *could* be that the independent variable is responsible, but there are other interpretations. In some situations, the direction of causality could be reversed. In others, there could be a third variable that is causing differences in both the independent and dependent variables. Quasi-experimental research is in the middle because the manipulation of the independent variable addresses some problems, but the lack of random assignment and experimental control fails to address others. Imagine, for example, that a researcher finds two similar schools, starts an antibullying program in one, and then finds fewer bullying incidents in that "treatment school" than in the "control school." There is no directionality problem because clearly the number of bullying incidents did not determine which school got the program. However, the lack of random assignment of children to schools could still mean that students in the treatment school differed from students in the control school in some other way that could explain the difference in bullying.

**FIGURE 7.1**
Experiments are generally high in internal validity, quasi-experiments lower, and correlational studies lower still.

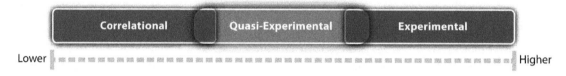

Internal Validity

Notice also in Figure 7.1 that there is some overlap in the internal validity of experiments, quasi-experiments, and correlational studies. For example, a poorly designed experiment that includes many confounding variables can be lower in internal validity than a well designed quasi-experiment with no obvious confounding variables.

## Key Takeaways

- Nonexperimental research is research that lacks the manipulation of an independent variable, control of extraneous variables through random assignment, or both.
- There are three broad types of nonexperimental research. Single-variable research focuses on a single variable rather than a relationship between variables. Correlational and quasi-experimental research focus on a statistical relationship but lack manipulation or random assignment. Qualitative research focuses on broader research questions, typically involves collecting large amounts of data from a small number of participants, and analyzes the data nonstatistically.
- In general, experimental research is high in internal validity, correlational research is low in internal validity, and quasi-experimental research is in between.

## Exercise

1. Discussion: For each of the following studies, decide which type of research design it is and explain why.
   a. A researcher conducts detailed interviews with unmarried teenage fathers to learn about how they feel and what they think about their role as fathers and summarizes their feelings in a written narrative.
   b. A researcher measures the impulsivity of a large sample of drivers and looks at the statistical relationship between this variable and the number of traffic tickets the drivers have received.

c. A researcher randomly assigns patients with low back pain either to a treatment involving hypnosis or to a treatment involving exercise. She then measures their level of low back pain after 3 months.

d. A college instructor gives weekly quizzes to students in one section of his course but no weekly quizzes to students in another section to see whether this has an effect on their test performance.

# 7.2 Correlational Research

## Learning Objectives

1. Define correlational research and give several examples.
2. Explain why a researcher might choose to conduct correlational research rather than experimental research or another type of nonexperimental research.

## What Is Correlational Research?

Correlational research is a type of nonexperimental research in which the researcher measures two variables and assesses the statistical relationship (i.e., the correlation) between them with little or no effort to control extraneous variables. There are essentially two reasons that researchers interested in statistical relationships between variables would choose to conduct a correlational study rather than an experiment. The first is that they do not believe that the statistical relationship is a causal one. For example, a researcher might evaluate the validity of a brief extraversion test by administering it to a large group of participants along with a longer extraversion test that has already been shown to be valid. This researcher might then check to see whether participants' scores on the brief test are strongly correlated with their scores on the longer one. Neither test score is thought to cause the other, so there is no independent variable to manipulate. In fact, the terms *independent variable* and *dependent variable* do not apply to this kind of research.

The other reason that researchers would choose to use a correlational study rather than an experiment is that the statistical relationship of interest is thought to be causal, but the researcher *cannot* manipulate the independent variable because it is impossible, impractical, or unethical. For example, Allen Kanner and his colleagues thought that the number of "daily hassles" (e.g., rude salespeople, heavy traffic) that people experience affects the number of physical and psychological symptoms they have (Kanner, Coyne, Schaefer, & Lazarus, 1981).[8] But because they could not *manipulate* the number of daily hassles their participants experienced, they had to settle for *measuring* the number of daily hassles—along with the number of symptoms—using self-report questionnaires. Although the strong positive relationship they found between these two variables is consistent with their idea that hassles cause symptoms, it is also consistent with the idea that symptoms cause hassles or that some third variable (e.g., neuroticism) causes both.

A common misconception among beginning researchers is that correlational research must involve two quantitative variables, such as scores on two extraversion tests or the number of hassles and number of symptoms people have experienced. However, the defining feature of correlational research is that the two variables are measured—neither one is manipulated—and this is true regardless of whether the variables are quantitative or categorical. Imagine, for example, that a researcher administers the Rosenberg Self-Esteem Scale to 50 American college students and 50 Japanese college students. Although this "feels" like a between-subjects experiment, it is a correlational study because the researcher did not manipulate the students' nationalities. The same is true of the study by Cacioppo and Petty comparing college faculty and factory workers in terms of their need for cognition. It is a correlational study because the researchers did not manipulate the participants' occupations.

Figure 7.2 shows data from a hypothetical study on the relationship between whether people make a daily list of things to do (a "to-do list") and stress. Notice that it is unclear whether this is an experiment or a correlational study because it is unclear whether the independent variable was manipulated. If the researcher randomly assigned some participants to make daily to-do lists and others not to, then it is an experiment. If the researcher simply asked participants whether they made daily to-do lists, then it is a correlational study. The distinction is important because if the study was an experiment, then it could be concluded that making the daily to-do lists reduced participants' stress. But if it was a correlational study, it could only be concluded that these variables are statistically related. Perhaps being stressed has a negative effect on people's ability to plan ahead (the directionality problem). Or perhaps people who are more conscientious are more likely to make to-do lists and less likely to be stressed (the third-variable problem). The crucial point is that what defines a study as experimental or correlational is not the variables being studied, nor whether the variables are quantitative or categorical, nor the type of graph or statistics used to analyze the data. It is *how* the study is conducted.

**FIGURE 7.2** Results of a Hypothetical Study on Whether People Who Make Daily To-Do Lists Experience Less Stress Than People Who Do Not Make Such Lists

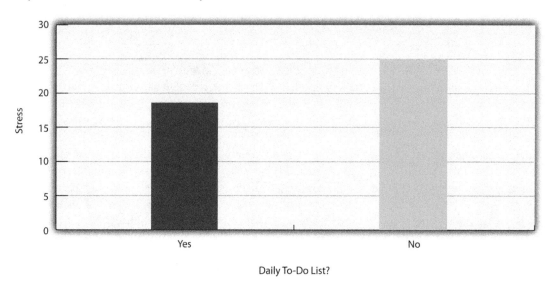

## Data Collection in Correlational Research

Again, the defining feature of correlational research is that neither variable is manipulated. It does not matter how or where the variables are measured. A researcher could have participants come to a laboratory to complete a computerized backward digit span task and a computerized risky decision-making task and then assess the relationship between participants' scores on the two tasks. Or a researcher could go to a shopping mall to ask people about their attitudes toward the environment and their shopping habits and then assess the relationship between these two variables. Both of these studies would be correlational because no independent variable is manipulated. However, because some approaches to data collection are strongly associated with correlational research, it makes sense to discuss them here. The two we will focus on are naturalistic observation and archival data. A third, survey research, is discussed in its own chapter.

## Naturalistic Observation

**Naturalistic observation** is an approach to data collection that involves observing people's behavior in the environment in which it typically occurs. Thus naturalistic observation is a type of "field research" (as opposed to a type of laboratory research). It could involve observing shoppers in a grocery store, children on a school playground, or psychiatric inpatients in their wards. Researchers engaged in naturalistic observation usually make their observations as unobtrusively as possible so that participants are often not aware that they are being studied. Ethically, this is considered to be acceptable if the participants remain anonymous and the behavior occurs in a public setting where people would not normally have an expectation of privacy. Grocery shoppers putting items into their shopping carts, for example, are engaged in public behavior that is easily observable by store employees and other shoppers. For this reason, most researchers would consider it ethically acceptable to observe them for a study. On the other hand, one of the arguments against the ethicality of the naturalistic observation of "bathroom behavior" discussed earlier in the book is that people have a reasonable expectation of privacy even in a public restroom and that this expectation was violated.

> **naturalistic observation**
>
> An approach to data collection in which the behavior of interest is observed in the environment in which it typically occurs.

Researchers Robert Levine and Ara Norenzayan used naturalistic observation to study differences in the "pace of life" across countries (Levine & Norenzayan, 1999).[9] One of their measures involved observing pedestrians in a large city to see how long it took them to walk 60 feet. They found that people in some countries walked reliably faster than people in other countries. For example, people in the United States and Japan covered 60 feet in about 12 seconds on average, while people in Brazil and Romania took close to 17 seconds.

Because naturalistic observation takes place in the complex and even chaotic "real world," there are two closely related issues that researchers must deal with before collecting data. The first is sampling. When, where, and under what conditions will the observations be made, and who exactly will be observed? Levine and Norenzayan described their sampling process as follows:

> *Male and female walking speed over a distance of 60 feet was measured in at least two locations in main downtown areas in each city. Measurements were taken during main business hours on clear summer days. All locations were flat, unobstructed, had broad sidewalks, and were sufficiently uncrowded to allow pedestrians to move at potentially maximum speeds. To control for the effects of socializing, only pedestrians walking alone were used. Children, individuals with obvious physical handicaps, and window-shoppers were not timed. Thirty-five men and 35 women were timed in most cities. (p. 186)*

Precise specification of the sampling process in this way makes data collection manageable for the observers, and it also provides some control over important extraneous variables. For example, by making their observations on clear summer days in all countries, Levine and Norenzayan controlled for effects of the weather on people's walking speeds.

The second issue is measurement. What specific behaviors will be observed? In Levine and Norenzayan's study, measurement was relatively straightforward. They simply measured out a 60-foot distance along a city sidewalk and then used a stopwatch to time participants as they walked over that distance. Often, however, the behaviors of interest are not so obvious or objective. For example, researchers Robert Kraut and Robert Johnston wanted to study bowlers' reactions to their shots, both when they were facing the pins and then when they turned toward their companions (Kraut & Johnston, 1979).[10] But what "reactions" should they observe? Based on previous research and their own pilot testing, Kraut and Johnston created a list of reactions that included "closed smile," "open smile," "laugh," "neutral face," "look down," "look away," and "face cover" (covering one's face with one's hands). The observers committed this list to memory and then practiced by coding the reactions of bowlers who had been videotaped. During the actual study, the observers spoke into an audio recorder, describing the reactions they observed. Among the most interesting results of this study was that bowlers rarely smiled while they still faced the pins. They were much more likely to smile after they turned toward their companions, suggesting that smiling is not purely an expression of happiness but also a form of social communication.

When the observations require a judgment on the part of the observers—as in Kraut and Johnston's study—this process is often described as **coding**. Coding generally requires clearly defining a set of target behaviors. The observers then categorize participants individually in terms of which behavior they have engaged in and the number of times they engaged in each behavior. The observers might even record the duration of each behavior. The target behaviors must be defined in such a way that different observers code them in the same way. This is the issue of interrater reliability. Researchers are expected to demonstrate the interrater reliability of their coding procedure by having multiple raters code the same behaviors independently and then showing that the different observers are in close agreement. Kraut and Johnston, for example, video recorded a subset of their participants' reactions and had two observers independently code them. The two observers showed that they agreed on the reactions that were exhibited 97% of the time, indicating good interrater reliability.

## Archival Data

Another approach to correlational research is the use of **archival data**, which are data that have already been collected for some other purpose. An example is a study by Brett Pelham and his colleagues on "implicit egotism"—the tendency for people to prefer people, places, and things that are similar to themselves (Pelham, Carvallo, & Jones, 2005).[11] In one study, they examined Social Security records to show that women with the names Virginia, Georgia, Louise, and Florence were more likely than other women to have moved to the states of Virginia, Georgia, Louisiana, and Florida, respectively.

As with naturalistic observation, measurement can be more or less straightforward when working with archival data. For example, counting the number of people named Virginia who live in various states based on Social Security records is relatively straightforward. But consider a study by Christopher Peterson and his colleagues on the relationship between optimism and health using data that had been collected many years before for a study on adult development (Peterson, Seligman, & Vaillant, 1988).[12] In the 1940s, healthy male college students had completed an open-ended questionnaire about difficult wartime experiences. In the late 1980s, Peterson and his colleagues reviewed the men's questionnaire responses to obtain a measure of explanatory style—their habitual ways of explaining bad events that happen to them. More pessimistic people tend to blame themselves and expect long-term negative consequences that affect many aspects of their lives, while more optimistic people tend to blame outside forces and expect limited negative consequences. To obtain a measure of explanatory style for each participant, the researchers used a procedure in which all negative events mentioned in the questionnaire responses, and any causal explanations for them, were identified and written on index cards. These were given to a separate group of raters who rated each explanation in terms of three separate dimensions of optimism-pessimism. These ratings were then averaged to produce an explanatory style score for each participant. The researchers then assessed the statistical relationship between the men's explanatory style as college students and archival measures of their health at approximately 60 years of age. The primary result was that the more optimistic the men were as college students, the healthier they were as older men. Pearson's *r* was +.25.

**FIGURE 7.3**

Naturalistic observation has revealed that bowlers tend to smile when they turn away from the pins and toward their companions, suggesting that smiling is not purely an expression of happiness but also a form of social communication.

Source: © Thinkstock

**coding**

An approach to measurement in naturalistic observation, in which target behaviors are specified ahead of time and observers watch for and record those specific behaviors.

**archival data**

Existing data that were collected or created for some other purpose. They can include school and hospital records, newspaper and magazine articles, Internet content, television shows, and many other things.

This is an example of **content analysis**—a family of systematic approaches to measurement using complex archival data. Just as naturalistic observation requires specifying the behaviors of interest and then noting them as they occur, content analysis requires specifying keywords, phrases, or ideas and then finding all occurrences of them in the data. These occurrences can then be counted, timed (e.g., the amount of time devoted to entertainment topics on the nightly news show), or analyzed in a variety of other ways.

**content analysis**

A family of techniques for analyzing archival data that generally involves identifying specific words, phrases, ideas, or other content in the data and then counting or summarizing their occurrence in other quantitative ways.

## Key Takeaways

- Correlational research involves measuring two variables and assessing the relationship between them, with no manipulation of an independent variable.
- Correlational research is not defined by where or how the data are collected. However, some approaches to data collection are strongly associated with correlational research. These include naturalistic observation (in which researchers observe people's behavior in the context in which it normally occurs) and the use of archival data that were already collected for some other purpose.

## Exercise

1. Discussion: For each of the following, decide whether it is most likely that the study described is experimental or correlational and explain why.

   a. An educational researcher compares the academic performance of students from the "rich" side of town with that of students from the "poor" side of town.

   b. A cognitive psychologist compares the ability of people to recall words that they were instructed to "read" with their ability to recall words that they were instructed to "imagine."

   c. A manager studies the correlation between new employees' college grade point averages and their first-year performance reports.

   d. An automotive engineer installs different stick shifts in a new car prototype, each time asking several people to rate how comfortable the stick shift feels.

   e. A food scientist studies the relationship between the temperature inside people's refrigerators and the amount of bacteria on their food.

   f. A social psychologist tells some research participants that they need to hurry over to the next building to complete a study. She tells others that they can take their time. Then she observes whether they stop to help a research assistant who is pretending to be hurt.

# 7.3 Quasi-Experimental Research

## Learning Objectives

1. Explain what quasi-experimental research is and distinguish it clearly from both experimental and correlational research.

2. Describe three different types of quasi-experimental research designs (nonequivalent groups, pretest-posttest, and interrupted time series) and identify examples of each one.

The prefix *quasi* means "resembling." Thus quasi-experimental research is research that resembles experimental research but is not true experimental research. Although the independent variable is manipulated, participants are not randomly assigned to conditions or orders of conditions (Cook & Campbell, 1979).[13] Because the independent variable is manipulated before the dependent variable is measured, quasi-experimental research eliminates the directionality problem. But because participants are not randomly assigned—making it likely that there are other differences between conditions—quasi-experimental research does not eliminate the problem of confounding variables. In terms of internal validity, therefore, quasi-experiments are generally somewhere between correlational studies and true experiments.

Quasi-experiments are most likely to be conducted in field settings in which random assignment is difficult or impossible. They are often conducted to evaluate the effectiveness of a treatment—perhaps a type of psychotherapy or an educational intervention. There are many different kinds of quasi-experiments, but we will discuss just a few of the most common ones here.

## Nonequivalent Groups Design

**nonequivalent groups design**

A between-subjects research design in which participants are not randomly assigned to conditions, usually because participants are in preexisting groups (e.g., students at different schools).

Recall that when participants in a between-subjects experiment are randomly assigned to conditions, the resulting groups are likely to be quite similar. In fact, researchers consider them to be equivalent. When participants are not randomly assigned to conditions, however, the resulting groups are likely to be dissimilar in some ways. For this reason, researchers consider them to be nonequivalent. A **nonequivalent groups design**, then, is a between-subjects design in which participants have not been randomly assigned to conditions.

Imagine, for example, a researcher who wants to evaluate a new method of teaching fractions to third graders. One way would be to conduct a study with a treatment group consisting of one class of third-grade students and a control group consisting of another class of third-grade students. This would be a nonequivalent groups design because the students are not randomly assigned to classes by the researcher, which means there could be important differences between them. For example, the parents of higher achieving or more motivated students might have been more likely to request that their children be assigned to Ms. Williams's class. Or the principal might have assigned the "troublemakers" to Mr. Jones's class because he is a stronger disciplinarian. Of course, the teachers' styles, and even the classroom environments, might be very different and might cause different levels of achievement or motivation among the students. If at the end of the study there was a difference in the two classes' knowledge of fractions, it might have been caused by the difference between the teaching methods—but it might have been caused by any of these confounding variables.

Of course, researchers using a nonequivalent groups design can take steps to ensure that their groups are as similar as possible. In the present example, the researcher could try to select two classes at the same school, where the students in the two classes have similar scores on a standardized math test and the teachers are the same sex, are close in age, and have similar teaching styles. Taking such steps would increase the internal validity of the study because it would eliminate some of the most important confounding variables. But without true random assignment of the students to conditions, there remains the possibility of other important confounding variables that the researcher was not able to control.

# Pretest-Posttest Design

In a **pretest-posttest design**, the dependent variable is measured once before the treatment is implemented and once after it is implemented. Imagine, for example, a researcher who is interested in the effectiveness of an antidrug education program on elementary school students' attitudes toward illegal drugs. The researcher could measure the attitudes of students at a particular elementary school during one week, implement the antidrug program during the next week, and finally, measure their attitudes again the following week. The pretest-posttest design is much like a within-subjects experiment in which each participant is tested first under the control condition and then under the treatment condition. It is unlike a within-subjects experiment, however, in that the order of conditions is not counterbalanced because it typically is not possible for a participant to be tested in the treatment condition first and then in an "untreated" control condition.

If the average posttest score is better than the average pretest score, then it makes sense to conclude that the treatment might be responsible for the improvement. Unfortunately, one often cannot conclude this with a high degree of certainty because there may be other explanations for why the posttest scores are better. One category of alternative explanations goes under the name of **history**. Other things might have happened between the pretest and the posttest. Perhaps an antidrug program aired on television and many of the students watched it, or perhaps a celebrity died of a drug overdose and many of the students heard about it. Another category of alternative explanations goes under the name of **maturation**. Participants might have changed between the pretest and the posttest in ways that they were going to anyway because they are growing and learning. If it were a yearlong program, participants might become less impulsive or better reasoners and this might be responsible for the change.

Another alternative explanation for a change in the dependent variable in a pretest-posttest design is **regression to the mean**. This refers to the statistical fact that an individual who scores extremely on a variable on one occasion will tend to score less extremely on the next occasion. For example, a bowler with a long-term average of 150 who suddenly bowls a 220 will almost certainly score lower in the next game. Her score will "regress" toward her mean score of 150. Regression to the mean can be a problem when participants are selected for further study *because* of their extreme scores. Imagine, for example, that only students who scored especially low on a test of fractions are given a special training program and then retested. Regression to the mean all but guarantees that their scores will be higher even if the training program has no effect. A closely related concept—and an extremely important one in psychological research—is **spontaneous remission**. This is the tendency for many medical and psychological problems to improve over time without any form of treatment. The common cold is a good example. If one were to measure symptom severity in 100 common cold sufferers today, give them a bowl of chicken soup every day, and then measure their symptom severity again in a week, they would probably be much improved. This does not mean that the chicken soup was responsible for the improvement, however, because they would have been much improved without any treatment at all. The same is true of many psychological problems. A group of severely depressed people today is likely to be less depressed on average in 6 months. In reviewing the results of several studies of treatments for depression, researchers Michael Posternak and Ivan Miller found that participants in waitlist control conditions improved an average of 10 to 15% before they received any treatment at all (Posternak & Miller, 2001).[14] Thus one must generally be very cautious about inferring causality from pretest-posttest designs.

## Does Psychotherapy Work?

Early studies on the effectiveness of psychotherapy tended to use pretest-posttest designs. In a classic 1952 article, researcher Hans Eysenck summarized the results of 24 such studies showing that about two thirds of patients improved between the pretest and the posttest (Eysenck,

## pretest-posttest design

A research design in which the dependent variable is measured (the pretest), a treatment is given, and the dependent variable is measured again (the posttest) to see if there is a change in the dependent variable from pretest to posttest.

## history

Refers collectively to extraneous events that can occur between a pretest and posttest or between the first and last measurements in a time series. It can provide alternative explanations for an observed change in the dependent variable.

## maturation

Refers collectively to extraneous developmental changes in participants that can occur between a pretest and posttest or between the first and last measurements in a time series. It can provide an alternative explanation for an observed change in the dependent variable.

## regression to the mean

The statistical fact that an individual who scores extremely on one occasion will tend to score less extremely on the next occasion.

## spontaneous remission

Improvement in a psychological or medical problem over time without any treatment.

1952).[15] But Eysenck also compared these results with archival data from state hospital and insurance company records showing that similar patients recovered at about the same rate *without* receiving psychotherapy. This suggested to Eysenck that the improvement that patients showed in the pretest-posttest studies might be no more than spontaneous remission. Note that Eysenck did not conclude that psychotherapy was ineffective. He merely concluded that there was no evidence that it was, and he wrote of "the necessity of properly planned and executed experimental studies into this important field" (p. 323). You can read the entire article here:

http://psychclassics.yorku.ca/Eysenck/psychotherapy.htm

Fortunately, many other researchers took up Eysenck's challenge, and by 1980 hundreds of experiments had been conducted in which participants were randomly assigned to treatment and control conditions, and the results were summarized in a classic book by Mary Lee Smith, Gene Glass, and Thomas Miller (Smith, Glass, & Miller, 1980).[16] They found that overall psychotherapy was quite effective, with about 80% of treatment participants improving more than the average control participant. Subsequent research has focused more on the conditions under which different types of psychotherapy are more or less effective.

**FIGURE 7.4**

In a classic 1952 article, researcher Hans Eysenck pointed out the shortcomings of the simple pretest-posttest design for evaluating the effectiveness of psychotherapy.

Source: ©Sirswindon, http://en.wikipedia.org/wiki/file:Hans.Eysenck.jpg

# Combination Designs

A type of quasi-experimental design that is generally better than either the nonequivalent groups design or the pretest-posttest design is one that combines elements of both. There is a treatment group that is given a pretest, receives a treatment, and then is given a posttest. But at the same time there is a control group that is given a pretest, does *not* receive the treatment, and then is given a posttest. The question, then, is not simply whether participants who receive the treatment improve but whether they improve *more* than participants who do not receive the treatment.

Imagine, for example, that students in one school are given a pretest on their attitudes toward drugs, then are exposed to an antidrug program (a kind of treatment), and finally are given a posttest on their attitudes toward drugs. If these students are more negative toward drugs in the posttest, this might be an effect of the antidrug program. But it might also be an effect of history (e.g., news of a celebrity drug overdose) or maturation (e.g., improved reasoning skills). For this reason, the researchers might include a control group of students in a similar school who are given the pretest, *not* exposed to the antidrug program, and then are given the posttest. If history or maturation was responsible for students' more negative attitudes in the posttest, we would expect to see this change in both schools. But if the antidrug program was responsible for students' more negative attitudes in the posttest, we would expect to see this change in the treatment school but not in the control school.

Finally, if participants in this kind of design are randomly assigned to conditions, it becomes a true experiment rather than a quasi experiment. In fact, it is the kind of experiment that Eysenck called for—and that has now been conducted many times—to demonstrate the effectiveness of psychotherapy.

## Key Takeaways

- Quasi-experimental research involves the manipulation of an independent variable without the random assignment of participants to conditions or orders of conditions. Among the important types are nonequivalent groups designs and pretest-posttest.
- Quasi-experimental research eliminates the directionality problem because it involves the manipulation of the independent variable. It does not eliminate the problem of confounding variables, however, because it does not involve random assignment to conditions. For these reasons, quasi-experimental research is generally higher in internal validity than correlational studies but lower than true experiments.

## Exercises

1. Practice: Imagine that two college professors decide to test the effect of giving daily quizzes on student performance in a statistics course. They decide that Professor A will give quizzes but Professor B will not. They will then compare the performance of students in their two sections on a common final exam. List five other variables that might differ between the two sections that could affect the results.

2. Discussion: Imagine that a group of obese children is recruited for a study in which their weight is measured, then they participate for 3 months in a program that encourages them to be more active, and finally their weight is measured again. Explain how each of the following might affect the results:

    a. regression to the mean

    b. spontaneous remission

    c. history

    d. maturation

# 7.4 Qualitative Research

## Learning Objectives

1. List several ways in which qualitative research differs from quantitative research in psychology.
2. Describe the strengths and weaknesses of qualitative research in psychology compared with quantitative research.
3. Give examples of qualitative research in psychology.

# What Is Qualitative Research?

**quantitative research**

Research that involves formulating focused research questions, collecting small amounts of data from a large number of participants, and summarizing the data using descriptive and inferential statistics.

This book is primarily about **quantitative research**. Quantitative researchers typically start with a focused research question or hypothesis, collect a small amount of data from each of a large number of individuals, describe the resulting data using statistical techniques, and draw general conclusions about some large population. Although this is by far the most common approach to conducting empirical research in psychology, there is an important alternative called qualitative research. Qualitative research originated in the disciplines of anthropology and sociology but is now used to study many psychological topics as well. Qualitative researchers generally begin with a less focused research question, collect large amounts of relatively "unfiltered" data from a relatively small number of individuals, and describe their data using nonstatistical techniques. They are usually less concerned with drawing general conclusions about human behavior than with understanding in detail the *experience* of their research participants.

Consider, for example, a study by researcher Per Lindqvist and his colleagues, who wanted to learn how the families of teenage suicide victims cope with their loss (Lindqvist, Johansson, & Karlsson, 2008).[17] They did not have a specific research question or hypothesis, such as, What percentage of family members join suicide support groups? Instead, they wanted to understand the variety of reactions that families had, with a focus on what it is like from *their* perspectives. To do this, they interviewed the families of 10 teenage suicide victims in their homes in rural Sweden. The interviews were relatively unstructured, beginning with a general request for the families to talk about the victim and ending with an invitation to talk about anything else that they wanted to tell the interviewer. One of the most important themes that emerged from these interviews was that even as life returned to "normal," the families continued to struggle with the question of why their loved one committed suicide. This struggle appeared to be especially difficult for families in which the suicide was most unexpected.

# The Purpose of Qualitative Research

Again, this book is primarily about quantitative research in psychology. The strength of quantitative research is its ability to provide precise answers to specific research questions and to draw general conclusions about human behavior. This is how we know that people have a strong tendency to obey authority figures, for example, or that female college students are not substantially more talkative than male college students. But while quantitative research is good at providing precise answers to specific research questions, it is not nearly as good at *generating* novel and interesting research questions. Likewise, while quantitative research is good at drawing general conclusions about human behavior, it is not nearly as good at providing detailed descriptions of the behavior of particular groups in particular situations. And it is not very good at all at communicating what it is actually like to be a member of a particular group in a particular situation.

But the relative weaknesses of quantitative research are the relative strengths of qualitative research. Qualitative research can help researchers to generate new and interesting research questions and hypotheses. The research of Lindqvist and colleagues, for example, suggests that there may be a general relationship between how unexpected a suicide is and how consumed the family is with trying to understand why the teen committed suicide. This relationship can now be explored using quantitative research. It is unclear whether this question would have arisen at all without the researchers sitting down with the families and listening to what they themselves wanted to say about their experience. Qualitative research can also provide rich and detailed descriptions of human behavior in the real-world contexts in which it occurs. Among qualitative researchers, this is often referred to as "thick description" (Geertz, 1973).[18] Similarly, qualitative research can convey a sense of what it is actually like to be a member of a particular group or in a particular situation—what qualitative researchers often refer to as the "lived experience" of the research participants. Lindqvist and colleagues, for example, describe how all the families spontaneously offered to show the interviewer the victim's bedroom or the place where the suicide occurred—revealing the importance of these physical locations to the families. It seems unlikely that a quantitative study would have discovered this.

# Data Collection and Analysis in Qualitative Research

As with correlational research, data collection approaches in qualitative research are quite varied and can involve naturalistic observation, archival data, artwork, and many other things. But one of the most common approaches, especially for psychological research, is to conduct **interviews**. Interviews in qualitative research tend to be unstructured—consisting of a small number of general questions or prompts that allow participants to talk about what is of interest to them. The researcher can follow up by asking more detailed questions about the topics that do come up. This was essentially the approach used by Lindqvist and colleagues in their research on the families of suicide survivors. Small groups of people who participate together in interviews focused on a particular topic or issue are often referred to as **focus groups**. The interaction among participants in a focus group can sometimes bring out more information than can be learned in a one-on-one interview. The use of focus groups has become a standard technique in business and industry among those who want to understand consumer tastes and preferences. The content of all focus group interviews is usually recorded and transcribed to facilitate later analyses.

Another approach to data collection in qualitative research is participant observation. In **participant observation**, researchers become active participants in the group or situation they are studying. The data they collect can include interviews (usually unstructured), their own notes based on their observations and interactions, documents, photographs, and other artifacts. The basic rationale for participant observation is that there may be important information that is only accessible to, or can be interpreted only by, someone who is an active participant in the group or situation. An example of participant observation comes from a study by sociologist Amy Wilkins (published in *Social Psychology Quarterly*) on a college-based religious organization that emphasized how happy its members were (Wilkins, 2008).[19] Wilkins spent 12 months attending and participating in the group's meetings and social events, and she interviewed several group members. In her study, Wilkins identified several ways in which the group "enforced" happiness—for example, by continually talking about happiness, discouraging the expression of negative emotions, and using happiness as a way to distinguish themselves from other groups.

## interviews

A data collection method in qualitative research. Interviews can be structured, semistructured, or unstructured—depending on how well specified the sequence of questions or prompts is.

## focus groups

A small group of people who participate together in an interview focused on a particular topic or issue.

## participant observation

An approach to data collection in qualitative research in which the researcher becomes an active participant in the group or situation under study.

## Data Analysis in Quantitative Research

Although quantitative and qualitative research generally differ along several important dimensions (e.g., the specificity of the research question, the type of data collected), it is the method of data *analysis* that distinguishes them more clearly than anything else. To illustrate this idea, imagine a team of researchers that conducts a series of unstructured interviews with recovering alcoholics to learn about the role of their religious faith in their recovery. Although this sounds like qualitative research, imagine further that once they collect the data, they code the data in terms of how often each participant mentions God (or a "higher power"), and they then use descriptive and inferential statistics to find out whether those who mention God more often are more successful in abstaining from alcohol. Now it sounds like quantitative research. In other words, the quantitative-qualitative distinction depends more on what researchers *do* with the data they have collected than with why or how they collected the data.

**grounded theory**

An approach to analyzing qualitative data in which repeating ideas are identified and grouped into broader themes. The themes are integrated in a theoretical narrative.

**theoretical narrative**

In grounded theory, a narrative interpretation of the broad themes that emerge from the data, usually supported by many direct quotations or examples from the data.

But what does qualitative data analysis look like? Just as there are many ways to collect data in qualitative research, there are many ways to analyze data. Here we focus on one general approach called **grounded theory** (Glaser & Strauss, 1967).[20] This approach was developed within the field of sociology in the 1960s and has gradually gained popularity in psychology. Remember that in quantitative research, it is typical for the researcher to start with a theory, derive a hypothesis from that theory, and then collect data to test that specific hypothesis. In qualitative research using grounded theory, researchers start with the data and develop a theory or an interpretation that is "grounded in" those data. They do this in stages. First, they identify ideas that are repeated throughout the data. Then they organize these ideas into a smaller number of broader themes. Finally, they write a **theoretical narrative**—an interpretation—of the data in terms of the themes that they have identified. This theoretical narrative focuses on the subjective experience of the participants and is usually supported by many direct quotations from the participants themselves.

As an example, consider a study by researchers Laura Abrams and Laura Curran, who used the grounded theory approach to study the experience of postpartum depression symptoms among low-income mothers (Abrams & Curran, 2009).[21] Their data were the result of unstructured interviews with 19 participants. Table 7.1 shows the five broad themes the researchers identified and the more specific repeating ideas that made up each of those themes. In their research report, they provide numerous quotations from their participants, such as this one from "Destiny:"

*Well, just recently my apartment was broken into and the fact that his Medicaid for some reason was cancelled so a lot of things was happening within the last two weeks all at one time. So that in itself I don't want to say almost drove me mad but it put me in a funk....Like I really was depressed. (p. 357)*

Their theoretical narrative focused on the participants' experience of their symptoms not as an abstract "affective disorder" but as closely tied to the daily struggle of raising children alone under often difficult circumstances.

TABLE 7.1 Themes and Repeating Ideas in a Study of Postpartum Depression Among Low-Income Mothers

| Theme | Repeating ideas |
|---|---|
| Ambivalence | "I wasn't prepared for this baby," "I didn't want to have any more children." |
| Caregiving overload | "Please stop crying," "I need a break," "I can't do this anymore." |
| Juggling | "No time to breathe," "Everyone depends on me," "Navigating the maze." |
| Mothering alone | "I really don't have any help," "My baby has no father." |
| Real-life worry | "I don't have any money," "Will my baby be OK?" "It's not safe here." |

# The Quantitative-Qualitative "Debate"

Given their differences, it may come as no surprise that quantitative and qualitative research in psychology and related fields do not coexist in complete harmony. Some quantitative researchers criticize qualitative methods on the grounds that they lack objectivity, are difficult to evaluate in terms of reliability and validity, and do not allow generalization to people or situations other than those actually studied. At the same time, some qualitative researchers criticize quantitative methods on the grounds that they overlook the richness of human behavior and experience and instead answer simple questions about easily quantifiable variables.

In general, however, qualitative researchers are well aware of the issues of objectivity, reliability, validity, and generalizability. In fact, they have developed a number of frameworks for addressing these issues (which are beyond the scope of our discussion). And in general, quantitative researchers are well aware of the issue of oversimplification. They do not believe that all human behavior and experience can be adequately described in terms of a small number of variables and the statistical relationships among them. Instead, they use simplification as a strategy for uncovering general principles of human behavior.

Many researchers from both the quantitative and qualitative camps now agree that the two approaches can and should be combined into what has come to be called **mixed-methods research** (Todd, Nerlich, McKeown, & Clarke, 2004).[22] (In fact, the studies by Lindqvist and colleagues and by Abrams and Curran both combined quantitative and qualitative approaches.) One approach to combining quantitative and qualitative research is to use qualitative research for hypothesis generation and quantitative research for hypothesis testing. Again, while a qualitative study might suggest that families who experience an unexpected suicide have more difficulty resolving the question of why, a well-designed quantitative study could test a hypothesis by measuring these specific variables for a large sample. A second approach to combining quantitative and qualitative research is referred to as **triangulation**. The idea is to use both quantitative and qualitative methods simultaneously to study the same general questions and to compare the results. If the results of the quantitative and qualitative methods converge on the same general conclusion, they reinforce and enrich each other. If the results diverge, then they suggest an interesting new question: Why do the results diverge and how can they be reconciled?

**mixed-methods research**

Research that uses both quantitative and qualitative methods.

**triangulation**

In mixed methods research, using multiple quantitative and qualitative methods to study the same topic, with the goal of converging on a single interpretation.

## Key Takeaways

- Qualitative research is an important alternative to quantitative research in psychology. It generally involves asking broader research questions, collecting more detailed data (e.g., interviews), and using nonstatistical analyses.
- Many researchers conceptualize quantitative and qualitative research as complementary and advocate combining them. For example, qualitative research can be used to generate hypotheses and quantitative research to test them.

## Exercise

1. Discussion: What are some ways in which a qualitative study of girls who play youth baseball would be likely to differ from a quantitative study on the same topic?

# Endnotes

1. Milgram, S. (1963). Behavioral study of obedience. *Journal of Abnormal and Social Psychology, 67,* 371–378.

2. Loftus, E. F., & Pickrell, J. E. (1995). The formation of false memories. *Psychiatric Annals, 25,* 720–725.

3. Cacioppo, J. T., & Petty, R. E. (1982). The need for cognition. *Journal of Personality and Social Psychology, 42,* 116–131.

4. Rosenhan, D. L. (1973). On being sane in insane places. *Science, 179,* 250–258.

5. Bushman, B. J., & Huesmann, L. R. (2001). Effects of televised violence on aggression. In D. Singer & J. Singer (Eds.), *Handbook of children and the media* (pp. 223–254). Thousand Oaks, CA: Sage.

6. Milgram, S. (1974). *Obedience to authority: An experimental view*. New York, NY: Harper & Row.

7. Rosenhan, D. L. (1973). On being sane in insane places. *Science, 179*, 250–258.

8. Kanner, A. D., Coyne, J. C., Schaefer, C., & Lazarus, R. S. (1981). Comparison of two modes of stress measurement: Daily hassles and uplifts versus major life events. *Journal of Behavioral Medicine, 4*, 1–39.

9. Levine, R. V., & Norenzayan, A. (1999). The pace of life in 31 countries. *Journal of Cross-Cultural Psychology, 30*, 178–205.

10. Kraut, R. E., & Johnston, R. E. (1979). Social and emotional messages of smiling: An ethological approach. *Journal of Personality and Social Psychology, 37*, 1539–1553.

11. Pelham, B. W., Carvallo, M., & Jones, J. T. (2005). Implicit egotism. *Current Directions in Psychological Science, 14*, 106–110.

12. Peterson, C., Seligman, M. E. P., & Vaillant, G. E. (1988). Pessimistic explanatory style is a risk factor for physical illness: A thirty-five year longitudinal study. *Journal of Personality and Social Psychology, 55*, 23–27.

13. Cook, T. D., & Campbell, D. T. (1979). *Quasi-experimentation: Design & analysis issues in field settings*. Boston, MA: Houghton Mifflin.

14. Posternak, M. A., & Miller, I. (2001). Untreated short-term course of major depression: A meta-analysis of studies using outcomes from studies using wait-list control groups. *Journal of Affective Disorders, 66*, 139–146.

15. Eysenck, H. J. (1952). The effects of psychotherapy: An evaluation. *Journal of Consulting Psychology, 16*, 319–324.

16. Smith, M. L., Glass, G. V., & Miller, T. I. (1980). *The benefits of psychotherapy*. Baltimore, MD: Johns Hopkins University Press.

17. Lindqvist, P., Johansson, L., & Karlsson, U. (2008). In the aftermath of teenage suicide: A qualitative study of the psychosocial consequences for the surviving family members. *BMC Psychiatry, 8*, 26. Retrieved from http://www.biomedcentral.com/1471-244X/8/26

18. Geertz, C. (1973). *The interpretation of cultures*. New York, NY: Basic Books.

19. Wilkins, A. (2008). "Happier than Non-Christians": Collective emotions and symbolic boundaries among evangelical Christians. *Social Psychology Quarterly, 71*, 281–301.

20. Glaser, B. G., & Strauss, A. L. (1967). *The discovery of grounded theory: Strategies for qualitative research*. Chicago, IL: Aldine.

21. Abrams, L. S., & Curran, L. (2009). "And you're telling me not to stress?" A grounded theory study of postpartum depression symptoms among low-income mothers. *Psychology of Women Quarterly, 33*, 351–362.

22. Todd, Z., Nerlich, B., McKeown, S., & Clarke, D. D. (2004) *Mixing methods in psychology: The integration of qualitative and quantitative methods in theory and practice*. London, UK: Psychology Press.

# CHAPTER 8
# Complex Research Designs

Researcher Simone Schnall and her colleagues were interested in whether feeling physically disgusted causes people to make harsher moral judgments (Schnall, Haidt, Clore, & Jordan, 2008).[1] They conducted an experiment in which they manipulated participants' feelings of disgust by testing them in either a clean room or a messy room that contained dirty dishes, an overflowing wastebasket, and a chewed-up pen. They also used a self-report questionnaire to measure the amount of attention that people pay to their own bodily sensations. They called this "private body consciousness." They measured their primary dependent variable, the harshness of people's moral judgments, by describing different behaviors (e.g., eating one's dead dog, failing to return a found wallet) and having participants rate the moral acceptability of each one on a scale of 1 to 7. They also measured some other dependent variables, including participants' willingness to eat at a new restaurant. Finally, the researchers asked participants to rate their current level of disgust and other emotions. The primary results of this study were that participants in the messy room were in fact more disgusted and made harsher moral judgments than participants in the clean room—but only if they scored relatively high in private body consciousness.

**FIGURE 8.1**
Research suggests that disgusting surroundings can cause people to make harsher moral judgments.

Source: © Thinkstock

The research designs we have considered so far have been simple—focusing on a question about one variable or about a statistical relationship between two variables. But in many ways the complex design of the experiment undertaken by Schnall and her colleagues is more typical of research in psychology. Fortunately, we have already covered the basic elements of such designs in previous chapters. In this chapter, we look closely at how and why researchers *combine* these basic elements into more complex designs. We start with complex experiments—considering first the inclusion of multiple dependent variables and then the inclusion of multiple independent variables. Finally, we look at complex correlational designs.

# 8.1 Multiple Dependent Variables

## Learning Objectives

1. Explain why researchers often include multiple dependent variables in their studies.
2. Explain what a manipulation check is and when it would be included in an experiment.

**multiple dependent variables**

More than one dependent variable in the same study. They can be measures of different variables, including a manipulation check, or different measures of the same construct.

Imagine that you have made the effort to find a research topic, review the research literature, formulate a question, design an experiment, obtain institutional review board (IRB) approval, recruit research participants, and manipulate an independent variable. It would seem almost wasteful to measure a single dependent variable. Even if you are primarily interested in the relationship between an independent variable and one primary dependent variable, there are usually several more questions that you can answer easily by including **multiple dependent variables**.

# Measures of Different Constructs

Often a researcher wants to know how an independent variable affects several distinct dependent variables. For example, Schnall and her colleagues were interested in how feeling disgusted affects the harshness of people's moral judgments, but they were also curious about how disgust affects other variables, such as people's willingness to eat in a restaurant. As another example, researcher Susan Knasko was interested in how different odors affect people's behavior (Knasko, 1992).[2] She conducted an experiment in which the independent variable was whether participants were tested in a room with no odor or in one scented with lemon, lavender, or dimethyl sulfide (which has a cabbagelike smell). Although she was primarily interested in how the odors affected people's creativity, she was also curious about how they affected people's moods and perceived health—and it was a simple enough matter to measure these dependent variables too. Although she found that creativity was unaffected by the ambient odor, she found that people's moods were lower in the dimethyl sulfide condition, and that their perceived health was greater in the lemon condition.

When an experiment includes multiple dependent variables, there is again a possibility of carryover effects. For example, it is possible that measuring participants' moods before measuring their perceived health could affect their perceived health or that measuring their perceived health before their moods could affect their moods. So the order in which multiple dependent variables are measured becomes an issue. One approach is to measure them in the same order for all participants—usually with the most important one first so that it cannot be affected by measuring the others. Another approach is to counterbalance, or systematically vary, the order in which the dependent variables are measured.

# Manipulation Checks

**manipulation check**

A measure of a manipulated independent variable—usually done at the end of the procedure—to confirm that the independent variable was successfully manipulated.

When the independent variable is a construct that can only be manipulated indirectly—such as emotions and other internal states—an additional measure of that independent variable is often included as a **manipulation check**. This is done to confirm that the independent variable was, in fact, successfully manipulated. For example, Schnall and her colleagues had their participants rate their level of disgust to be sure that those in the messy room actually felt more disgusted than those in the clean room. Manipulation checks are usually done at the end of the procedure to be sure that the effect of the manipulation lasted throughout the entire procedure and to avoid calling unnecessary attention to the manipulation.

Manipulation checks become especially important when the manipulation of the independent variable turns out to have no effect on the dependent variable. Imagine, for example, that you exposed participants to happy or sad movie music—intending to put them in happy or sad moods—but you found that this had no effect on the number of happy or sad childhood events they recalled. This could be because being in a happy or sad mood has no effect on memories for childhood events. But it could also be that the music was ineffective at putting participants in happy or sad moods. A manipulation check—in this case, a measure of participants' moods—would help resolve this uncertainty. If it showed that you had successfully manipulated participants' moods, then it would appear that there is indeed no effect of mood on memory for childhood events. But if it showed that you did not successfully manipulate participants' moods, then it would appear that you need a more effective manipulation to answer your research question.

# Measures of the Same Construct

Another common approach to including multiple dependent variables is to operationally define and measure the same construct, or closely related ones, in different ways. Imagine, for example, that a researcher conducts an experiment on the effect of daily exercise on stress. The dependent variable, stress, is a construct that can be operationally defined in different ways. For this reason, the researcher might have participants complete the paper-and-pencil Perceived Stress Scale *and* measure their levels of the stress hormone cortisol. This is an example of the use of converging operations. If the researcher finds that the different measures are affected by exercise in the same way, then he or she can be confident in the conclusion that exercise affects the more general construct of stress.

When multiple dependent variables are different measures of the same construct—especially if they are measured on the same scale—researchers have the option of combining them into a single measure of that construct. Recall that Schnall and her colleagues were interested in the harshness of people's moral judgments. To measure this construct, they presented their participants with seven different scenarios describing morally questionable behaviors and asked them to rate the moral acceptability of each one. Although they could have treated each of the seven ratings as a separate dependent variable, these researchers combined them into a single dependent variable by computing their mean.

When researchers combine dependent variables in this way, they are treating them collectively as a multiple-response measure of a single construct. The advantage of this is that multiple-response measures are generally more reliable than single-response measures. However, it is important to make sure the individual dependent variables are correlated with each other by computing an internal consistency measure such as Cronbach's $\alpha$. If they are not correlated with each other, then it does not make sense to combine them into a measure of a single construct. If they have poor internal consistency, then they should be treated as separate dependent variables.

## Key Takeaways

- Researchers in psychology often include multiple dependent variables in their studies. The primary reason is that this easily allows them to answer more research questions with minimal additional effort.
- When an independent variable is a construct that is manipulated indirectly, it is a good idea to include a manipulation check. This is a measure of the independent variable typically given at the end of the procedure to confirm that it was successfully manipulated.
- Multiple measures of the same construct can be analyzed separately or combined to produce a single multiple-item measure of that construct. The latter approach requires that the measures taken together have good internal consistency.

## Exercises

1. Practice: List three independent variables for which it would be good to include a manipulation check. List three others for which a manipulation check would be unnecessary.
2. Practice: Imagine a study in which the independent variable is whether the room where participants are tested is warm (80°) or cool (65°). List three dependent variables that you might

treat as measures of separate variables. List three more that you might combine and treat as measures of the same underlying construct.

# 8.2 Multiple Independent Variables

## Learning Objectives

1. Explain why researchers often include multiple independent variables in their studies.
2. Define factorial design, and use a factorial design table to represent and interpret simple factorial designs.
3. Distinguish between main effects and interactions, and recognize and give examples of each.
4. Sketch and interpret bar graphs and line graphs showing the results of studies with simple factorial designs.

Just as it is common for studies in psychology to include multiple dependent variables, it is also common for them to include multiple independent variables. Schnall and her colleagues studied the effect of both disgust and private body consciousness in the same study. Researchers' inclusion of multiple independent variables in one experiment is further illustrated by the following actual titles from various professional journals:

- The Effects of Temporal Delay and Orientation on Haptic Object Recognition
- Opening Closed Minds: The Combined Effects of Intergroup Contact and Need for Closure on Prejudice
- Effects of Expectancies and Coping on Pain-Induced Intentions to Smoke
- The Effect of Age and Divided Attention on Spontaneous Recognition
- The Effects of Reduced Food Size and Package Size on the Consumption Behavior of Restrained and Unrestrained Eaters

Just as including multiple dependent variables in the same experiment allows one to answer more research questions, so too does including multiple independent variables in the same experiment. For example, instead of conducting one study on the effect of disgust on moral judgment and another on the effect of private body consciousness on moral judgment, Schnall and colleagues were able to conduct one study that addressed both questions. But including multiple independent variables also allows the researcher to answer questions about whether the effect of one independent variable depends on the level of another. This is referred to as an interaction between the independent variables. Schnall and her colleagues, for example, observed an interaction between disgust and private body consciousness because the effect of disgust depended on whether participants were high or low in private body consciousness. As we will see, interactions are often among the most interesting results in psychological research.

# Factorial Designs

## Overview

By far the most common approach to including multiple independent variables in an experiment is the factorial design. In a **factorial design**, each level of one independent variable (which can also be called a **factor**) is combined with each level of the others to produce all possible combinations. Each combination, then, becomes a condition in the experiment. Imagine, for example, an experiment on the effect of cell phone use (yes vs. no) and time of day (day vs. night) on driving performance. This is shown in the **factorial design table** in Figure 8.2. The columns of the table represent cell phone use, and the rows represent time of day. The four cells of the table represent the four possible combinations or conditions: using a cell phone during the day, not using a cell phone during the day, using a cell phone at night, and not using a cell phone at night. This particular design is a 2 × 2 (read "two-by-two") factorial design because it combines two variables, each of which has two levels. If one of the independent variables had a third level (e.g., using a handheld cell phone, using a hands-free cell phone, and not using a cell phone), then it would be a 3 × 2 factorial design, and there would be six distinct conditions. Notice that the number of possible conditions is the product of the numbers of levels. A 2 × 2 factorial design has four conditions, a 3 × 2 factorial design has six conditions, a 4 × 5 factorial design would have 20 conditions, and so on.

**factorial design**

A research design with multiple independent variables in which each level of one independent variable is combined with each level of the others to produce all possible conditions.

**factor**

An independent variable in a factorial design. Also in factor analysis, one of the underlying constructs that is assumed to account for correlations among multiple variables.

**factorial design table**

A table used to represent a factorial design. The rows represent the levels of one independent variable, the columns represent the levels of a second independent variable, and each cell represents a condition.

**FIGURE 8.2** Factorial Design Table Representing a 2 × 2 Factorial Design

In principle, factorial designs can include any number of independent variables with any number of levels. For example, an experiment could include the type of psychotherapy (cognitive vs. behavioral), the length of psychotherapy (2 weeks vs. 2 months), and the sex of the psychotherapist (female vs. male). This would be a 2 × 2 × 2 factorial design and would have eight conditions. Figure 8.3 shows one way to represent this design. In practice, it is unusual for there to be more than three independent variables with more than two or three levels each because the number of conditions can quickly become unmanageable. For example, adding a fourth independent variable with three levels (e.g., therapist experience: low vs. medium vs. high) to the current example would make it a $2 \times 2 \times 2 \times 3$ factorial design with 24 distinct conditions. In the rest of this section, we will focus on designs with two independent variables. The general principles discussed here extend in a straight-forward way to more complex factorial designs.

**FIGURE 8.3** Factorial Design Table Representing a 2 × 2 × 2 Factorial Design

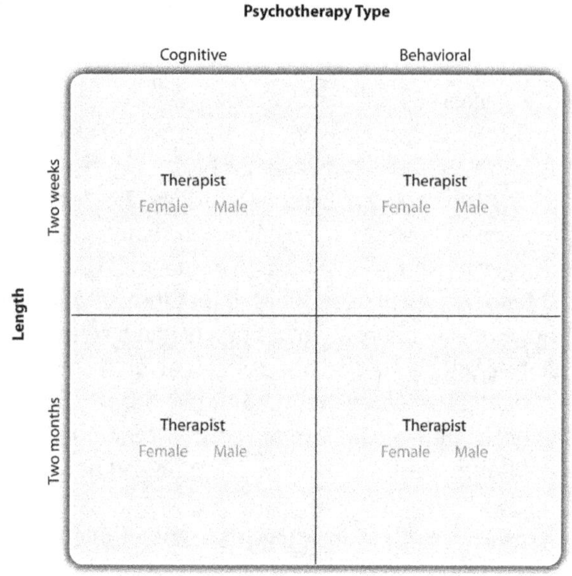

## Assigning Participants to Conditions

**between-subjects factorial design**

A factorial design in which each independent variable is manipulated between subjects so that each participant is tested in only one condition.

**within-subjects factorial design**

A factorial design in which each independent variable is manipulated within subjects so that each participant is tested in all conditions.

**mixed factorial design**

A factorial design in which at least one independent variable is manipulated between subjects and at least one is manipulated within subjects.

Recall that in a simple between-subjects design, each participant is tested in only one condition. In a simple within-subjects design, each participant is tested in all conditions. In a factorial experiment, the decision to take the between-subjects or within-subjects approach must be made separately for each independent variable. In a **between-subjects factorial design**, all of the independent variables are manipulated between subjects. For example, each participant could be tested either while using a cell phone *or* while not using a cell phone and either during the day *or* during the night. This would mean that each participant was tested in one and only one of the four conditions. In a **within-subjects factorial design**, all of the independent variables are manipulated within subjects. All participants could be tested both while using a cell phone *and* while not using a cell phone and both during the day *and* during the night. This would mean that each participant was tested in all four conditions. The advantages and disadvantages of these two approaches are the same as those discussed in Chapter 6. The between-subjects design is conceptually simpler, avoids carryover effects, and minimizes the time and effort for each participant. The within-subjects design is more efficient for the researcher and controls extraneous participant variables.

It is also possible to manipulate one independent variable between subjects and another within subjects. This is called a **mixed factorial design**. For example, a researcher might choose to treat cell phone use as a within-subjects factor by testing the same participants both while using a cell phone and while not using a cell phone (while counterbalancing the order of these two conditions). But he or she might choose to treat time of day as a between-subjects factor by testing each participant either during the day or during the night (perhaps because this only requires them to come in for testing once). Thus each participant in this mixed design would be tested in two of the four conditions.

Regardless of whether the design is between subjects, within subjects, or mixed, the actual assignment of participants to conditions or orders of conditions is typically done randomly.

# Nonmanipulated Independent Variables

In many factorial designs, one of the independent variables is a **nonmanipulated independent variable**. The researchers measure it but do not manipulate it. The study by Schnall and colleagues is a good example. One independent variable was disgust, which they manipulated by testing participants in a clean room or a messy room. The other was private body consciousness, which the researchers simply measured. Another example is a study by Halle Brown and colleagues in which participants were exposed to several words that they were later asked to recall (Brown, Kosslyn, Delamater, Fama, & Barsky, 1999).[3] The manipulated independent variable was the type of word. Some were negative health-related words (e.g., *tumor*, *coronary*), and others were not health related (e.g., *election*, *geometry*). The nonmanipulated independent variable was whether participants were high or low in hypochondriasis (excessive concern with ordinary bodily symptoms). The result of this study was that the participants high in hypochondriasis were better than those low in hypochondriasis at recalling the health-related words, but they were no better at recalling the non-health-related words.

Such studies are extremely common, and there are several points worth making about them. First, nonmanipulated independent variables are usually participant variables (private body consciousness, hypochondriasis, self-esteem, and so on), and as such they are by definition between-subjects factors. For example, people are either low in hypochondriasis or high in hypochondriasis; they cannot be tested in both of these conditions. Second, such studies are generally considered to be experiments as long as at least one independent variable is manipulated, regardless of how many nonmanipulated independent variables are included. Third, it is important to remember that causal conclusions can only be drawn about the manipulated independent variable. For example, Schnall and her colleagues were justified in concluding that disgust affected the harshness of their participants' moral judgments because they manipulated that variable and randomly assigned participants to the clean or messy room. But they would not have been justified in concluding that participants' private body consciousness affected the harshness of their participants' moral judgments because they did not manipulate that variable. It could be, for example, that having a strict moral code and a heightened awareness of one's body are both caused by some third variable (e.g., neuroticism). Thus it is important to be aware of which variables in a study are manipulated and which are not.

> **nonmanipulated independent variable**
>
> In a factorial design, a variable (usually a participant variable) that is treated as an independent variable but is not actually manipulated by the researcher.

# Graphing the Results of Factorial Experiments

The results of factorial experiments with two independent variables can be graphed by representing one independent variable on the x-axis and representing the other by using different kinds of bars or lines. (The y-axis is always reserved for the dependent variable.) Figure 8.4 shows results for two hypothetical factorial experiments. The top panel shows the results of a 2 × 2 design. Time of day (day vs. night) is represented by different locations on the x-axis, and cell phone use (no vs. yes) is represented by different-colored bars. (It would also be possible to represent cell phone use on the x-axis and time of day as different-colored bars. The choice comes down to which way seems to communicate the results most clearly.) The bottom panel of Figure 8.4 shows the results of a 4 × 2 design in which one of the variables is quantitative. This variable, psychotherapy length, is represented along the x-axis, and the other variable (psychotherapy type) is represented by differently formatted lines. This is a line graph rather than a bar graph because the variable on the x-axis is quantitative with a small number of distinct levels.

**FIGURE 8.4** Two Ways to Plot the Results of a Factorial Experiment With Two Independent Variables

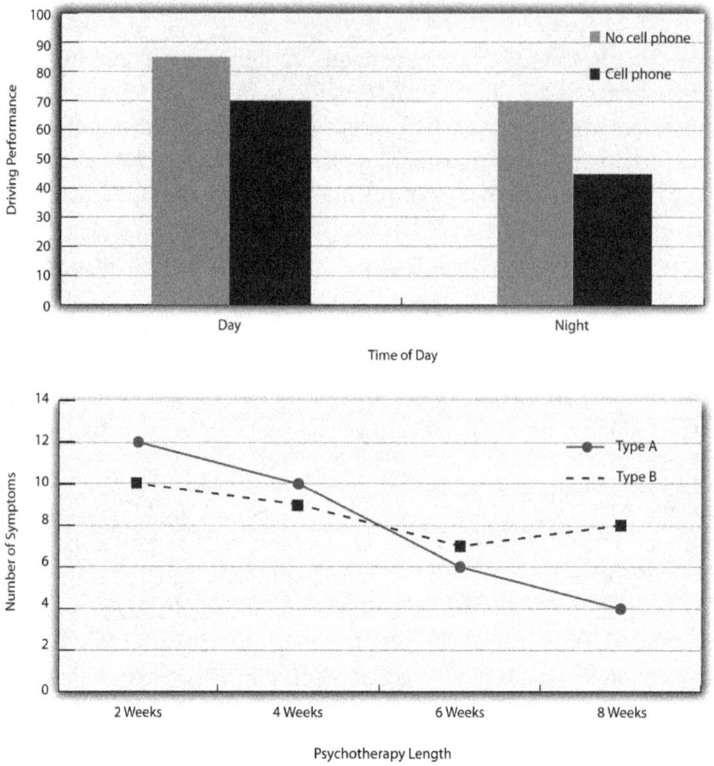

# Main Effects and Interactions

**main effect**

In a factorial design, the effect of one independent variable averaged across levels of all other independent variables.

In factorial designs, there are two kinds of results that are of interest: main effects and interaction effects (which are also called just "interactions"). A **main effect** is the statistical relationship between one independent variable and a dependent variable—averaging across the levels of the other independent variable. Thus there is one main effect to consider for each independent variable in the study. The top panel of Figure 8.4 shows a main effect of cell phone use because driving performance was better, on average, when participants were not using cell phones than when they were. The blue bars are, on average, higher than the red bars. It also shows a main effect of time of day because driving performance was better, on average, during the day than during the night. The "day" bars are, on average, higher than the "night" bars. Main effects are independent of each other in the sense that whether or not there is a main effect of one independent variable says nothing about whether or not there is a main effect of the other. The bottom panel of Figure 8.4, for example, shows a clear main effect of psychotherapy length. The longer the psychotherapy, the better it worked. But it also shows no overall advantage of one type of psychotherapy over the other.

**interaction**

In a factorial design, when the effect of one independent variable depends on the level of another independent variable.

There is an **interaction** effect (or just "interaction") when the effect of one independent variable depends on the level of another. Although this might seem complicated, you probably have an intuitive understanding of interactions already. It would not surprise you, for example, to hear that the effect of receiving psychotherapy is stronger among people who are highly motivated to change than among people who are not motivated to change. This is an interaction because the effect of one independent variable (whether or not one receives psychotherapy) depends on the level of another (motivation to change). Schnall and her colleagues also demonstrated an interaction because the effect of whether the room was clean or messy on participants' moral judgments depended on whether the participants were low or high in private body consciousness. If they were high in private body consciousness, then those in the messy room made harsher judgments. If they were low in private body consciousness, then whether the room was clean or messy did not matter.

The effect of one independent variable can depend on the level of the other in different ways. This is shown in Figure 8.5. In the top panel, one independent variable has an effect at one level of the second independent variable but no effect at the other. (This is much like the study of Schnall and her colleagues where there was an effect of disgust for those high in private body consciousness but not for those low in private body consciousness.) In the middle panel, one independent variable has a stronger effect at one level of the second independent variable than at the other level. This is like the hypothetical driving example where there was a stronger effect of using a cell phone at night than during the day. In the bottom panel, one independent variable has an effect at both levels of the second independent variable, but the effects are in opposite directions. This is called a **crossover interaction**. One example of a crossover interaction comes from a study by Kathy Gilliland on the effect of caffeine on the verbal test scores of introverts and extroverts (Gilliland, 1980).[4] Introverts performed better than extroverts when they had not ingested any caffeine. But extroverts performed better than introverts when they had ingested 4 mg of caffeine per kilogram of body weight. Figure 8.6 shows examples of these same kinds of interactions when one of the independent variables is quantitative and the results are plotted in a line graph. Note that in a crossover interaction, the two lines literally "cross over" each other.

**crossover interaction**

An interaction in which one independent variable has opposite effects at different levels of another independent variable.

**FIGURE 8.5** Bar Graphs Showing Three Types of Interactions
In the top panel, one independent variable has an effect at one level of the second independent variable but not at the other. In the middle panel, one independent variable has a stronger effect at one level of the second independent variable than at the other. In the bottom panel, one independent variable has the opposite effect at one level of the second independent variable than at the other.

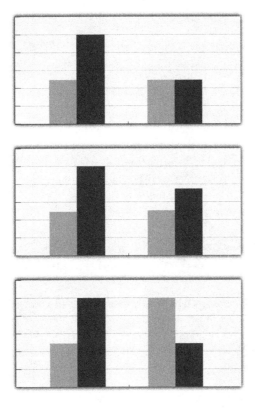

**FIGURE 8.6** Line Graphs Showing Three Types of Interactions
In the top panel, one independent variable has an effect at one level of the second independent variable but not at the other. In the middle panel, one independent variable has a stronger effect at one level of the second independent variable than at the other. In the bottom panel, one independent variable has the opposite effect at one level of the second independent variable than at the other.

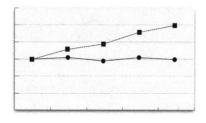

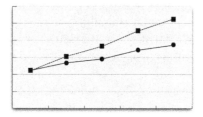

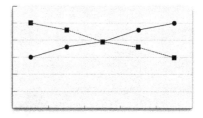

In many studies, the primary research question is about an interaction. The study by Brown and her colleagues was inspired by the idea that people with hypochondriasis are especially attentive to any negative health-related information. This led to the hypothesis that people high in hypochondriasis would recall negative health-related words more accurately than people low in hypochondriasis but recall non-health-related words about the same as people low in hypochondriasis. And of course this is exactly what happened.

## Key Takeaways

- Researchers often include multiple independent variables in their experiments. The most common approach is the factorial design, in which each level of one independent variable is combined with each level of the others to create all possible conditions.

- In a factorial design, the main effect of an independent variable is its overall effect averaged across all other independent variables. There is one main effect for each independent variable.

- There is an interaction between two independent variables when the effect of one depends on the level of the other. Some of the most interesting research questions and results in psychology are specifically about interactions.

1. Practice: Return to the five bulleted article titles presented at the beginning of this section. For each one, identify the independent variables and the dependent variable.
2. Practice: Create a factorial design table for an experiment on the effects room temperature and noise level on performance on the SAT. Be sure to indicate whether each independent variable will be manipulated between subjects or within subjects and explain why.

# 8.3 Complex Correlational Designs

## Learning Objectives

1. Explain some reasons that researchers use complex correlational designs.
2. Create and interpret a correlation matrix.
3. Describe how researchers can use correlational research to explore causal relationships among variables—including the limits of this approach.

As we have already seen, researchers conduct correlational studies rather than experiments when they are interested in noncausal relationships or when they are interested in causal relationships where the independent variable cannot be manipulated for practical or ethical reasons. In this section, we look at some approaches to complex correlational research that involve measuring several variables and assessing the relationships among them.

## Correlational Studies With Factorial Designs

We have already seen that factorial experiments can include manipulated independent variables or a combination of manipulated and nonmanipulated independent variables. But factorial designs can also include *only* nonmanipulated independent variables, in which case they are no longer experiments but correlational studies. Consider a hypothetical study in which a researcher measures both the moods and the self-esteem of several participants—categorizing them as having either a positive or negative mood and as being either high or low in self-esteem—along with their willingness to have unprotected sexual intercourse. This can be conceptualized as a 2 × 2 factorial design with mood (positive vs. negative) and self-esteem (high vs. low) as between-subjects factors. (Willingness to have unprotected sex is the dependent variable.) This design can be represented in a factorial design table and the results in a bar graph of the sort we have already seen. The researcher would consider the main effect of sex, the main effect of self-esteem, and the interaction between these two independent variables.

Again, because neither independent variable in this example was manipulated, it is a correlational study rather than an experiment. (The similar study by MacDonald and Martineau, 2002,[5] was an experiment because they manipulated their participants' moods.) This is important because, as always, one must be cautious about inferring causality from correlational studies because of the directionality and third-variable problems. For example, a main effect of participants' moods on their willingness to have unprotected sex might be caused by any other variable that happens to be correlated with their moods.

# Assessing Relationships Among Multiple Variables

Most complex correlational research, however, does not fit neatly into a factorial design. Instead, it involves measuring several variables—often both categorical and quantitative—and then assessing the statistical relationships among them. For example, researchers Nathan Radcliffe and William Klein studied a sample of middle-aged adults to see how their level of optimism (measured by using a short questionnaire called the Life Orientation Test) relates to several other variables related to having a heart attack (Radcliffe & Klein, 2002).[6] These included their health, their knowledge of heart attack risk factors, and their beliefs about their own risk of having a heart attack. They found that more optimistic participants were healthier (e.g., they exercised more and had lower blood pressure), knew more about heart attack risk factors, and correctly believed their own risk to be lower than that of their peers.

**correlation matrix**

A table that shows the correlations among several variables.

This approach is often used to assess the validity of new psychological measures. For example, when John Cacioppo and Richard Petty created their Need for Cognition Scale—a measure of the extent to which people like to think and value thinking—they used it to measure the need for cognition for a large sample of college students, along with three other variables: intelligence, socially desirable responding (the tendency to give what one thinks is the "appropriate" response), and dogmatism (Caccioppo & Petty, 1982).[7] The results of this study are summarized in Table 8.1, which is a **correlation matrix** showing the correlation (Pearson's $r$) between every possible pair of variables in the study. For example, the correlation between the need for cognition and intelligence was +.39, the correlation between intelligence and socially desirable responding was -.02, and so on. (Only half the matrix is filled in because the other half would contain exactly the same information. Also, because the correlation between a variable and itself is always +1.00, these values are replaced with dashes throughout the matrix.) In this case, the overall pattern of correlations was consistent with the researchers' ideas about how scores on the need for cognition should be related to these other constructs.

**TABLE 8.1** Correlation Matrix Showing Correlations Among the Need for Cognition and Three Other Variables Based on Research by Cacioppo and Petty

|  | Need for cognition | Intelligence | Social desirability | Dogmatism |
|---|---|---|---|---|
| Need for cognition | — |  |  |  |
| Intelligence | +.39 | — |  |  |
| Social desirability | +.08 | +.02 | — |  |
| Dogmatism | −.27 | −.23 | +.03 | — |

**factor analysis**

A complex statistical technique that organizes several variables into clusters where there are strong correlations among the variables within a cluster but weak correlations among the variables between clusters. Each cluster is interpreted as representing a different underlying variable or factor.

When researchers study relationships among a large number of conceptually similar variables, they often use a complex statistical technique called **factor analysis**. In essence, factor analysis organizes the variables into a smaller number of clusters, such that they are strongly correlated within each cluster but weakly correlated between clusters. Each cluster is then interpreted as multiple measures of the same underlying construct. These underlying constructs are also called "factors." For example, when people perform a wide variety of mental tasks, factor analysis typically organizes them into two main factors—one that researchers interpret as mathematical intelligence (arithmetic, quantitative estimation, spatial reasoning, and so on) and another that they interpret as verbal intelligence (grammar, reading comprehension, vocabulary, and so on). The Big Five personality factors have been identified through factor analyses of people's scores on a large number of more specific traits. For example, measures of warmth, gregariousness, activity level, and positive emotions tend to be highly correlated with each other and are interpreted as representing the construct of extroversion. As a final example, researchers Peter Rentfrow and Samuel Gosling asked more than 1,700 college students to rate how much they liked 14 different popular genres of music (Rentfrow & Gosling, 2008).[8] They then submitted these 14 variables to a factor analysis, which identified four distinct factors. The researchers called them *Reflective and Complex* (blues, jazz, classical, and folk), *Intense and Rebellious* (rock, alternative, and heavy metal), *Upbeat and Conventional* (country, soundtrack, religious, pop), and *Energetic and Rhythmic* (rap/hip-hop, soul/funk, and electronica).

Two additional points about factor analysis are worth making here. One is that factors are not categories. Factor analysis does not tell us that people are *either* extroverted *or* conscientious or that they like *either* "reflective and complex" music *or* "intense and rebellious" music. Instead, factors are constructs that operate independently of each other. So people who are high in extroversion might be high or low in conscientiousness, and people who like reflective and complex music might or might not also like intense and rebellious music. The second point is that factor analysis reveals only the underlying structure of the variables. It is up to researchers to interpret and label the factors and to explain the origin of that particular factor structure. For example, one reason that extroversion and the other Big Five operate as separate factors is that they appear to be controlled by different genes (Plomin, DeFries, McClean, & McGuffin, 2008).[9]

# Exploring Causal Relationships

Another important use of complex correlational research is to explore possible causal relationships among variables. This might seem surprising given that "correlation does not imply causation." It is true that correlational research cannot unambiguously establish that one variable causes another. Complex correlational research, however, can often be used to rule out other plausible interpretations.

The primary way of doing this is through the **statistical control** of potential third variables. Instead of controlling these variables by random assignment or by holding them constant as in an experiment, the researchers measure them and include them in the statistical analysis. Consider some research by Paul Piff and his colleagues, who hypothesized that being lower in socioeconomic status (SES) causes people to be more generous (Piff, Kraus, Côté, Hayden Cheng, & Keltner, 2011).[10] They measured their participants' SES and had them play the "dictator game." They told participants that each would be paired with another participant in a different room. (In reality, there was no other participant.) Then they gave each participant 10 points (which could later be converted to money) to split with the "partner" in whatever way the participant decided. Because the participants were the "dictators," they could even keep all 10 points for themselves if they wanted to.

**statistical control**

In complex correlational research, accounting for third variables by measuring them and including them in the analysis.

As these researchers expected, participants who were lower in SES tended to give away more of their points than participants who were higher in SES. This is consistent with the idea that being lower in SES causes people to be more generous. But there are also plausible third variables that could explain this relationship. It could be, for example, that people who are lower in SES tend to be more religious and that it is their greater religiosity that causes them to be more generous. Or it could be that people who are lower in SES tend to come from ethnic groups that emphasize generosity more than other ethnic groups. The researchers dealt with these potential third variables, however, by measuring them and including them in their statistical analyses. They found that neither religiosity nor ethnicity was correlated with generosity and were therefore able to rule them out as alternative explanations of their results. This does not prove that SES causes greater generosity because there could still be other third variables that the researchers did not measure. But by ruling out some of the most plausible third variables, the researchers made a stronger case for SES as the cause of the greater generosity.

**multiple regression**

A statistical technique that describes the relationship between multiple independent variables and a single dependent variable in terms of an equation that shows the separate contribution of each independent variable to the dependent variable.

Many studies of this type use a statistical technique called **multiple regression**. This involves measuring several independent variables ($X_1$, $X_2$, $X_3$,...$X_i$), all of which are possible causes of a single dependent variable ($Y$). The result of a multiple regression analysis is an equation that expresses the dependent variable as an additive combination of the independent variables. This regression equation has the following general form:

$$b_1X_1 + b_2X_2 + b_3X_3 + ... + b_iX_i = Y.$$

The quantities $b_1$, $b_2$, and so on are regression weights that indicate how large a contribution an independent variable makes, on average, to the dependent variable. Specifically, they indicate how much the dependent variable changes for each one-unit change in the independent variable.

The advantage of multiple regression is that it can show whether an independent variable makes a contribution to a dependent variable *over and above* the contributions made by other independent variables. As a hypothetical example, imagine that a researcher wants to know how the independent variables of income and health relate to the dependent variable of happiness. This is tricky because income and health are themselves related to each other. Thus if people with greater incomes tend to be happier, then perhaps this is only because they tend to be healthier. Likewise, if people who are healthier tend to be happier, perhaps this is only because they tend to make more money. But a multiple regression analysis including both income and happiness as independent variables would show whether each one makes a contribution to happiness when the other is taken into account. (Research like this, by the way, has shown both income and health make extremely small contributions to happiness except in the case of severe poverty or illness; Diener, 2000.[11])

The examples discussed in this section only scratch the surface of how researchers use complex correlational research to explore possible causal relationships among variables. It is important to keep in mind, however, that purely correlational approaches cannot unambiguously establish that one variable causes another. The best they can do is show patterns of relationships that are consistent with some causal interpretations and inconsistent with others.

## Key Takeaways

- Researchers often use complex correlational research to explore relationships among several variables in the same study.
- Complex correlational research can be used to explore possible causal relationships among variables using techniques such as multiple regression. Such designs can show patterns of relationships that are consistent with some causal interpretations and inconsistent with others, but they cannot unambiguously establish that one variable causes another.

## Exercises

1. Practice: Make a correlation matrix for a hypothetical study including the variables of depression, anxiety, self-esteem, and happiness. Include the Pearson's *r* values that you would expect.
2. Discussion: Imagine a correlational study that looks at intelligence, the need for cognition, and high school students' performance in a critical-thinking course. A multiple regression analysis shows that intelligence is not related to performance in the class but that the need for cognition is. Explain what this study has shown in terms of what causes good performance in the critical-thinking course.

# Endnotes

1. Schnall, S., Haidt, J., Clore, G. L., & Jordan, A. H. (2008). Disgust as embodied moral judgment. *Personality and Social Psychology Bulletin, 34,* 1096–1109.

2. Knasko, S. C. (1992). Ambient odor's effect on creativity, mood, and perceived health. *Chemical Senses, 17,* 27–35.

3. Brown, H. D., Kosslyn, S. M., Delamater, B., Fama, A., & Barsky, A. J. (1999). Perceptual and memory biases for health-related information in hypochondriacal individuals. *Journal of Psychosomatic Research, 47,* 67–78.

4. Gilliland, K. (1980). The interactive effect of introversion-extroversion with caffeine induced arousal on verbal performance. *Journal of Research in Personality, 14,* 482–492.

5. MacDonald, T. K., & Martineau, A. M. (2002). Self-esteem, mood, and intentions to use condoms: When does low self-esteem lead to risky health behaviors? *Journal of Experimental Social Psychology, 38,* 299–306.

6. Radcliffe, N. M., & Klein, W. M. P. (2002). Dispositional, unrealistic, and comparative optimism: Differential relations with knowledge and processing of risk information and beliefs about personal risk. *Personality and Social Psychology Bulletin, 28,* 836–846.

7. Cacioppo, J. T., & Petty, R. E. (1982). The need for cognition. *Journal of Personality and Social Psychology, 42,* 116–131.

8. Rentfrow, P. J., & Gosling, S. D. (2008). The do re mi's of everyday life: The structure and personality correlates of music preferences. *Journal of Personality and Social Psychology, 84,* 1236–1256.

9. Plomin, R., DeFries, J. C., McClearn, G. E., & McGuffin, P. (2008). *Behavioral genetics* (5th ed.). New York, NY: Worth.

10. Piff, P. K., Kraus, M. W., Côté, S., Hayden Cheng, B., & Keltner, D. (2011). Having less, giving more: The influence of social class on prosocial behavior. *Journal of Personality and Social Psychology, 99,* 771–784.

11. Diener, E. (2000). Subjective well-being: The science of happiness, and a proposal for a national index. *American Psychologist, 55,* 34–43.

# CHAPTER 9

# Survey Research

Shortly after the terrorist attacks in New York City and Washington, DC, in September of 2001, researcher Jennifer Lerner and her colleagues conducted an Internet-based survey of nearly 2,000 Americans ranging in age from 13 to 88 (Lerner, Gonzalez, Small, & Fischhoff, 2003).[1] They asked participants about their reactions to the attacks and for their judgments of various terrorism-related and other risks. Among the results were that the participants tended to overestimate most risks, that females did so more than males, and that there were no differences between teens and adults. The most interesting result, however, had to do with the fact that some participants were "primed" to feel anger by asking what made them angry about the attacks and by presenting a photograph and audio clip intended to evoke anger. Others were primed to feel fear by asking what made them fearful about the attacks and by presenting a photograph and audio clip intended to evoke fear. As the researchers hypothesized, the participants who were primed to feel anger perceived less risk than the participants who had been primed to feel fear—showing how risk perceptions are strongly tied to specific emotions.

The study by Lerner and her colleagues is an example of survey research in psychology—the topic of this chapter. We begin with an overview of survey research, including its definition, some history, and a bit about who conducts it and why. We then look at survey responding as a psychological process and the implications of this for constructing good survey questionnaires. Finally, we consider some issues related to actually conducting survey research, including sampling the participants and collecting the data.

# 9.1 Overview of Survey Research

## Learning Objectives

1. Define what survey research is, including its two important characteristics.
2. Describe several different ways that survey research can be used and give some examples.

## What Is Survey Research?

**Survey research** is a quantitative approach that has two important characteristics. First, the variables of interest are measured using self-reports. In essence, survey researchers ask their participants (who are often called "respondents" in survey research) to report directly on their own thoughts, feelings, and behaviors. Second, considerable attention is paid to the issue of sampling. In particular, survey researchers have a strong preference for large random samples because they provide the most accurate estimates of what is true in the population. In fact, survey research may be the only approach in psychology in which random sampling is routinely used. Beyond these two characteristics, almost anything goes in survey research. Surveys can be long or short. They can be conducted in person, by telephone, through the mail, or over the Internet. They can be about voting

**survey research**

A quantitative research approach that uses self-report measures and large, carefully selected samples.

intentions, consumer preferences, social attitudes, health, or anything else that it is possible to ask people about and receive meaningful answers.

Most survey research is nonexperimental. It is used to describe single variables (e.g., the percentage of voters who prefer one presidential candidate or another, the prevalence of schizophrenia in the general population) and also to assess statistical relationships between variables (e.g., the relationship between income and health). But surveys can also be experimental. The study by Lerner and her colleagues is a good example. Their use of self-report measures and a large national sample identifies their work as survey research. But their manipulation of an independent variable (anger vs. fear) to assess its effect on a dependent variable (risk judgments) also identifies their work as experimental.

# History and Uses of Survey Research

Survey research may have its roots in English and American "social surveys" conducted around the turn of the 20th century by researchers and reformers who wanted to document the extent of social problems such as poverty (Converse, 1987).[2] By the 1930s, the U.S. government was conducting surveys to document economic and social conditions in the country. The need to draw conclusions about the entire population helped spur advances in sampling procedures. At about the same time, several researchers who had already made a name for themselves in market research—studying consumer preferences for American businesses—turned their attention to election polling. A watershed event was the presidential election of 1936 between Alf Landon and Franklin Roosevelt. A magazine called *Literary Digest* conducted a survey by sending ballots (which were also subscription requests) to millions of Americans. Based on this "straw poll," the editors predicted that Landon would win in a landslide. At the same time, the new pollsters were using scientific methods with much smaller samples to predict just the opposite—that Roosevelt would win in a landslide. In fact, one of them, George Gallup, publicly criticized the methods of *Literary Digest* before the election and all but guaranteed that his prediction would be correct. And of course it was. (We will consider the reasons that Gallup was right later in this chapter.)

From market research and election polling, survey research made its way into several academic fields, including political science, sociology, and public health—where it continues to be one of the primary approaches to collecting new data. Beginning in the 1930s, psychologists made important advances in questionnaire design, including techniques that are still used today, such as the Likert scale. (See "What Is a Likert Scale?" in Section 2.) Survey research has a strong historical association with the social psychological study of attitudes, stereotypes, and prejudice. Early attitude researchers were also among the first psychologists to seek larger and more diverse samples than the convenience samples of college students that were routinely used in psychology (and still are).

Survey research continues to be important in psychology today. For example, survey data have been instrumental in estimating the prevalence of various mental disorders and identifying statistical relationships among those disorders and with other factors. The National Comorbidity Survey is a large-scale mental health survey conducted in the United States (see http://www.hcp.med.harvard.edu/ncs). In just one part of this survey, nearly 10,000 adults were given a structured mental health interview in their homes in 2002 and 2003. Table 9.1 presents results on the lifetime prevalence of some anxiety, mood, and substance use disorders. (Lifetime prevalence is the percentage of the population that develops the problem sometime in their lifetime.) Obviously, this kind of information can be of great use both to basic researchers seeking to understand the causes and correlates of mental disorders and also to clinicians and policymakers who need to understand exactly how common these disorders are.

**TABLE 9.1** Some Lifetime Prevalence Results From the National Comorbidity Survey

| Lifetime prevalence* | | | |
|---|---|---|---|
| Disorder | Total | Female | Male |
| Generalized anxiety disorder | 5.7 | 7.1 | 4.2 |
| Obsessive-compulsive disorder | 2.3 | 3.1 | 1.6 |
| Major depressive disorder | 16.9 | 20.2 | 13.2 |
| Bipolar disorder | 4.4 | 4.5 | 4.3 |
| Alcohol abuse | 13.2 | 7.5 | 19.6 |
| Drug abuse | 8.0 | 4.8 | 11.6 |
| *The lifetime prevalence of a disorder is the percentage of people in the population that develop that disorder at any time in their lives. | | | |

And as the opening example makes clear, survey research can even be used to conduct experiments to test specific hypotheses about causal relationships between variables. Such studies, when conducted on large and diverse samples, can be a useful supplement to laboratory studies conducted on college students. Although this is not a typical use of survey research, it certainly illustrates the flexibility of this approach.

## Key Takeaways

- Survey research is a quantitative approach that features the use of self-report measures on carefully selected samples. It is a flexible approach that can be used to study a wide variety of basic and applied research questions.
- Survey research has its roots in applied social research, market research, and election polling. It has since become an important approach in many academic disciplines, including political science, sociology, public health, and, of course, psychology.

## Exercise

1. Discussion: Think of a question that each of the following professionals might try to answer using survey research.
    a. a social psychologist
    b. an educational researcher
    c. a market researcher who works for a supermarket chain
    d. the mayor of a large city
    e. the head of a university police force

# 9.2 Constructing Survey Questionnaires

## Learning Objectives

1. Describe the cognitive processes involved in responding to a survey item.
2. Explain what a context effect is and give some examples.
3. Create a simple survey questionnaire based on principles of effective item writing and organization.

The heart of any survey research project is the survey questionnaire itself. Although it is easy to think of interesting questions to ask people, constructing a good survey questionnaire is not easy at all. The problem is that the answers people give can be influenced in unintended ways by the wording of the items, the order of the items, the response options provided, and many other factors. At best, these influences add noise to the data. At worst, they result in systematic biases and misleading results. In this section, therefore, we consider some principles for constructing survey questionnaires to minimize these unintended effects and thereby maximize the reliability and validity of respondents' answers.

## Survey Responding as a Psychological Process

Before looking at specific principles of survey questionnaire construction, it will help to consider survey responding as a psychological process.

### A Cognitive Model

Figure 9.1 presents a model of the cognitive processes that people engage in when responding to a survey item (Sudman, Bradburn, & Schwarz, 1996).[3] Respondents must interpret the question, retrieve relevant information from memory, form a tentative judgment, convert the tentative judgment into one of the response options provided (e.g., a rating on a 1-to-7 scale), and finally edit their response as necessary.

**FIGURE 9.1** Model of the Cognitive Processes Involved in Responding to a Survey Item

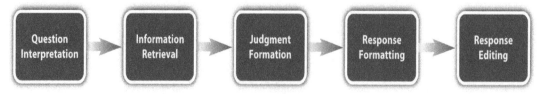

Consider, for example, the following questionnaire item:

How many alcoholic drinks do you consume in a typical day?

- _____ a lot more than average
- _____ somewhat more than average
- _____ average
- _____ somewhat fewer than average
- _____ a lot fewer than average

Although this item at first seems straightforward, it poses several difficulties for respondents. First, they must interpret the question. For example, they must decide whether "alcoholic drinks" include beer and wine (as opposed to just hard liquor) and whether a "typical day" is a typical weekday, typical weekend day, or both. Once they have interpreted the question, they must retrieve relevant information from memory to answer it. But what information should they retrieve, and how should they go about retrieving it? They might think vaguely about some recent occasions on which they drank alcohol, they might carefully try to recall and count the number of alcoholic drinks they consumed last week, or they might retrieve some existing beliefs that they have about themselves (e.g., "I am not much of a drinker"). Then they must use this information to arrive at a tentative judgment about how many alcoholic drinks they consume in a typical day. For example, this might mean dividing the number of alcoholic drinks they consumed last week by seven to come up with an average number per day. Then they must format this tentative answer in terms of the response options actually provided. In this case, the options pose additional problems of interpretation. For example, what does "average" mean, and what would count as "somewhat more" than average? Finally, they must decide whether they want to report the response they have come up with or whether they want to edit it in some way. For example, if they believe that they drink much more than average, they might not want to report this for fear of looking bad in the eyes of the researcher.

From this perspective, what at first appears to be a simple matter of asking people how much they drink (and receiving a straightforward answer from them) turns out to be much more complex.

## Context Effects on Questionnaire Responses

Again, this complexity can lead to unintended influences on respondents' answers. These are often referred to as **context effects** because they are not related to the content of the item but to the context in which the item appears (Schwarz & Strack, 1990).[4] For example, there is an **item-order effect** when the order in which the items are presented affects people's responses. One item can change how participants interpret a later item or change the information that they retrieve to respond to later items. For example, researcher Fritz Strack and his colleagues asked college students about both their general life satisfaction and their dating frequency (Strack, Martin, & Schwarz, 1988).[5] When the life satisfaction item came first, the correlation between the two was only –.12, suggesting that the two variables are only weakly related. But when the dating frequency item came first, the correlation between the two was +.66, suggesting that those who date more have a strong tendency to be more satisfied with their lives. Reporting the dating frequency first made that information more accessible in memory so that they were more likely to base their life satisfaction rating on it.

The response options provided can also have unintended effects on people's responses (Schwarz, 1999).[6] For example, when people are asked how often they are "really irritated" and given response options ranging from "less than once a year" to "more than once a month," they tend to think of major irritations and report being irritated infrequently. But when they are given response options ranging from "less than once a day" to "several times a month," they tend to think of minor irritations and report being irritated frequently. People also tend to assume that middle response options represent what is normal or typical. So if they think of themselves as normal or typical, they tend to choose middle response options. For example, people are likely to report watching

**context effect**

An unintended effect of the context in which a response is made. In within-subjects experiments, this can be an effect of being tested in one condition on how participants perceive stimuli or interpret their task and therefore how they respond in later conditions. In survey research, this can be an effect of the surrounding items or the response scale on responses to a particular item.

**item-order effect**

The effect of responding to one survey item on responses to a later survey item.

more television when the response options are centered on a middle option of 4 hours than when centered on a middle option of 2 hours.

# Writing Survey Questionnaire Items

## Types of Items

**open-ended item**

A questionnaire item that asks a question and allows respondents to respond in whatever way they want.

Questionnaire items can be either open-ended or closed-ended. **Open-ended items** simply ask a question and allow participants to answer in whatever way they choose. The following are examples of open-ended questionnaire items.

- "What is the most important thing to teach children to prepare them for life?"
- "Please describe a time when you were discriminated against because of your age."
- "Is there anything else you would like to tell us about?"

Open-ended items are useful when researchers do not know how participants might respond or want to avoid influencing their responses. They tend to be used when researchers have more vaguely defined research questions—often in the early stages of a research project. Open-ended items are relatively easy to write because there are no response options to worry about. However, they take more time and effort on the part of participants, and they are more difficult for the researcher to analyze because the answers must be transcribed, coded, and submitted to some form of content analysis.

**closed-ended item**

A questionnaire item that asks a question and provides a set of response options for respondents to choose from.

**Closed-ended items** ask a question and provide a set of response options for participants to choose from. The alcohol item just mentioned is an example, as are the following:

How old are you?

- _____ Under 18
- _____ 18 to 34
- _____ 35 to 49
- _____ 50 to 70
- _____ Over 70

On a scale of 0 (no pain at all) to 10 (worst pain ever experienced), how much pain are you in right now?

Have you ever in your adult life been depressed for a period of two weeks or more?

Closed-ended items are used when researchers have a good idea of the different responses that participants might make. They are also used when researchers are interested in a well-defined variable or construct such as participants' level of agreement with some statement, perceptions of risk, or frequency of a particular behavior. Closed-ended items are more difficult to write because they must include an appropriate set of response options. However, they are relatively quick and easy for participants to complete. They are also much easier for researchers to analyze because the responses can be easily converted to numbers and entered into a spreadsheet. For these reasons, closed-ended items are much more common.

**rating scale**

An ordered set of response options to a closed-ended questionnaire item.

All closed-ended items include a set of response options from which a participant must choose. For categorical variables like sex, race, or political party preference, the categories are usually listed and participants choose the one (or ones) that they belong to. For quantitative variables, a rating scale is typically provided. A **rating scale** is an ordered set of responses that participants must choose from. Figure 9.2 shows several examples. The number of response options on a typical rating scale ranges from 3 to 11—although 5 and 7 are probably most common. The first rating scale in Figure 9.2 is a five-point agreement scale that allows respondents to choose one of five levels of agreement expressed verbally. The second rating scale in Figure 9.2 is a 7-point likelihood scale that allows respondents to choose a number from 1 to 7 to indicate how likely an event is. This scale also includes the verbal anchors "Extremely Unlikely" and "Extremely Likely" at the ends of the scale to help respondents calibrate their responses. The third rating scale in Figure 9.2 is a friendliness scale. It is a "visual-analog scale," consisting of a horizontal like with the verbal anchors "Extremely Unfriendly" and "Extremely Friendly." This allows respondents to place a mark (or click) anywhere along the horizontal line to indicate the magnitude of their response.

**FIGURE 9.2** Example Rating Scales for Closed-Ended Questionnaire Items

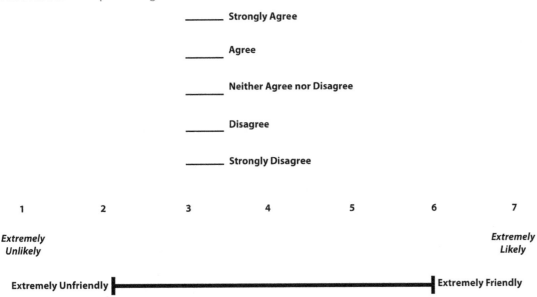

## What Is a Likert Scale?

In reading about psychological research, you are likely to encounter the term *Likert scale*. Although this term is sometimes used to refer to almost any rating scale (e.g., a 0-to-10 life satisfaction scale), it has a much more precise meaning.

In the 1930s, researcher Rensis Likert (pronounced LICK-ert) created a new approach for measuring people's attitudes (Likert, 1932).[7] It involves presenting people with several statements—including both favorable and unfavorable statements—about some person, group, or idea. Respondents then express their agreement or disagreement with each statement on a 5-point scale: *Strongly Agree, Agree, Neither Agree nor Disagree, Disagree, Strongly Disagree*. Numbers are assigned to each response (with reverse coding as necessary) and then summed across all items to produce a score representing the attitude toward the person, group, or idea. The entire set of items came to be called a Likert scale.

Thus unless you are measuring people's attitude toward something by assessing their level of agreement with several statements about it, it is best not to call it a Likert scale. You are probably just using a "rating scale."

## Writing Effective Items

We can now consider some principles of writing questionnaire items that minimize unintended context effects and maximize the reliability and validity of participants' responses. A rough guideline for writing questionnaire items is provided by the BRUSO model (Peterson, 2000).[8] An acronym, **BRUSO** stands for "brief," "relevant," "unambiguous," "specific," and "objective." Effective questionnaire items are *brief* and to the point. They avoid long, overly technical, or unnecessary words. This makes them easier for respondents to understand and faster for them to complete.

**BRUSO**

A prescriptive model for writing good questionnaire items. They should be brief, relevant, unambiguous, specific, and objective.

Effective questionnaire items are also *relevant* to the research question. If a respondent's sexual orientation, marital status, or income is not relevant, then it is best not to ask about it. Again, this makes the questionnaire faster to complete, but it also avoids annoying respondents with what they will rightly perceive as irrelevant or even "nosy" questions. Effective questionnaire items are also *unambiguous*; they can be interpreted in only one way. Part of the problem with the alcohol item presented earlier in this section is that different respondents might have different ideas about what constitutes "an alcoholic drink" or "a typical day." Effective questionnaire items are also *specific*, so that it is clear to respondents what their response *should* be about and clear to researchers what it *is* about. A common problem here is closed-ended items that are "double barreled." They ask about two conceptually separate issues but allow only one response. For example, "Please rate the extent to which you have been feeling anxious and depressed." This item should probably be split into two separate items—one about anxiety and one about depression. Finally, effective questionnaire items are *objective* in the sense that they do not reveal the researcher's own opinions or lead participants to answer in a particular way. Table 9.2 shows some examples of poor and effective questionnaire items based on the BRUSO criteria.

**TABLE 9.2** BRUSO Model of Writing Effective Questionnaire Items, Plus Examples

| Criterion | Poor | Effective |
|---|---|---|
| B—Brief | "Are you now or have you ever been the possessor of a firearm?" | "Have you ever owned a gun?" |
| R—Relevant | "What is your sexual orientation?" | Do not include this item unless it is clearly relevant to the research. |
| U—Unambiguous | "Are you a gun person?" | "Do you currently own a gun?" |
| S—Specific | "How much have you read about the new gun control measure and sales tax?" | "How much have you read about the new gun control measure?" "How much have you read about the new sales tax?" |
| O—Objective | "How much do you support the new gun control measure?" | "What is your view of the new gun control measure?" |

For closed-ended items, it is also important to create an appropriate response scale. For categorical variables, the categories presented should generally be mutually exclusive and exhaustive. Mutually exclusive categories do not overlap. For a religion item, for example, the categories of *Christian* and *Catholic* are not mutually exclusive but *Protestant* and *Catholic* are. Exhaustive categories cover all possible responses. Although *Protestant* and *Catholic* are mutually exclusive, they are not exhaustive because there are many other religious categories that a respondent might select: *Jewish*, *Hindu*, *Buddhist*, and so on. In many cases, it is not feasible to include every possible category, in which case an *Other* category, with a space for the respondent to fill in a more specific response, is a good solution. If respondents could belong to more than one category (e.g., race), they should be instructed to choose all categories that apply.

For rating scales, five or seven response options generally allow about as much precision as respondents are capable of. However, numerical scales with more options can sometimes be appropriate. For dimensions such as attractiveness, pain, and likelihood, a 0-to-10 scale will be familiar to many respondents and easy for them to use. Regardless of the number of response options, the most extreme ones should generally be "balanced" around a neutral or modal midpoint. An example of an unbalanced rating scale measuring perceived likelihood might look like this:

*Unlikely | Somewhat Likely | Likely | Very Likely | Extremely Likely*

A balanced version might look like this:

*Extremely Unlikely | Somewhat Unlikely | As Likely as Not | Somewhat Likely | Extremely Likely*

Note, however, that a middle or neutral response option does not have to be included. Researchers sometimes choose to leave it out because they want to encourage respondents to think more deeply about their response and not simply choose the middle option by default.

Numerical rating scales often begin at 1 and go up to 5 or 7. However, they can also begin at 0 if the lowest response option means the complete absence of something (e.g., no pain). They can also have 0 as their midpoint, but it is important to think about how this might change people's interpretation of the response options. For example, when asked to rate how successful in life they have been on a 0-to-10 scale, many people use numbers in the lower half of the scale because they interpret this to mean that they have been only somewhat successful in life. But when asked to rate how successful they have been in life on a –5 to +5 scale, very few people use numbers in the lower half of the scale because they interpret negative numbers to mean they have actually been *unsuccessful* in life (Schwarz, 1999).[9]

# Formatting the Questionnaire

Writing effective items is only one part of constructing a survey questionnaire. For one thing, every survey questionnaire should have a written or spoken introduction that serves two basic functions (Peterson, 2000).[10] One is to encourage respondents to participate in the survey. In many types of research, such encouragement is not necessary either because participants do not know they are in a study (as in naturalistic observation) or because they are part of a subject pool and have already shown their willingness to participate by signing up and showing up for the study. Survey research usually catches respondents by surprise when they answer their phone, go to their mailbox, or check their e-mail—and the researcher must make a good case for why they should agree to participate. Thus the introduction should briefly explain the purpose of the survey and its importance, provide information about the sponsor of the survey (university-based surveys tend to generate higher response rates), acknowledge the importance of the respondent's participation, and describe any incentives for participating.

The second function of the introduction is to establish informed consent. Remember that this means describing to respondents everything that might affect their decision to participate. This includes the topics covered by the survey, the amount of time it is likely to take, the respondent's option to withdraw at any time, confidentiality issues, and so on. Written consent forms are not typically used in survey research, so it is important that this part of the introduction be well documented and presented clearly and in its entirety to every respondent.

The introduction should be followed by the substantive questionnaire items. But first, it is important to present clear instructions for completing the questionnaire, including examples of how to use any unusual response scales. Remember that this is the point at which respondents are usually most interested and least fatigued, so it is good practice to start with the most important items for purposes of the research and proceed to less important items. Items should also be grouped by topic or by type. For example, items using the same rating scale (e.g., a 5-point agreement scale) should be grouped together if possible to make things faster and easier for respondents. Demographic items are often presented last because they are least interesting to participants but also easy to answer in the event respondents have become tired or bored. Of course, any survey should end with an expression of appreciation to the respondent.

## Key Takeaways

- Responding to a survey item is itself a complex cognitive process that involves interpreting the question, retrieving information, making a tentative judgment, putting that judgment into the required response format, and editing the response.

- Survey questionnaire responses are subject to numerous context effects due to question wording, item order, response options, and other factors. Researchers should be sensitive to such effects when constructing surveys and interpreting survey results.
- Survey questionnaire items are either open-ended or closed-ended. Open-ended items simply ask a question and allow respondents to answer in whatever way they want. Closed-ended items ask a question and provide several response options that respondents must choose from.
- According to the BRUSO model, questionnaire items should be brief, relevant, unambiguous, specific, and objective.

## Exercises

1. Discussion: Write a survey item and then write a short description of how someone might respond to that item based on the cognitive model of survey responding (or choose any item on the Rosenberg Self-Esteem Scale).
2. Practice: Write survey questionnaire items for each of the following general questions. In some cases, a series of items, rather than a single item, might be necessary.

   a. How much does the respondent use Facebook?

   b. How much exercise does the respondent get?

   c. How likely does the respondent think it is that the incumbent will be reelected in the next presidential election?

   d. To what extent does the respondent experience "road rage"?

# 9.3 Conducting Surveys

## Learning Objectives

1. Explain the difference between probability and nonprobability sampling, and describe the major types of probability sampling.
2. Define sampling bias in general and nonresponse bias in particular. List some techniques that can be used to increase the response rate and reduce nonresponse bias.
3. List the four major ways to conduct a survey along with some pros and cons of each.

In this section, we consider how to go about conducting a survey. We first consider the issue of sampling, followed by some different methods of actually collecting survey data.

# Sampling

Essentially all psychological research involves sampling—selecting a sample to study from the population of interest. Sampling falls into two broad categories. **Probability sampling** occurs when the researcher can specify the probability that each member of the population will be selected for the sample. **Nonprobability sampling** occurs when the researcher cannot specify these probabilities. Most psychological research involves nonprobability sampling. Convenience sampling—studying individuals who happen to be nearby and willing to participate—is a very common form of non-probability sampling used in psychological research.

Survey researchers, however, are much more likely to use some form of probability sampling. This is because the goal of most survey research is to make accurate estimates about what is true in a particular population, and these estimates are most accurate when based on a probability sample. For example, it is important for survey researchers to base their estimates of election outcomes—which are often decided by only a few percentage points—on probability samples of likely registered voters.

Compared with nonprobability sampling, probability sampling requires a very clear specification of the population, which of course depends on the research questions to be answered. The population might be all registered voters in the state of Arkansas, all American consumers who have purchased a car in the past year, women in the United States over 40 years old who have received a mammogram in the past decade, or all the alumni of a particular university. Once the population has been specified, probability sampling requires a **sampling frame**. This is essentially a list of all the members of the population from which to select the respondents. Sampling frames can come from a variety of sources, including telephone directories, lists of registered voters, and hospital or insurance records. In some cases, a map can serve as a sampling frame, allowing for the selection of cities, streets, or households.

There are a variety of different probability sampling methods. **Simple random sampling** is done in such a way that each individual in the population has an equal probability of being selected for the sample. Conceptually, this is like putting the names of all individuals in the sampling frame into a box, mixing them up, and then drawing out the number needed for the sample. Given that most sampling frames take the form of computer files, random sampling is more likely to involve computerized sorting or selection of respondents.

A common alternative to simple random sampling is **stratified random sampling**, in which the population is divided into different subgroups or "strata" (usually based on demographic characteristics) and then a random sample is taken from each "stratum." Stratified random sampling can be used to select a sample in which the proportion of respondents in each of various subgroups matches the proportion in the population. For example, because about 12.5% of the U.S. population is black, stratified random sampling can be used to ensure that a survey of 1,000 American adults includes about 125 black respondents. Stratified random sampling can also be used to sample extra respondents from particularly small subgroups—allowing valid conclusions to be drawn about those subgroups. For example, because Asian Americans make up a fairly small percentage of the U.S. population (about 4.5%), a simple random sample of 1,000 American adults might include too few Asian Americans to draw any conclusions about them as distinct from any other subgroup. If this is important to the research question, however, then stratified random sampling could be used to ensure that enough Asian American respondents are included in the sample to draw valid conclusions about Asian Americans as a whole.

Yet another type of probability sampling is **cluster sampling**, in which larger clusters of individuals are randomly sampled and then individuals within each cluster are randomly sampled. For example, to select a sample of small-town residents in the United States, a researcher might randomly select several small towns and then randomly select several individuals within each town. Cluster sampling is especially useful for surveys that involve face-to-face interviewing because it minimizes the amount of traveling that the interviewers must do. For example, instead of traveling

**probability sampling**

An approach to sampling in which the researcher can specify the probability that each member of the population will be selected.

**nonprobability sampling**

An approach to sampling in which the researcher cannot specify the probability that each member of the population will be selected. Convenience sampling is an example.

**sampling frame**

A list of all the members of the population, from which the actual sample is selected.

**simple random sampling**

Sampling where each member of the population has an equal probability of being selected.

**stratified random sampling**

Sampling where the population is first divided into different subgroups or strata and a separate random sample is selected from each stratum.

**cluster sampling**

Sampling where larger clusters of individuals (e.g., cities, households) are sampled first and then individuals are sampled from these clusters.

to 200 small towns to interview 200 residents, a research team could travel to 10 small towns and interview 20 residents of each. The National Comorbidity Survey was done using a form of cluster sampling.

How large does a survey sample need to be? In general, this depends on two factors. One is the level of confidence in the result that the researcher wants. The larger the sample, the closer any statistic based on that sample will tend to be to the corresponding value in the population. The other factor is the budget of the study. Larger samples provide greater confidence, but they take more time, effort, and money to obtain. Taking these two factors into account, most survey research uses sample sizes that range from about 100 to about 1,000.

## Sample Size and Population Size

Why is a sample of 1,000 considered to be adequate for most survey research—even when the population is much larger than that? Consider, for example, that a sample of only 1,000 registered voters is generally considered a good sample of the roughly 120 million registered voters in the U.S. population—even though it includes only about 0.0008% of the population! The answer is a bit surprising.

One part of the answer is that a statistic based on a larger sample will tend to be closer to the population value. Imagine, for example, that in a sample of 100 registered voters, exactly 50% say they intend to vote for the incumbent. It can be shown mathematically that there is a 95% chance that the true percentage in the population is between 40 and 60. But if there are 1,000 voters in the sample, there is a 95% chance that the true percentage is between 47 and 53. This "95% confidence interval" (often called the "margin of error") continues to shrink as the sample size increases but it does so at a slower rate. For example, if there are 2,000 voters in the sample, the 95% confidence interval only shrinks to 48 to 52. In many situations, the small increase in confidence beyond a sample size of 1,000 is not considered to be worth the additional time, effort, and money.

Another part of the answer—and perhaps the more surprising part—is that these confidence intervals depend only on the size of the sample and not on the size of the population. So a sample of 1,000 would produce a 95% confidence interval of 47 to 53 regardless of whether the population size was a hundred thousand, a million, or a hundred million.

# Sampling Bias

**sampling bias**

Occurs when a sample is selected in such a way that it is not representative of the entire population and therefore produces inaccurate results.

**nonresponse bias**

A type of sampling bias in which those who do not respond to the survey differ systematically from those who do, producing misleading results.

Probability sampling was developed in large part to address the issue of sampling bias. **Sampling bias** occurs when a sample is selected in such a way that it is not representative of the entire population and therefore produces inaccurate results. This was the reason that the *Literary Digest* straw poll was so far off in its prediction of the 1936 presidential election. The mailing lists used came largely from telephone directories and lists of registered automobile owners, which overrepresented wealthier people, who were more likely to vote for Landon. Gallup was successful because he knew about this bias and found ways to sample less wealthy people as well.

There is one form of sampling bias that even careful random sampling is subject to. It is almost never the case that everyone selected for the sample actually responds to the survey. Some may have died or moved away, and others may decline to participate because they are too busy, are not interested in the survey topic, or do not participate in surveys on principle. If these survey nonresponders differ from survey responders in systematic ways, then this can produce **nonresponse bias**. For example, in a mail survey on alcohol consumption, researcher Vivienne Lahaut and colleagues found that only about half the sample responded after the initial contact and two followup reminders (Lahaut, Jansen, van de Mheen, & Garretsen, 2002).[11] The danger here is that the half who responded might have different patterns of alcohol consumption than the half who did not, which could lead to inaccurate conclusions on the part of the researchers. So to test for nonresponse bias, the researchers later made unannounced visits to the homes of a subset of the nonresponders—coming back up to five times if they did not find them at home. They found that the original nonresponders included an especially high proportion of abstainers (nondrinkers), which meant that their estimates of alcohol consumption based only on the original responders were too high.

Although there are methods for statistically correcting for nonresponse bias, they are based on assumptions about the nonresponders—for example, that they are more similar to late responders than to early responders—which may not be correct. For this reason, the best approach to minimizing nonresponse bias is to minimize the number of nonresponders—that is, to maximize the response rate. There is a large research literature on the factors that affect survey response rates (Groves et al., 2004).[12] In general, in-person interviews have the highest response rates, followed by telephone surveys, and then mail and Internet surveys. Among the other factors that increase response rates are sending potential respondents a short prenotification message informing them that they will be asked to participate in a survey in the near future and sending simple follow-up reminders to nonresponders after a few weeks. The perceived length and complexity of the survey also makes a difference, which is why it is important to keep survey questionnaires as short, simple, and on topic as possible. Finally, offering an incentive—especially cash—is a reliable way to increase response rates.

# Conducting the Survey

The four main ways to conduct surveys are through in-person interviews, by telephone, through the mail, and over the Internet. As with other aspects of survey design, the choice depends on both the researcher's goals and the budget. In-person interviews have the highest response rates and provide the closest personal contact with respondents. Personal contact can be important, for example, when the interviewer must see and make judgments about respondents, as is the case with some mental health interviews. But in-person interviewing is by far the most costly approach. Telephone surveys have lower response rates and still provide some personal contact with respondents. They can also be costly but are generally less so than in-person interviews. Mail surveys are less costly still but generally have even lower response rates—making them most susceptible to nonresponse bias.

Not surprisingly, Internet surveys are becoming more common. They are increasingly easy to construct and use (see "Online Survey Creation"). Although initial contact can be made by mail with a link provided to the survey, this approach does not necessarily produce higher response rates than an ordinary mail survey. A better approach is to make initial contact by e-mail with a link directly to the survey. This can work well when the population consists of the members of an organization who have known e-mail addresses and regularly use them (e.g., a university community). For other populations, it can be difficult or impossible to find a comprehensive list of e-mail addresses to serve as a sampling frame. Alternatively, a request to participate in the survey with a link to it can be posted on websites known to be visited by members of the population. But again it is very difficult to get anything approaching a random sample this way because the members of the population who visit the websites are likely to be different from the population as a whole. However, Internet survey methods are in rapid development. Because of their low cost and because more people are online than ever before, Internet surveys are becoming the dominant approach to survey data collection.

### Online Survey Creation

There are now several online tools for creating online questionnaires. After a questionnaire is created, a link to it can then be e-mailed to potential respondents or embedded in a web page. The following websites are among those that offer free accounts. Although the free accounts limit the number of questionnaire items and the number of respondents, they can be useful for doing small-scale surveys and for practicing the principles of good questionnaire construction.

- Polldaddy: http://www.polldaddy.com
- Qualtrics: http://www.qualtrics.com
- QuestionPro: http://www.questionpro.com
- SurveyMonkey: http://www.surveymonkey.com
- Zoomerang: http://www.zoomerang.com

## Key Takeaways

- Survey research usually involves probability sampling, in which each member of the population has a known probability of being selected for the sample. Types of probability sampling include simple random sampling, stratified random sampling, and cluster sampling.

- Sampling bias occurs when a sample is selected in such a way that it is not representative of the population and therefore produces inaccurate results. The most pervasive form of sampling bias is nonresponse bias, which occurs when people who do not respond to the survey differ in important ways from people who do respond. The best way to minimize nonresponse bias is to maximize the response rate by prenotifying respondents, sending them reminders, constructing questionnaires that are short and easy to complete, and offering incentives.

- Surveys can be conducted in person, by telephone, through the mail, and on the Internet. In-person interviewing has the highest response rates but is the most expensive. Mail and Internet surveys are less expensive but have much lower response rates. Internet surveys are becoming the dominant approach because of their low cost.

## Exercises

1. Discussion: If possible, identify an appropriate sampling frame for each of the following populations. If there is no appropriate sampling frame, explain why.

    a. students at a particular college or university
    b. adults living in the state of Nevada
    c. households in Little Rock, Arkansas
    d. people with low self-esteem

2. Practice: Use one of the online survey creation tools to create a 10-item survey questionnaire on a topic of your choice.

## Endnotes

1. Lerner, J. S., Gonzalez, R. M., Small, D. A., & Fischhoff, B. (2003). Effects of fear and anger on perceived risks of terrorism: A national field experiment. *Psychological Science, 14*, 144–150.
2. Converse, J. M. (1987). *Survey research in the United States: Roots and emergence, 1890–1960.* Berkeley, CA: University of California Press.

3. Sudman, S., Bradburn, N. M., & Schwarz, N. (1996). *Thinking about answers: The application of cognitive processes to survey methodology*. San Francisco, CA: Jossey-Bass.

4. Schwarz, N., & Strack, F. (1990). Context effects in attitude surveys: Applying cognitive theory to social research. In W. Stroebe & M. Hewstone (Eds.), *European review of social psychology* (Vol. 2, pp. 31–50). Chichester, UK: Wiley.

5. Strack, F., Martin, L. L., & Schwarz, N. (1988). Priming and communication: The social determinants of information use in judgments of life satisfaction. *European Journal of Social Psychology, 18*, 429–442.

6. Schwarz, N. (1999). Self-reports: How the questions shape the answers. *American Psychologist, 54*, 93–105.

7. Likert, R. (1932). A technique for the measurement of attitudes. *Archives of Psychology, 140*, 1–55.

8. Peterson, R. A. (2000). *Constructing effective questionnaires*. Thousand Oaks, CA: Sage.

9. Schwarz, N. (1999). Self-reports: How the questions shape the answers. *American Psychologist, 54*, 93–105.

10. Peterson, R. A. (2000). *Constructing effective questionnaires*. Thousand Oaks, CA: Sage.

11. Lahaut, V. M. H. C. J., Jansen, H. A. M., van de Mheen, D., & Garretsen, H. F. L. (2002). Non-response bias in a sample survey on alcohol consumption. *Alcohol and Alcoholism, 37*, 256–260.

12. Groves, R. M., Fowler, F. J., Couper, M. P., Lepkowski, J. M., Singer, E., & Tourangeau, R. (2004). *Survey methodology*. Hoboken, NJ: Wiley.

# CHAPTER 10
# Single-Subject Research

Researcher Vance Hall and his colleagues were faced with the challenge of increasing the extent to which six disruptive elementary school students stayed focused on their schoolwork (Hall, Lund, & Jackson, 1968).[1] For each of several days, the researchers carefully recorded whether or not each student was doing schoolwork every 10 seconds during a 30-minute period. Once they had established this baseline, they introduced a treatment. The treatment was that when the student was doing schoolwork, the teacher gave him or her positive attention in the form of a comment like "good work" or a pat on the shoulder. The result was that all of the students dramatically increased their time spent on schoolwork and decreased their disruptive behavior during this treatment phase. For example, a student named Robbie originally spent 25% of his time on schoolwork and the other 75% "snapping rubber bands, playing with toys from his pocket, and talking and laughing with peers" (p. 3). During the treatment phase, however, he spent 71% of his time on schoolwork and only 29% on other activities. Finally, when the researchers had the teacher stop giving positive attention, the students all decreased their studying and increased their disruptive behavior. This confirmed that it was, in fact, the positive attention that was responsible for the increase in studying. This was one of the first studies to show that attending to positive behavior—and ignoring negative behavior—could be a quick and effective way to deal with problem behavior in an applied setting.

**FIGURE 10.1**
Single-subject research has shown that positive attention from a teacher for studying can increase studying and decrease disruptive behavior.

Source: © Thinkstock

Most of this book is about what can be called group research, which typically involves studying a large number of participants and combining their data to draw general conclusions about human behavior. The study by Hall and his colleagues, in contrast, is an example of single-subject research, which typically involves studying a small number of participants and focusing closely on each individual. In this chapter, we consider this alternative approach. We begin with an overview of single-subject research, including some assumptions on which it is based, who conducts it, and why they do. We then look at some basic single-subject research designs and how the data from those designs are analyzed. Finally, we consider some of the strengths and weaknesses of single-subject research as compared with group research and see how these two approaches can complement each other.

# 10.1 Overview of Single-Subject Research

## Learning Objectives

1. Explain what single-subject research is, including how it differs from other types of psychological research.
2. Explain what case studies are, including some of their strengths and weaknesses.
3. Explain who uses single-subject research and why.

# What Is Single-Subject Research?

**single-subject research**

A type of quantitative research that involves examining in detail the behavior of each of a small number of participants.

**group research**

A type of quantitative research that involves studying a large number of participants and examining their behavior in terms of means, standard deviations, and other group-level statistics.

**case study**

A detailed description of an individual case.

**Single-subject research** is a type of quantitative research that involves studying the behavior of each of a small number of participants in detail. Note that the term *single-subject* does not mean that only one participant is studied; it is more typical for there to be somewhere between two and 10 participants. (This is why single-subject research designs are sometimes called small-*n* designs, where *n* is the statistical symbol for the sample size.) Single-subject research can be contrasted with **group research**, which typically involves studying large numbers of participants and examining their behavior primarily in terms of group means, standard deviations, and so on. The majority of this book is devoted to understanding group research, which is the most common approach in psychology. But single-subject research is an important alternative, and it is the primary approach in some areas of psychology.

Before continuing, it is important to distinguish single-subject research from two other approaches, both of which involve studying a small number of participants in detail. One is qualitative research, which focuses on understanding people's subjective experience by collecting relatively unstructured data (e.g., detailed interviews) and analyzing those data using narrative rather than quantitative techniques. (Qualitative research is discussed more thoroughly in Chapter 7.) Single-subject research, in contrast, focuses on understanding objective behavior through experimental manipulation and control, collecting highly structured data, and analyzing those data quantitatively.

It is also important to distinguish single-subject research from case studies. A **case study** is a detailed description of an individual, which can include both qualitative and quantitative analyses. (Case studies that include only qualitative analyses can be considered a type of qualitative research.) The history of psychology is filled with influential cases studies, such as Sigmund Freud's description of "Anna O." (see "The Case of "Anna O."") and John Watson and Rosalie Rayner's description of Little Albert (Watson & Rayner, 1920),[2] who learned to fear a white rat—along with other furry objects—when the researchers made a loud noise while he was playing with the rat. Case studies can be useful for suggesting new research questions and for illustrating general principles. They can also help researchers understand rare phenomena, such as the effects of damage to a specific part of the human brain. As a general rule, however, case studies cannot substitute for carefully designed group or single-subject research studies. One reason is that case studies usually do not allow researchers to determine whether specific events are causally related, or even related at all. For example, if a patient is described in a case study as having been sexually abused as a child and then as having developed an eating disorder as a teenager, there is no way to determine whether these two events had anything to do with each other. A second reason is that an individual case can always be unusual in some way and therefore be unrepresentative of people more generally. Thus case studies have serious problems with both internal and external validity.

## The Case of "Anna O."

Sigmund Freud used the case of a young woman he called "Anna O." to illustrate many principles of his theory of psychoanalysis (Freud, 1961).[3] (Her real name was Bertha Pappenheim, and she was an early feminist who went on to make important contributions to the field of social work.) Anna had come to Freud's colleague Josef Breuer around 1880 with a variety of odd physical and psychological symptoms. One of them was that for several weeks she was unable to drink any fluids. According to Freud,

> She would take up the glass of water that she longed for, but as soon as it touched her lips she would push it away like someone suffering from hydrophobia....She lived only on fruit, such as melons, etc., so as to lessen her tormenting thirst (p. 9).

But according to Freud, a breakthrough came one day while Anna was under hypnosis.

> [S]he grumbled about her English "lady-companion," whom she did not care for, and went on to describe, with every sign of disgust, how she had once gone into this lady's room and how her little dog—horrid creature!—had drunk out of a glass there. The patient had said nothing, as she had wanted to be polite. After giving further energetic expression to the anger she had held back, she asked for something to drink, drank a large quantity of water without any difficulty, and awoke from her hypnosis with the glass at her lips; and thereupon the disturbance vanished, never to return.

Freud's interpretation was that Anna had repressed the memory of this incident along with the emotion that it triggered and that this was what had caused her inability to drink. Furthermore, her recollection of the incident, along with her expression of the emotion she had repressed, caused the symptom to go away.

As an illustration of Freud's theory, the case study of Anna O. is quite effective. As evidence for the theory, however, it is essentially worthless. The description provides no way of knowing whether Anna had really repressed the memory of the dog drinking from the glass, whether this repression had caused her inability to drink, or whether recalling this "trauma" relieved the symptom. It is also unclear from this case study how typical or atypical Anna's experience was.

**FIGURE 10.2**
"Anna O." was the subject of a famous case study used by Freud to illustrate the principles of psychoanalysis.

Source: http://en.wikipedia.org/wiki/File:Pappenheim_1882.jpg

# Assumptions of Single-Subject Research

Again, single-subject research involves studying a small number of participants and focusing intensively on the behavior of each one. But why take this approach instead of the group approach? There are several important assumptions underlying single-subject research, and it will help to consider them now.

First and foremost is the assumption that it is important to focus intensively on the behavior of individual participants. One reason for this is that group research can hide individual differences and generate results that do not represent the behavior of any individual. For example, a treatment that has a positive effect for half the people exposed to it but a negative effect for the other half would, on average, appear to have no effect at all. Single-subject research, however, would likely reveal these individual differences. A second reason to focus intensively on individuals is that sometimes it is the behavior of a particular individual that is primarily of interest. A school psychologist, for example, might be interested in changing the behavior of a particular disruptive student. Although previous published research (both single-subject and group research) is likely to provide some guidance on how to do this, conducting a study on this student would be more direct and probably more effective.

A second assumption of single-subject research is that it is important to discover causal relationships through the manipulation of an independent variable, the careful measurement of a dependent variable, and the control of extraneous variables. For this reason, single-subject research is often considered a type of experimental research with good internal validity. Recall, for example, that Hall and his colleagues measured their dependent variable (studying) many times—first under a no-treatment control condition, then under a treatment condition (positive teacher attention), and then again under the control condition. Because there was a clear increase in studying when the treatment was introduced, a decrease when it was removed, and an increase when it was reintroduced, there is little doubt that the treatment was the cause of the improvement.

A third assumption of single-subject research is that it is important to study strong and consistent effects that have biological or social importance. Applied researchers, in particular, are interested in treatments that have substantial effects on important behaviors and that can be implemented reliably in the real-world contexts in which they occur. This is sometimes referred to as **social validity** (Wolf, 1976).[4] The study by Hall and his colleagues, for example, had good social validity because it showed strong and consistent effects of positive teacher attention on a behavior that is of obvious importance to teachers, parents, and students. Furthermore, the teachers found the treatment easy to implement, even in their often chaotic elementary school classrooms.

**social validity**

The extent to which a single-subject study focuses on an intervention that has a substantial effect on an important behavior and can be implemented reliably in the real-world contexts (e.g., by teachers in a classroom) in which that behavior occurs.

# Who Uses Single-Subject Research?

Single-subject research has been around as long as the field of psychology itself. In the late 1800s, one of psychology's founders, Wilhelm Wundt, studied sensation and consciousness by focusing intensively on each of a small number of research participants. Herman Ebbinghaus's research on memory and Ivan Pavlov's research on classical conditioning are other early examples, both of which are still described in almost every introductory psychology textbook.

In the middle of the 20th century, B. F. Skinner clarified many of the assumptions underlying single-subject research and refined many of its techniques (Skinner, 1938).[5] He and other researchers then used it to describe how rewards, punishments, and other environmental factors affect behavior over time. This work was carried out primarily using nonhuman subjects—mostly rats and pigeons. This approach, which Skinner called the **experimental analysis of behavior**—remains an important subfield of psychology and continues to rely almost exclusively on single-subject research. For excellent examples of this work, look at any issue of the *Journal of the Experimental Analysis of Behavior*. By the 1960s, many researchers were interested in using this approach to conduct applied research primarily with humans—a subfield now called **applied behavior analysis** (Baer, Wolf, & Risley, 1968).[6] Applied behavior analysis plays an especially important role in contemporary research on developmental disabilities, education, organizational behavior, and health, among many other areas. Excellent examples of this work (including the study by Hall and his colleagues) can be found in the *Journal of Applied Behavior Analysis*.

**experimental analysis of behavior**

A subfield of psychology founded by B. F. Skinner that uses single-subject research—often with nonhuman animals—to study relationships primarily between environmental conditions and objectively observable behaviors.

**applied behavior analysis**

A subfield of psychology that uses single-subject research and applies the principles of behavior analysis to real-world problems in areas that include education, developmental disabilities, organizational behavior, and health behavior.

Although most contemporary single-subject research is conducted from the behavioral perspective, it can in principle be used to address questions framed in terms of any theoretical perspective. For example, a studying technique based on cognitive principles of learning and memory could be evaluated by testing it on individual high school students using the single-subject approach. The single-subject approach can also be used by clinicians who take any theoretical perspective—behavioral, cognitive, psychodynamic, or humanistic—to study processes of therapeutic change with individual clients and to document their clients' improvement (Kazdin, 1982).[7]

## Key Takeaways

- Single-subject research—which involves testing a small number of participants and focusing intensively on the behavior of each individual—is an important alternative to group research in psychology.

- Single-subject studies must be distinguished from case studies, in which an individual case is described in detail. Case studies can be useful for generating new research questions, for studying rare phenomena, and for illustrating general principles. However, they cannot substitute for carefully controlled experimental or correlational studies because they are low in internal and external validity.
- Single-subject research has been around since the beginning of the field of psychology. Today it is most strongly associated with the behavioral theoretical perspective, but it can in principle be used to study behavior from any perspective.

## Exercises

1. Practice: Find and read a published article in psychology that reports new single-subject research. (Try searching PsycINFO or Google Scholar using the key term *single-subject design*.) Write a short summary of the study.
2. Practice: Find and read a published case study in psychology. (Try searching PsycINFO or Google Scholar using the key term *case study*.) Then do the following:
    a. Describe one problem related to internal validity.
    b. Describe one problem related to external validity.
    c. Generate one hypothesis suggested by the case study that might be interesting to test in a systematic single-subject or group study.

# 10.2 Single-Subject Research Designs

## Learning Objectives

1. Describe the basic elements of a single-subject research design.
2. Design simple single-subject studies using reversal and multiple-baseline designs.
3. Explain how single-subject research designs address the issue of internal validity.
4. Interpret the results of simple, single-subject studies based on the visual inspection of graphed data.

## General Features of Single-Subject Designs

Before looking at any specific single-subject research designs, it will be helpful to consider some features that are common to most of them. Many of these features are illustrated in Figure 10.3, which shows the results of a generic single-subject study. First, the dependent variable (represented on the y-axis of the graph) is measured repeatedly over time (represented by the x-axis) at regular intervals. Second, the study is divided into distinct phases, and the participant is tested under one condition per phase. The conditions are often designated by capital letters: A, B, C, and so on. Thus Figure 10.3 represents a design in which the participant was tested first in one condition (A), then tested in another condition (B), and finally retested in the original condition (A). (This is called a reversal design and will be discussed in more detail shortly.)

**FIGURE 10.3** Results of a Generic Single-Subject Study Illustrating Several Principles of Single-Subject Research

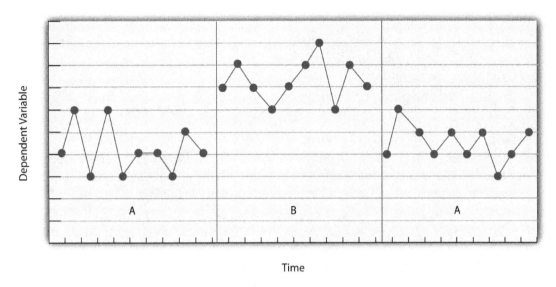

Another important aspect of single-subject research is that the change from one condition to the next does not usually occur after a fixed amount of time or number of observations. Instead, it depends on the participant's behavior. Specifically, the researcher waits until the participant's behavior in one condition becomes fairly consistent from observation to observation before changing conditions. This is sometimes referred to as the **steady state strategy** (Sidman, 1960).[8] The idea is that when the dependent variable has reached a steady state, then any change across conditions will be relatively easy to detect. Recall that we encountered this same principle when discussing experimental research more generally. The effect of an independent variable is easier to detect when the "noise" in the data is minimized.

**steady state strategy**

In single-subject research, allowing behavior to become fairly consistent from one observation to the next before changing conditions. This makes any effect of the treatment easier to detect.

# Reversal Designs

**reversal design**

A single-subject research design that begins with a baseline condition with no treatment, followed by the introduction of a treatment, and after that a return to the baseline condition. It can include additional treatment conditions and returns to baseline.

**ABA design**

The simplest reversal design, in which there is a baseline condition (A), followed by a treatment condition (B), followed by a return to baseline (A).

**baseline**

A condition in a single-subject research design in which the dependent variable is measured repeatedly in the absence of any treatment. Most designs begin with a baseline condition, and many return to the baseline condition at least once.

The most basic single-subject research design is the **reversal design**, also called the **ABA design**. During the first phase, A, a **baseline** is established for the dependent variable. This is the level of responding before any treatment is introduced, and therefore the baseline phase is a kind of control condition. When steady state responding is reached, phase B begins as the researcher introduces the treatment. There may be a period of adjustment to the treatment during which the behavior of interest becomes more variable and begins to increase or decrease. Again, the researcher waits until that dependent variable reaches a steady state so that it is clear whether and how much it has changed. Finally, the researcher removes the treatment and again waits until the dependent variable reaches a steady state. This basic reversal design can also be extended with the reintroduction of the treatment (ABAB), another return to baseline (ABABA), and so on.

The study by Hall and his colleagues was an ABAB reversal design. Figure 10.4 approximates the data for Robbie. The percentage of time he spent studying (the dependent variable) was low during the first baseline phase, increased during the first treatment phase until it leveled off, decreased during the second baseline phase, and again increased during the second treatment phase.

**FIGURE 10.4** An Approximation of the Results for Hall and Colleagues' Participant Robbie in Their ABAB Reversal Design

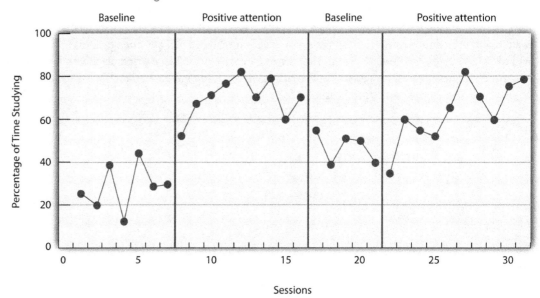

Why is the reversal—the removal of the treatment—considered to be necessary in this type of design? Why use an ABA design, for example, rather than a simpler AB design? Notice that an AB design is essentially an interrupted time-series design applied to an individual participant. Recall that one problem with that design is that if the dependent variable changes after the treatment is introduced, it is not always clear that the treatment was responsible for the change. It is possible that something else changed at around the same time and that this confounding variable is responsible for the change in the dependent variable. But if the dependent variable changes with the introduction of the treatment and then changes *back* with the removal of the treatment, it is much clearer that the treatment (and removal of the treatment) is the cause. In other words, the reversal greatly increases the internal validity of the study.

There are close relatives of the basic reversal design that allow for the evaluation of more than one treatment. In a **multiple-treatment reversal design**, a baseline phase is followed by separate phases in which different treatments are introduced. For example, a researcher might establish a baseline of studying behavior for a disruptive student (A), then introduce a treatment involving positive attention from the teacher (B), and then switch to a treatment involving mild punishment for not studying (C). The participant could then be returned to a baseline phase before reintroducing each treatment—perhaps in the reverse order as a way of controlling for carryover effects. This particular multiple-treatment reversal design could also be referred to as an ABCACB design.

In an **alternating treatments design**, two or more treatments are alternated relatively quickly on a regular schedule. For example, positive attention for studying could be used one day and mild punishment for not studying the next, and so on. Or one treatment could be implemented in the morning and another in the afternoon. The alternating treatments design can be a quick and effective way of comparing treatments, but only when the treatments are fast acting.

**multiple-treatment reversal design**

A single-subject research design in which phases that introduce different treatments are alternated.

**alternating treatments design**

A single-subject research design in which multiple treatments are alternated rapidly on a regular schedule.

## Multiple-Baseline Designs

There are two potential problems with the reversal design—both of which have to do with the removal of the treatment. One is that if a treatment is working, it may be unethical to remove it. For example, if a treatment seemed to reduce the incidence of self-injury in a developmentally disabled child, it would be unethical to remove that treatment just to show that the incidence of self-injury increases. The second problem is that the dependent variable may not return to baseline when the treatment is removed. For example, when positive attention for studying is removed, a student might continue to study at an increased rate. This could mean that the positive attention had a lasting effect on the student's studying, which of course would be good. But it could also mean that the positive attention was not really the cause of the increased studying in the first place. Perhaps something else happened at about the same time as the treatment—for example, the student's parents might have started rewarding him for good grades.

One solution to these problems is to use a **multiple-baseline design**, which is represented in Figure 10.5. In one version of the design, a baseline is established for each of several participants, and the treatment is then introduced for each one. In essence, each participant is tested in an AB design. The key to this design is that the treatment is introduced at a different *time* for each participant. The idea is that if the dependent variable changes when the treatment is introduced for one participant, it might be a coincidence. But if the dependent variable changes when the treatment is introduced for multiple participants—especially when the treatment is introduced at different times for the different participants—then it is extremely unlikely to be a coincidence.

**multiple-baseline design**

A single-subject research design in which multiple baselines are established for different participants, different dependent variables, or different contexts and the treatment is introduced at a different time for each baseline.

**FIGURE 10.5** Results of a Generic Multiple-Baseline Study
The treatment is introduced at a different time on each baseline. The different baselines can be for different participants (as shown here), different dependent variables, or different settings.

# Participant 1

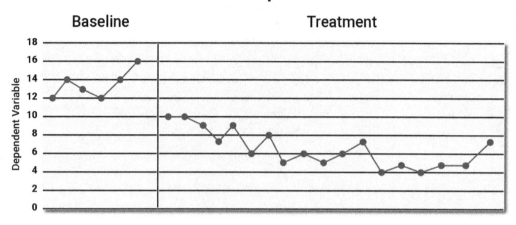

# Participant 2

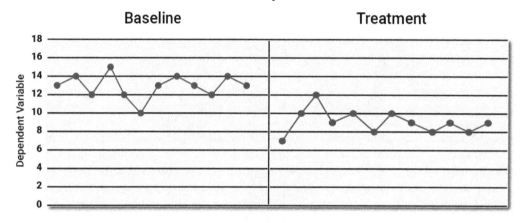

# Participant 3

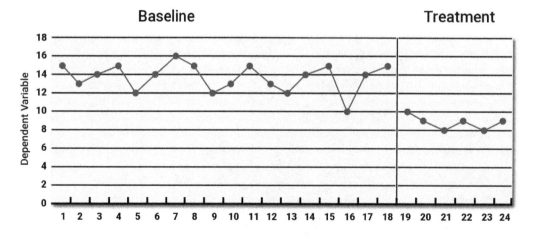

As an example, consider a study by Scott Ross and Robert Horner (Ross & Horner, 2009).[9] They were interested in how a school-wide bullying prevention program affected the bullying behavior of particular problem students. At each of three different schools, the researchers studied two students who had regularly engaged in bullying. During the baseline phase, they observed the students for 10-minute periods each day during lunch recess and counted the number of aggressive behaviors they exhibited toward their peers. (The researchers used handheld computers to help record the data.) After two weeks, they implemented the program at one school. After two more weeks, they implemented it at the second school. And after two more weeks, they implemented it at the third school. They found that the number of aggressive behaviors exhibited by each student dropped shortly after the program was implemented at his or her school. Notice that if the researchers had only studied one school or if they had introduced the treatment at the same time at all three schools, then it would be unclear whether the reduction in aggressive behaviors was due to the bullying program or something else that happened at about the same time it was introduced (e.g., a holiday, a television program, a change in the weather). But with their multiple-baseline design, this kind of coincidence would have to happen three separate times—a very unlikely occurrence—to explain their results.

In another version of the multiple-baseline design, multiple baselines are established for the same participant but for different dependent variables, and the treatment is introduced at a different time for each dependent variable. Imagine, for example, a study on the effect of setting clear goals on the productivity of an office worker who has two primary tasks: making sales calls and writing reports. Baselines for both tasks could be established. For example, the researcher could measure the number of sales calls made and reports written by the worker each week for several weeks. Then the goal-setting treatment could be introduced for one of these tasks, and at a later time the same treatment could be introduced for the other task. The logic is the same as before. If productivity increases on one task after the treatment is introduced, it is unclear whether the treatment caused the increase. But if productivity increases on both tasks after the treatment is introduced—especially when the treatment is introduced at two different times—then it seems much clearer that the treatment was responsible.

In yet a third version of the multiple-baseline design, multiple baselines are established for the same participant but in different settings. For example, a baseline might be established for the amount of time a child spends reading during his free time at school and during his free time at home. Then a treatment such as positive attention might be introduced first at school and later at home. Again, if the dependent variable changes after the treatment is introduced in each setting, then this gives the researcher confidence that the treatment is, in fact, responsible for the change.

# Data Analysis in Single-Subject Research

In addition to its focus on individual participants, single-subject research differs from group research in the way the data are typically analyzed. As we have seen throughout the book, group research involves combining data across participants. Group data are described using statistics such as means, standard deviations, Pearson's $r$, and so on to detect general patterns. Finally, inferential statistics are used to help decide whether the result for the sample is likely to generalize to the population. Single-subject research, by contrast, relies heavily on a very different approach called **visual inspection**. This means plotting individual participants' data as shown throughout this chapter, looking carefully at those data, and making judgments about whether and to what extent the independent variable had an effect on the dependent variable. Inferential statistics are typically not used.

**visual inspection**

The primary approach to data analysis in single-subject research, which involves graphing the data and making a judgment as to whether and to what extent the independent variable affected the dependent variable.

**level**

One factor that is considered in the visual inspection of single-subject data. The overall level of the dependent variable within a condition.

**trend**

One factor that is considered in the visual inspection of single-subject data. An increase or decrease in the independent variable over several observations.

**latency**

One factor that is considered in the visual inspection of single-subject data. The time between the change in conditions and the change in the dependent variable.

In visually inspecting their data, single-subject researchers take several factors into account. One of them is changes in the **level** of the dependent variable from condition to condition. If the dependent variable is much higher or much lower in one condition than another, this suggests that the treatment had an effect. A second factor is **trend**, which refers to gradual increases or decreases in the dependent variable across observations. If the dependent variable begins increasing or decreasing with a change in conditions, then again this suggests that the treatment had an effect. It can be especially telling when a trend changes directions—for example, when an unwanted behavior is increasing during baseline but then begins to decrease with the introduction of the treatment. A third factor is **latency**, which is the time it takes for the dependent variable to begin changing after a change in conditions. In general, if a change in the dependent variable begins shortly after a change in conditions, this suggests that the treatment was responsible.

In the top panel of Figure 10.6, there are fairly obvious changes in the level and trend of the dependent variable from condition to condition. Furthermore, the latencies of these changes are short; the change happens immediately. This pattern of results strongly suggests that the treatment was responsible for the changes in the dependent variable. In the bottom panel of Figure 10.6, however, the changes in level are fairly small. And although there appears to be an increasing trend in the treatment condition, it looks as though it might be a continuation of a trend that had already begun during baseline. This pattern of results strongly suggests that the treatment was not responsible for any changes in the dependent variable—at least not to the extent that single-subject researchers typically hope to see.

**FIGURE 10.6**
Visual inspection of the data suggests an effective treatment in the top panel but an ineffective treatment in the bottom panel.

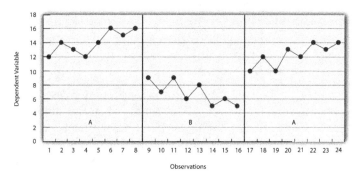

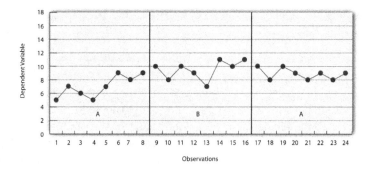

The results of single-subject research can also be analyzed using statistical procedures—and this is becoming more common. There are many different approaches, and single-subject researchers continue to debate which are the most useful. One approach parallels what is typically done in group research. The mean and standard deviation of each participant's responses under each condition are computed and compared, and inferential statistical tests such as the *t* test or analysis of variance are applied (Fisch, 2001).[10] (Note that averaging *across* participants is less common.) Another approach is to compute the **percentage of nonoverlapping data** (PND) for each participant (Scruggs & Mastropieri, 2001).[11] This is the percentage of responses in the treatment condition that are more extreme than the most extreme response in a relevant control condition. In the study of Hall and his colleagues, for example, all measures of Robbie's study time in the first treatment condition were greater than the highest measure in the first baseline, for a PND of 100%. The greater the percentage of nonoverlapping data, the stronger the treatment effect. Still, formal statistical approaches to data analysis in single-subject research are generally considered a supplement to visual inspection, not a replacement for it.

**percentage of nonoverlapping data**

A statistic sometimes used in single-subject research. The percentage of observations in a treatment condition that are more extreme than the most extreme observation in a relevant baseline condition.

## Key Takeaways

- Single-subject research designs typically involve measuring the dependent variable repeatedly over time and changing conditions (e.g., from baseline to treatment) when the dependent variable has reached a steady state. This approach allows the researcher to see whether changes in the independent variable are causing changes in the dependent variable.

- In a reversal design, the participant is tested in a baseline condition, then tested in a treatment condition, and then returned to baseline. If the dependent variable changes with the introduction of the treatment and then changes back with the return to baseline, this provides strong evidence of a treatment effect.

- In a multiple-baseline design, baselines are established for different participants, different dependent variables, or different settings—and the treatment is introduced at a different time on each baseline. If the introduction of the treatment is followed by a change in the dependent variable on each baseline, this provides strong evidence of a treatment effect.

- Single-subject researchers typically analyze their data by graphing them and making judgments about whether the independent variable is affecting the dependent variable based on level, trend, and latency.

## Exercises

1. Practice: Design a simple, single-subject study (using either a reversal or multiple-baseline design) to answer the following questions. Be sure to specify the treatment, operationally define the dependent variable, decide when and where the observations will be made, and so on.

   a. Does positive attention from a parent increase a child's toothbrushing behavior?

   b. Does self-testing while studying improve a student's performance on weekly spelling tests?

   c. Does regular exercise help relieve depression?

2. Practice: Create a graph that displays the hypothetical results for the study you designed in Exercise 1. Write a paragraph in which you describe what the results show. Be sure to comment on level, trend, and latency.

# 10.3 The Single-Subject Versus Group "Debate"

Single-subject research is similar to group research—especially experimental group research—in many ways. They are both quantitative approaches that try to establish causal relationships by manipulating an independent variable, measuring a dependent variable, and controlling extraneous variables. But there are important differences between these approaches too, and these differences sometimes lead to disagreements. It is worth addressing the most common points of disagreement between single-subject researchers and group researchers and how these disagreements can be resolved. As we will see, single-subject research and group research are probably best conceptualized as complementary approaches.

## Data Analysis

One set of disagreements revolves around the issue of data analysis. Some advocates of group research worry that visual inspection is inadequate for deciding whether and to what extent a treatment has affected a dependent variable. One specific concern is that visual inspection is not sensitive enough to detect weak effects. A second is that visual inspection can be unreliable, with different researchers reaching different conclusions about the same set of data (Danov & Symons, 2008).[12] A third is that the results of visual inspection—an overall judgment of whether or not a treatment was effective—cannot be clearly and efficiently summarized or compared across studies (unlike the measures of relationship strength typically used in group research).

In general, single-subject researchers share these concerns. However, they also argue that their use of the steady state strategy, combined with their focus on strong and consistent effects, minimizes most of them. If the effect of a treatment is difficult to detect by visual inspection because the effect is weak or the data are noisy, then single-subject researchers look for ways to increase the strength of the effect or reduce the noise in the data by controlling extraneous variables (e.g., by administering the treatment more consistently). If the effect is still difficult to detect, then they are likely to consider it neither strong enough nor consistent enough to be of further interest. Many single-subject researchers also point out that statistical analysis is becoming increasingly common and that many of them are using it as a supplement to visual inspection—especially for the purpose of comparing results across studies (Scruggs & Mastropieri, 2001).[13]

Turning the tables, some advocates of single-subject research worry about the way that group researchers analyze their data. Specifically, they point out that focusing on group means can be highly misleading. Again, imagine that a treatment has a strong positive effect on half the people exposed to it and an equally strong negative effect on the other half. In a traditional between-subjects experiment, the positive effect on half the participants in the treatment condition would be statistically cancelled out by the negative effect on the other half. The mean for the treatment group would then be the same as the mean for the control group, making it seem as though the treatment had no effect when in fact it had a strong effect on every single participant!

But again, group researchers share this concern. Although they do focus on group statistics, they also emphasize the importance of examining distributions of individual scores. For example, if some participants were positively affected by a treatment and others negatively affected by it, this would produce a bimodal distribution of scores and could be detected by looking at a histogram of the data. The use of within-subjects designs is another strategy that allows group researchers to observe effects at the individual level and to specify what percentage of individuals exhibit strong, medium, weak, and even negative effects.

# External Validity

The second issue about which single-subject and group researchers sometimes disagree has to do with external validity—the ability to generalize the results of a study beyond the people and situation actually studied. In particular, advocates of group research point out the difficulty in knowing whether results for just a few participants are likely to generalize to others in the population. Imagine, for example, that in a single-subject study, a treatment has been shown to reduce self-injury for each of two developmentally disabled children. Even if the effect is strong for these two children, how can one know whether this treatment is likely to work for other developmentally disabled children?

Again, single-subject researchers share this concern. In response, they note that the strong and consistent effects they are typically interested in—even when observed in small samples—are likely to generalize to others in the population. Single-subject researchers also note that they place a strong emphasis on replicating their research results. When they observe an effect with a small sample of participants, they typically try to replicate it with another small sample—perhaps with a slightly different type of participant or under slightly different conditions. Each time they observe similar results, they rightfully become more confident in the generality of those results. Single-subject researchers can also point to the fact that the principles of classical and operant conditioning—most of which were discovered using the single-subject approach—have been successfully generalized across an incredibly wide range of species and situations.

And again turning the tables, single-subject researchers have concerns of their own about the external validity of group research. One extremely important point they make is that studying large groups of participants does not entirely solve the problem of generalizing to other *individuals*. Imagine, for example, a treatment that has been shown to have a small positive effect on average in a large group study. It is likely that although many participants exhibited a small positive effect, others exhibited a large positive effect, and still others exhibited a small negative effect. When it comes to applying this treatment to another large *group*, we might be fairly sure that it will have a small effect on average. But when it comes to applying this treatment to another *individual*, we cannot be sure whether it will have a small, a large, or even a negative effect. Another point that single-subject researchers make is that group researchers also face a similar problem when they study a single situation and then generalize their results to other situations. For example, researchers who conduct a study on the effect of cell phone use on drivers on a closed oval track probably want to apply their results to drivers in many other real-world driving situations. But notice that this requires generalizing from a single situation to a population of situations. Thus the ability to generalize is based on much more than just the sheer number of participants one has studied. It requires a careful consideration of the similarity of the participants *and* situations studied to the population of participants and situations that one wants to generalize to (Shadish, Cook, & Campbell, 2002).[14]

# Single-Subject and Group Research as Complementary Methods

As with quantitative and qualitative research, it is probably best to conceptualize single-subject research and group research as complementary methods that have different strengths and weaknesses and that are appropriate for answering different kinds of research questions (Kazdin, 1982).[15] Single-subject research is particularly good for testing the effectiveness of treatments on individuals when the focus is on strong, consistent, and biologically or socially important effects. It is especially useful when the behavior of particular individuals is of interest. Clinicians who work with only one individual at a time may find that it is their only option for doing systematic quantitative research.

Group research, on the other hand, is good for testing the effectiveness of treatments at the group level. Among the advantages of this approach is that it allows researchers to detect weak effects, which can be of interest for many reasons. For example, finding a weak treatment effect might lead to refinements of the treatment that eventually produce a larger and more meaningful effect. Group research is also good for studying interactions between treatments and participant characteristics. For example, if a treatment is effective for those who are high in motivation to change and ineffective for those who are low in motivation to change, then a group design can detect this much more efficiently than a single-subject design. Group research is also necessary to answer questions that cannot be addressed using the single-subject approach, including questions about independent variables that cannot be manipulated (e.g., number of siblings, extroversion, culture).

Finally, it is important to understand that the single-subject and group approaches represent different research traditions. This factor is probably the most important one affecting which approach a researcher uses. Researchers in the experimental analysis of behavior and applied behavior analysis learn to conceptualize their research questions in ways that are amenable to the single-subject approach. Researchers in most other areas of psychology learn to conceptualize their research questions in ways that are amenable to the group approach. At the same time, there are many topics in psychology in which research from the two traditions have informed each other and been successfully integrated. One example is research suggesting that both animals and humans have an innate "number sense"—an awareness of how many objects or events of a particular type have they have experienced without actually having to count them (Dehaene, 2011).[16] Single-subject research with rats and birds and group research with human infants have shown strikingly similar abilities in those populations to discriminate small numbers of objects and events. This number sense—which probably evolved long before humans did—may even be the foundation of humans' advanced mathematical abilities.

## Key Takeaways

- Differences between single-subject research and group research sometimes lead to disagreements between single-subject and group researchers. These disagreements center on the issues of data analysis and external validity (especially generalization to other people).
- Single-subject research and group research are probably best seen as complementary methods, with different strengths and weaknesses, that are appropriate for answering different kinds of research questions.

## Exercises

1. Discussion: Imagine you have conducted a single-subject study showing a positive effect of a treatment on the behavior of a man with social anxiety disorder. Your research has been criticized on the grounds that it cannot be generalized to others. How could you respond to this criticism?

2. Discussion: Imagine you have conducted a group study showing a positive effect of a treatment on the behavior of a group of people with social anxiety disorder, but your research has been criticized on the grounds that "average" effects cannot be generalized to individuals. How could you respond to this criticism?

3. Practice: Redesign as a group study the study by Hall and his colleagues described at the beginning of this chapter. List the strengths and weaknesses of your new study compared with the original study.

4. Practice: The generation effect refers to the fact that people who generate information as they are learning it (e.g., by self-testing) recall it better later than do people who simply review information. Design a single-subject study on the generation effect applied to college students learning brain anatomy.

# Endnotes

1. Hall, R. V., Lund, D., & Jackson, D. (1968). Effects of teacher attention on study behavior. *Journal of Applied Behavior Analysis, 1*, 1–12.
2. Watson, J. B., & Rayner, R. (1920). Conditioned emotional reactions. *Journal of Experimental Psychology, 3*, 1–14.
3. Freud, S. (1961). *Five lectures on psycho-analysis*. New York, NY: Norton.
4. Wolf, M. (1976). Social validity: The case for subjective measurement or how applied behavior analysis is finding its heart. *Journal of Applied Behavior Analysis, 11*, 203–214.
5. Skinner, B. F. (1938). *The behavior of organisms: An experimental analysis*. New York, NY: Appleton-Century-Crofts.
6. Baer, D. M., Wolf, M. M., & Risley, T. R. (1968). Some current dimensions of applied behavior analysis. *Journal of Applied Behavior Analysis, 1*, 91–97.
7. Kazdin, A. E. (1982). *Single-case research designs: Methods for clinical and applied settings*. New York, NY: Oxford University Press.
8. Sidman, M. (1960). *Tactics of scientific research: Evaluating experimental data in psychology*. Boston, MA: Authors Cooperative.
9. Ross, S. W., & Horner, R. H. (2009). Bully prevention in positive behavior support. *Journal of Applied Behavior Analysis, 42*, 747–759.
10. Fisch, G. S. (2001). Evaluating data from behavioral analysis: Visual inspection or statistical models. *Behavioural Processes, 54*, 137–154.
11. Scruggs, T. E., & Mastropieri, M. A. (2001). How to summarize single-participant research: Ideas and applications. *Exceptionality, 9*, 227–244.
12. Danov, S. E., & Symons, F. E. (2008). A survey evaluation of the reliability of visual inspection and functional analysis graphs. *Behavior Modification, 32*, 828–839.
13. Scruggs, T. E., & Mastropieri, M. A. (2001). How to summarize single-participant research: Ideas and applications. *Exceptionality, 9*, 227–244.
14. Shadish, W. R., Cook, T. D., & Campbell, D. T. (2002). *Experimental and quasi-experimental designs for generalized causal inference*. Boston, MA: Houghton Mifflin.
15. Kazdin, A. E. (1982). *Single-case research designs: Methods for clinical and applied settings*. New York, NY: Oxford University Press.
16. Dehaene, S. (2011). *The number sense: How the mind creates mathematics* (2nd ed.). New York, NY: Oxford.

# CHAPTER 11
# Presenting Research

*Research is complete only when the results are shared with the scientific community.*

— American Psychological Association (2006, p. 9)[1]

Imagine that you have identified an interesting research question, reviewed the relevant literature, designed and conducted an empirical study, and drawn your conclusions. There is still one more step in the process of conducting scientific research. It is time to add your research to the literature so that others can learn from it and build on it. Remember that science is a social process—a large-scale collaboration among many researchers distributed across space and time. For this reason, it could be argued that unless you make your research public in some form, you are not really engaged in science at all.

In this chapter, we look at how to present your research effectively. We begin with a discussion of American Psychological Association (APA) style—the primary approach to writing taken by researchers in psychology and related fields. Then we consider how to write an APA-style empirical research report. Finally, we look at some of the many other ways in which researchers present their work, including review and theoretical articles, theses and other student papers, and talks and posters at professional meetings.

# 11.1 American Psychological Association (APA) Style

## Learning Objectives

1. Define APA style and list several of its most important characteristics.
2. Identify three levels of APA style and give examples of each.
3. Identify multiple sources of information about APA style.

# What Is APA Style?

**APA style** is a set of guidelines for writing in psychology and related fields. These guidelines are set down in the ***Publication Manual of the American Psychological Association*** (APA, 2006).[2] The *Publication Manual* originated in 1929 as a short journal article that provided basic standards for preparing manuscripts to be submitted for publication. It was later expanded and published as a book by the association and is now in its sixth edition. The primary purpose of APA style is to facilitate scientific communication by promoting clear writing and by standardizing the organization and content of research articles and book chapters. It is easier to write about research when you know what information to present, the order in which to present it, and even the style in which to present it. Likewise, it is easier to read about research when it is presented in familiar and expected ways.

APA style is best thought of as a "genre" of writing that is appropriate for presenting the results of psychological research—especially in academic and professional contexts. It is not synonymous with "good writing" in general. You would not write a literary analysis for an English class, even if it were based on psychoanalytic concepts, in APA style. You would write it in Modern Language Association (MLA) style instead. And you would not write a newspaper article, even if it were about a new breakthrough in behavioral neuroscience, in APA style. You would write it in Associated Press (AP) style instead. At the same time, you would not write an empirical research report in MLA style, in AP style, or in the style of a romance novel, an e-mail to a friend, or a shopping list. You would write it in APA style. Part of being a good writer in general is adopting a style that is appropriate to the writing task at hand. For writing about psychological research, this is APA style.

# The Levels of APA Style

Because APA style consists of a large number and variety of guidelines—the *Publication Manual* is nearly 300 pages long—it can be useful to think about it in terms of three basic levels. The first is the overall **organization** of an article (covered in Chapter 2 of the *Publication Manual*). Empirical research reports, in particular, have several distinct sections that always appear in the same order:

1. **Title page.** Presents the article title and author names and affiliations.
2. **Abstract.** Summarizes the research.
3. **Introduction.** Describes previous research and the rationale for the current study.
4. **Method.** Describes how the study was conducted.
5. **Results.** Describes the results of the study.
6. **Discussion.** Summarizes the study and discusses its implications.
7. **References.** Lists the references cited throughout the article.

The second level of APA style can be referred to as **high-level style** (covered in Chapter 3 of the *Publication Manual*), which includes guidelines for clear writing. There are two important themes here. One is that APA-style writing is formal rather than informal. It adopts a tone that is appropriate for communicating with professional colleagues—other researchers and practitioners—who share an interest in the topic. Beyond this shared interest, however, these colleagues are not necessarily similar to the writer or to each other. A graduate student in California might be writing an article that will be read by a young psychotherapist in New York City and a respected professor of psychology in Tokyo. Thus formal writing avoids slang, contractions, pop culture references, humor, and other elements that would be acceptable in talking with a friend or in writing informally.

The second theme of high-level APA style is that it is straightforward. This means that it communicates ideas as simply and clearly as possible, putting the focus on the ideas themselves and not on how they are communicated. Thus APA-style writing minimizes literary devices such as metaphor, imagery, irony, suspense, and so on. Again, humor is kept to a minimum. Sentences are short and direct. Technical terms must be used, but they are used to improve communication, not simply to make the writing sound more "scientific." For example, if participants immersed their hands in a bucket of ice water, it is better just to write this than to write that they "were subjected to a pain-inducement apparatus." At the same time, however, there is no better way to communicate that a between-subjects design was used than to use the term "between-subjects design."

## APA Style and the Values of Psychology

Robert Madigan and his colleagues have argued that APA style has a deeper purpose that even many researchers do not recognize (Madigan, Johnson, & Linton, 1995).[3] Specifically, it promotes psychologists' scientific values and assumptions. From this perspective, many features of APA style that at first seem arbitrary actually make good sense. Following are several features of APA-style writing and the scientific values or assumptions they reflect.

**TABLE 11.1**

| APA style feature | Scientific value or assumption |
|---|---|
| There are very few direct quotations of other researchers. | The phenomena and theories of psychology are objective and do not depend on the specific words a particular researcher used to describe them. |
| Criticisms are directed at other researchers' work but not at them personally. | The focus of scientific research is on drawing general conclusions about the world, not on the personalities of particular researchers. |
| There are many references and reference citations. | Scientific research is a large-scale collaboration among many researchers. |
| Empirical research reports are organized with specific sections in a fixed order. | There is an ideal approach to conducting empirical research in psychology (even if this ideal is not always achieved in actual research). |
| Researchers tend to "hedge" their conclusions, e.g., "The results *suggest* that…" | Scientific knowledge is tentative and always subject to revision based on new empirical results. |

Another important element of high-level APA style is the avoidance of language that is biased against particular groups. This is not only to avoid offending people—why would you want to offend people who are interested in your work?—but also for the sake of scientific objectivity and accuracy. For example, the term *sexual orientation* should be used instead of *sexual preference* because people do not generally experience their orientation as a "preference," nor is it as easily changeable as this term suggests (Committee on Lesbian and Gay Concerns, APA, 1991).[4]

The general principles for avoiding biased language are fairly simple. First, be sensitive to labels by avoiding terms that are offensive or have negative connotations. This includes terms that identify people with a disorder or other problem they happen to have. For example, *patients with schizophrenia* is better than *schizophrenics*. Second, use more specific terms rather than more general ones. For example, *Mexican Americans* is better than *Hispanics* if everyone in the group is, in fact, Mexican American. Third, avoid objectifying research participants. Instead, acknowledge their active contribution to the research. For example, "The *students completed* the questionnaire" is better than "The *subjects were administered* the questionnaire." Note that this principle also makes for clearer, more engaging writing. Table 11.2 shows several more examples that follow these general principles.

**TABLE 11.2** Examples of Avoiding Biased Language

| Instead of... | Use... |
|---|---|
| man, men | men and women, people |
| firemen | firefighters |
| homosexuals, gays, bisexuals | lesbians, gay men, bisexual men, bisexual women |
| minority | specific group label (e.g., hispanic) |
| neurotics | people scoring high in neuroticism |
| special children | children with learning disabilities |

The previous edition of the *Publication Manual* strongly discouraged the use of the term *subjects* (except for nonhumans) and strongly encouraged the use of *participants* instead. The current edition, however, acknowledges that *subjects* can still be appropriate in referring to human participants in areas in which it has traditionally been used (e.g., basic memory research). But it also encourages the use of more specific terms when possible: *college students, children, respondents,* and so on.

**low-level style**

The most specific level of APA style. It refers to the extensive rules pertaining to spelling, grammar, the formatting of reference and reference citations, the creation of tables and figures, and so on.

The third level of APA style can be referred to as **low-level style** (covered in Chapter 4 through Chapter 7 of the *Publication Manual*.) Low-level style includes all the specific guidelines pertaining to spelling, grammar, references and reference citations, numbers and statistics, figures and tables, and so on. There are so many low-level guidelines that even experienced professionals need to consult the *Publication Manual* from time to time. Table 11.3 contains some of the most common types of APA style errors based on an analysis of manuscripts submitted to one professional journal over a 6-year period (Onwuegbuzie, Combs, Slate, & Frels, 2010).[5] These errors were committed by professional researchers but are probably similar to those that students commit the most too. See also "Online APA-Style Resources""Online APA-Style Resources" in this section and, of course, the *Publication Manual* itself.

**TABLE 11.3** Top 10 APA Style Errors

| Error type | Example |
|---|---|
| 1. Use of numbers | Failing to use numerals for 10 and above |
| 2. Hyphenation | Failing to hyphenate compound adjectives that precede a noun (e.g., "role playing technique" should be "role-playing technique") |
| 3. Use of *et al.* | Failing to use it after a reference is cited for the first time |
| 4. Headings | Not capitalizing headings correctly |
| 5. Use of *since* | Using *since* to mean *because* |
| 6. Tables and figures | Not formatting them in APA style; repeating information that is already given in the text |
| 7. Use of commas | Failing to use a comma before *and* or *or* in a series of three or more elements |
| 8. Use of abbreviations | Failing to spell out a term completely before introducing an abbreviation for it |
| 9. Spacing | Not consistently double-spacing between lines |
| 10. Use of & in references | Using *&* in the text or *and* in parentheses |

## Online APA-Style Resources

The best source of information on APA style is the *Publication Manual* itself. However, there are also many good websites on APA style, which do an excellent job of presenting the basics for beginning researchers. Here are a few of them.

- American Psychological Association's APA-style website: http://www.apastyle.org
- Doc Scribe's APA Basic for Research Papers: http://www.docstyles.com/apaindex.html
- Purdue Owl Online Writing Lab: http://owl.english.purdue.edu/owl/section/2/10/

# APA-Style References and Citations

Because science is a large-scale collaboration among researchers, references to the work of other researchers are extremely important. Their importance is reflected in the extensive and detailed set of rules for formatting and using them.

## References

At the end of an APA-style article or book chapter is a list that contains **references** to all the works cited in the text (and *only* the works cited in the text). The reference list begins on its own page, with the heading, "References," centered in upper and lower case. The references themselves are then listed alphabetically according to the last names of the first named author. (As in the rest of an APA-style manuscript, *everything* is double-spaced.) Many different kinds of works might be cited in APA-style articles and book chapters, including magazine articles, websites, government documents, and even television shows. Of course, you should consult the *Publication Manual* or "Online APA-Style Resources" for details on how to format them. Here we will focus on formatting references for the three most common kinds of works cited in APA style: journal articles, books, and book chapters.

**references**

The formatted publication information about a work that is cited in an APA-style article or book chapter. The references appear in a reference list at the end of the article or book chapter. "Reference" can also mean the work itself.

### Journal Articles

For journal articles, the generic format for a reference is as follows:

Author, A. A., Author, B. B., & Author, C. C. (year). Title of article. *Title of Journal, xx*, pp–pp. doi:xx.xxxxxxxxxx

Here is a concrete example:

Adair, J. G., & Vohra, N. (2003). The explosion of knowledge, references, and citations: Psychology's unique response to a crisis. *American Psychologist, 58*, 15–23. doi: 10.1037/0003-066X.58.1.15

There are several things to notice here. The reference includes a hanging indent. That is, the first line of the reference is not indented but all subsequent lines are. The authors' names appear in the same order as on the article, which reflects the authors' relative contributions to the research. Only the authors' last names and initials appear, and the names are separated by commas with an ampersand (&) between the last two. This is true even when there are only two authors. Only the first word of the article title is capitalized. The only exceptions are for words that are proper nouns or adjectives (e.g., "Freudian") or if there is a subtitle, in which case the first word of the subtitle is also capitalized. In the journal title, however, all the important words are capitalized. The journal title and volume number are italicized. At the very end of the reference is the digital object identifier (DOI), which provides a permanent link to the location of the article on the Internet. Include this if it is available. It can generally be found in the record for the item on an electronic database (e.g., PsycINFO) and is usually displayed on the first page of the published article.

## Books

For a book, the generic format and a concrete example are as follows:

Author, A. A. (year). *Title of book*. Location: Publisher.

Milgram, S. (1974). *Obedience to authority: An experimental view*. New York, NY: Harper & Row.

## Book Chapters

For a chapter in an edited book, the generic format and a concrete example are as follows:

Author, A. A., Author, B. B., & Author, C. C. (year). Title of chapter. In A. A. Editor, B. B. Editor, & C. C. Editor (Eds.), *Title of book* (pp. xxx–xxx). Location: Publisher.

Lilienfeld, S. O., & Lynn, S. J. (2003). Dissociative identity disorder: Multiple personalities, multiple controversies. In S. O. Lilienfeld, S. J. Lynn, & J. M. Lohr (Eds.), *Science and pseudoscience in clinical psychology* (pp. 109–142). New York, NY: Guilford Press.

Notice that references for books and book chapters are similar to those for journal articles, but there are several differences too. For an edited book, the names of the editors appear with their first and middle initials followed by their last names (not the other way around)—with the abbreviation "Eds." (or "Ed.," if there is only one) appearing in parentheses immediately after the final editor's name. Only the first word of a book title is capitalized (with the exceptions noted for article titles), and the entire title is italicized. For a chapter in an edited book, the page numbers of the chapter appear in parentheses after the book title with the abbreviation "pp." Finally, both formats end with the location and name of the publisher, separated by a colon.

## Reference Citations

**reference citation**

In the text of an APA-style article or book chapter, a mention of a specific reference. APA-style reference citations provide the authors' last names and the year of publication.

When you refer to another researcher's idea, you must include a **reference citation** in the text to the work in which that idea originally appeared and a full reference to that work in the reference list. What counts as an idea that must be cited? In general, this includes phenomena discovered by other researchers, theories they have developed, hypotheses they have derived, and specific methods they have used (e.g., specific questionnaires or stimulus materials). Citations should also appear for factual information that is not common knowledge so that other researchers can check that information for themselves. For example, in an article on the effect of cell phone use on driving ability, the writer might cite official statistics on the number of cell phone–related accidents that occur each year. Among the ideas that do not need citations are widely shared methodological and statistical concepts (e.g., between-subjects design, *t* test) and statements that are so broad that they would be difficult for anyone to argue with (e.g., "Working memory plays a role in many daily activities."). Be careful, though, because "common knowledge" about human behavior is often incorrect. Therefore, when in doubt, find an appropriate reference to cite or remove the questionable assertion.

When you cite a work in the text of your manuscript, there are two ways to do it. The parenthetical style of citation follows the idea that needs to be cited and includes the authors' last names and the year of publication in parentheses. Here are two examples:

*People can be surprisingly obedient to authority figures (Burger, 2008; Milgram, 1963).*

*Recent evidence suggests that men and women are about equally talkative (Mehl, Vazire, Ramirez-Esparza, Slatcher, & Pennebaker, 2007).*

Notice several things. One is that only the authors' last names are used; there are no first names or initials. Another is that this style of citation is often placed at the very end of the sentence, which minimizes its disruption to the flow of that sentence. Finally, notice that when there are multiple citations in the same set of parentheses, they are organized alphabetically by the name of the first author and separated by semicolons.

The second way to cite a work in the text of your manuscript is the narrative style, which uses the authors' last names as part of the sentence, followed immediately by the year of publication in parentheses. Here are two examples:

*Burger (2008) conducted a replication of Milgram's (1963) original obedience study.*

*Although many people believe that women are more talkative than men, Mehl, Vazire, Ramirez-Esparza, Slatcher, and Pennebaker (2007) found essentially no difference in the number of words spoken by male and female college students.*

Notice that for this style of citation the authors' names are treated grammatically as names of people. It is better to write "a replication of Milgram's (1963) study" than "a replication of Milgram (1963)." Second, when there are two authors the names are not separated by commas, but when there are three or more authors they are. Third, the word *and* (rather than an ampersand) is used to join the authors' names. Fourth, the year follows immediately after the final author's name. An additional point, which is not illustrated in these examples but is illustrated in the sample paper in Section 2, is that the year only needs to be included the first time a particular work is cited in the same paragraph.

There are no strict rules for deciding which of the two citation styles to use. Most articles and book chapters contain a mixture of the two, although the parenthetical style is much more common. The parenthetical style works well when you are discussing a general idea and especially when you want to include multiple citations for the same idea. The narrative style works well when you want to emphasize the person who conducted the research—for example, if you were comparing the theories of two prominent researchers. It also works well when you are describing a particular study in detail.

The third most common error in Table 11.3 has to do with the use of *et al.* This is an abbreviation for the Latin term *et alia*, which means "and others." In APA style, if an article or a book chapter has three, four, or five authors, you should include all their names when you first cite that work. After that, however, you should use the first author's name followed by "et al." If there are six or more authors, then "et al." should be used right from the start. Here are some examples:

> *Recall that Mehl et al. (2007) found that women and men spoke about the same number of words per day on average.*

> *There is a strong positive correlation between the number of daily hassles and the number of symptoms people experience (Kanner et al., 1981).*

Notice that there is no comma between the first author's name and "et al." Notice also that there is no period after "et" but there is one after "al." This is because "et" is a complete word and "al." is an abbreviation for the word *alia*.

## Key Takeaways

- APA style is a set of guidelines for writing in psychology. It is the genre of writing that psychologists use to communicate about their research with other researchers and practitioners.
- APA style can be seen as having three levels. There is the organization of a research article, the high-level style that includes writing in a formal and straightforward way, and the low-level style that consists of many specific rules of grammar, spelling, formatting of references, and so on.
- References and reference citations are an important part of APA style. There are specific rules for formatting references and for citing them in the text of an article.

## Exercises

1. Practice: Find a description of a research study in a popular magazine, newspaper, blog, or website. Then identify five specific differences between how that description is written and how it would be written in APA style.
2. Practice: Find and correct the errors in the following fictional APA-style references and citations.
   a. Walters, F. T., and DeLeon, M. (2010). Relationship Between Intrinsic Motivation and Accuracy of Academic Self-Evaluations Among High School Students. *Educational Psychology Quarterly*, 23, 234–256.
   b. Moore, Lilia S. (2007). Ethics in survey research. In M. Williams & P. L. Lee (eds.), Ethical Issues in Psychology (pp. 120–156), Boston, Psychological Research Press.

   c. Vang, C., Dumont, L. S., and Prescott, M. P. found that left-handed people have a stronger preference for abstract art than right-handed people (2006).
   d. This result has been replicated several times (Williamson, 1998; Pentecost & Garcia, 2006; Armbruster, 2011)

# 11.2 Writing a Research Report in American Psychological Association (APA) Style

## Learning Objectives

1. Identify the major sections of an APA-style research report and the basic contents of each section.
2. Plan and write an effective APA-style research report.

In this section, we look at how to write an APA-style **empirical research report**, an article that presents the results of one or more new studies. Recall that the standard sections of an empirical research report provide a kind of outline. Here we consider each of these sections in detail, including what information it contains, how that information is formatted and organized, and tips for writing each section. At the end of this section is a sample APA-style research report that illustrates many of these principles.

**empirical research report**

A type of journal article in which the author reports on a new empirical research study.

## Sections of a Research Report

### Title Page and Abstract

An APA-style research report begins with a **title page**. The title is centered in the upper half of the page, with each important word capitalized. The title should clearly and concisely (in about 12 words or fewer) communicate the primary variables and research questions. This sometimes requires a main title followed by a subtitle that elaborates on the main title, in which case the main title and subtitle are separated by a colon. Here are some titles from recent issues of professional journals published by the APA.

**title page**

The first page of an APA-style manuscript, containing the title, author names and affiliations, and author note.

- Sex Differences in Coping Styles and Implications for Depressed Mood
- Effects of Aging and Divided Attention on Memory for Items and Their Contexts
- Computer-Assisted Cognitive Behavioral Therapy for Child Anxiety: Results of a Randomized Clinical Trial
- Virtual Driving and Risk Taking: Do Racing Games Increase Risk-Taking Cognitions, Affect, and Behavior?

Below the title are the authors' names and, on the next line, their institutional affiliation—the university or other institution where the authors worked when they conducted the research. As we have already seen, the authors are listed in an order that reflects their contribution to the research. When multiple authors have made equal contributions to the research, they often list their names alphabetically or in a randomly determined order.

---

### It's *Soooo* Cute!

How Informal Should an Article Title Be?

In some areas of psychology, the titles of many empirical research reports are informal in a way that is perhaps best described as "cute." They usually take the form of a play on words or a well-known expression that relates to the topic under study. Here are some examples from recent issues of the *Journal of Personality and Social Psychology*.

- "Let's Get Serious: Communicating Commitment in Romantic Relationships"
- "Home Alone: Why People Believe Others' Social Lives are Richer than Their Own"
- "Don't Hide Your Happiness! Positive Emotion Dissociation, Social Connectedness, and Psychological Functioning"
- "Forbidden Fruit: Inattention to Attractive Alternatives Provokes Implicit Relationship Reactance"

Individual researchers differ quite a bit in their preference for such titles. Some use them regularly, while others never use them. What might be some of the pros and cons of using cute article titles?

---

Articles that are being submitted for publication may have a few additional elements. One is a short version of the title called the running head that appears in all capital letters in the upper left corner of each page. On the title page only, the running head is preceded by "Running Head:" (in upper and lower case). The title page can also include an author note that lists the authors' full institutional affiliations, any acknowledgments the authors wish to make to agencies that funded the research or to colleagues who commented on it, and contact information for the authors. For student papers that are not being submitted for publication—including theses—running heads and author notes may not be necessary.

**abstract**

A short summary (approximately 200 words) of a research article. In an APA-style manuscript, the abstract appears on the second page.

The **abstract** is a short (150 to 200 words) summary of the study. It is on the second page of the manuscript and is headed with the word *Abstract*. The first line is not indented. The abstract presents the research question, a summary of the method, the basic results, and the most important conclusions.

## Introduction

**introduction**

The first major section of an APA-style empirical research report. It typically includes an opening, a literature review, and a closing.

The **introduction** begins on the third page of the manuscript. The heading at the top of this page is the full title of the manuscript, with each important word capitalized as on the title page. The introduction includes three distinct subsections, although these are typically not identified by separate headings. The opening introduces the research question and explains why it is interesting, the literature review discusses relevant previous research, and the closing restates the research question and comments on the method used to answer it.

## The Opening

The **opening**, which is usually a paragraph or two in length, introduces the research question and explains why it is interesting. To capture the reader's attention, researcher Daryl Bem recommends starting with general observations about the topic under study, expressed in ordinary language (not technical jargon)—observations that are about people and their behavior (not about researchers or their research; Bem, 2003).[6] The use of concrete examples in the opening is often very useful. According to Bem, this would be a poor way to begin a research report:

*Festinger's theory of cognitive dissonance received a great deal of attention during the latter part of the 20th century (p. 191)*

The following would be much better:

*The individual who holds two beliefs that are inconsistent with one another may feel uncomfortable. For example, the person who knows that he or she enjoys smoking but believes it to be unhealthy may experience discomfort arising from the inconsistency or disharmony between these two thoughts or cognitions. This feeling of discomfort was called cognitive dissonance by social psychologist Leon Festinger (1957), who suggested that individuals will be motivated to remove this dissonance in whatever way they can (p. 191).*

After capturing the reader's attention, the opening should go on to introduce the research question and explain why it is interesting. Will the answer fill a gap in the literature? Will it provide a test of an important theory? Does it have practical implications? Giving readers a clear sense of what the research is about and why they should care about it will motivate them to continue reading the literature review—and will help them make sense of it.

**opening**

The first paragraph or two of the introduction of an APA-style empirical report. It introduces the research question and explains why it is interesting.

## Breaking the Rules

Researcher Larry Jacoby reported several studies showing that a word that people see or hear repeatedly can seem more familiar—even when they do not recall the repetitions—and that this tendency is especially pronounced among older adults. He opened his article with the following humorous anecdote (Jacoby, 1999).[7]

*A friend whose mother is suffering symptoms of Alzheimer's disease (AD) tells the story of taking her mother to visit a nursing home, preliminary to her mother's moving there. During an orientation meeting at the nursing home, the rules and regulations were explained, one of which regarded the dining room. The dining room was described as similar to a fine restaurant except that tipping was not required. The absence of tipping was a central theme in the orientation lecture, mentioned frequently to emphasize the quality of care along with the advantages of having paid in advance. At the end of the meeting, the friend's mother was asked whether she had any questions. She replied that she only had one question: "Should I tip?" (p. 3).*

Although both humor and personal anecdotes are generally discouraged in APA-style writing, this example is a highly effective way to start because it both engages the reader and provides an excellent real-world example of the topic under study.

## The Literature Review

**literature review**

A written summary of previous research on a topic. It constitutes the bulk of the introduction of an APA-style empirical research report.

Immediately after the opening comes the **literature review**, which describes relevant previous research on the topic and can be anywhere from several paragraphs to several pages in length. However, the literature review is not simply a list of past studies. Instead, it constitutes a kind of argument for why the research question is worth addressing. By the end of the literature review, readers should be convinced that the research question makes sense and that the present study is a logical next step in the ongoing research process.

Like any effective argument, the literature review must have some kind of structure. For example, it might begin by describing a phenomenon in a general way along with several studies that demonstrate it, then describing two or more competing theories of the phenomenon, and finally presenting a hypothesis to test one or more of the theories. Or it might describe one phenomenon, then describe another phenomenon that seems inconsistent with the first one, then propose a theory that resolves the inconsistency, and finally present a hypothesis to test that theory. In applied research, it might describe a phenomenon or theory, then describe how that phenomenon or theory applies to some important real-world situation, and finally suggest a way to test whether it does, in fact, apply to that situation.

Looking at the literature review in this way emphasizes a few things. First, it is extremely important to start with an outline of the main points that you want to make, organized in the order that you want to make them. The basic structure of your argument, then, should be apparent from the outline itself. Second, it is important to emphasize the structure of your argument in your writing. One way to do this is to begin the literature review by summarizing your argument even before you begin to make it. "In this article, I will describe two apparently contradictory phenomena, present a new theory that has the potential to resolve the apparent contradiction, and finally present a novel hypothesis to test the theory." Another way is to open each paragraph with a sentence that summarizes the main point of the paragraph and links it to the preceding points. These opening sentences provide the "transitions" that many beginning researchers have difficulty with. Instead of beginning a paragraph by launching into a description of a previous study, such as "Williams (2004) found that...," it is better to start by indicating something about why you are describing this particular study. Here are some simple examples:

*Another example of this phenomenon comes from the work of Williams (2004).*

*Williams (2004) offers one explanation of this phenomenon.*

*An alternative perspective has been provided by Williams (2004).*

*We used a method based on the one used by Williams (2004).*

Finally, remember that your goal is to construct an argument for why your research question is interesting and worth addressing—not necessarily why your favorite answer to it is correct. In other words, your literature review must be balanced. If you want to emphasize the generality of a phenomenon, then of course you should discuss various studies that have demonstrated it. However, if there are other studies that have failed to demonstrate it, you should discuss them too. Or if you are proposing a new theory, then of course you should discuss findings that are consistent with that theory. However, if there are other findings that are inconsistent with it, again, you should discuss them too. It is acceptable to argue that the *balance* of the research supports the existence of a phenomenon or is consistent with a theory (and that is usually the best that researchers in psychology can hope for), but it is not acceptable to *ignore* contradictory evidence. Besides, a large part of what makes a research question interesting is uncertainty about its answer.

## The Closing

The **closing** of the introduction—typically the final paragraph or two—usually includes two important elements. The first is a clear statement of the main research question or hypothesis. This statement tends to be more formal and precise than in the opening and is often expressed in terms of operational definitions of the key variables. The second is a brief overview of the method and some comment on its appropriateness. Here, for example, is how Darley and Latané (1968)[8] concluded the introduction to their classic article on the bystander effect:

**closing**

The last paragraph or two of the introduction of an APA-style empirical research report. It restates the research question and comments on the method.

> *These considerations lead to the hypothesis that the more bystanders to an emergency, the less likely, or the more slowly, any one bystander will intervene to provide aid. To test this proposition it would be necessary to create a situation in which a realistic "emergency" could plausibly occur. Each subject should also be blocked from communicating with others to prevent his getting information about their behavior during the emergency. Finally, the experimental situation should allow for the assessment of the speed and frequency of the subjects' reaction to the emergency. The experiment reported below attempted to fulfill these conditions (p. 378).*

Thus the introduction leads smoothly into the next major section of the article—the method section.

## Method

**method section**

The section of an APA-style empirical research report in which the method is described in detail. At minimum, it includes a participants subsection and a design and procedure subsections.

The **method section** is where you describe how you conducted your study. An important principle for writing a method section is that it should be clear and detailed enough that other researchers could replicate the study by following your "recipe." This means that it must describe all the important elements of the study—basic demographic characteristics of the participants, how they were recruited, whether they were randomly assigned, how the variables were manipulated or measured, how counterbalancing was accomplished, and so on. At the same time, it should avoid irrelevant details such as the fact that the study was conducted in Classroom 37B of the Industrial Technology Building or that the questionnaire was double-sided and completed using pencils.

The method section begins immediately after the introduction ends with the heading "Method" (not "Methods") centered on the page. Immediately after this is the subheading "Participants," left justified and in italics. The participants subsection indicates how many participants there were, the number of women and men, some indication of their age, other demographics that may be relevant to the study, and how they were recruited, including any incentives given for participation.

After the participants section, the structure can vary a bit. In one approach, the participants section is followed by a design and procedure subsection, which describes the rest of the method. This works well for methods that are relatively simple and can be described adequately in a few paragraphs. In a second approach, the participants section is followed by separate design and procedure subsections. This works well when both the design and the procedure are relatively complicated and each requires multiple paragraphs.

What is the difference between design and procedure? The design of a study is its overall structure. What were the independent and dependent variables? Was the independent variable manipulated, and if so, was it manipulated between or within subjects? How were the variables operationally defined? The procedure is how the study was carried out. It often works well to describe the procedure in terms of what the participants did rather than what the researchers did. For example, the participants gave their informed consent, read a set of instructions, completed a block of four practice trials, completed a block of 20 test trials, completed two questionnaires, and were debriefed and excused.

In a third approach to organizing a method section, the participants subsection is followed by a materials subsection before the design and procedure subsections. This works well when there are complicated materials to describe. This might mean multiple questionnaires, written vignettes that participants read and respond to, perceptual stimuli, and so on. The heading of this subsection can be modified to reflect its content. Instead of "Materials," it can be "Questionnaires," "Stimuli," and so on.

# Results

The **results section** is where you present the main results of the study, including the results of the statistical analyses. Although it does not include the raw data—individual participants' responses or scores—researchers should save their raw data and make them available to other researchers who request them. Some journals now make the raw data available online.

Although there are no standard subsections, it is still important for the results section to be logically organized. Typically, it begins with certain preliminary issues. One is whether any participants or responses were excluded from the analyses and why. The rationale for excluding data should be described clearly so that other researchers can decide whether it is appropriate. A second preliminary issue is how multiple responses were combined to produce the primary variables in the analyses. For example, if participants rated the attractiveness of 20 stimulus people, you might have to explain that you began by computing the mean attractiveness rating for each participant. Or if they recalled as many items as they could from study list of 20 words, did you count the number correctly recalled, compute the percentage correctly recalled, or perhaps compute the number correct minus the number incorrect? A third preliminary issue is the reliability of the measures. This is where you would present test-retest correlations, Cronbach's $\alpha$, or other statistics to show that the measures are consistent across time and across items. A final preliminary issue is whether the manipulation was successful. This is where you would report the results of any manipulation checks.

The results section should then tackle the primary research questions, one at a time. Again, there should be a clear organization. One approach would be to answer the most general questions and then proceed to answer more specific ones. Another would be to answer the main question first and then to answer secondary ones. Regardless, Bem (2003)[9] suggests the following basic structure for discussing each new result:

1. Remind the reader of the research question.
2. Give the answer to the research question in words.
3. Present the relevant statistics.
4. Qualify the answer if necessary.
5. Summarize the result.

Notice that only Step 3 necessarily involves numbers. The rest of the steps involve presenting the research question and the answer to it in words. In fact, the basic results should be clear even to a reader who skips over the numbers.

**results section**

The section of an APA-style empirical research report in which the results are described in detail.

# Discussion

The **discussion** is the last major section of the research report. Discussions usually consist of some combination of the following elements:

- Summary of the research
- Theoretical implications
- Practical implications
- Limitations
- Suggestions for future research

The discussion typically begins with a summary of the study that provides a clear answer to the research question. In a short report with a single study, this might require no more than a sentence. In a longer report with multiple studies, it might require a paragraph or even two. The summary is often followed by a discussion of the theoretical implications of the research. Do the results provide support for any existing theories? If not, how *can* they be explained? Although you

**discussion**

The final major section of an APA-style empirical research report. It typically includes a summary of the research, a discussion of theoretical and practical implications of the study, limitations of the study, and suggestions for future research.

do not have to provide a definitive explanation or detailed theory for your results, you at least need to outline one or more possible explanations. In applied research—and often in basic research—there is also some discussion of the practical implications of the research. How can the results be used, and by whom, to accomplish some real-world goal?

The theoretical and practical implications are often followed by a discussion of the study's limitations. Perhaps there are problems with its internal or external validity. Perhaps the manipulation was not very effective or the measures not very reliable. Perhaps there is some evidence that participants did not fully understand their task or that they were suspicious of the intent of the researchers. Now is the time to discuss these issues and how they might have affected the results. But do not overdo it. All studies have limitations, and most readers will understand that a different sample or different measures might have produced different results. Unless there is good reason to think they *would* have, however, there is no reason to mention these routine issues. Instead, pick two or three limitations that seem like they could have influenced the results, explain how they could have influenced the results, and suggest ways to deal with them.

Most discussions end with some suggestions for future research. If the study did not satisfactorily answer the original research question, what will it take to do so? What *new* research questions has the study raised? This part of the discussion, however, is not just a list of new questions. It is a discussion of two or three of the most important unresolved issues. This means identifying and clarifying each question, suggesting some alternative answers, and even suggesting ways they could be studied.

Finally, some researchers are quite good at ending their articles with a sweeping or thought-provoking conclusion. Darley and Latané (1968),[10] for example, ended their article on the bystander effect by discussing the idea that whether people help others may depend more on the situation than on their personalities. Their final sentence is, "If people understand the situational forces that can make them hesitate to intervene, they may better overcome them" (p. 383). However, this kind of ending can be difficult to pull off. It can sound overreaching or just banal and end up detracting from the overall impact of the article. It is often better simply to end when you have made your final point (although you should avoid ending on a limitation).

## References

The references section begins on a new page with the heading "References" centered at the top of the page. All references cited in the text are then listed in the format presented earlier. They are listed alphabetically by the last name of the first author. If two sources have the same first author, they are listed alphabetically by the last name of the second author. If all the authors are the same, then they are listed chronologically by the year of publication. Everything in the reference list is double-spaced both within and between references.

## Appendixes, Tables, and Figures

**appendix**

An optional section at the end of an APA-style manuscript used to present important supplemental material.

Appendixes, tables, and figures come after the references. An **appendix** is appropriate for supplemental material that would interrupt the flow of the research report if it were presented within any of the major sections. An appendix could be used to present lists of stimulus words, questionnaire items, detailed descriptions of special equipment or unusual statistical analyses, or references to the studies that are included in a meta-analysis. Each appendix begins on a new page. If there is only one, the heading is "Appendix," centered at the top of the page. If there is more than one, the headings are "Appendix A," "Appendix B," and so on, and they appear in the order they were first mentioned in the text of the report.

After any appendixes come tables and then figures. Tables and figures are both used to present results. Figures can also be used to illustrate theories (e.g., in the form of a flowchart), display stimuli, outline procedures, and present many other kinds of information. Each table and figure appears on its own page. Tables are numbered in the order that they are first mentioned in the text ("Table 1," "Table 2," and so on). Figures are numbered the same way ("Figure 1," "Figure 2," and so on). A brief explanatory title, with the important words capitalized, appears above each table. Each figure is given a brief explanatory caption, where (aside from proper nouns or names) only the first word of each sentence is capitalized. More details on preparing APA-style tables and figures are presented later in the book.

## Sample APA-Style Research Report

Figure 11.1, Figure 11.2, Figure 11.3, and Figure 11.4 show some sample pages from an APA-style empirical research report written by master's student Jenica Wilson at California State University, Fresno. Her study was about the relationship between people's social class—based on their family income, parents' education, and sense of standing in their community—and their perceptions of the riskiness of a wide variety of behaviors, including disagreeing with a supervisor, bungee jumping, and investing in the stock market. What she found was that people who were higher in social class tended to perceive these behaviors to be less risky than did people who were lower in social class. The main purpose of these figures, though, is to illustrate the basic organization and formatting of an APA-style empirical research report.

**FIGURE 11.1** Title Page and Abstract
This student paper does not include the author note on the title page. The abstract appears on its own page.

**FIGURE 11.2** Introduction and Method

Note that the introduction is headed with the full title, and the method section begins immediately after the introduction ends.

**FIGURE 11.3** Results and Discussion

The discussion begins immediately after the results section ends.

**FIGURE 11.4** References and Figure

If there were appendixes or tables, they would come before the figure.

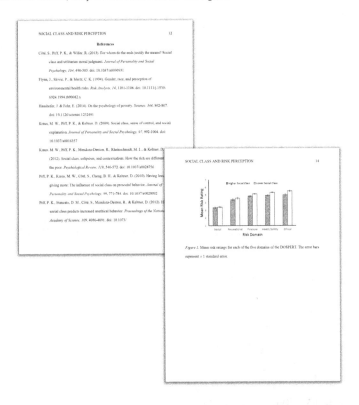

## Key Takeaways

- An APA-style empirical research report consists of several standard sections. The main ones are the abstract, introduction, method, results, discussion, and references.

- The introduction consists of an opening that presents the research question, a literature review that describes previous research on the topic, and a closing that restates the research question and comments on the method. The literature review constitutes an argument for why the current study is worth doing.

- The method section describes the method in enough detail that another researcher could replicate the study. At a minimum, it consists of a participants subsection and a design and procedure subsection.

- The results section describes the results in an organized fashion. Each primary result is presented in terms of statistical results but also explained in words.

- The discussion typically summarizes the study, discusses theoretical and practical implications and limitations of the study, and offers suggestions for further research.

## Exercises

1. Practice: Look through an issue of a general interest professional journal (e.g., *Psychological Science*). Read the opening of the first five articles and rate the effectiveness of each one from 1 (*very ineffective*) to 5 (*very effective*). Write a sentence or two explaining each rating.

2. Practice: Find a recent article in a professional journal and identify where the opening, literature review, and closing of the introduction begin and end.

3. Practice: Find a recent article in a professional journal and highlight in a different color each of the following elements in the discussion: summary, theoretical implications, practical implications, limitations, and suggestions for future research.

# 11.3 Other Presentation Formats

## Learning Objectives

1. List several ways that researchers in psychology can present their research and the situations in which they might use them.
2. Describe how final manuscripts differ from copy manuscripts in American Psychological Association (APA) style.
3. Describe the purpose of talks and posters at professional conferences.
4. Prepare a short conference-style talk and simple poster presentation.

Writing an empirical research report in APA style is only one way to present new research in psychology. In this section, we look at several other important ways.

## Other Types of Manuscripts

Section 2 focused on writing empirical research reports to be submitted for publication in a professional journal. However, there are other kinds of manuscripts that are written in APA style, many of which will not be submitted for publication elsewhere. Here we look at a few of them.

### Review and Theoretical Articles

**review article**

A type of journal article in which the author summarizes previous research on a particular topic.

**theoretical article**

A type of journal article in which the author presents a new theory or evaluates existing theories.

Recall that **review articles** summarize research on a particular topic without presenting new empirical results. When these articles present a new theory, they are often called **theoretical articles**. Review and theoretical articles are structured much like empirical research reports, with a title page, an abstract, references, appendixes, tables, and figures, and they are written in the same high-level and low-level style. Because they do not report the results of new empirical research, however, there is no method or results section. Of course, the body of the manuscript should still have a logical organization and include an opening that identifies the topic and explains its importance, a literature review that organizes previous research (identifying important relationships among concepts or gaps in the literature), and a closing or conclusion that summarizes the main conclusions and suggests directions for further research or discusses theoretical and practical implications. In a theoretical article, of course, much of the body of the manuscript is devoted to presenting the new theory. Theoretical and review articles are usually divided into sections, each with a heading that is appropriate to that section. The sections and headings can vary considerably from article to article (unlike in an empirical research report). But whatever they are, they should help organize the manuscript and make the argument clear.

# Final Manuscripts

Until now, we have focused on the formatting of manuscripts that will be submitted to a professional journal for publication. These are referred to as **copy manuscripts**. Many features of a copy manuscript—consistent double-spacing, the running head, and the placement of tables and figures at the end—are intended to make it easier to edit and typeset on its way to publication. The published journal article looks quite different from the copy manuscript. For example, the title and author information, the abstract, and the beginning of the introduction generally appear on the same page rather than on separate pages. In contrast, other types of manuscripts are prepared by the author in their final form with no intention of submitting them for publication elsewhere. These are called **final manuscripts** and include dissertations, theses, and other student papers.

Final manuscripts can differ from copy manuscripts in a number of ways that make them easier to read. This can include putting tables and figures close to where they are discussed so that the reader does not have to flip to the back of the manuscript to see them. It can also include variations in line spacing that improve readability—such as using single spacing for table titles and figure captions or triple spacing between major sections or around tables and figures. Dissertations and theses can differ from copy manuscripts in additional ways. They may have a longer abstract, a special acknowledgments page, a table of contents, and so on. For student papers, it is important to check with the course instructor about formatting specifics. In a research methods course, papers are usually required to be written as though they were copy manuscripts being submitted for publication.

**copy manuscript**

A manuscript prepared according to APA style to be submitted for publication to a professional journal.

**final manuscript**

A manuscript (such as a dissertation, thesis, or student paper) prepared in its final form that will not be submitted for publication in a professional journal.

# Conference Presentations

One of the ways that researchers in psychology share their research with each other is by presenting it at **professional conferences**. (Although some professional conferences in psychology are devoted mainly to issues of clinical practice, we are concerned here with those that focus on research.) Professional conferences can range from small-scale events involving a dozen researchers who get together for an afternoon to large-scale events involving thousands of researchers who meet for several days. Although researchers attending a professional conference are likely to discuss their work with each other informally, there are two more formal types of presentation: oral presentations ("talks") and posters. Presenting a talk or poster at a conference usually requires submitting an abstract of the research to the conference organizers in advance and having it accepted for presentation—although the peer review process is typically not as rigorous as it is for manuscripts submitted to a professional journal.

**professional conference**

A meeting at which researchers in a particular field gather to share their research.

## Professional Conferences

Here are links to the websites for several large national conferences and a link to a website that lists several regional conferences that feature the work of undergraduate students.

American Psychological Association Convention: http://www.apa.org/convention

Association for Psychological Science Conference: http://www.psychologicalscience.org/index.php/convention

Society for Personality and Social Psychology Conference: http://www.spsp.org/?page=Convention

Psychonomic Society Annual Meeting: http://www.psychonomic.org/page/meetings

Undergraduate Research Conferences in Psychology: https://www.psychonomic.org/page/2018annualmeeting

# Oral Presentations

**oral presentation**

A presentation at a professional conference in which presenters stand in front of an audience and tell them about their research, usually with the aid of a slide show. Such presentations, which are informally called "talks," can last anywhere from 10 minutes to an hour.

In an **oral presentation**, or "talk," the presenter stands in front of an audience of other researchers and tells them about his or her research—usually with the help of a slide show. Talks usually last from 10 to 20 minutes, with the last few minutes reserved for questions from the audience. At larger conferences, talks are typically grouped into sessions lasting an hour or two in which all the talks are on the same general topic.

In preparing a talk, presenters should keep several general principles in mind. The first is that the number of slides should be no more than about one per minute of the talk. The second is that a talk is generally structured like an APA-style research report. There is a slide with the title and authors, a few slides to help provide the background, a few more to help describe the method, a few for the results, and a few for the conclusions. The third is that the presenter should look at the audience members and speak to them in a conversational tone that is less formal than APA-style writing but more formal than a conversation with a friend. The slides should not be the focus of the presentation; they should act as visual aids. As such, they should present main points in bulleted lists or simple tables and figures.

# Posters

**poster**

A simple written presentation that is posted on a bulletin board during a poster session at a professional conference. The presenter stands near the poster and interacts with other researchers who are interested in the research.

**poster session**

A one- or two-hour session at a professional conference in which several researchers present their posters, often on related topics.

Another way to present research at a conference is in the form of a **poster**. A poster is typically presented during a one- to two-hour **poster session** that takes place in a large room at the conference site. Presenters set up their posters on bulletin boards arranged around the room and stand near them. Other researchers then circulate through the room, read the posters, and talk to the presenters. In essence, poster sessions are a grown-up version of the school science fair. But there is nothing childish about them. Posters are used by professional researchers in all scientific disciplines and they are becoming increasingly common. At a recent Association for Psychological Science conference, nearly 2,000 posters were presented across 16 separate poster sessions. Among the reasons posters are so popular is that they encourage meaningful interaction among researchers.

Although a poster can consist of several sheets of paper that are attached separately to the bulletin board, it is now more common for them to consist of a single large sheet of paper. Either way, the information is organized into distinct sections, including a title, author names and affiliations, an introduction, a method section, a results section, a discussion or conclusions section, references, and acknowledgments. Although posters can include an abstract, this may not be necessary because the poster itself is already a brief summary of the research. Figure 11.5 shows two different ways that the information on a poster might be organized.

**FIGURE 11.5** Two Possible Ways to Organize the Information on a Poster

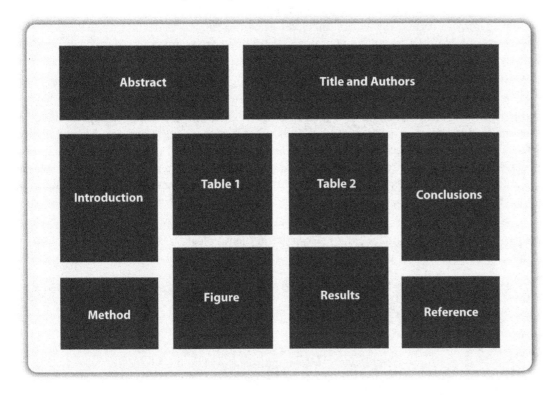

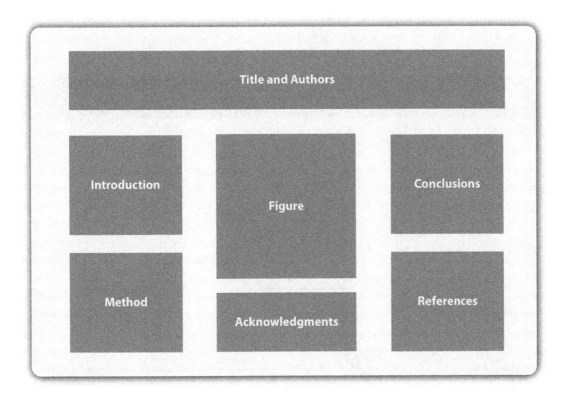

Given the conditions under which posters are often presented—for example, in crowded ballrooms where people are also eating, drinking, and socializing—they should be constructed so that they present the main ideas behind the research in as simple and clear a way as possible. The font sizes on a poster should be large—perhaps 72 points for the title and authors' names and 28 points for the main text. The information should be organized into sections with clear headings, and text should be blocked into sentences or bulleted points rather than paragraphs. It is also better for it to be organized in columns and flow from top to bottom rather than to be organized in rows that flow across the poster. This makes it easier for multiple people to read at the same time without bumping into each other. Posters often include elements that add visual interest, such as colorful figures, copies of visual stimuli, or photographs of the research apparatus. They can also include purely decorative elements, although it is best not to overdo these.

Again, a primary reason that posters are becoming such a popular way to present research is that they facilitate interaction among researchers. Many presenters immediately offer to describe their research to visitors and use the poster as a visual aid. At the very least, it is important for presenters to stand by their posters, greet visitors, offer to answer questions, and be prepared for questions and even the occasional critical comment. It is generally a good idea to have a more detailed write-up of the research available for visitors who want more information, to offer to send them a detailed write-up, or to provide contact information so that they can request more information later.

For more information on preparing and presenting both talks and posters, see the website of Psi Chi, the International Honor Society in Psychology: https://www.psichi.org/?RES_ConvPresent#.W0UDO1Mvy3d.

**FIGURE 11.6**
New research is often presented in the form of posters at professional conferences.

Source: Photo courtesy of Brandy Jaramillo

## Key Takeaways

- Research in psychology can be presented in several different formats. In addition to APA-style empirical research reports, there are theoretical and review articles; final manuscripts, including dissertations, theses, and student papers; and talks and posters at professional conferences.
- Talks and posters at professional conferences follow some APA style guidelines but are considerably less detailed than APA-style research reports. Their function is to present new research to interested researchers and facilitate further interaction among researchers.

## Exercise

1. Discussion: Do an Internet search using search terms such as *psychology* and *poster* to find three examples of posters that have been presented at conferences. Based on information in this chapter, what are the main strengths and main weaknesses of each poster?

# Endnotes

1. American Psychological Association. (2006). *Publication Manual of the American Psychological Association* (6th ed.). Washington, DC: American Psychological Association.
2. American Psychological Association. (2006). *Publication Manual of the American Psychological Association* (6th ed.). Washington, DC: American Psychological Association.
3. Madigan, R., Johnson, S., & Linton, P. (1995). The language of psychology: APA style as epistemology. *American Psychologist, 50*, 428–436.
4. Committee on Lesbian and Gay Concerns, American Psychological Association. (1991). Avoiding heterosexual bias in language. *American Psychologist, 46*, 973–974. Retrieved from http://www.apa.org/pi/lgbt/resources/language.aspx
5. Onwuegbuzie, A. J., Combs, J. P., Slate, J. R., & Frels, R. K. (2010). Editorial: Evidence-based guidelines for avoiding the most common APA errors in journal article submissions. *Research in the Schools, 16*, ix–xxxvi.
6. Bem, D. J. (2003). Writing the empirical journal article. In J. M. Darley, M. P. Zanna, & H. R. Roediger III (Eds.), *The compleat academic: A practical guide for the beginning social scientist* (2nd ed.). Washington, DC: American Psychological Association.
7. Jacoby, L. (1999). Ironic Effects of Repetition: Measuring Age-Related Differences in Memory. *Journal of Experimental Psychology: Learning, Memory, and Cognition, 25*, 3-22.
8. Darley, J. M., & Latané, B. (1968). Bystander intervention in emergencies: Diffusion of responsibility. *Journal of Personality and Social Psychology, 4*, 377–383.
9. Bem, D. J. (2003). Writing the empirical journal article. In J. M. Darley, M. P. Zanna, & H. R. Roediger III (Eds.), *The compleat academic: A practical guide for the beginning social scientist* (2nd ed.). Washington, DC: American Psychological Association.

10. Darley, J. M., & Latané, B. (1968). Bystander intervention in emergencies: Diffusion of responsibility. *Journal of Personality and Social Psychology, 4*, 377–383.

# Descriptive Statistics

At this point, we need to consider the basics of data analysis in psychological research in more detail. In this chapter, we focus on descriptive statistics—a set of techniques for summarizing and displaying the data from your sample. We look first at some of the most common techniques for describing single variables, followed by some of the most common techniques for describing statistical relationships between variables. We then look at ways to present descriptive statistics—in writing, in graphs, and in tables—that would be appropriate for an APA-style research report. We end with some practical advice for organizing and carrying out your analyses.

## 12.1 Describing Single Variables

### Learning Objectives

1. Use frequency tables and histograms to display and interpret the distribution of a variable.
2. Compute and interpret the mean, median, and mode of a distribution and identify situations in which the mean, median, or mode is the most appropriate measure of central tendency.
3. Compute and interpret the range and standard deviation of a distribution.
4. Compute and interpret percentile ranks and $z$ scores.

**Descriptive statistics** refers to a set of techniques for summarizing and displaying data. Although in most cases the primary research question will be about one or more statistical relationships between variables, it is also important to describe each variable individually. For this reason, we begin by looking at some of the most common techniques for describing single variables.

**descriptive statistics**

A set of techniques for summarizing and displaying data.

## The Distribution of a Variable

Every variable has a **distribution**, which is the way the scores are distributed across the levels of that variable. For example, in a sample of 100 college students, the distribution of the variable "number of siblings" might be such that 10 of them have no siblings, 30 have one sibling, 40 have two siblings, and so on. In the same sample, the distribution of the variable "sex" might be such that 44 have a score of "male" and 56 have a score of "female."

**distribution**

The way the scores on a variable are distributed across the levels of that variable.

# Frequency Tables

One way to display the distribution of a variable is in a **frequency table**. Table 12.1, for example, is a frequency table showing a hypothetical distribution of scores on the Rosenberg Self-Esteem Scale for a sample of 40 college students. The first column lists the values of the variable—the possible scores on the Rosenberg scale—and the second column lists the frequency of each score. This table shows that there were three students who had self-esteem scores of 24, five who had self-esteem scores of 23, and so on. From a frequency table like this, you can quickly see several important aspects of a distribution, including the range of scores (from 15 to 24), the most and least common scores (22 and 17, respectively), and any extreme scores that stand out from the rest.

**TABLE 12.1** Frequency Table Showing a Hypothetical Distribution of Scores on the Rosenberg Self-Esteem Scale

| Self-esteem | Frequency |
| --- | --- |
| 24 | 3 |
| 23 | 5 |
| 22 | 10 |
| 21 | 8 |
| 20 | 5 |
| 19 | 3 |
| 18 | 3 |
| 17 | 0 |
| 16 | 2 |
| 15 | 1 |

There are a few other points worth noting about frequency tables. First, the levels listed in the first column usually go from the highest at the top to the lowest at the bottom, and they usually do not extend beyond the highest and lowest scores in the data. Second, when there are many different scores across a wide range of values, it is often better to create a grouped frequency table, in which the first column lists ranges of values and the second column lists the frequency of scores in each range. Table 12.2, for example, is a grouped frequency table showing a hypothetical distribution of simple reaction times for a sample of 20 participants. In a grouped frequency table, the ranges must all be of equal width, and there are usually between five and 15 of them. Finally, frequency tables can also be used for categorical variables, in which case the levels are category labels, which are often listed from the most frequent at the top to the least frequent at the bottom.

**TABLE 12.2** A Grouped Frequency Table Showing a Hypothetical Distribution of Reaction Times

| Reaction time (ms) | Frequency |
| --- | --- |
| 241–260 | 1 |
| 221–240 | 2 |
| 201–220 | 2 |
| 181–200 | 9 |
| 161–180 | 4 |
| 141–160 | 2 |

## Histograms

A **histogram** is a graphical display of a distribution. It presents the same information as a frequency table but in a way that is even quicker and easier to grasp. The histogram in Figure 12.1 presents the distribution of self-esteem scores in Table 12.1. The x-axis of the histogram represents the variable and the y-axis represents frequency. When the variable is quantitative, as in this example, there is usually no gap between the bars. When the variable is categorical, however, there is usually a small gap between them. (The gap at 17 in this histogram reflects the fact that there were no scores of 17 in this data set.)

**histogram**

A graph for displaying the distribution of a variable. The x-axis represents the values of the variable, and the y-axis represents the frequency of each score.

**FIGURE 12.1** Histogram Showing the Distribution of Self-Esteem Scores Presented in Table 12.1

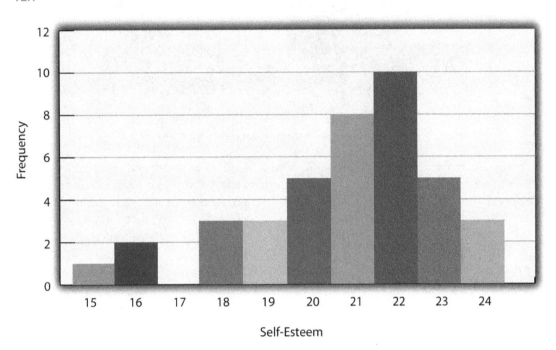

## Distribution Shapes

When the distribution of a quantitative variable is displayed in a histogram, it has a shape. The shape of the distribution of self-esteem scores in Figure 12.1 is typical. There is a peak somewhere near the middle of the distribution and "tails" that taper in either direction from the peak. The distribution of Figure 12.1 is unimodal, meaning it has one distinct peak, but distributions can also be bimodal, meaning they have two distinct peaks. Figure 12.2, for example, shows a hypothetical bimodal distribution of scores on the Beck Depression Inventory. Distributions can also have more than two distinct peaks, but these are relatively rare in psychological research.

**FIGURE 12.2** Histogram Showing a Hypothetical Bimodal Distribution of Scores on the Beck Depression Inventory

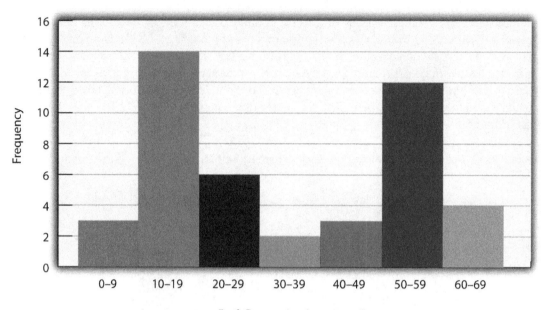

symmetrical

Refers to a distribution in which the left and right sides are near mirror images of each other.

Another characteristic of the shape of a distribution is whether it is symmetrical or skewed. The distribution in the center of Figure 12.3 is **symmetrical**. Its left and right halves are mirror images of each other. The distribution on the left is negatively **skewed**, with its peak shifted toward the upper end of its range and a relatively long negative tail. The distribution on the right is positively skewed, with its peak toward the lower end of its range and a relatively long positive tail.

skewed

Refers to an asymmetrical distribution. A positively skewed distribution has a relatively long positive tail, and a negatively skewed distribution has a relatively long negative tail.

**FIGURE 12.3** Histograms Showing Negatively Skewed, Symmetrical, and Positively Skewed Distributions

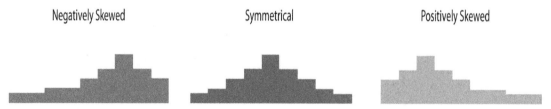

outlier

An extreme score that is far removed from the rest of the scores in the distribution.

An **outlier** is an extreme score that is much higher or lower than the rest of the scores in the distribution. Sometimes outliers represent truly extreme scores on the variable of interest. For example, on the Beck Depression Inventory, a single clinically depressed person might be an outlier in a sample of otherwise happy and high-functioning peers. However, outliers can also represent errors or misunderstandings on the part of the researcher or participant, equipment malfunctions, or similar problems. We will say more about how to interpret outliers and what to do about them later in this chapter.

## Measures of Central Tendency and Variability

It is also useful to be able to describe the characteristics of a distribution more precisely. Here we look at how to do this in terms of two important characteristics: their central tendency and their variability.

# Central Tendency

The **central tendency** of a distribution is its middle—the point around which the scores in the distribution tend to cluster. (Another term for central tendency is *average*.) Looking back at Figure 12.1, for example, we can see that the self-esteem scores tend to cluster around the values of 20 to 22. Here we will consider the three most common measures of central tendency: the mean, the median, and the mode.

The **mean** of a distribution (symbolized $M$) is the sum of the scores divided by the number of scores. As a formula, it looks like this:

$$M = \frac{\Sigma X}{N}$$

In this formula, the symbol $\Sigma$ (the Greek letter sigma) is the summation sign and means to sum across the values of the variable $X$. $N$ represents the number of scores. The mean is by far the most common measure of central tendency, and there are some good reasons for this. It usually provides a good indication of the central tendency of a distribution, and it is easily understood by most people. In addition, the mean has statistical properties that make it especially useful in doing inferential statistics.

An alternative to the mean is the median. The **median** is the middle score in the sense that half the scores in the distribution are above it and half are below it. The simplest way to find the median is to organize the scores from lowest to highest and locate the score in the middle. Consider, for example, the following set of seven scores:

8 4 12 14 3 2 3

To find the median, simply rearrange the scores from lowest to highest and locate the one in the middle.

2 3 3 4 8 12 14

In this case, the median is 4 because there are three scores lower than 4 and three scores higher than 4. When there is an even number of scores, there are two scores in the middle of the distribution, in which case the median is the value halfway between them. For example, if we were to add a score of 15 to these data, there would be two scores (both 4 and 8) in the middle of the distribution, and the median would be halfway between them (6).

One final measure of central tendency is the mode. The **mode** is the most frequent score in a distribution. In the self-esteem distribution presented in Table 12.1 and Figure 12.1, for example, the mode is 22. More students had that score than any other. The mode is the only measure of central tendency that can also be used for categorical variables.

In a distribution that is both unimodal and symmetrical, the mean, median, and mode will be very close to each other at the peak of the distribution. In a bimodal or asymmetrical distribution, the mean, median, and mode can be quite different. In a bimodal distribution, the mean and median will tend to be between the peaks, while the mode will be at the tallest peak. In a skewed distribution, the mean will differ from the median in the direction of the skew (i.e., the direction of the longer tail). For highly skewed distributions, the mean can be pulled so far in the direction of the skew that it is no longer a good measure of the central tendency of that distribution. Imagine, for example, a set of four simple reaction times of 200, 250, 280, and 250 milliseconds (ms). The mean is 245 ms. But the addition of one more score of 5,000 ms—perhaps because the participant was not paying attention—would raise the mean to 1,445 ms. Not only is this measure of central tendency greater than 80% of the scores in the distribution, it does not represent the behavior of *anyone* in the distribution very well. This is why researchers often prefer the median for highly skewed distributions (such as distributions of reaction times).

**central tendency**

The middle of a distribution. The mean, median, and mode are measures of central tendency.

**mean**

The most common measure of central tendency. The sum of the scores divided by the number of scores.

**median**

A measure of central tendency. The value such that half the scores in the distribution are above it and half are below it.

**mode**

A measure of central tendency. The most frequently occurring score in the distribution.

Keep in mind, though, that you are not required to choose a single measure of central tendency in analyzing your data. Each one provides slightly different information, and all of them can be useful.

## Measures of Variability

The **variability** of a distribution is the extent to which the scores vary around their central tendency. Consider the two distributions in Figure 12.4, both of which have the same central tendency. The mean, median, and mode of each distribution are 10. Notice, however, that the two distributions differ in terms of their variability. The top one has relatively low variability, with all the scores relatively close to the center. The bottom one has relatively high variability, with the scores spread across a much greater range.

**FIGURE 12.4** Histograms Showing Hypothetical Distributions With the Same Mean, Median, and Mode (10) but With Low Variability (Top) and High Variability (Bottom)

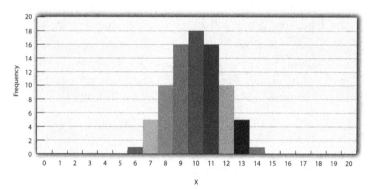

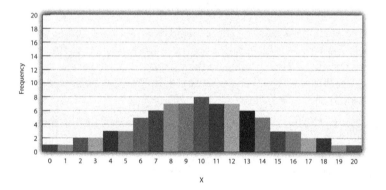

One simple measure of variability is the **range**, which is simply the difference between the highest and lowest scores in the distribution. The range of the self-esteem scores in Table 12.1, for example, is the difference between the highest score (24) and the lowest score (15). That is, the range is 24 – 15 = 9. Although the range is easy to compute and understand, it can be misleading when there are outliers. Imagine, for example, an exam on which all the students scored between 90 and 100. It has a range of 10. But if there was a single student who scored 20, the range would increase to 80—giving the impression that the scores were quite variable when in fact only one student differed substantially from the rest.

By far the most common measure of variability is the standard deviation. The **standard deviation** of a distribution is, roughly speaking, the average distance between the scores and the mean. For example, the standard deviations of the distributions in Figure 12.4 are 1.69 for the top distribution and 4.30 for the bottom one. That is, while the scores in the top distribution differ from the mean by about 1.69 units on average, the scores in the bottom distribution differ from the mean by about 4.30 units on average.

Computing the standard deviation involves a slight complication. Specifically, it involves finding the difference between each score and the mean, squaring each difference, finding the mean of these squared differences, and finally finding the square root of that mean. The formula looks like this:

$$SD = \sqrt{\frac{\Sigma(X-M)^2}{N}}$$

The computations for the standard deviation are illustrated for a small set of data in Table 12.3. The first column is a set of eight scores that has a mean of 5. The second column is the difference between each score and the mean. The third column is the square of each of these differences. Notice that although the differences can be negative, the squared differences are always positive—meaning that the standard deviation is always positive. At the bottom of the third column is the mean of the squared differences, which is also called the **variance** (symbolized $SD^2$). Although the variance is itself a measure of variability, it generally plays a larger role in inferential statistics than in descriptive statistics. Finally, below the variance is the square root of the variance, which is the standard deviation.

**standard deviation**

The most common measure of variability. The square root of the mean of the squared differences between the scores and the mean. Also the square root of the variance.

**variance**

A measure of variability. The mean of the squared differences between the scores and the mean. Also the square of the standard deviation.

**TABLE 12.3** Computations for the Standard Deviation

| X | X – M | (X – M)$^2$ |
|---|---|---|
| 3 | –2 | 4 |
| 5 | 0 | 0 |
| 4 | –1 | 1 |
| 2 | –3 | 9 |
| 7 | 2 | 4 |
| 6 | 1 | 1 |
| 5 | 0 | 0 |
| 8 | 3 | 9 |
| M = 5 | | $SD^2 = \frac{28}{8} = 3.50$ |
| | | $SD = \sqrt{3.50} = 1.87$ |

## N or N – 1?

If you have already taken a statistics course, you may have learned to divide the sum of the squared differences by $N - 1$ rather than by $N$ when you compute the variance and standard deviation. Why is this?

By definition, the standard deviation is the square root of the mean of the squared differences. This implies dividing the sum of squared differences by $N$, as in the formula just presented. Computing the standard deviation this way is appropriate when your goal is simply to describe the variability in a sample. And learning it this way emphasizes that the variance is in fact the *mean* of the squared differences—and the standard deviation is the square root of this *mean*.

However, most calculators and software packages divide the sum of squared differences by $N - 1$. This is because the standard deviation of a sample tends to be a bit lower than the standard deviation of the population the sample was selected from. Dividing the sum of squares by $N - 1$ corrects for this tendency and results in a better estimate of the population standard deviation. Because researchers generally think of their data as representing a sample selected from a larger population—and because they are generally interested in drawing conclusions about the population—it makes sense to routinely apply this correction.

## Percentile Ranks and z Scores

**percentile rank**

A measure of the location of a score within its distribution. The percentage of scores below a particular score.

In many situations, it is useful to have a way to describe the location of an individual score within its distribution. One approach is the percentile rank. The **percentile rank** of a score is the percentage of scores in the distribution that are lower than that score. Consider, for example, the distribution in Table 12.1. For any score in the distribution, we can find its percentile rank by counting the number of scores in the distribution that are lower than that score and converting that number to a percentage of the total number of scores. Notice, for example, that five of the students represented by the data in Table 12.1 had self-esteem scores of 23. In this distribution, 32 of the 40 scores (80%) are lower than 23. Thus each of these students has a percentile rank of 80. (It can also be said that they scored "at the 80th percentile.") Percentile ranks are often used to report the results of standardized tests of ability or achievement. If your percentile rank on a test of verbal ability were 40, for example, this would mean that you scored higher than 40% of the people who took the test.

**z score**

A measure of the location of a score within its distribution. The score minus the mean, divided by the standard deviation.

Another approach is the z score. The **z score** for a particular individual is the difference between that individual's score and the mean of the distribution, divided by the standard deviation of the distribution:

$$z = \frac{X - M}{SD}$$

A z score indicates how far above or below the mean a raw score is, but it expresses this in terms of the standard deviation. For example, in a distribution of intelligence quotient (IQ) scores with a mean of 100 and a standard deviation of 15, an IQ score of 110 would have a z score of (110 - 100) / 15 = +0.67. In other words, a score of 110 is 0.67 standard deviations (approximately two thirds of a standard deviation) above the mean. Similarly, a raw score of 85 would have a z score of (85 - 100) / 15 = -1.00. In other words, a score of 85 is one standard deviation below the mean.

There are several reasons that z scores are important. Again, they provide a way of describing where an individual's score is located within a distribution and are sometimes used to report the results of standardized tests. They also provide one way of defining outliers. For example, outliers are sometimes defined as scores that have z scores less than -3.00 or greater than +3.00. In other words, they are defined as scores that are more than three standard deviations from the mean. Finally, z scores play an important role in understanding and computing other statistics, as we will see shortly.

### Online Descriptive Statistics

Although many researchers use commercially available software such as SPSS and Excel to analyze their data, there are several free online analysis tools that can also be extremely useful. Many allow you to enter or upload your data and then make one click to conduct several descriptive statistical analyses. Among them are the following.

- SciStatCalc: http://scistatcalc.blogspot.co.uk
- Simple Interactive Statistical Analysis: http://www.quantitativeskills.com/sisa/

- Social Science Statistics: http://www.socscistatistics.com/descriptive/Default.aspx
- VassarStats: http://vassarstats.net

## Key Takeaways

- Every variable has a distribution—a way that the scores are distributed across the levels. The distribution can be described using a frequency table and histogram. It can also be described in words in terms of its shape, including whether it is unimodal or bimodal, and whether it is symmetrical or skewed.
- The central tendency, or middle, of a distribution can be described precisely using three statistics—the mean, median, and mode. The mean is the sum of the scores divided by the number of scores, the median is the middle score, and the mode is the most common score.
- The variability, or spread, of a distribution can be described precisely using the range and standard deviation. The range is the difference between the highest and lowest scores, and the standard deviation is roughly the average amount by which the scores differ from the mean.
- The location of a score within its distribution can be described using percentile ranks or $z$ scores. The percentile rank of a score is the percentage of scores below that score, and the $z$ score is the difference between the score and the mean divided by the standard deviation.

## Exercises

1. Practice: Make a frequency table and histogram for the following data. Then write a short description of the shape of the distribution in words.

   11, 8, 9, 12, 9, 10, 12, 13, 11, 13, 12, 6, 10, 17, 13, 11, 12, 12, 14, 14

2. Practice: For the data in Exercise 1, compute the mean, median, mode, standard deviation, and range.
3. Practice: Using the data in Exercises 1 and 2, find (a) the percentile ranks for scores of 9 and 14 and (b) the $z$ scores for scores of 8 and 12.

# 12.2 Describing Statistical Relationships

## Learning Objectives

1. Describe differences between groups in terms of their means and standard deviations, and in terms of Cohen's $d$.
2. Describe correlations between quantitative variables in terms of Pearson's $r$.

As we have seen throughout this book, most interesting research questions in psychology are about statistical relationships between variables. Recall that there is a statistical relationship between two variables when the average score on one differs systematically across the levels of the other. In this section, we revisit the two basic forms of statistical relationship introduced earlier in the book—differences between groups or conditions and relationships between quantitative variables—and we consider how to describe them in more detail.

# Differences Between Groups or Conditions

Differences between groups or conditions are usually described in terms of the mean and standard deviation of each group or condition. For example, Thomas Ollendick and his colleagues conducted a study in which they evaluated two, one-session treatments for simple phobias in children (Ollendick et al., 2009).[1] They randomly assigned children with an intense fear (e.g., to dogs) to one of three conditions. In the exposure condition, the children actually confronted the object of their fear under the guidance of a trained therapist. In the education condition, they learned about phobias and some strategies for coping with them. In the waitlist control condition, they were waiting to receive a treatment after the study was over. The severity of each child's phobia was then rated on a 1-to-8 scale by a clinician who did not know which treatment the child had received. (This was one of several dependent variables.) The mean fear rating in the education condition was 4.83 with a standard deviation of 1.52, while the mean fear rating in the exposure condition was 3.47 with a standard deviation of 1.77. The mean fear rating in the control condition was 5.56 with a standard deviation of 1.21. In other words, both treatments worked, but the exposure treatment worked better than the education treatment. As we have seen, differences between group or condition means can be presented in a bar graph like that in Figure 12.5, where the heights of the bars represent the group or condition means. We will look more closely at creating APA-style bar graphs shortly.

**FIGURE 12.5** Bar Graph Showing Mean Clinician Phobia Ratings for Children in Two Treatment Conditions

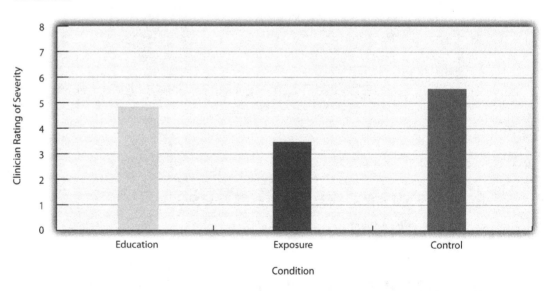

It is also important to be able to describe the strength of a statistical relationship, which is often referred to as the **effect size**. The most widely used measure of effect size for differences between group or condition means is called **Cohen's d**, which is the difference between the two means divided by the standard deviation:

$$d = \frac{M_1 - M_2}{SD}$$

In this formula, it does not really matter which mean is $M_1$ and which is $M_2$. If there is a treatment group and a control group, the treatment group mean is usually $M_1$ and the control group mean is $M_2$. Otherwise, the larger mean is usually $M_1$ and the smaller mean $M_2$ so that Cohen's d turns out to be positive. The standard deviation in this formula is usually a kind of average of the two group standard deviations called the pooled-within groups standard deviation. To compute the pooled within-groups standard deviation, add the sum of the squared differences for Group 1 to the sum of squared differences for Group 2, divide this by the sum of the two sample sizes, and then take the square root of that. Informally, however, the standard deviation of either group can be used instead.

Conceptually, Cohen's d is the difference between the two means expressed in standard deviation units. (Notice its similarity to a z score, which expresses the difference between an individual score and a mean in standard deviation units.) A Cohen's d of 0.50 means that the two group means differ by 0.50 standard deviations (half a standard deviation). A Cohen's d of 1.20 means that they differ by 1.20 standard deviations. But how should we interpret these values in terms of the strength of the relationship or the size of the difference between the means? Table 12.4 presents some guidelines for interpreting Cohen's d values in psychological research (Cohen, 1992).[2] Values near 0.20 are considered small, values near 0.50 are considered medium, and values near 0.80 are considered large. Thus a Cohen's d value of 0.50 represents a medium-sized difference between two means, and a Cohen's d value of 1.20 represents a very large difference in the context of psychological research. In the research by Ollendick and his colleagues, there was a large difference ($d = 0.82$) between the exposure and education conditions.

**TABLE 12.4** Guidelines for Referring to Cohen's d and Pearson's r Values as "Strong," "Medium," or "Weak"

| Relationship strength | Cohen's d | Pearson's r |
|---|---|---|
| Strong/large | ± 0.80 | ± 0.50 |
| Medium | ± 0.50 | ± 0.30 |
| Weak/small | ± 0.20 | ± 0.10 |

Cohen's d is useful because it has the same meaning regardless of the variable being compared or the scale it was measured on. A Cohen's d of 0.20 means that the two group means differ by 0.20 standard deviations whether we are talking about scores on the Rosenberg Self-Esteem scale, reaction time measured in milliseconds, number of siblings, or diastolic blood pressure measured in millimeters of mercury. Not only does this make it easier for researchers to communicate with each other about their results, it also makes it possible to combine and compare results across different studies using different measures.

Be aware that the term *effect size* can be misleading because it suggests a causal relationship—that the difference between the two means is an "effect" of being in one group or condition as opposed to another. Imagine, for example, a study showing that a group of exercisers is happier on average than a group of nonexercisers, with an "effect size" of $d = 0.35$. If the study was an experiment—with participants randomly assigned to exercise and no-exercise conditions—then one could conclude that exercising caused a small to medium increase in happiness. If the study was correlational, however, then one could conclude only that the exercisers were happier than the nonexercisers by a small to medium amount. In other words, simply calling the difference an "effect size" does not change the fact that "correlation does not imply causation."

---

**effect size**

Another name for measures of relationship strength, including Cohen's d and Pearson's r.

**Cohen's d**

A measure of relationship strength or "effect size" for a difference between two groups or conditions.

## Sex Differences Expressed as Cohen's *d*

Researcher Janet Shibley Hyde has looked at the results of numerous studies on psychological sex differences and expressed the results in terms of Cohen's *d* (Hyde, 2007).[3] Following are a few of the values she has found, averaging across several studies in each case. (Note that because she always treats the mean for men as $M_1$ and the mean for women as $M_2$, positive values indicate that men score higher and negative values indicate that women score higher.)

**TABLE 12.5**

| | |
|---|---|
| Mathematical problem solving | +0.08 |
| Reading comprehension | −0.09 |
| Smiling | −0.40 |
| Aggression | +0.50 |
| Attitudes toward casual sex | +0.81 |
| Leadership effectiveness | −0.02 |

Hyde points out that although men and women differ by a large amount on some variables (e.g., attitudes toward casual sex), they differ by only a small amount on the vast majority. In many cases, Cohen's *d* is less than 0.10, which she terms a "trivial" difference. (The difference in talkativeness discussed in Chapter 1 was also trivial: *d* = 0.06.) Although researchers and nonresearchers alike often emphasize sex *differences*, Hyde has argued that it makes at least as much sense to think of men and women as fundamentally *similar*. She refers to this as the "gender similarities hypothesis."

**FIGURE 12.6**
Research on psychological sex differences has shown that there is essentially no difference in the leadership effectiveness of women and men.

Source: © Thinkstock

## Correlations Between Quantitative Variables

As we have seen throughout the book, many interesting statistical relationships take the form of correlations between quantitative variables. For example, researchers Kurt Carlson and Jacqueline

Conard conducted a study on the relationship between the alphabetical position of the first letter of people's last names (from A = 1 to Z = 26) and how quickly those people responded to consumer appeals (Carlson & Conard, 2011).[4] In one study, they sent e-mails to a large group of MBA students, offering free basketball tickets from a limited supply. The result was that the further toward the end of the alphabet students' last names were, the faster they tended to respond. These results are summarized in Figure 12.7.

**FIGURE 12.7** Line Graph Showing the Relationship Between the Alphabetical Position of People's Last Names and How Quickly Those People Respond to Offers of Consumer Goods

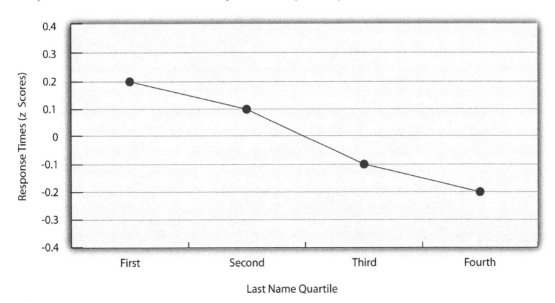

Such relationships are often presented using line graphs or scatterplots, which show how the level of one variable differs across the range of the other. In the line graph in Figure 12.7, for example, each point represents the mean response time for participants with last names in the first, second, third, and fourth quartiles (or quarters) of the name distribution. It clearly shows how response time tends to decline as people's last names get closer to the end of the alphabet. The scatterplot in Figure 12.8, which is reproduced from Chapter 5, shows the relationship between 25 research methods students' scores on the Rosenberg Self-Esteem Scale given on two occasions a week apart. Here the points represent individuals, and we can see that the higher students scored on the first occasion, the higher they tended to score on the second occasion. In general, line graphs are used when the variable on the x-axis has (or is organized into) a small number of distinct values, such as the four quartiles of the name distribution. Scatterplots are used when the variable on the x-axis has a large number of values, such as the different possible self-esteem scores.

**FIGURE 12.8** Statistical Relationship Between Several College Students' Scores on the Rosenberg Self-Esteem Scale Given on Two Occasions a Week Apart

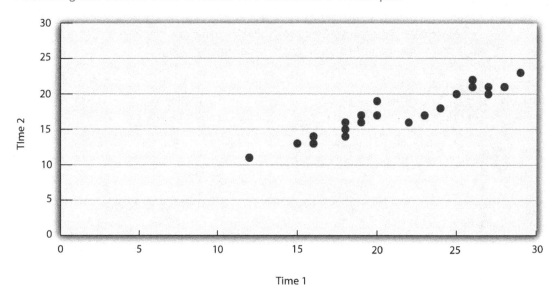

The data presented in Figure 12.8 provide a good example of a positive relationship, in which higher scores on one variable tend to be associated with higher scores on the other (so that the points go from the lower left to the upper right of the graph). The data presented in Figure 12.7 provide a good example of a negative relationship, in which higher scores on one variable tend to be associated with lower scores on the other (so that the points go from the upper left to the lower right).

**nonlinear relationship**

A statistical relationship in which as the *X* variable increases, the *Y* variable does not increase or decrease at a constant rate. Such relationships are best described by a curved line.

Both of these examples are also linear relationships, in which the points are reasonably well fit by a single straight line. **Nonlinear relationships** are those in which the points are better fit by a curved line. Figure 12.9, for example, shows a hypothetical relationship between the amount of sleep people get per night and their level of depression. In this example, the line that best fits the points is a curve—a kind of upside down "U"—because people who get about eight hours of sleep tend to be the least depressed, while those who get too little sleep and those who get too much sleep tend to be more depressed. Nonlinear relationships are not uncommon in psychology, but a detailed discussion of them is beyond the scope of this book.

**FIGURE 12.9** A Hypothetical Nonlinear Relationship Between How Much Sleep People Get per Night and How Depressed They Are

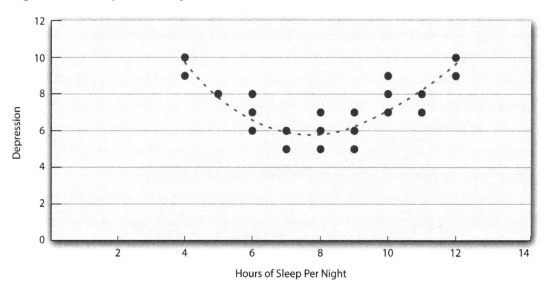

As we saw earlier in the book, the strength of a correlation between quantitative variables is typically measured using a statistic called Pearson's *r*. As Figure 12.10 shows, its possible values range from −1.00 to +1.00. A value of 0 means there is no relationship between the two variables. In addition to his guidelines for interpreting Cohen's *d*, Cohen offered guidelines for interpreting Pearson's *r* in psychological research (see Table 12.4). Values near ±.10 are considered small, values near ± .30 are considered medium, and values near ±.50 are considered large. Notice that the sign of Pearson's *r* is unrelated to its strength. Pearson's *r* values of +.30 and −.30, for example, are equally strong; it is just that one represents a moderate positive relationship and the other a moderate negative relationship. Like Cohen's *d*, Pearson's *r* is also referred to as a measure of "effect size" even though the relationship may not be a causal one.

**FIGURE 12.10** Pearson's *r* Ranges From −1.00 (Representing the Strongest Possible Negative Relationship), Through 0 (Representing No Relationship), to +1.00 (Representing the Strongest Possible Positive Relationship)

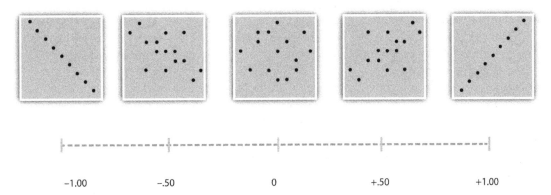

| −1.00 | −.50 | 0 | +.50 | +1.00 |

The computations for Pearson's *r* are more complicated than those for Cohen's *d*. Although you may never have to do them by hand, it is still instructive to see how. Computationally, Pearson's *r* is the "mean cross-product of *z* scores." To compute it, one starts by transforming all the scores to *z* scores. For the *X* variable, subtract the mean of *X* from each score and divide each difference by the standard deviation of *X*. For the *Y* variable, subtract the mean of *Y* from each score and divide each difference by the standard deviation of *Y*. Then, for each individual, multiply the two *z* scores together to form a cross-product. Finally, take the mean of the cross-products. The formula looks like this:

$$r = \frac{\sum (z_x z_y)}{N}$$

Table 12.6 illustrates these computations for a small set of data. The first column lists the scores for the *X* variable, which has a mean of 4.00 and a standard deviation of 1.90. The second column is the *z* score for each of these raw scores. The third and fourth columns list the raw scores for the *Y* variable, which has a mean of 40 and a standard deviation of 11.78, and the corresponding *z* scores. The fifth column lists the cross-products. For example, the first one is 0.00 multiplied by −0.85, which is equal to 0.00. The second is 1.58 multiplied by 1.19, which is equal to 1.88. The mean of these cross-products, shown at the bottom of that column, is Pearson's *r*, which in this case is +.53. There are other formulas for computing Pearson's *r* by hand that may be quicker. This approach, however, is much clearer in terms of communicating conceptually what Pearson's *r* is.

**TABLE 12.6** Sample Computations for Pearson's *r*

| *X* | $z_x$ | *Y* | $z_y$ | $z_x z_y$ |
|---|---|---|---|---|
| 4 | 0.00 | 30 | −0.85 | 0.00 |
| 7 | 1.58 | 54 | 1.19 | 1.88 |
| 2 | −1.05 | 23 | −1.44 | 1.52 |

| X | zx | Y | zy | zxzy |
|---|---|---|---|---|
| 5 | 0.53 | 43 | 0.26 | 0.13 |
| 2 | −1.05 | 50 | 0.85 | −0.89 |
| $M_X = 4.00$ | | $M_y = 40.00$ | | $r = 0.53$ |
| $SD_X = 1.90$ | | $SD_y = 11.78$ | | |

**restriction of range**

When the data used to assess a statistical relationship include a limited range of scores on either the *X* or *Y* variable, relative to the range of scores in the population. This makes the statistical relationships appear weaker than it actually is.

There are two common situations in which the value of Pearson's *r* can be misleading. One is when the relationship under study is nonlinear. Even though Figure 12.9 shows a fairly strong relationship between depression and sleep, Pearson's *r* would be close to zero because the points in the scatterplot are not well fit by a single straight line. This means that it is important to make a scatterplot and confirm that a relationship is approximately linear before using Pearson's *r*. The other is when one or both of the variables have a limited range in the sample relative to the population. This is referred to as **restriction of range**. Assume, for example, that there is a strong negative correlation between people's ages and their enjoyment of hip hop music as shown by the scatterplot in Figure 12.11. Based on the entire range of ages show, from 18 to 83, Pearson's *r* is −.77. However, if we were to collect data only from 18- to 24-year-olds—represented by the shaded area of Figure 12.11—then the relationship would seem to be quite weak. In fact, Pearson's *r* for this restricted range of ages is 0. It is a good idea, therefore, to design studies to avoid restriction of range. For example, if age is one of your primary variables, then you can plan to collect data from people of a wide range of ages. Because restriction of range is not always anticipated or easily avoidable, however, it is good practice to examine your data for possible restriction of range and to interpret Pearson's *r* in light of it. (There are also statistical methods to correct Pearson's *r* for restriction of range, but they are beyond the scope of this book).

**FIGURE 12.11** Hypothetical Data Showing How a Strong Overall Correlation Can Appear to Be Weak When One Variable Has a Restricted Range
The overall correlation here is −.77, but the correlation for the 18- to 24-year-olds (in the blue box) is 0.

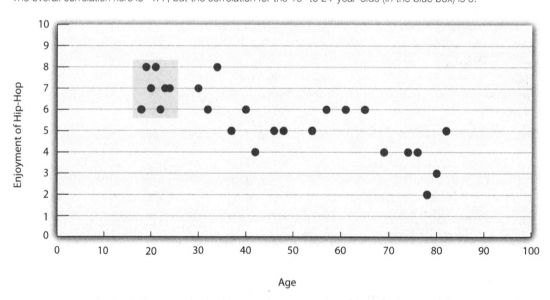

## Key Takeaways

- Differences between groups or conditions are typically described in terms of the means and standard deviations of the groups or conditions or in terms of Cohen's *d* and are presented in bar graphs.

- Cohen's *d* is a measure of relationship strength (or effect size) for differences between two group or condition means. It is the difference of the means divided by the standard deviation. In general, values of ±0.20, ±0.50, and ±0.80 can be considered small, medium, and large, respectively.

- Correlations between quantitative variables are typically described in terms of Pearson's *r* and presented in line graphs or scatterplots.

- Pearson's *r* is a measure of relationship strength (or effect size) for relationships between quantitative variables. It is the mean cross-product of the two sets of *z* scores. In general, values of ±.10, ±.30, and ±.50 can be considered small, medium, and large, respectively.

## Exercises

1. Practice: The following data represent scores on the Rosenberg Self-Esteem Scale for a sample of 10 Japanese college students and 10 American college students. (Although hypothetical, these data are consistent with empirical findings [Schmitt & Allik, 2005].[5]) Compute the means and standard deviations of the two groups, make a bar graph, compute Cohen's *d*, and describe the strength of the relationship in words.

| Japan | United States |
|---|---|
| 25 | 27 |
| 20 | 30 |
| 24 | 34 |
| 28 | 37 |
| 30 | 26 |
| 32 | 24 |
| 21 | 28 |
| 24 | 35 |
| 20 | 33 |
| 26 | 36 |

2. Practice: The hypothetical data that follow are extroversion scores and the number of Facebook friends for 15 college students. Make a scatterplot for these data, compute Pearson's *r*, and describe the relationship in words.

| Extroversion | Facebook Friends |
|---|---|
| 8 | 75 |
| 10 | 315 |
| 4 | 28 |
| 6 | 214 |
| 12 | 176 |
| 14 | 95 |
| 10 | 120 |
| 11 | 150 |
| 4 | 32 |
| 13 | 250 |
| 5 | 99 |

| Extroversion | Facebook Friends |
|---|---|
| 7 | 136 |
| 8 | 185 |
| 11 | 88 |
| 10 | 144 |

# 12.3 Expressing Your Results

## Learning Objectives

1. Write out simple descriptive statistics in American Psychological Association (APA) style.
2. Interpret and create simple APA-style graphs—including bar graphs, line graphs, and scatterplots.
3. Interpret and create simple APA-style tables—including tables of group or condition means and correlation matrixes.

Once you have conducted your descriptive statistical analyses, you will need to present them to others. In this section, we focus on presenting descriptive statistical results in writing, in graphs, and in tables—following American Psychological Association (APA) guidelines for written research reports. These principles can be adapted easily to other presentation formats such as posters and slide shows.

## Presenting Descriptive Statistics in Writing

When you have a small number of results to report, it is often most efficient to write them out. There are a few important APA style guidelines here. First, statistical results are always presented in the form of numerals rather than words and are usually rounded to two decimal places (e.g., "2.00" rather than "two" or "2"). They can be presented either in the narrative description of the results or parenthetically—much like reference citations. Here are some examples:

The mean age of the participants was 22.43 years with a standard deviation of 2.34.

- Among the low self-esteem participants, those in a negative mood expressed stronger intentions to have unprotected sex ($M$ = 4.05, $SD$ = 2.32) than those in a positive mood ($M$ = 2.15, $SD$ = 2.27).

- The treatment group had a mean of 23.40 ($SD$ = 9.33), while the control group had a mean of 20.87 ($SD$ = 8.45).

- The test-retest correlation was .96.

- There was a moderate negative correlation between the alphabetical position of respondents' last names and their response time ($r$ = −.27).

Notice that when presented in the narrative, the terms *mean* and *standard deviation* are written out, but when presented parenthetically, the symbols $M$ and $SD$ are used instead. Notice also that it is especially important to use parallel construction to express similar or comparable results in similar ways. The third example is *much* better than the following nonparallel alternative:

- The treatment group had a mean of 23.40 (*SD* = 9.33), while 20.87 was the mean of the control group, which had a standard deviation of 8.45.

# Presenting Descriptive Statistics in Graphs

When you have a large number of results to report, you can often do it more clearly and efficiently with a graph. When you prepare graphs for an APA-style research report, there are some general guidelines that you should keep in mind. First, the graph should always add important information rather than repeat information that already appears in the text or in a table. (If a graph presents information more clearly or efficiently, then you should keep the graph and eliminate the text or table.) Second, graphs should be as simple as possible. For example, the *Publication Manual* discourages the use of color unless it is absolutely necessary (although color can still be an effective element in posters, slide show presentations, or textbooks.) Third, graphs should be interpretable on their own. A reader should be able to understand the basic result based only on the graph and its caption and should not have to refer to the text for an explanation.

There are also several more technical guidelines for graphs that include the following:

- Layout
  - The graph should be slightly wider than it is tall.
  - The independent variable should be plotted on the *x*-axis and the dependent variable on the *y*-axis.
  - Values should increase from left to right on the *x*-axis and from bottom to top on the *y*-axis.
- Axis Labels and Legends
  - Axis labels should be clear and concise and include the units of measurement if they do not appear in the caption.
  - Axis labels should be parallel to the axis.
  - Legends should appear within the boundaries of the graph.
  - Text should be in the same simple font throughout and differ by no more than four points.
- Captions
  - Captions should briefly describe the figure, explain any abbreviations, and include the units of measurement if they do not appear in the axis labels.
  - Captions in an APA manuscript should be typed on a separate page that appears at the end of the manuscript. See Chapter 11 for more information.

## Bar Graphs

**error bars**

In bar graphs and line graphs, vertical lines that show the amount of variability around the mean in each group or condition. They typically extend upward and downward one standard error from the top of each bar or point.

**standard error**

The standard deviation divided by the square root of the sample size. Often used for error bars in graphs.

As we have seen throughout this book, bar graphs are generally used to present and compare the mean scores for two or more groups or conditions. The bar graph in Figure 12.12 is an APA-style version of Figure 12.5. Notice that it conforms to all the guidelines listed. A new element in Figure 12.12 is the smaller vertical bars that extend both upward and downward from the top of each main bar. These are **error bars**, and they represent the variability in each group or condition. Although they sometimes extend one standard deviation in each direction, they are more likely to extend one standard error in each direction (as in Figure 12.12). The **standard error** is the standard deviation of the group divided by the square root of the sample size of the group. One reason the standard error is used is that, in general, a difference between group means that is greater than two standard errors is statistically significant. Thus one can "see" whether a difference between means is statistically significant based on a bar graph with error bars.

**FIGURE 12.12** Sample APA-Style Bar Graph, With Error Bars Representing the Standard Errors, Based on Research by Ollendick and Colleagues

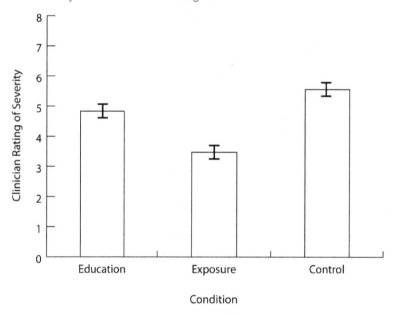

*Figure X.* Mean clinician's rating of phobia severity for participants receiving the education treatment and the exposure treatment. Error bars represent standard errors.

## Line Graphs

**line graph**

A graph used to show the relationship between two quantitative variables. For each level of the *X* variable, there is a point representing the mean of the *Y* variable. The points are connected by lines.

**Line graphs** are used to present correlations between quantitative variables when the independent variable has, or is organized into, a relatively small number of distinct levels. Each point in a line graph represents the mean score on the dependent variable for participants at one level of the independent variable. Figure 12.13 is an APA-style version of the results of Carlson and Conard (2011). Notice that it includes error bars representing the standard error and conforms to all the stated guidelines.

**FIGURE 12.13** Sample APA-Style Line Graph Based on Research by Carlson and Conard (2011)

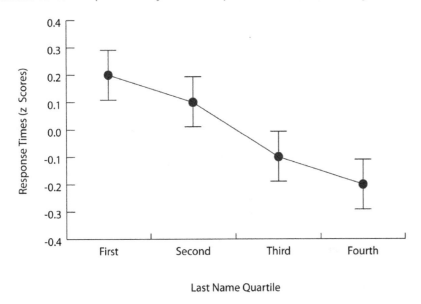

*Figure X.* Mean response time by the alphabetical position of respondents' names in the alphabet. Response times are expressed as z scores. Error bars represent standard errors.

In most cases, the information in a line graph could just as easily be presented in a bar graph. In Figure 12.13, for example, one could replace each point with a bar that reaches up to the same level and leave the error bars right where they are. This emphasizes the fundamental similarity of the two types of statistical relationship. Both are differences in the average score on one variable across levels of another. The convention followed by most researchers, however, is to use a bar graph when the variable plotted on the *x*-axis is categorical and a line graph when it is quantitative.

## Scatterplots

**Scatterplots** are used to present relationships between quantitative variables when the variable on the *x*-axis (typically the independent variable) has a large number of levels. Each point in a scatterplot represents an individual rather than the mean for a group of individuals, and there are no lines connecting the points. The graph in Figure 12.14 is an APA-style version of Figure 12.8, which illustrates two additional points. First, when two or more individuals fall at exactly the same point on the graph, one way this can be indicated is by offsetting the points slightly along the *x*-axis. Other ways are by displaying the number of individuals in parentheses next to the point or by making the point larger or darker in proportion to the number of individuals. Second, the straight line that best fits the points in the scatterplot, which is called the regression line, can also be included.

**scatterplot**

A graph used to show the correlation between two quantitative variables. For each individual, there is a point representing that individual's score on both the *X* and *Y* variables.

**FIGURE 12.14** Sample APA-Style Scatterplot

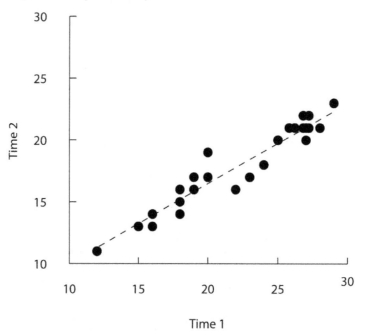

*Figure X.* Relationship between scores on the Rosenberg self-esteem scale taken by 25 research methods students on two occasions one week apart. Pearson's r =.96.

# Expressing Descriptive Statistics in Tables

Like graphs, tables can be used to present large amounts of information clearly and efficiently. The same general principles apply to tables as apply to graphs. They should add important information to the presentation of your results, be as simple as possible, and be interpretable on their own. Again, we focus here on tables for an APA-style manuscript.

The most common use of tables is to present several means and standard deviations—usually for complex research designs with multiple independent and dependent variables. Figure 12.15, for example, shows the results of a hypothetical study similar to the one by MacDonald and Martineau (2002)[6] discussed in Chapter 5. (The means in Figure 12.15 are the means reported by MacDonald and Martineau, but the standard errors are not.) Recall that these researchers categorized participants as having low or high self-esteem, put them into a negative or positive mood, and measured their intentions to have unprotected sex. Although not mentioned in Chapter 5, they also measured participants' attitudes toward unprotected sex. Notice that the table includes horizontal lines spanning the entire table at the top and bottom, and just beneath the column headings. Furthermore, every column has a heading—including the leftmost column—and there are additional headings spanning two or more columns that help to organize the information and present it more efficiently. Finally, notice that APA-style tables are numbered consecutively starting at 1 (Table 1, Table 2, and so on) and given a brief but clear and descriptive title.

FIGURE 12.15 Sample APA-Style Table Presenting Means and Standard Deviations

**Table X**

*Means and Standard Deviations of Intentions to Have Unprotected Sex and Attitudes Toward*
*Unprotected Sex as a Function of Both Mood and Self-Esteem*

| Self-Esteem | Negative mood | | | Positive mood | |
|---|---|---|---|---|---|
| | M | SD | | M | SD |
| Intentions | | | | | |
| High | 2.46 | 1.97 | | 2.45 | 2.00 |
| Low | 4.05 | 2.32 | | 2.15 | 2.27 |
| Attitudes | | | | | |
| High | 1.65 | 2.23 | | 1.82 | 2.32 |
| Low | 1.95 | 2.01 | | 1.23 | 1.75 |

Another common use of tables is to present correlations—usually measured by Pearson's *r*—among several variables. This is called a **correlation matrix**. Figure 12.16 is a correlation matrix based on a study by David McCabe and colleagues (McCabe, Roediger, McDaniel, Balota, & Hambrick, 2010).[7] They were interested in the relationships between working memory and several other variables. We can see from the table that the correlation between working memory and executive function, for example, was an extremely strong .96, that the correlation between working memory and vocabulary was a medium .27, and that all the measures except vocabulary tend to decline with age. Notice here that only half the table is filled in because the other half would have identical values. For example, the Pearson's *r* value in the upper right corner (working memory and age) would be the same as the one in the lower left corner (age and working memory). The correlation of a variable with itself is always 1.00, so these values are replaced by dashes to make the table easier to read.

**correlation matrix**

A table that shows the correlations among several variables.

FIGURE 12.16 Sample APA-Style Table (Correlation Matrix) Based on Research by McCabe and Colleagues

**Table X**

*Correlations Between Five Cognitive Variables and Age*

| Measure | 1 | 2 | 3 | 4 | 5 |
|---|---|---|---|---|---|
| 1. Working memory | — | | | | |
| 2. Executive function | .96 | — | | | |
| 3. Processing speed | .78 | .78 | — | | |
| 4. Vocabulary | .27 | .45 | .08 | — | |
| 5. Episodic memory | .73 | .75 | .52 | .38 | — |
| 6. Age | –.59 | –.56 | –.82 | .22 | –.41 |

As with graphs, precise statistical results that appear in a table do not need to be repeated in the text. Instead, the writer can note major trends and alert the reader to details (e.g., specific correlations) that are of particular interest.

- In an APA-style article, simple results are most efficiently presented in the text, while more complex results are most efficiently presented in graphs or tables.
- APA style includes several rules for presenting numerical results in the text. These include using words only for numbers less than 10 that do not represent precise statistical results, and rounding results to two decimal places, using words (e.g., "mean") in the text and symbols (e.g., "*M*") in parentheses.
- APA style includes several rules for presenting results in graphs and tables. Graphs and tables should add information rather than repeating information, be as simple as possible, and be interpretable on their own with a descriptive caption (for graphs) or a descriptive title (for tables).

## Exercise

1. Practice: In a classic study, men and women rated the importance of physical attractiveness in both a short-term mate and a long-term mate (Buss & Schmitt, 1993).[8] The means and standard deviations are as follows. Men / Short Term: $M = 5.67$, $SD = 2.34$; Men / Long Term: $M = 4.43$, $SD = 2.11$; Women / Short Term: $M = 5.67$, $SD = 2.48$; Women / Long Term: $M = 4.22$, $SD = 1.98$. Present these results (a) in writing, (b) in a graph, and (c) in a table.

# 12.4 Conducting Your Analyses

## Learning Objective

1. Describe the steps involved in preparing and analyzing a typical set of raw data.

Even when you understand the statistics involved, analyzing data can be a complicated process. It is likely that for each of several participants, there are data for several different variables: demographics such as sex and age, one or more independent variables, one or more dependent variables, and perhaps a manipulation check. Furthermore, the "raw" (unanalyzed) data might take several different forms—completed paper-and-pencil questionnaires, computer files filled with numbers or text, videos, or written notes—and these may have to be organized, coded, or combined in some way. There might even be missing, incorrect, or just "suspicious" responses that must be dealt with. In this section, we consider some practical advice to make this process as organized and efficient as possible.

## Prepare Your Data for Analysis

Whether your raw data are on paper or in a computer file (or both), there are a few things you should do before you begin analyzing them. First, be sure they do not include any information that might identify individual participants and be sure that you have a secure location where you can store the data and a separate secure location where you can store any consent forms. Unless the data are highly sensitive, a locked room or password-protected computer is usually good enough. It is also a good idea to make photocopies or backup files of your data and store them in yet another secure location—at least until the project is complete. Professional researchers usually keep a copy of their raw data and consent forms for several years in case questions about the procedure, the data, or participant consent arise after the project is completed.

Next, you should check your **raw data** to make sure that they are complete and appear to have been accurately recorded (whether it was participants, you, or a computer program that did the recording). At this point, you might find that there are illegible or missing responses, or obvious misunderstandings (e.g., a response of "12" on a 1-to-10 rating scale). You will have to decide whether such problems are severe enough to make a participant's data unusable. If information about the main independent or dependent variable is missing, or if several responses are missing or suspicious, you may have to exclude that participant's data from the analyses. If you do decide to exclude any data, do not throw them away or delete them because you or another researcher might want to see them later. Instead, set them aside and keep notes about why you decided to exclude them because you will need to report this information.

Now you are ready to enter your data in a spreadsheet program or, if it is already in a computer file, to format it for analysis. You can use a general spreadsheet program like Microsoft Excel or a statistical analysis program like SPSS to create your **data file**. (Data files created in one program can usually be converted to work with other programs.) The most common format is for each row to represent a participant and for each column to represent a variable (with the variable name at the top of each column). A sample data file is shown in Table 12.7. The first column contains participant identification numbers. This is followed by columns containing demographic information (sex and age), independent variables (mood, four self-esteem items, and the total of the four self-esteem items), and finally dependent variables (intentions and attitudes). Categorical variables can usually be entered as category labels (e.g., "M" and "F" for male and female) or as numbers (e.g., "0" for negative mood and "1" for positive mood). Although category labels are often clearer, some analyses might require numbers.

**raw data**

Data in the form in which they were originally collected (e.g., completed questionnaires).

**data file**

A computer file that contains data formatted for statistical analysis.

**TABLE 12.7** Sample Data File

| ID | SEX | AGE | MOOD | SE1 | SE2 | SE3 | SE4 | TOTAL | INT | ATT |
|----|-----|-----|------|-----|-----|-----|-----|-------|-----|-----|
| 1 | M | 20 | 1 | 2 | 3 | 2 | 3 | 10 | 6 | 5 |
| 2 | F | 22 | 1 | 1 | 0 | 2 | 1 | 4 | 4 | 4 |
| 3 | F | 19 | 0 | 2 | 2 | 2 | 2 | 8 | 2 | 3 |
| 4 | F | 24 | 0 | 3 | 3 | 2 | 3 | 11 | 5 | 6 |

If you have multiple-response measures—such as the self-esteem measure in Table 12.7—you could combine the items by hand and then enter the total score in your spreadsheet. However, it is much better to enter each response as a separate variable in the spreadsheet—as with the self-esteem measure in Table 12.7—and use the software to combine them (e.g., using the "AVERAGE" function in Excel or the "Compute" function in SPSS). Not only is this approach more accurate, but it allows you to detect and correct errors, to assess internal consistency, and to analyze individual responses if you decide to do so later.

## Preliminary Analyses

Before turning to your primary research questions, there are often several preliminary analyses to conduct. For multiple-response measures, you should assess the internal consistency of the measure. Statistical programs like SPSS will allow you to compute Cronbach's α or Cohen's κ. If this is beyond your comfort level, you can still compute and evaluate a split-half correlation. (See the "Internal Consistency" section of Chapter 5 Section 2 for more on the split-half correlation.)

Next, you should analyze each important variable separately. (This is not necessary for manipulated independent variables, of course, because you as the researcher determined what the distribution would be.) Make histograms for each one, note their shapes, and compute the common measures of central tendency and variability. Be sure you understand what these statistics *mean* in terms of the variables you are interested in. For example, a distribution of self-report happiness ratings on a 1-to-10-point scale might be unimodal and negatively skewed with a mean of 8.25 and a standard deviation of 1.14. But what this *means* is that most participants rated themselves fairly high on the happiness scale, with a small number rating themselves noticeably lower.

Now is the time to identify outliers, examine them more closely, and decide what to do about them. You might discover that what at first appears to be an outlier is the result of a response being entered incorrectly in the data file, in which case you only need to correct the data file and move on. Alternatively, you might suspect that an outlier represents some other kind of error, misunderstanding, or lack of effort by a participant. For example, in a reaction time distribution in which most participants took only a few seconds to respond, a participant who took 3 minutes to respond would be an outlier. It seems likely that this participant did not understand the task (or at least was not paying very close attention). Also, including his or her reaction time would have a large impact on the mean and standard deviation for the sample. In situations like this, it can be justifiable to exclude the outlying response or participant from the analyses. If you do this, however, you should keep notes on which responses or participants you have excluded and why, and apply those same criteria consistently to every response and every participant. When you present your results, you should indicate how many responses or participants you excluded and the specific criteria that you used. And again, do not literally throw away or delete the data that you choose to exclude. Just set them aside because you or another researcher might want to see them later.

Keep in mind that outliers do not *necessarily* represent an error, misunderstanding, or lack of effort. They might represent truly extreme responses or participants. For example, in one large college student sample, the vast majority of participants reported having had fewer than 15 sexual partners, but there were also a few extreme scores of 60 or 70 (Brown & Sinclair, 1999).[9] Although these scores might represent errors, misunderstandings, or even intentional exaggerations, it is also plausible that they represent honest and even accurate estimates. One strategy here would be to use the median and other statistics that are not strongly affected by the outliers. Another would be to analyze the data both including and excluding any outliers. If the results are essentially the same, which they often are, then it makes sense to leave the outliers. If the results differ depending on whether the outliers are included or excluded them, then both analyses can be reported and the differences between them discussed.

## Answer Your Research Questions

Finally, you are ready to answer your primary research questions. If you are interested in a difference between group or condition means, you can compute the relevant group or condition means and standard deviations, make a bar graph to display the results, and compute Cohen's *d*. If you are interested in a correlation between quantitative variables, you can make a line graph or scatterplot (be sure to check for nonlinearity and restriction of range) and compute Pearson's *r*.

At this point, you may also explore your data for other interesting results that might provide the basis for future research (and material for the discussion section of your paper). Daryl Bem (2003) suggests that you:

*[e]xamine [your data] from every angle. Analyze the sexes separately. Make up new composite indexes. If a datum suggests a new hypothesis, try to find additional evidence for it elsewhere in the data. If you see dim traces of interesting patterns, try to reorganize the data to bring them into bolder relief. If there are participants you don't like, or trials, observers, or interviewers who gave you anomalous results, drop them (temporarily). Go on a fishing expedition for something—anything—interesting. (p. 186–187)[10]*

It is important to be cautious, however, because complex sets of data are likely to include "patterns" that occurred entirely by chance. Thus results discovered while "fishing" should be replicated in at least one new study before being presented as new phenomena in their own right.

# Understand Your Descriptive Statistics

In the next chapter, we will consider inferential statistics—a set of techniques for deciding whether the results for your sample are likely to apply to the population. Although inferential statistics are important for reasons that will be explained shortly, beginning researchers sometimes forget that their descriptive statistics really tell "what happened" in their study. For example, imagine that a treatment group of 50 participants has a mean score of 34.32 ($SD$ = 10.45), a control group of 50 participants has a mean score of 21.45 ($SD$ = 9.22), and Cohen's $d$ is an extremely strong 1.31. Although conducting and reporting inferential statistics (like a $t$ test) would certainly be a required part of any formal report on this study, it should be clear from the descriptive statistics alone that the treatment worked. Or imagine that a scatterplot shows an indistinct "cloud" of points and Pearson's $r$ is a trivial -.02. Again, although conducting and reporting inferential statistics would be a required part of any formal report on this study, it should be clear from the descriptive statistics alone that the variables are essentially unrelated. The point is that you should always be sure that you thoroughly understand your results at a descriptive level first, and then move on to the inferential statistics.

## Key Takeaways

- Raw data must be prepared for analysis by examining them for possible errors, organizing them, and entering them into a spreadsheet program.
- Preliminary analyses on any data set include checking the reliability of measures, evaluating the effectiveness of any manipulations, examining the distributions of individual variables, and identifying outliers.
- Outliers that appear to be the result of an error, a misunderstanding, or a lack of effort can be excluded from the analyses. The criteria for excluded responses or participants should be applied in the same way to all the data and described when you present your results. Excluded data should be set aside rather than destroyed or deleted in case they are needed later.
- Descriptive statistics tell the story of what happened in a study. Although inferential statistics are also important, it is essential to understand the descriptive statistics first.

## Exercise

1. Discussion: What are at least two reasonable ways to deal with each of the following outliers based on the discussion in this chapter? (a) A participant estimating ordinary people's heights estimates one woman's height to be "84 inches" tall. (b) In a study of memory for ordinary objects, one participant scores 0 out of 15. (c) In response to a question about how many "close friends" she has, one participant writes "32."

# Endnotes

1. Ollendick, T. H., Öst, L.-G., Reuterskiöld, L., Costa, N., Cederlund, R., Sirbu, C.,...Jarrett, M. A. (2009). One-session treatments of specific phobias in youth: A randomized clinical trial in the United States and Sweden. *Journal of Consulting and Clinical Psychology, 77*, 504–516.

2. Cohen, J. (1992). A power primer. *Psychological Bulletin, 112*, 155–159.

3. Hyde, J. S. (2007). New directions in the study of gender similarities and differences. *Current Directions in Psychological Science, 16*, 259–263.

4. Carlson, K. A., & Conard, J. M. (2011). The last name effect: How last name influences acquisition timing. *Journal of Consumer Research*. doi: 10.1086/658470

5. Schmitt, D. P., & Allik, J. (2005). Simultaneous administration of the Rosenberg Self-Esteem Scale in 53 nations: Exploring the universal and culture-specific features of global self-esteem. *Journal of Personality and Social Psychology, 89*, 623–642.

6. MacDonald, T. K., & Martineau, A. M. (2002). Self-esteem, mood, and intentions to use condoms: When does low self-esteem lead to risky health behaviors? *Journal of Experimental Social Psychology, 38*, 299–306.

7. McCabe, D. P., Roediger, H. L., McDaniel, M. A., Balota, D. A., & Hambrick, D. Z. (2010). The relationship between working memory capacity and executive functioning. *Neuropsychology, 243*, 222–243.

8. Buss, D. M., & Schmitt, D. P. (1993). Sexual strategies theory: A contextual evolutionary analysis of human mating. *Psychological Review, 100*, 204–232.

9. Brown, N. R., & Sinclair, R. C. (1999). Estimating number of lifetime sexual partners: Men and women do it differently. *The Journal of Sex Research, 36*, 292–297.

10. Bem, D. J. (2003). Writing the empirical journal article. In J. M. Darley, M. P. Zanna, & H. L. Roediger III (Eds.), *The compleat academic: A career guide* (2nd ed., pp. 185–219). Washington, DC: American Psychological Association.

# CHAPTER 13
# Inferential Statistics

Recall that Matias Mehl and his colleagues, in their study of sex differences in talkativeness, found that the women in their sample spoke a mean of 16,215 words per day and the men a mean of 15,669 words per day (Mehl, Vazire, Ramirez-Esparza, Slatcher, & Pennebaker, 2007).[1] But despite this sex difference in their sample, they concluded that there was no evidence of a sex difference in talkativeness in the population. Recall also that Allen Kanner and his colleagues, in their study of the relationship between daily hassles and symptoms, found a correlation of +.60 in their sample (Kanner, Coyne, Schaefer, & Lazarus, 1981).[2] But they concluded that this means there *is* a relationship between hassles and symptoms in the population. This raises the question of how researchers can say whether their sample result reflects something that is true of the population.

The answer to this question is that they use a set of techniques called inferential statistics, which is what this chapter is about. We focus, in particular, on null hypothesis testing, the most common approach to inferential statistics in psychological research. We begin with a conceptual overview of null hypothesis testing, including its purpose and basic logic. Then we look at several null hypothesis testing techniques for drawing conclusions about differences between means and about correlations between quantitative variables. Finally, we consider a few other important ideas related to null hypothesis testing, including some that can be helpful in planning new studies and interpreting results. We also look at some long-standing criticisms of null hypothesis testing and some ways of dealing with these criticisms.

# 13.1 Understanding Null Hypothesis Testing

## Learning Objectives

1. Explain the purpose of null hypothesis testing, including the role of sampling error.
2. Describe the basic logic of null hypothesis testing.
3. Describe the role of relationship strength and sample size in determining statistical significance and make reasonable judgments about statistical significance based on these two factors.

# The Purpose of Null Hypothesis Testing

**parameter**

A numerical summary (e.g., mean, standard deviation) of a population. A numerical summary of a sample is called a "statistic."

As we have seen, psychological research typically involves measuring one or more variables for a sample and computing descriptive statistics for that sample. In general, however, the researcher's goal is not to draw conclusions about that sample but to draw conclusions about the population that the sample was selected from. Thus researchers must use sample statistics to draw conclusions about the corresponding values in the population. These corresponding values in the population are called **parameters**. Imagine, for example, that a researcher measures the number of depressive symptoms exhibited by each of 50 clinically depressed adults and computes the mean number of symptoms. The researcher probably wants to use this sample statistic (the mean number of symptoms for the sample) to draw conclusions about the corresponding population parameter (the mean number of symptoms for clinically depressed adults).

**sampling error**

Random variation in a statistic from sample to sample.

Unfortunately, sample statistics are not perfect estimates of their corresponding population parameters. This is because there is a certain amount of random variability in any statistic from sample to sample. The mean number of depressive symptoms might be 8.73 in one sample of clinically depressed adults, 6.45 in a second sample, and 9.44 in a third—even though these samples are selected randomly from the same population. Similarly, the correlation (Pearson's $r$) between two variables might be +.24 in one sample, −.04 in a second sample, and +.15 in a third—again, even though these samples are selected randomly from the same population. This random variability in a statistic from sample to sample is called **sampling error**. (Note that the term *error* here refers to random variability and does not imply that anyone has made a mistake. No one "commits a sampling error.")

One implication of this is that when there is a statistical relationship in a sample, it is not always clear that there is a statistical relationship in the population. A small difference between two group means in a sample might indicate that there is a small difference between the two group means in the population. But it could also be that there is no difference between the means in the population and that the difference in the sample is just a matter of sampling error. Similarly, a Pearson's $r$ value of −.29 in a sample might mean that there is a negative relationship in the population. But it could also be that there is no relationship in the population and that the relationship in the sample is just a matter of sampling error.

In fact, any statistical relationship in a sample can be interpreted in two ways:

1. There is a relationship in the population, and the relationship in the sample reflects this.
2. There is no relationship in the population, and the relationship in the sample reflects only sampling error.

The purpose of null hypothesis testing is simply to help researchers decide between these two interpretations.

# The Logic of Null Hypothesis Testing

**Null hypothesis testing** is a formal approach to deciding between two interpretations of a statistical relationship in a sample. One interpretation is called the **null hypothesis** (often symbolized $H_0$ and read as "H-naught"). This is the idea that there is no relationship in the population and that the relationship in the sample reflects only sampling error. Informally, the null hypothesis is that the sample relationship "occurred by chance." The other interpretation is called the **alternative hypothesis** (often symbolized as $H_1$). This is the idea that there is a relationship in the population and that the relationship in the sample reflects this relationship in the population.

Although there are many specific null hypothesis testing techniques, they are all based on the same general logic. The steps are as follows:

1. Assume for the moment that the null hypothesis is true. There is no relationship between the variables in the population.

2. Determine how likely the sample relationship would be if this were the case.

3. If the sample relationship would be extremely unlikely, then **reject the null hypothesis** in favor of the alternative hypothesis. Otherwise, **fail to reject the null hypothesis** and continue to assume that there is no relationship in the population.

Following this logic, we can begin to understand why Mehl and his colleagues concluded that there is no difference in talkativeness between women and men in the population. In essence, they asked the following question: "If there were no difference in the population, how likely is it that we would find a small difference of $d = 0.06$ in our sample?" Their answer to this question was that this would not be at all unlikely if the null hypothesis were true. Therefore, they did not reject the null hypothesis and concluded that there is no evidence of a sex difference in the population. We can also see why Kanner and his colleagues concluded that there is a correlation between hassles and symptoms in the population. They asked, "If there were no correlation in the population, how likely is it that we would find a strong correlation of $+.60$ in our sample?" Their answer to this question was that this sample relationship would be extremely unlikely if the null hypothesis were true. Therefore, they rejected the null hypothesis in favor of the alternative hypothesis—concluding that there is a positive correlation between these variables in the population.

**null hypothesis testing**

A formal approach to deciding whether a sample relationship is due to chance (the null hypothesis) or reflects a real relationship in the population (the alternative hypothesis).

**null hypothesis**

The idea that there is no statistical relationship between two variables in the population and that any relationship in a sample is due to chance. Often abbreviated $H_0$.

**alternative hypothesis**

The idea that there is a statistical relationship between two variables in the population and that any relationship in a sample reflects that real relationship. Often abbreviated $H_1$.

**reject the null hypothesis**

In null hypothesis testing, the conclusion that the null hypothesis is false. The sample relationship reflects a real relationship in the population.

**fail to reject the null hypothesis**

In null hypothesis testing, the tentative conclusion that the null hypothesis is true. The sample relationship is due to chance. Sometimes expressed as "retain the null hypothesis" (although never as "accept the null hypothesis").

**p value**

In null hypothesis testing, the probability of a sample result at least as extreme as the one obtained if the null hypothesis were true.

**α (alpha)**

In null hypothesis testing, the criterion for deciding that a p value is low enough to reject the null hypothesis. In psychological research, it is almost always set to .05.

**statistically significant**

Used to describe a result for which the null hypothesis has been rejected.

A crucial step in null hypothesis testing is finding the likelihood of the sample result if the null hypothesis were true. This probability is called the **p value**. A low p value means that the sample result would be unlikely if the null hypothesis were true and leads to the rejection of the null hypothesis. A high p value means that the sample result would be likely if the null hypothesis were true and leads to the failure to reject the null hypothesis. But how low must the p value be before the sample result is considered unlikely enough to reject the null hypothesis? In null hypothesis testing, this criterion is called **α (alpha)** and is almost always set to .05 (or 5%). If there is less than a 5% chance of a result as extreme as the sample result—if the null hypothesis were true—then the null hypothesis is rejected. When this happens, the result is said to be **statistically significant**. If there is greater than a 5% chance of a result as extreme as the sample result when the null hypothesis is true, then the null hypothesis is not rejected. This does not necessarily mean that the researcher accepts the null hypothesis as true—only that there is not currently enough evidence to conclude that it is false. Researchers sometimes use the expression "retain the null hypothesis" rather than "fail to reject the null hypothesis," but they never use the expression "accept the null hypothesis."

## The Misunderstood p Value

The p value is one of the most misunderstood quantities in psychological research (Cohen, 1994).[3] Even professional researchers misinterpret it, and it is not unusual for such misinterpretations to appear in statistics textbooks!

The most common misinterpretation is that the p value is the probability that the null hypothesis is true—that the sample result occurred by chance. For example, a misguided researcher might say that because the p value is .02, there is only a 2% chance that the result is due to chance and a 98% chance that it reflects a real relationship in the population. But this is *incorrect*. The p value is really the probability of a result at least as extreme as the sample result *if* the null hypothesis *were* true. So a p value of .02 means that if the null hypothesis were true, a sample result at least this extreme would occur only 2% of the time.

You can avoid this misunderstanding by remembering that the p value is not the probability that any particular *hypothesis* is true or false. Instead, it is the probability of obtaining the *sample result* if the null hypothesis were true.

# Role of Sample Size and Relationship Strength

Recall that null hypothesis testing involves answering the question, "If the null hypothesis were true, what is the probability of a sample result as extreme as this one?" In other words, "What is the p value?" It can be helpful to see that the answer to this question depends on just two considerations: the strength of the relationship and the size of the sample. Specifically, the stronger the sample relationship and the larger the sample, the less likely the result would be if the null hypothesis were true. That is, the lower the p value would be. This should make sense. Imagine a study in which a sample of 500 women is compared with a sample of 500 men in terms of some psychological characteristic, and Cohen's d is a strong 0.50. If there were really no sex difference in the population, then a result this strong based on such a large sample should seem highly unlikely. Now imagine a similar study in which a sample of three women is compared with a sample of three men, and Cohen's d is a small 0.10. If there were no sex difference in the population, then a relationship this weak based on such a small sample should seem fairly likely. And this is precisely why the null hypothesis would be rejected in the first example and retained in the second.

Of course, sometimes the relationship can be weak and the sample large, or the relationship can be strong and the sample small. In these cases, the two considerations trade off against each other so that a weak relationship can be statistically significant if the sample is large enough and a strong relationship can be statistically significant even if the sample is small. Table 13.1

shows roughly how relationship strength and sample size combine to determine whether a sample result is statistically significant. The columns of the table represent the three levels of relationship strength: weak, medium, and strong. The rows represent four sample sizes that can be considered small, medium, large, and extra large in the context of psychological research. Thus each cell in the table represents a combination of relationship strength and sample size. If a cell contains the word *Yes*, then this combination would be statistically significant for both Cohen's $d$ and Pearson's $r$. If it contains the word *No*, then it would not be statistically significant for either. There is one cell where the decision for $d$ and $r$ would be different and another where it might be different depending on some additional considerations, which are discussed in Section 2.

**TABLE 13.1** How Relationship Strength and Sample Size Combine to Determine Whether a Result Is Statistically Significant

|  | Relationship strength | | |
| --- | --- | --- | --- |
| Sample Size | Weak | Medium | Strong |
| Small ($N$ = 20) | No | No | $d$ = Maybe<br>$r$ = Yes |
| Medium ($N$ = 50) | No | Yes | Yes |
| Large ($N$ = 100) | $d$ = Yes<br>$r$ = No | Yes | Yes |
| Extra large ($N$ = 500) | Yes | Yes | Yes |

Although Table 13.1 provides only a rough guideline, it shows very clearly that weak relationships based on medium or small samples are never statistically significant and that strong relationships based on medium or larger samples are always statistically significant. If you keep this in mind, you will often know whether a result is statistically significant based on the descriptive statistics alone. It is extremely useful to be able to develop this kind of intuitive judgment. One reason is that it allows you to develop expectations about how your formal null hypothesis tests are going to come out, which in turn allows you to detect problems in your analyses. For example, if your sample relationship is strong and your sample is medium, then you would expect to reject the null hypothesis. If for some reason your formal null hypothesis test indicates otherwise, then you need to double-check your computations and interpretations. A second reason is that the ability to make this kind of intuitive judgment is an indication that you understand the basic logic of this approach in addition to being able to do the computations.

## Intuitive Null Hypothesis Testing

In many cases, you can tell whether a result is statistically significant just by looking at the descriptive statistics and taking into account the relationship strength and the sample size. Try your hand at this kind of "intuitive null hypothesis testing" with the examples below. Refer to Table 13.1 if you need help.

- A treatment group ($N$ = 124) scores higher than a control group ($N$ = 119), with a Cohen's $d$ of 0.92. Is this result statistically significant?
- The correlation between extroversion and sense of humor was $r$ = +.04 for a sample of 21 college students. Is this result statistically significant?
- One group ($N$ = 13) hears a joke told by a man and rates the funniness of the joke. Another group ($N$ =12) hears the same joke told by a woman and rates the funniness of the joke. The mean in the first group is 7.50 ($SD$ = 3.20) and the mean in the second group is 7.20 ($SD$ = 2.80). Is this result statistically significant?
- A sample of 213 managers complete a measure of conscientiousness. The correlation between their conscientiousness scores and their annual salaries is $r$ = +.44. Is this result statistically significant?

# Statistical Significance Versus Practical Significance

Table 13.1 illustrates another extremely important point. A statistically significant result is not necessarily a strong one. Even a very weak result can be statistically significant if it is based on a large enough sample. This is closely related to Janet Shibley Hyde's argument about sex differences (Hyde, 2007).[4] The differences between women and men in mathematical problem solving and reading comprehension are statistically significant. But the word *significant* can cause people to interpret these differences as strong and important—perhaps even important enough to influence the college courses they take or even who they vote for. As we have seen, however, these statistically significant differences are actually quite weak—perhaps even "trivial."

**practical significance**

The importance of a research result in some real-world context. Research results can be statistically significant without having any practical significance. In clinical practice, practical significance is called "clinical significance."

This is why it is important to distinguish between the *statistical* significance of a result and the *practical* significance of that result. **Practical significance** refers to the importance or usefulness of the result in some real-world context. Many sex differences are statistically significant—and may even be interesting for purely scientific reasons—but they are not practically significant. In clinical practice, this same concept is often referred to as "clinical significance." For example, a study on a new treatment for social phobia might show that it produces a statistically significant positive effect. Yet this effect might not be strong enough to justify the time, effort, and other costs of putting it into practice—especially if easier and cheaper treatments that work almost as well already exist. Although statistically significant, this result would be said to lack practical or clinical significance.

## Key Takeaways

- Null hypothesis testing is a formal approach to deciding whether a statistical relationship in a sample reflects a real relationship in the population or is just due to chance.
- The logic of null hypothesis testing involves assuming that the null hypothesis is true, finding how likely the sample result would be if this assumption were correct, and then making a decision. If the sample result would be unlikely if the null hypothesis were true, then it is rejected in favor of the alternative hypothesis. If it would not be unlikely, then the null hypothesis is retained.
- The probability of obtaining the sample result if the null hypothesis were true (the *p* value) is based on two considerations: relationship strength and sample size. Reasonable judgments about whether a sample relationship is statistically significant can often be made by quickly considering these two factors.
- Statistical significance is not the same as relationship strength or importance. Even weak relationships can be statistically significant if the sample size is large enough. It is important to consider relationship strength and the practical significance of a result in addition to its statistical significance.

## Exercises

1. Discussion: Imagine a study showing that people who eat more broccoli tend to be happier. Explain for someone who knows nothing about statistics why the researchers would conduct a null hypothesis test.
2. Practice: Do "intuitive null hypothesis testing" (referring to Table 13.1 as necessary) to decide whether each of the following results is statistically significant.
   a. The correlation between two variables is $r = -.78$ based on a sample size of 137.

   b. The mean score on a psychological characteristic for women is 25 (*SD* = 5) and the mean score for men is 24 (*SD* = 5). There were 12 women and 10 men in the study.

   c. In a memory experiment, the mean number of items recalled by the 40 participants in Condition A was greater than the mean number of items recalled by the 40 participants in Condition B. Cohen's *d* was 0.50.

   d. In another memory experiment, the mean scores for participants in Conditions A and B came out exactly the same!

   e. A student finds a correlation of *r* = .04 between the number of units enrolled in and the stress levels of the other 23 students in his research methods class.

# 13.2 Some Basic Null Hypothesis Tests

## Learning Objectives

1. Conduct and interpret one-sample, dependent-samples, and independent-samples *t* tests.
2. Interpret the results of one-way, repeated measures, and factorial ANOVAs.
3. Conduct and interpret null hypothesis tests of Pearson's *r*.

In this section, we look at several common null hypothesis testing procedures. The emphasis here is on providing enough information to allow you to conduct and interpret the most basic versions. In most cases, the online statistical analysis tools mentioned in Chapter 12 will handle the computations—as will programs such as Microsoft Excel and SPSS.

## The *t* Test

As we have seen throughout this book, many studies in psychology focus on the difference between two means. The most common null hypothesis test for this type of statistical relationship is the **t test**. In this section, we look at three types of *t* tests that are used for slightly different research designs: the one-sample *t* test, the dependent-samples *t* test, and the independent-samples *t* test.

**t test**

A family of null hypothesis tests used to compare two means.

# One-Sample *t* Test

**one-sample *t* test**

A null hypothesis test used to compare one sample mean with a hypothetical population mean that provides an interesting standard of comparison.

**test statistic**

In null hypothesis testing, a statistic such as *t* or *F* that is computed only to help find the *p* value for the sample result.

The **one-sample *t* test** is used to compare a sample mean (*M*) with a hypothetical population mean ($\mu_0$) that provides some interesting standard. The null hypothesis is that the mean for the population ($\mu$) is equal to the hypothetical population mean: $\mu = \mu_0$. The alternative hypothesis is that the mean for the population is different from the hypothetical population mean: $\mu \neq \mu_0$. To decide between these two hypotheses, we need to find the probability of the sample mean (or one more extreme) if the null hypothesis were true. But finding this *p* value requires first computing a test statistic called *t*. (A **test statistic** is a statistic that is computed only to help find the *p* value.) The formula for *t* is as follows:

$$t = \frac{M - \mu_0}{\left(\frac{SD}{\sqrt{N}}\right)}$$

Again, *M* is the sample mean and $\mu_0$ is the hypothetical population mean of interest. *SD* is the sample standard deviation and *N* is the sample size.

The reason the *t* statistic (or any test statistic) is useful is that we know how it is distributed when the null hypothesis is true. As shown in Figure 13.1, the distribution of the *t* statistic is unimodal and symmetrical, and it has a mean of 0. Its precise shape depends on a statistical concept called the degrees of freedom, which for a one-sample *t* test is *N* - 1. (There are 24 degrees of freedom for the distribution shown in Figure 13.1.) The important point is that knowing this distribution makes it possible to find the *p* value for any *t* score. Consider, for example, a *t* score of +1.50 based on a sample of 25. The probability of a *t* score at least this extreme is just the proportion of *t* scores in the distribution that are at least this extreme. For now, let us define *extreme* as being far from zero in either the positive or negative direction. Thus the *p* value for a *t* score of +1.50 is the proportion of *t* scores that are greater than +1.50 *or* less than –1.50. As Figure 13.1 shows, this proportion is .14 or 14%.

**FIGURE 13.1** Distribution of *t* Scores (With 24 Degrees of Freedom) When the Null Hypothesis Is True
This example shows that 7% of *t* scores are greater than +1.50 and 7% of *t* scores are less than –1.50.

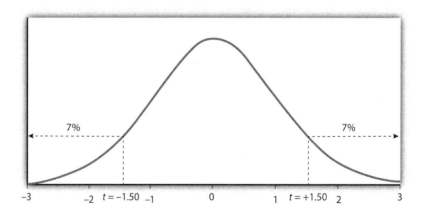

Fortunately, we do not have to deal directly with the distribution of *t* scores. If we were to enter our sample data and hypothetical mean of interest into one of the online statistical tools in Chapter 12 or into a program like SPSS (Excel does not have a one-sample *t* test function), the output would include both the *t* score and the *p* value. At this point, the rest of the procedure is simple. If *p* is less than .05, we reject the null hypothesis and conclude that the population mean differs from the hypothetical mean of interest. If *p* is greater than .05, we fail to reject the null hypothesis and conclude that the population mean does not differ from the hypothetical mean of interest. (Again, technically, we conclude only that we do not have enough evidence to conclude that it *does* differ.)

## "Looking Up" the *p* Value

Many statistics textbooks still include extensive tables that allow you to look up the "critical value" of *t* for many different degrees of freedom. If the *t* score for your sample is more extreme than the critical value, then your *p* value is less than .05 and your result is statistically significant. Before there were personal computers, tables like these were the only way that most people could know for sure whether their results were statistically significant. Today, however, you can use your computer, tablet, or phone to look up the exact *p* value for any *t* score and degrees of freedom. Here are two easy-to-use online *p* value calculators for doing just this.

- For Differences Between Two Means:
    - http://www.socscistatistics.com/pvalues/tdistribution.aspx
    - http://vassarstats.net/tabs_t.html
- For Correlations Between Quantitative Variables:
    - http://www.socscistatistics.com/pvalues/pearsondistribution.aspx
    - http://vassarstats.net/tabs_r.html

Thus far, we have considered what is called a **two-tailed test**, where we reject the null hypothesis if the *t* score for the sample is extreme in either direction. This makes sense when we believe that the sample mean could differ from the hypothetical population mean in either direction. But it is also possible to do a **one-tailed test**, where we reject the null hypothesis only if the *t* score for the sample is extreme in one direction, which we specify before collecting the data. This makes sense when we have good reason to expect the sample mean will differ from the hypothetical population mean in one direction and not the other. The only thing that changes when we do a one-tailed test is the *p* value. Again, Figure 13.1 shows a *t* score of +1.90 with 24 degrees of freedom has a two-tailed *p* value of .07. However, if we had specified before collecting the data that we expected the sample mean to be greater than the hypothetical mean, then we could do a one-tailed test where the *p* value is the probability of a *t* score *greater* than +1.90. This one-tailed *p* value is only .035, which is exactly half the two-tailed *p* value. Notice that in this example, the result is not statistically significant by a two-tailed test but it is statistically significant by a one-tailed test. This illustrates an advantage of one-tailed tests over two-tailed tests. The disadvantage of one-tailed tests is that if the sample mean differs from the hypothetical population mean in the unexpected direction, then there is no chance at all of rejecting the null hypothesis.

**two-tailed test**

A null hypothesis test (e.g., a *t* test or test of Pearson's *r*) in which the null hypothesis is rejected if the sample result is extreme in either direction. Used when the researcher does not have a strong expectation about the direction of the relationship.

**one-tailed test**

A null hypothesis test (e.g., a *t* test or test of Pearson's *r*) in which the null hypothesis is rejected only if the sample result is extreme in one direction specified before the data are collected. Used when the researcher has a strong expectation about the direction of the relationship.

## Example One-Sample *t* Test

Imagine that a health psychologist is interested in the accuracy of college students' estimates of the number of calories in a chocolate chip cookie. He shows the cookie to a sample of 10 students and asks each one to estimate the number of calories in it. Because the actual number of calories in the cookie is 250, this is the hypothetical population mean of interest ($\mu_0$). The null hypothesis is that the mean estimate for the population ($\mu$) is 250. Because he has no real sense of whether the students will underestimate or overestimate the number of calories, he decides to do a two-tailed test. Now imagine further that the participants' actual estimates are as follows:

$$250, 280, 200, 150, 175, 200, 200, 220, 180, 250.$$

The mean estimate for the sample (*M*) is 212.00 calories and the standard deviation (*SD*) is 39.17. The health psychologist can now compute the *t* score for his sample:

$$t = \frac{212 - 250}{\left(\frac{39.17}{\sqrt{10}}\right)} = -3.07$$

If he were to enter this $t$ score and 9 degrees of freedom (remember the degrees of freedom is the sample size minus one) into one of the online $p$ value calculators, it would tell him that the two-tailed p value was .013. Because this is less than .05, the health psychologist would reject the null hypothesis and conclude that college students tend to underestimate the number of calories in a chocolate chip cookie. If he were to enter his means, standard deviations, and sample sizes—or his raw data—into one of the online analysis tools in Chapter 12, he would get the same results.

Finally, if this researcher had gone into this study with good reason to expect that college students underestimate the number of calories, then he could have done a one-tailed test instead of a two-tailed test. The only thing this would change is the $p$ value, which would be .007. However, if it turned out that college students overestimated the number of calories—no matter how much they overestimated it—the researcher would not have been able to reject the null hypothesis using the one-tailed test.

## The Dependent-Samples $t$ Test

**dependent-samples $t$ test**

A null hypothesis test used to compare two means for one sample measured at two different times or under two different conditions—as in a pretest-posttest or within-subjects design.

**difference score**

The difference between an individual's score at one time or under one condition and that individual's score at a second time or under a second condition. The dependent-samples $t$ test is in essence a one-sample $t$ test on a set of difference scores.

The **dependent-samples $t$ test** (sometimes called the paired-samples $t$ test) is used to compare two means for the same sample tested at two different times or under two different conditions. This makes it appropriate for pretest-posttest designs or within-subjects experiments. The null hypothesis is that the means at the two times or under the two conditions are the same in the population. The alternative hypothesis is that they are not the same. This test can also be one-tailed if the researcher has good reason to expect the difference goes in a particular direction.

It helps to think of the dependent-samples $t$ test as a special case of the one-sample $t$ test. However, the first step in the dependent-samples $t$ test is to reduce the two scores for each participant to a single **difference score** by taking the difference between them. At this point, the dependent-samples $t$ test becomes a one-sample $t$ test on the difference scores. The hypothetical population mean ($\mu_0$) of interest is 0 because this is what the mean difference score would be if there were no difference on average between the two times or two conditions. We can now think of the null hypothesis as being that the mean difference score in the population is 0 ($\mu_0 = 0$) and the alternative hypothesis as being that the mean difference score in the population is not 0 ($\mu_0 \neq 0$).

### Example Dependent-Samples $t$ Test

Imagine that the health psychologist now knows that people tend to underestimate the number of calories in junk food and has developed a short training program to improve their estimates. To test the effectiveness of this program, he conducts a pretest-posttest study in which 10 participants estimate the number of calories in a chocolate chip cookie before the training program and then again afterward. Because he expects the program to increase the participants' estimates, he decides to do a one-tailed test. Now imagine further that the pretest estimates are

230, 250, 280, 175, 150, 200, 180, 210, 220, 190

and that the posttest estimates (for the same participants in the same order) are

250, 260, 250, 200, 160, 200, 200, 180, 230, 240.

The difference scores, then, are as follows:

+20, +10, −30, +25, +10, 0, +20, −30, +10, +50.

Note that it does not matter whether the first set of scores is subtracted from the second or the second from the first as long as it is done the same way for all participants. In this example, it makes sense to subtract the pretest estimates from the posttest estimates so that positive difference scores mean that the estimates went up after the training and negative difference scores mean the estimates went down.

The mean of the difference scores is 8.50 with a standard deviation of 27.27. The health psychologist can now compute the $t$ score for his sample as follows:

$$t = \frac{8.5 - 0}{\left(\frac{27.27}{\sqrt{10}}\right)} = 1.11$$

If he were to enter this $t$ score and 9 degrees of freedom (remember the degrees of freedom is the sample size minus one) into one of the online $p$ value calculators, it would tell him that the two-tailed $p$ value was .148 and the one-tailed $p$ value was .074. Either way, because the $p$ value is greater than .05, he would fail to reject the null hypothesis and conclude that the training program does not increase people's calorie estimates. Again, if he were to enter his means, standard deviations, and sample sizes—or his raw data—into one of the online analysis tools in Chapter 12, he would get these same results.

## The Independent-Samples $t$ Test

The **independent-samples $t$ test** is used to compare the means of two separate samples ($M_1$ and $M_2$). The two samples might have been tested under different conditions in a between-subjects experiment, or they could be preexisting groups in a correlational design (e.g., women and men, extroverts and introverts). The null hypothesis is that the means of the two populations are the same: $\mu_1 = \mu_2$. The alternative hypothesis is that they are not the same: $\mu_1 \neq \mu_2$. Again, the test can be one-tailed if the researcher has good reason to expect the difference goes in a particular direction.

**independent-samples $t$ test**

A null hypothesis test used to compare means for two separate samples—as in a between-subjects design.

The $t$ statistic here is a bit more complicated because it must take into account two sample means, two standard deviations, and two sample sizes. The formula is as follows:

$$t = \frac{M_1 - M_2}{\sqrt{\frac{SD_1^2}{n_1} + \frac{SD_2^2}{n_2}}}$$

Notice that this formula includes squared standard deviations (variances) that appear inside the square root symbol. Also, lowercase $n_1$ and $n_2$ refer to the sample sizes in the two groups or condition (as opposed to capital $N$, which generally refers to the total sample size). The only additional thing to know here is that there are $N - 2$ degrees of freedom for the independent-samples $t$ test.

### Example Independent-Samples $t$ Test

Now the health psychologist wants to compare the calorie estimates of people who regularly eat junk food with the estimates of people who rarely eat junk food. He believes the difference could come out in either direction so he decides to conduct a two-tailed test. He collects data from a sample of eight participants who eat junk food regularly and seven participants who rarely eat junk food. The data are as follows:

Junk food eaters: 180, 220, 150, 85, 200, 170, 150, 190

Non–junk food eaters: 200, 240, 190, 175, 200, 300, 240

The mean for the junk food eaters is 220.71 with a standard deviation of 41.23. The mean for the non–junk food eaters is 168.12 with a standard deviation of 42.66. He can now compute his $t$ score as follows:

$$t = \frac{220.71 - 168.12}{\sqrt{\frac{41.23^2}{8} + \frac{42.66^2}{7}}} = 2.42$$

If he were to enter this $t$ score and 13 degrees of freedom (remember the degrees of freedom is the sample size minus two) into one of the online $p$ value calculators, it would tell him that the two-tailed $p$ value was .031 and the one-tailed $p$ value was .015. Either way, because the $p$ value is less than .05, he would reject the null hypothesis and conclude that people who eat junk food regularly make lower calorie estimates than people who eat it rarely. And if he were to enter his means, standard deviations, and sample sizes—or his raw data—into one of the online analysis tools in Chapter 12, he would get these same results.

# The Analysis of Variance

**analysis of variance (ANOVA)**

A null hypothesis test used to compare means for more than two groups or conditions.

When there are more than two groups or condition means to be compared, the most common null hypothesis test is the **analysis of variance (ANOVA)**. In this section, we look primarily at the **one-way ANOVA**, which is used for between-subjects designs with a single independent variable. We then briefly consider some other versions of the ANOVA that are used for within-subjects and factorial research designs.

**one-way ANOVA**

A null hypothesis test used to compare more than two means in a between-subjects design with one independent variable.

## One-Way ANOVA

The one-way ANOVA is used to compare the means of more than two samples ($M_1$, $M_2...M_G$) in a between-subjects design. The null hypothesis is that all the means are equal in the population: $\mu_1 = \mu_2 = ... = \mu_G$. The alternative hypothesis is that not all the means in the population are equal.

**mean squares between groups ($MS_B$)**

In an analysis of variance, an estimate for the population variance based only on differences among the group or condition means.

The test statistic for the ANOVA is called $F$. It is a ratio of two estimates of the population variance based on the sample data. One estimate of the population variance is called the **mean squares between groups ($MS_B$)** and is based on the differences among the sample means. The other is called the **mean squares within groups ($MS_W$)** and is based on the differences among the scores within each group. The $F$ statistic is the ratio of the $MS_B$ to the $MS_W$ and can therefore be expressed as follows:

$$F = \frac{MS_B}{MS_W}$$

**mean squares within groups ($MS_W$)**

In an analysis of variance, an estimate of the population variance based on the variability within each group or condition.

Again, the reason that $F$ is useful is that we know how it is distributed when the null hypothesis is true. As shown in Figure 13.2, this distribution looks quite different from the $t$ distribution. It is unimodal but positively skewed with values that cluster around 1. The precise shape of the distribution depends on both the number of groups and the sample size, and there are degrees of freedom value associated with each of these. The between-groups degrees of freedom is the number of groups minus one: $df_B = (G - 1)$. The within-groups degrees of freedom is the total sample size minus the number of groups: $df_W = N - G$. Again, knowing the distribution of $F$ when the null hypothesis is true allows us to find the $p$ value.

**FIGURE 13.2** Distribution of the *F* Ratio With 2 and 37 Degrees of Freedom When the Null Hypothesis Is True

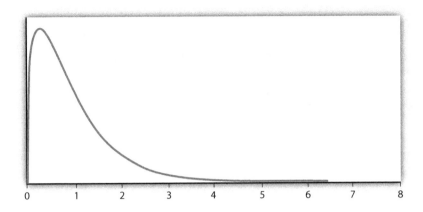

The online tools in Chapter 12 and statistical software such as Excel and SPSS will compute *F* and find the *p* value. If *p* is less than .05, then we reject the null hypothesis and conclude that there are differences among the group means in the population. If *p* is greater than .05, then we fail to reject the null hypothesis and conclude that there are no differences.

## Example One-Way ANOVA

Imagine that the health psychologist wants to compare the calorie estimates of psychology majors, nutrition majors, and professional dieticians. He collects the following data:

Psych majors: 200, 180, 220, 160, 150, 200, 190, 200

Nutrition majors: 190, 220, 200, 230, 160, 150, 200, 210, 195

Dieticians: 220, 250, 240, 275, 250, 230, 200, 240

The means are 187.50 ($SD$ = 23.14), 195.00 ($SD$ = 27.77), and 238.13 ($SD$ = 22.35), respectively. So it appears that dieticians made substantially more accurate estimates on average. The researcher would almost certainly enter these data into a program such as Excel or SPSS, which would compute *F* for him and find the *p* value. Table 13.2 shows the output of the one-way ANOVA function in Excel for these data. This is referred to as an ANOVA table. It shows that $MS_B$ is 5,971.88, $MS_W$ is 602.23, and their ratio, *F*, is 9.92. The *p* value is .0009. Because this is below .05, the researcher would reject the null hypothesis and conclude that the mean calorie estimates for the three groups are not the same in the population. Notice that the ANOVA table also includes the "sum of squares" (*SS*) for between groups and for within groups. These values are computed on the way to finding $MS_B$ and $MS_W$ but are not typically reported by the researcher.

**TABLE 13.2** Typical One-Way ANOVA Output From Excel

| ANOVA | | | | | | |
|---|---|---|---|---|---|---|
| *Source of variation* | *SS* | *df* | *MS* | *F* | *p-value* | *F* crit |
| Between groups | 11,943.75 | 2 | 5,971.875 | 9.916234 | 0.000928 | 3.4668 |
| Within groups | 12,646.88 | 21 | 602.2321 | | | |
| Total | 24,590.63 | 23 | | | | |

# ANOVA Elaborations

## Post Hoc Comparisons

**post hoc comparisons**

Statistical comparison of selected pairs of group or condition means following a statistically significant ANOVA result. Usually done using one of several modified *t*-test procedures.

When we reject the null hypothesis in a one-way ANOVA, we conclude that the group means are not all the same in the population. But this can indicate different things. With three groups, it can indicate that all three means are significantly different from each other. Or it can indicate that one of the means is significantly different from the other two, but the other two are not significantly different from each other. It could be, for example, that the mean calorie estimates of psychology majors, nutrition majors, and dieticians are all significantly different from each other. Or it could be that the mean for dieticians is significantly different from the means for psychology and nutrition majors, but the means for psychology and nutrition majors are not significantly different from each other. For this reason, statistically significant one-way ANOVA results are typically followed up with a series of **post hoc comparisons** of selected pairs of group means to determine which are different from which others.

One approach to post hoc comparisons would be to conduct a series of independent-samples *t* tests comparing each group mean to each of the other group means. But there is a problem with this approach. In general, if we conduct a *t* test when the null hypothesis is true, we have a 5% chance of mistakenly rejecting the null hypothesis (see Section 3 for more on such Type I errors). If we conduct several *t* tests when the null hypothesis is true, the chance of mistakenly rejecting *at least one* null hypothesis increases with each test we conduct. Thus researchers do not usually make post hoc comparisons using standard *t* tests because there is too great a chance that they will mistakenly reject at least one null hypothesis. Instead, they use one of several modified *t* test procedures—among them the Bonferonni procedure, Fisher's least significant difference (LSD) test, and Tukey's honestly significant difference (HSD) test. The details of these approaches are beyond the scope of this book, but it is important to understand their purpose. It is to keep the risk of mistakenly rejecting a true null hypothesis to an acceptable level (close to 5%).

## Repeated-Measures ANOVA

**repeated-measures ANOVA**

A null hypothesis test used to compare means for one sample at more than two times or under more than two conditions in a within-subjects design.

Recall that the one-way ANOVA is appropriate for between-subjects designs in which the means being compared come from separate groups of participants. It is not appropriate for within-subjects designs in which the means being compared come from the same participants tested under different conditions or at different times. This requires a slightly different approach, called the **repeated-measures ANOVA**. The basics of the repeated-measures ANOVA are the same as for the one-way ANOVA. The main difference is that measuring the dependent variable multiple times for each participant allows for a more refined measure of $MS_W$. Imagine, for example, that the dependent variable in a study is a measure of reaction time. Some participants will be faster or slower than others because of stable individual differences in their nervous systems, muscles, and other factors. In a between-subjects design, these stable individual differences would simply add to the variability within the groups and increase the value of $MS_W$. In a within-subjects design, however, these stable individual differences can be measured and subtracted from the value of $MS_W$. This lower value of $MS_W$ means a higher value of $F$ and a more sensitive test.

## Factorial ANOVA

**factorial ANOVA**

A null hypothesis test used to test both main effects and interactions in a factorial design.

When more than one independent variable is included in a factorial design, the appropriate approach is the **factorial ANOVA**. Again, the basics of the factorial ANOVA are the same as for the one-way and repeated-measures ANOVAs. The main difference is that it produces an $F$ ratio and $p$ value for each main effect and for each interaction. Returning to our calorie estimation example, imagine that the health psychologist tests the effect of participant major (psychology vs. nutrition) and food type (cookie vs. hamburger) in a factorial design. A factorial ANOVA would produce separate $F$ ratios and $p$ values for the main effect of major, the main effect of food type, and the interaction between major and food. Appropriate modifications must be made depending on whether the design is between subjects, within subjects, or mixed.

# Testing Pearson's $r$

For relationships between quantitative variables, where Pearson's $r$ is used to describe the strength of those relationships, the appropriate null hypothesis test is a test of Pearson's $r$. The basic logic is exactly the same as for other null hypothesis tests. In this case, the null hypothesis is that there is no relationship in the population. We can use the Greek lowercase rho ($\rho$) to represent the relevant parameter: $\rho = 0$. The alternative hypothesis is that there is a relationship in the population: $\rho \neq 0$. As with the $t$ test, this test can be two-tailed if the researcher has no expectation about the direction of the relationship or one-tailed if the researcher expects the relationship to go in a particular direction.

It is possible to use Pearson's $r$ for the sample to compute a $t$ score with $N - 2$ degrees of freedom and then to proceed as for a $t$ test. However, because of the way it is computed, Pearson's $r$ can also be treated as its own test statistic. Statistical software such as SPSS generally computes Pearson's $r$ and provides the associated $p$ value. If you have already computed Pearson's r and just need the $p$ value, you can enter your value of $r$ and your sample size in one of the online $p$ value calculators. As always, if the $p$ value is less than .05, we reject the null hypothesis and conclude that there is a relationship between the variables in the population. If the $p$ value is greater than .05, we fail to reject the null hypothesis and conclude that there is no relationship in the population.

## Example Test of Pearson's $r$

Imagine that the health psychologist is interested in the correlation between people's calorie estimates and their weight. He has no expectation about the direction of the relationship, so he decides to conduct a two-tailed test. He computes the correlation for a sample of 22 college students and finds that Pearson's $r$ is -.21. The statistical software he uses tells him that the $p$ value is .348. It is greater than .05, so he fails to reject the null hypothesis and concludes that there is no relationship between people's calorie estimates and their weight.

## Key Takeaways

- To compare two means, the most common null hypothesis test is the $t$ test. The one-sample $t$ test is used for comparing one sample mean with a hypothetical population mean of interest, the dependent-samples $t$ test is used to compare two means in a within-subjects design, and the independent-samples $t$ test is used to compare two means in a between-subjects design.

- To compare more than two means, the most common null hypothesis test is the analysis of variance (ANOVA). The one-way ANOVA is used for between-subjects designs with one independent variable, the repeated-measures ANOVA is used for within-subjects designs, and the factorial ANOVA is used for factorial designs.

- A null hypothesis test of Pearson's $r$ is used to compare a sample value of Pearson's $r$ with a hypothetical population value of 0.

## Exercises

1. Practice: Use one of the online tools, Excel, or SPSS to reproduce the one-sample *t* test, dependent-samples *t* test, independent-samples *t* test, and one-way ANOVA for the four sets of calorie estimation data presented in this section.

2. Practice: A sample of 25 college students rated their friendliness on a scale of 1 (*Much Lower Than Average*) to 7 (*Much Higher Than Average*). Their mean rating was 5.30 with a standard deviation of 1.50. Conduct a one-sample *t* test comparing their mean rating with a hypothetical mean rating of 4 (*Average*). The question is whether college students have a tendency to rate themselves as friendlier than average.

3. Practice: Use the online tools in this section to decide whether each of the following Pearson's *r* values is statistically significant for both a one-tailed and a two-tailed test. (a) The correlation between height and IQ is +.13 in a sample of 35. (b) For a sample of 88 college students, the correlation between how disgusted they felt and the harshness of their moral judgments was +.23. (c) The correlation between the number of daily hassles and positive mood is −.43 for a sample of 30 middle-aged adults.

# 13.3 Additional Considerations

## Learning Objectives

1. Define Type I and Type II errors, explain why they occur, and identify some steps that can be taken to minimize their likelihood.

2. Define statistical power, explain its role in the planning of new studies, and use online tools to compute the statistical power of simple research designs.

3. List some criticisms of conventional null hypothesis testing, along with some ways of dealing with these criticisms.

In this section, we consider a few other issues related to null hypothesis testing, including some that are useful in planning studies and interpreting results. We even consider some long-standing criticisms of null hypothesis testing, along with some steps that researchers in psychology have taken to address them.

## Errors in Null Hypothesis Testing

In null hypothesis testing, the researcher tries to draw a reasonable conclusion about the population based on the sample. Unfortunately, this conclusion is not guaranteed to be correct. This is illustrated by Table 13.3. The rows of this table represent the two possible decisions that we can make in null hypothesis testing: to reject or retain the null hypothesis. The columns represent the two possible states of the world: The null hypothesis is false or it is true. The four cells of the table, then, represent the four distinct outcomes of a null hypothesis test. Two of the outcomes—rejecting the null hypothesis when it is false and retaining it when it is true—are correct decisions. The other two—rejecting the null hypothesis when it is true and retaining it when it is false—are errors.

**TABLE 13.3** Two Types of Correct Decisions and Two Types of Errors in Null Hypothesis Testing

|  | True state of the world | |
|---|---|---|
| Decision | $H_0$ False | $H_0$ True |
| Reject $H_0$ | Correct decision | Type 1 Error |
| Fail to reject $H_0$ | Type II error | Correct decision |

Rejecting the null hypothesis when it is true is called a **Type I error**. This means that we have concluded that there is a relationship in the population when in fact there is not. Type I errors occur because even when there is no relationship in the population, sampling error alone will occasionally produce an extreme result. In fact, when the null hypothesis is true and $\alpha$ is .05, we will mistakenly reject the null hypothesis 5% of the time. (This is why $\alpha$ is sometimes referred to as the "Type I error rate.") Retaining the null hypothesis when it is false is called a **Type II error**. This means that we have concluded that there is no relationship in the population when in fact there is. In practice, Type II errors occur primarily because the research design lacks adequate statistical power to detect the relationship (e.g., the sample is too small). We will have more to say about statistical power shortly.

In principle, it is possible to reduce the chance of a Type I error by setting $\alpha$ to something less than .05. Setting it to .01, for example, would mean that if the null hypothesis is true, then there is only a 1% chance of mistakenly rejecting it. But making it harder to reject true null hypotheses also makes it harder to reject false ones and therefore increases the chance of a Type II error. Similarly, it is possible to reduce the chance of a Type II error by setting $\alpha$ to something greater than .05 (e.g., .10). But making it easier to reject false null hypotheses also makes it easier to reject true ones and therefore increases the chance of a Type I error. This provides some insight into why the convention is to set $\alpha$ to .05. There is some agreement among researchers that this keeps the rates of both Type I and Type II errors at acceptable levels.

The possibility of committing Type I and Type II errors has several important implications for interpreting the results of our own and others' research. One is that we should be cautious about interpreting the results of any individual study because there is a chance that it reflects a Type I or Type II error. This is why researchers consider it important to replicate their studies. Each time researchers replicate a study and find a similar result, they rightly become more confident that the result represents a real phenomenon and not just a Type I or Type II error.

**Type I error**

In null hypothesis testing, rejecting the null hypothesis when it is true.

**Type II error**

In null hypothesis testing, failing to reject the null hypothesis when it is false.

# Statistical Power

The **statistical power** of a research design is the probability of rejecting the null hypothesis given the sample size and expected relationship strength. For example, the statistical power of a study with 50 participants and an expected Pearson's $r$ of +.30 in the population is .59. That is, there is a 59% chance of rejecting the null hypothesis if indeed the population correlation is +.30. Statistical power is the complement of the probability of committing a Type II error. So in this example, the probability of committing a Type II error would be 1 − .59 = .41. Clearly, researchers should be interested in the power of their research designs if they want to avoid making Type II errors. In particular, they should make sure their research design has adequate power before collecting data. A common guideline is that a power of .80 is adequate. This means that there is an 80% chance of rejecting the null hypothesis for the expected relationship strength.

The topic of how to compute power for various research designs and null hypothesis tests is beyond the scope of this book. However, there are online tools that allow you to do this by entering your sample size, expected relationship strength, and $\alpha$ level for various hypothesis tests (see "Computing Power Online"). In addition, Table 13.4 shows the sample size needed to achieve power

**statistical power**

The probability of rejecting the null hypothesis for a given sample size and expected relationship strength.

of .80 for weak, medium, and strong relationships for a two-tailed independent-samples *t* test and for a two-tailed test of Pearson's *r*. Notice that this table amplifies the point made earlier about relationship strength, sample size, and statistical significance. In particular, weak relationships require very large samples to provide adequate statistical power.

**TABLE 13.4** Sample Sizes Needed to Achieve Statistical Power of .80 for Different Expected Relationship Strengths for an Independent-Samples *t* Test and a Test of Pearson's *r*

| Null Hypothesis Test | | |
| --- | --- | --- |
| Relationship Strength | Independent-Samples *t* Test | Test of Pearson's *r* |
| Strong ($d = .80$, $r = .50$) | 52 | 28 |
| Medium ($d = .50$, $r = .30$) | 128 | 84 |
| Weak ($d = .20$, $r = .10$) | 788 | 782 |

What should you do if you discover that your research design does not have adequate power? Imagine, for example, that you are conducting a between-subjects experiment with 20 participants in each of two conditions and that you expect a medium difference ($d = .50$) in the population. The statistical power of this design is only .34. That is, even if there is a medium difference in the population, there is only about a one in three chance of rejecting the null hypothesis and about a two in three chance of committing a Type II error. Given the time and effort involved in conducting the study, this probably seems like an unacceptably low chance of rejecting the null hypothesis and an unacceptably high chance of committing a Type II error.

Given that statistical power depends primarily on relationship strength and sample size, there are essentially two steps you can take to increase statistical power: increase the strength of the relationship or increase the sample size. Increasing the strength of the relationship can sometimes be accomplished by using a stronger manipulation or by more carefully controlling extraneous variables to reduce the amount of noise in the data (e.g., by using a within-subjects design rather than a between-subjects design). The usual strategy, however, is to increase the sample size. For any expected relationship strength, there will always be some sample large enough to achieve adequate power.

### Computing Power Online

The following links are to tools that allow you to compute statistical power for various research designs and null hypothesis tests by entering information about the expected relationship strength, the sample size, and the α level. They also allow you to compute the sample size necessary to achieve your desired level of power (e.g., .80). The first is an online tool. The second is a free downloadable program called G*Power.

- Rollin Brant's Sample Size / Power Calculator: https://www.stat.ubc.ca/~rollin/stats/ssize/
- G*Power: http://gpower.hhu.de/

# Problems With Null Hypothesis Testing, and Some Solutions

Again, null hypothesis testing is the most common approach to inferential statistics in psychology. It is not without its critics, however. In fact, in recent years the criticisms have become so prominent that the American Psychological Association (APA) convened a task force to make recommendations about how to deal with them (Wilkinson & Task Force on Statistical Inference, 1999).[5] In this section, we consider some of the criticisms and some of the recommendations.

## Criticisms of Null Hypothesis Testing

Some criticisms of null hypothesis testing focus on researchers' misunderstanding of it. We have already seen, for example, that the $p$ value is widely misinterpreted as the probability that the null hypothesis is true. (Recall that it is really the probability of the sample result *if* the null hypothesis were true.) A closely related misinterpretation is that $1 - p$ is the probability of replicating a statistically significant result. In one study, 60% of a sample of professional researchers thought that a $p$ value of .01—for an independent-samples $t$ test with 20 participants in each group—meant there was a 99% chance of replicating the statistically significant result (Oakes, 1986).[6] Our earlier discussion of power should make it clear that this is too optimistic. As Table 13.3 shows, even if there were a large difference between means in the population, it would require 26 participants per group to achieve a power of .80. And the program G*Power shows that it would require 59 participants per group to achieve a power of .99.

Another set of criticisms focuses on the logic of null hypothesis testing. To many, the strict convention of rejecting the null hypothesis when $p$ is less than .05 and failing to reject it when $p$ is greater than .05 makes little sense. This criticism does not have to do with the specific value of .05 but with the idea that there should be any rigid dividing line between results that are considered statistically significant and results that are not. Imagine two studies on the same statistical relationship with similar sample sizes. One has a $p$ value of .04 and the other a $p$ value of .06. Although the two studies have produced essentially the same result, the former is likely to be considered interesting and worthy of publication and the latter simply not significant. This convention is likely to prevent perfectly good research from being published.

Yet another set of criticisms focus on the idea that null hypothesis testing—even when understood and carried out correctly—is simply not very informative. Recall that the null hypothesis says there is no relationship between variables in the population (e.g., Cohen's $d$ or Pearson's $r$ is precisely 0). So to reject the null hypothesis is simply to say that there is *some* nonzero relationship in the population. But this is not really saying very much. Imagine if the discipline of chemistry could tell us only that there is *some* relationship between the temperature of a gas and its volume—as opposed to providing a precise equation to describe that relationship. Some critics even argue that the relationship between two variables in the population is never precisely 0 if it is carried out to enough decimal places. In other words, the null hypothesis is never literally true. So rejecting it does not tell us anything we did not already know!

To be fair, many researchers have come to the defense of null hypothesis testing. One of them, Robert Abelson, has argued that when it is correctly understood and carried out, null hypothesis testing does serve an important purpose (Abelson, 1995).[7] Especially when dealing with new phenomena, it gives researchers a principled way to convince others that their results should not be dismissed as mere chance occurrences.

## What to Do?

Even those who defend null hypothesis testing recognize many of the problems with it. But what should be done? Some suggestions now appear in the *Publication Manual*. One is that each null hypothesis test should be accompanied by an effect size measure such as Cohen's $d$ or Pearson's $r$. By doing so, the researcher provides an estimate of how strong the relationship in the population is—not just whether there is one or not. (Remember that the $p$ value cannot substitute as a measure of relationship strength because it also depends on the sample size. Even a very weak result can be statistically significant if the sample is large enough.)

**confidence interval**

A range of values computed in such a way that for some specified percentage of the time (usually 95%) the population parameter of interest will lie within that range.

Another suggestion is to use confidence intervals rather than null hypothesis tests. A **confidence interval** around a statistic is a range of values that is computed in such a way that for some percentage of the time (usually 95%) the population parameter will lie within that range. For example, a sample of 20 college students might have a mean calorie estimate for a chocolate chip cookie of 200 with a 95% confidence interval of 160 to 240. In other words, there is a very good chance that the mean calorie estimate for the population of college students lies between 160 and 240. Advocates of confidence intervals argue that they are much easier to interpret than null hypothesis tests. Another advantage of confidence intervals is that they provide the information necessary to do null hypothesis tests should anyone want to. In this example, the sample mean of 200 is significantly different at the .05 level from any hypothetical population mean that lies outside the confidence interval. So the confidence interval of 160 to 240 tells us that the sample mean is statistically significantly different from any hypothetical population mean that is outside this range.

**Bayesian statistics**

An alternative approach to inferential statistics in which the researcher specifies the probability that the null hypothesis and important alternative hypotheses are true before conducting a study, conducts the study, and then computes revised probabilities based on the data.

Finally, there are more radical solutions to the problems of null hypothesis testing that involve using very different approaches to inferential statistics. **Bayesian statistics**, for example, is an approach in which the researcher specifies the probability that the null hypothesis and any important alternative hypotheses are true before conducting the study. The researcher conducts the study and then updates the probabilities based on the data. It is too early to say whether this approach will become common in psychological research. For now, null hypothesis testing—supported by effect size measures and confidence intervals—remains the dominant approach.

## Key Takeaways

- The decision to reject or retain the null hypothesis is not guaranteed to be correct. A Type I error occurs when one rejects the null hypothesis when it is true. A Type II error occurs when one fails to reject the null hypothesis when it is false.
- The statistical power of a research design is the probability of rejecting the null hypothesis given the expected relationship strength in the population and the sample size. Researchers should make sure that their studies have adequate statistical power before conducting them.
- Null hypothesis testing has been criticized on the grounds that researchers misunderstand it, that it is illogical, and that it is uninformative. Others argue that it serves an important purpose—especially when used with effect size measures, confidence intervals, and other techniques. It remains the dominant approach to inferential statistics in psychology.

## Exercises

1. Discussion: A researcher compares the effectiveness of two forms of psychotherapy for social phobia using an independent-samples $t$ test.
    a. Explain what it would mean for the researcher to commit a Type I error.
    b. Explain what it would mean for the researcher to commit a Type II error.
2. Discussion: Imagine that you conduct a $t$ test and the $p$ value is .02. How could you explain what this $p$ value means to someone who is not already familiar with null hypothesis testing? Be sure to avoid the common misinterpretations of the $p$ value.

# Endnotes

1. Mehl, M. R., Vazire, S., Ramirez-Esparza, N., Slatcher, R. B., & Pennebaker, J. W. (2007). Are women really more talkative than men? *Science, 317*, 82.

2. Kanner, A. D., Coyne, J. C., Schaefer, C., & Lazarus, R. S. (1981). Comparison of two modes of stress measurement: Daily hassles and uplifts versus major life events. *Journal of Behavioral Medicine, 4*, 1–39.

3. Cohen, J. (1994). The world is round: $p < .05$. *American Psychologist, 49*, 997–1003.

4. Hyde, J. S. (2007). New directions in the study of gender similarities and differences. *Current Directions in Psychological Science, 16*, 259–263.

5. Wilkinson, L., & Task Force on Statistical Inference. (1999). Statistical methods in psychology journals: Guidelines and explanations. *American Psychologist, 54*, 594–604.

6. Oakes, M. (1986). *Statistical inference: A commentary for the social and behavioral sciences.* Chichester, UK: Wiley.

7. Abelson, R. P. (1995). *Statistics as principled argument.* Mahwah, NJ: Erlbaum.

# CHAPTER 14
# The Big Picture

> *Do not interpret a single study's results as having importance independent of the effects reported elsewhere in the relevant literature. The thinking presented in a single study may turn the movement of the literature, but the results in a single study are important primarily as one contribution to a mosaic of study effects. (Wilkinson & APA Task Force on Statistical Inference, 1999, p. 602).*[1]

As you probably know, a mosaic is a piece of artwork that consists of many tiles or bits of glass that fit together to form a larger pattern. The quotation above makes the point that individual studies, like the individual tiles in a mosaic, can be difficult to interpret on their own. We have to look at many of them all together to see the larger pattern.

In this chapter, we start by considering several reasons to be cautious when interpreting the results of individual studies. We then look at meta-analysis, which is a systematic approach to integrating the results of multiple studies to see the larger pattern. Along the way, we address some criticisms of the way psychological research has been traditionally conducted and some important questions about its reliability. We end with a discussion of several ways that researchers in psychology are working collectively to improve their research practices to produce more reliable results and make better scientific progress.

**FIGURE 14.1** A Colorful Mosaic
Like the individual tiles in a mosaic, individual research studies are meaningful only when we see how they fit together into a larger pattern.

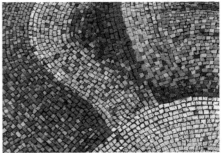

Source: © Shutterstock, Inc.

# 14.1 Why Individual Studies Can Be Misleading

## Learning Objectives

1. List several reasons that published research results can be misleading or even wrong.
2. Explain publication bias and its implications for interpreting published research.
3. Explain why some people say the field of psychology is experiencing a "replication crisis."

Researchers Travis Carter, Melissa Ferguson, and Ran Hassin were interested in the idea that simple exposure to the American flag might have an effect on Americans' political beliefs (Carter, Ferguson, & Hassin, 2011).[2] They started by showing people photographs of buildings and asked them to estimate the time of day the photographs were taken. In one condition, some of the photographs included an American flag. In another condition, there were no flags. They then had participants complete a self-report measure of their political beliefs. The main result—which reinforced something they had found in an earlier study—was that participants exposed to the American flag expressed more conservative political beliefs, and this difference was statistically significant. The researchers suggested that this occurs because the American flag is associated more with the conservative Republican party than the liberal Democratic party and therefore automatically activates (or "primes") conservative ideas in people's minds. According to all the standards presented in this book, this appears to be a well-conducted study, an extremely interesting empirical result, and a plausible theory to account for that result. Furthermore, it was published in a respected (and highly selective) professional journal: *Psychological Science*. The problem, however, is that the conclusion was wrong. Subsequent research strongly suggests that there is *no* flag priming effect.

In this section, we consider several reasons that the results of individual studies can be misleading or even wrong. We also consider how often misleading or wrong results make their way into the published research literature.

## Type I and Type II Errors

Recall that researchers generally use null hypothesis testing to decide whether the relationship in their sample reflects a relationship in the population (the result is "statistically significant") or whether it occurred by chance (the result is "not statistically significant"). Recall also that this decision is a kind of educated guess based on the strength of the sample relationship and the size of the sample. This means that no matter which decision the researchers make, it could be wrong. A Type I error is when researchers decide a result is statistically significant when there is actually *no* relationship in the population. (This is what appears to have happened in the flag priming study.) A Type II error occurs when researchers decide a result is not statistically significant when there actually *is* a relationship in the population. (See Chapter 13 "Inferential Statistics" for more details.) The point here is that any individual research result can be wrong even when the researchers have done everything right.

## Publication Bias and the File Drawer Problem

**publication bias**

A bias in favor of publishing statistically significant results over statistically nonsignificant results.

When Type I errors occur, their negative effect can be amplified by **publication bias**. This refers to a bias among researchers and journal editors in favor of publishing statistically significant results and against publishing nonsignificant results. Imagine, for example, an experiment on whether eating chocolate causes people to feel more romantic. Participants are randomly assigned to eat or not eat chocolate before completing a romantic feelings questionnaire. Imagine further that there turns out to be a statistically significant difference in romantic feelings, with participants in the chocolate condition scoring higher than participants in the control condition. The researchers are likely to consider the study a success and to submit it to a professional journal, where the journal editor and reviewers are likely to find the result interesting and worthy of publication. But imagine that instead there turns out to be no difference. In this case, the researchers are likely to consider the study a failure and decide not to submit it to a professional journal. Or if they do submit it, the journal editor and reviewers are likely to find the result uninteresting and not worthy of publication.

Publication bias is problematic from a purely logical standpoint. If a research question is worth asking, then the answer should be worth knowing regardless of what it turns out to be. But publication bias also leads to the **file drawer problem** (Rosenthal, 1979).[3] While statistically significant results are published, statistically nonsignificant results are stashed away in researchers' file drawers (or nowadays, in folders on their hard drives) where no one but the original researchers know about them. Thus when you read a published study with a statistically significant result, you have no idea how many similar studies have been conducted with nonsignificant results. Imagine, for example, that there is one published study in which chocolate eaters scored higher in romantic feelings than a control group. But at the same time there are 19 unpublished studies (stashed away in researchers' file drawers) in which there was no difference. The problem is that *all* of the studies together strongly suggest that there is no "chocolate effect" on people's romantic feelings, but most researchers will only know about the one published study that suggests that there is.

# Researcher Degrees of Freedom

It has also become clear in recent years that the problems of Type I errors and publication bias are compounded by several fairly common research practices. Researcher Joseph Simmons and his colleagues[4] have discussed what they call **researcher degrees of freedom**. These are certain decisions that researchers make during the research process, including when to stop collecting data, whether to exclude any participants from the analyses (and which ones), which analyses to do, and which dependent variables and conditions to report. The idea is that researchers are generally free to try out many different possibilities in their search for statistically significant results. Researchers Stephen Lindsay and colleagues (Lindsay, Simons, & Lilienfeld, 2016)[5] give a good sense of this.

> *Imagine you conduct a study testing whether symmetrical faces are more attractive than asymmetrical ones. Suppose that you find no overall difference in attractiveness, so you test whether the effect differed as a function of the gender of the participant and the gender of the face. Looking at the means, you see that men found symmetry attractive for faces of both genders, whereas women found symmetry attractive in women's faces but asymmetry attractive in men's faces. That interesting interaction pattern was not statistically significant. Examining the data more closely, though, you notice that some faces were rated as maximally attractive by almost everyone, so you drop those faces from the analysis because they might obscure a real effect. Moreover, some participants were older than the rest and their ratings don't seem to fit the pattern, so you exclude their data, too. Now the interaction becomes statistically significant. "Eureka!" you cry.*

This example illustrates two important researcher degrees of freedom: which data to exclude and which analyses to do. Another one is deciding when to stop collecting data. Some researchers look at their data periodically while they are testing participants. If the result is not statistically significant they test a few more, look again, and repeat. If at some point they look at their data and the result *is* statistically significant, they immediately stop testing participants.

Yet another researcher degree of freedom is including multiple dependent variables in a study but "dropping" some of them when reporting the results. Imagine, for example, that we gave participants a romantic feelings questionnaire and also asked them to report the number of dates they would like to go on in the next month and to rate how much they enjoy love songs. If the result turned out to be statistically significant only for the number of dates, we might be tempted to write a research report that features that dependent variable but does not mention the other two. A similar researcher degree of freedom is when researchers include multiple conditions in a study but drop some of them when reporting the results.

The problem with researcher degrees of freedom is that if you analyze any set of data in enough different ways, you are very likely to find *some* result that is statistically significant just by chance (a Type I error). In fact, Simmons and his colleagues showed that researchers who take advantage of all these researcher degrees of freedom in a relatively simple study can increase their chance of finding a statistically significant result to more than 60%. This is when there are *no* statistical relationships among the variables studied in the population.

**researcher degrees of freedom**

Decisions that researchers can make during the research process that increase the chances of making a Type I error. These include when to stop collecting data, whether to exclude any participants from the analyses, which analyses to do, and which dependent variables and conditions to report.

### Lucky Shots

Imagine your friend has posted an impressive video of himself making a basketball free throw with his back to the basket. He tosses the ball up over his head and *swish!* Although this seems impressive, what would you think if you learned that he took video of himself attempting 99 shots before one of them finally went in, and then he edited and posted the video of that *one* shot.

**FIGURE 14.2**
Reporting only research results that "worked" is like posting a video of the one time in 100 you made a trick basketball shot.

Source: © Shutterstock, Inc.

This is a bit like a researcher conducting a complex study, looking at many different results from that study (e.g., for different dependent variables or different comparisons between conditions), and then only reporting the one that turned out to be statistically significant.

In both cases, your first impression is that you are seeing something real and reliable. But once you know about the many attempts it took to achieve that outcome, it looks like nothing more than a lucky shot.

It is important to emphasize that taking advantage of researcher degrees of freedom to find statistically significant results (which has also come to be called "*p*-hacking") does not necessarily imply bad intent on the part of researchers. On the contrary, this approach has been fairly common and accepted for decades. It is only recently that researchers have come to understand how large an influence it can have on Type I error rates.

## The "Replication Crisis"

The problems discussed in this section have prompted many researchers to ask a fundamental question. To what extent do the results reported in the research literature reflect real psychological phenomena as opposed to Type I errors? Certainly, to the extent that they reflect real psychological phenomena, other researchers should be able to replicate the studies and obtain the same results. But can they?

**replication crisis**

The idea that many results in psychology cannot be replicated and therefore do not reflect real psychological phenomena.

Consider one large and varied set of phenomena known as social priming effects. After being exposed to stimuli related to some social stereotype (e.g., of the elderly), people supposedly begin to think, feel, and act in ways that are consistent with the "primed" stereotype. The flag priming effect reported by Carter and colleagues is a good example. American flags are associated with political conservatives, so exposure to American flags supposedly causes people to express more conservative political views. Another famous example comes from the work of researchers John Bargh and colleagues (Bargh, Chen, & Burrows, 1996)[6]. College students who were exposed to words related to being elderly (e.g., retirement) walked more slowly down the hallway afterwards than college students exposed to other kinds of words. As it turns out, however, many of these published social priming results have been difficult or impossible for other researchers to replicate (Abbott, 2013)[7].

Some observers have even suggested that the field of psychological research is experiencing a full-blown **replication crisis**.

In response to this concern, many researchers have begun to address the issue of replicability directly. A group called the Open Science Collaboration (2015)[8] organized a large-scale *Reproducibility Project* (http://osf.io/ezcuj/). A team of 270 researchers conducted direct replications of a representative sample of 100 studies published in three professional journals during 2008. One finding was that only slightly more than a third of results were successfully replicated.

Another large-scale attempt to assess the replicability of psychological research was the Many Labs Replication Project (https://osf.io/wx7ck/). This large group of researchers replicated 13 classic and contemporary psychological studies in an online format with 36 different samples for each study (Klein et al., 2014).[9] In this case, 11 of the 13 results were successfully replicated. (One of the ones that was not successfully replicated was the flag priming study. The overall Cohen's *d* for that study was a minuscule 0.03.) One surprising outcome of this replication project was how variable the results for each study were across the different samples—even when they had used identical procedures. One of the studies, for example, looked at gender differences in implicit attitudes toward math. The original study had found a Cohen's *d* of about 1.00, with men having more positive attitudes than women. Although this study was successfully replicated with a mean Cohen's *d* of 0.53, the individual replication attempts had Cohen's *d* values ranging from essentially zero to greater than 1.00.

It seems clear from these initial attempts to assess the replicability of psychological research that many published research do, in fact, replicate. But many—perhaps the majority—do not. Regardless of whether this constitutes a "crisis," it is clearly a problem. We will discuss some proposed solutions to this problem in Section 14.3.

One final note is that all of the problems we have been discussing here—Type I errors, publication bias, the file drawer problem, researcher degrees of freedom, and replication failures—are not unique to psychology. They affect other fields as well, especially the biomedical sciences. In fact, one of the landmark articles about the extent of these problems was written by an epidemiologist and published in a medical journal, *PLOS Medicine*. Its title: *Why Most Published Research Findings are False* (Ioannidis, 2005).[10]

## Key Takeaways

- The results of any individual study do not necessarily reflect what is true in the population. A Type I error occurs when a sample result is statistically significant but there is no statistical relationship in the population. A Type II error is when a sample result is not statistically significant but there is a statistically relationship in the population.

- Publication bias refers to a bias toward publishing statistically significant results rather than nonsignificant results. This means that the published research literature probably contains a high proportion of Type I errors.

- Researcher degrees of freedom are decisions that researchers often make while conducting their study and analyzing their data. These include looking at the data before deciding to test more participants, excluding some of the data from analysis, and dropping dependent variables and conditions that did not "work." These practices also increase the Type I error rate, producing many "false positive" results.

- Some observers have commented that there is a "replication crisis" in psychology because many published research results have proved difficult or impossible to replicate.

## Exercises

1. Discussion: Imagine that you are a young researcher and have just found that 20 people who ate chocolate reported more romantic feelings on average than 20 people who did not eat chocolate. The $p$ value was .03.  What are the pros and cons of immediately submitting the study for publication versus first conducting a replication? Be sure to consider the pros and cons for you personally and the pros and cons for the scientific community.
2. Discussion: Based on the results of the Reproducibility Project and the Many Labs Replication Project, argue both for and against the idea that there is a replication "crisis" in psychological research.

# 14.2 Meta-Analysis

## Learning Objectives

1. Explain what meta-analysis is and why it is important.
2. Describe the steps in a basic meta-analysis.

Imagine that you are interested in existing research on sex differences in the personality trait of narcissism. The first study you look at shows a large and statistically significant difference, with the men scoring higher in narcissism than the women. Good. That makes sense. But then the second study you look at shows a smaller and nonsignificant difference. And in the third study the women actually scored slightly higher than the men! You could not be blamed for wanting to give up at this point. How can you possibly make sense of all these conflicting results?

One thing to keep in mind, though, is that this kind of variability in results is to be expected. One reason is that the different studies probably used different types of samples (e.g., students vs. non-students), different materials (e.g., alternative narcissism measures), and different procedures (e.g., in person vs. online). So some of the variability in results is probably related to these methodological differences. But another reason is that even when a study is repeated in exactly the same way, the results can still vary widely due to chance alone. This was one of the lessons of the Many Labs Replication Project.

Another thing to keep in mind is that trying to understand the results of research on gender differences in narcissism (or on any research question) by looking at individual studies one by one is a bit like trying to "see" a large mosaic by looking at the individual tiles one by one. You will not get a clear and accurate impression of the overall pattern. This is what meta-analysis is for.

### Sex Differences in Narcissism

The example of sex differences in narcissism is a good one in part because researcher Emily Grijalva and her colleagues recently conducted a meta-analysis of research on exactly this question.[11] They found 355 different studies (including 136 unpublished ones) with a total of 470,846 participants! Although there was considerable variability in the results of the individual studies, when they were all aggregated it became clear that on average men were slightly more narcissistic than women, with a mean Cohen's *d* of 0.26.

# Meta-Analysis Basics

**Meta-analysis** is a set of techniques for finding all the studies that address a particular research question and then combining the results of those studies statistically to see the overall pattern. Many of its basic techniques were introduced by researchers Mary Lee Smith and Gene Glass in their review of the effectiveness of psychotherapy in the late 1970s (Smith & Glass, 1977).[12] The literature at that time included hundreds of experiments in which people with psychological problems had been randomly assigned to a psychotherapy condition or to a control condition and their degree of improvement had been measured and compared. But, as with the narcissism example above, there was considerable variability in the results of these studies. Psychotherapy often seemed to work but sometimes it did not. And occasionally it seemed to hurt more than it helped. Other researchers had read and summarized this literature but their conclusions seemed to reveal their preexisting biases more than anything else. Pro-psychotherapy researchers tended to focus on the positive results and explain away the negative ones. Anti-psychotherapy researchers did the opposite. Smith and Glass realized that they needed a way to quantify the results of each study and then analyze those results statistically. When they did this, they found that the mean effect of psychotherapy across all the studies was strong and positive and that the variability among the studies was not much more than would be expected by chance.

The rationale for meta-analysis can be appreciated by analogy to "regular" statistical analysis. Imagine you measure the narcissism levels of 100 college students. To understand these data you would *not* look carefully at each individual's narcissism, speculate about what caused it to be high or low, and then try to combine the 100 scores (or to compare the men's and women's scores) in your head. There is no way you could do this thoroughly, accurately, and without bias. What you *would* do is analyze these scores statistically. You would compute the overall mean, compare the means for men and women, and so on. Now imagine instead that you have 100 studies, each of which compared men and women in terms of narcissism. Before the development of meta-analysis, a researcher reviewing this literature might have looked carefully at each study's result, speculated about what caused that result, and then tried to combine the 100 results in his or her head. But clearly this approach has the same shortcomings as it does when trying to understand the scores of the 100 college students; it is unlikely to be thorough, accurate, and without bias. A much better approach would be to analyze the study results statistically. Each study in this approach is like a "participant" and each study result (the size of the sex difference) is like the "score" for that participant. You would then use statistics to find the overall mean of these study results and to see how they relate to other characteristics of the studies (e.g., in-person studies vs. online studies). This is the essence of meta-analysis.

**meta-analysis**

A set of techniques for finding all the studies that address a particular research question and then combining the results of those studies statistically to see the overall pattern.

### Meta-Analysis Everywhere!

*Psychological Bulletin* is the premier journal for publishing review articles—articles that summarize all the research on a particular topic. Below are all the titles from two recent issues of this journal, and you can see that every single one involves a meta-analysis. You can also see that meta-analysis is being applied to an extremely wide range of research topics.

- *Automatic Imitation: A Meta-Analysis*
- *The Relation of Attachment Security Status to Effortful Self-Regulation: A Meta-Analysis*
- *The Meta-Analysis of Longitudinal Associations Between Substance Use and Interpersonal Attachment Security*
- *Emotion Fingerprints or Emotion Populations? A Meta-Analytic Investigation of Autonomic Features of Emotion Categories*
- *Is Bilingualism Associated with Enhanced Executive Functioning in Adults? A Meta-Analytic Review*
- *Normative Changes in Interests from Adolescence to Adulthood: A Meta-Analysis of Longitudinal Studies*

# Steps in a Meta-Analysis

Again, meta-analysis refers to a set of techniques for finding and statistically combining the results of research studies. This set of techniques is large and varied and undergoing continual refinement. At a very basic level, though, all meta-analyses involve the following steps.

1) *Identify the Research Question.* The meta-analyst starts by identifying the research question of interest. This question needs to be fairly specific and expressed in terms of a relationship between variables. It could be about a difference between groups (e.g., Do people who receive psychotherapy improve more than people who do not receive psychotherapy?). Or it could be about a correlation between quantitative variables (e.g., Are stress and physical symptoms positively correlated)?

2) *Find All the Research that Addresses that Question.* The meta-analyst now finds as much research as possible that addresses that question. Published research is generally easy to find using online databases. But remember that published research tends to be biased toward stronger and statistically significant results, so the meta-analyst must also find as much unpublished research as possible. To do this, it is typical for the meta-analyst to contact other researchers in the field, post messages to relevant online forums, and search through conference programs.

3) *Find or Compute the Effect Size in Each Study* – The meta-analyst then reduces each study's results to a single effect size measure—usually Cohen's *d* for a question about a difference between groups or Pearson's *r* for a question about a correlation between quantitative variables. This is easy if the authors of the original study provided this information in their article. But many times the original authors did not provide effect sizes so that the meta-analyst must compute or infer them based on information that was, in fact, provided.

4) *Combine All the Effect Sizes into a Single Overall Effect Size.* The meta-analyst then computes the mean of all the effect sizes as an estimate of the overall effect size in the population. In general, the individual effect sizes are weighted by the size of the sample because larger samples tend to produce more accurate results than smaller samples. So, for example, a study with 500 participants would contribute more to the overall mean effect size than a study with 50 participants.

5) *Test Potential Moderators of the Effect Size.* In a meta-analysis, a moderator is a study characteristic related to the effect size. For example, the meta-analyst can check to see whether published studies produced stronger effects than unpublished studies (as a way of testing for publication

bias) or whether in-person studies produced stronger effects than online studies. In Smith and Glass's meta-analysis, some of the different studies involved several different types of psychotherapy. Thus the type of psychotherapy was a potential moderator of the effect. Surprisingly, when Smith and Glass compared the effect sizes across the different types of psychotherapy, they found essentially no difference!

# Meta-Analysis Example

To get a better sense of how meta-analysis works, consider the following example. Researchers Robert Lull and Brad Bushman were interested in the effect of violent media content on people's memory for advertising (Lull & Bushman, 2014). Essentially, they wanted to know whether violence in a television show affects people's memory for products that are advertised during that show. (This was actually just one part of a larger meta-analysis on the effects of both sexual and violent content on product memory, attitudes, and purchasing intentions. For simplicity, though, we focus just on the effect of violence on product memory.) A researcher casually reading through the literature on this question would find many different measures and operational definitions. Furthermore, some of the studies show significant positive effects, some null effects, and some negative effects.

But Lull and Bushman decided to step back and try to see the big picture by doing a meta-analysis. They began by systematically searching PsycINFO and other databases for research that included the keywords *violence, aggression, advertising, commercials, memory, recall,* and so on. They also searched the reference lists of the articles they found for citations to work that had not been published in a professional journal, including unpublished studies, conference presentations, and graduate student theses and dissertations. Next they read the titles and abstracts of all the articles to identify studies that met the following criteria. 1) There was an experimental condition in which participants were exposed to violent media content. 2) There was a control condition in which participants were exposed to non-violent media content. 3) Participants were also exposed to an advertisement and their memory for the brand of the product was measured.

Lull and Bushman found a total of 24 relevant references that included 31 distinct studies (with 3,907 participants) that met their criteria. They then found Cohen's $d$ for each of these 31 studies. In computing Cohen's $d$, they always subtracted the mean memory score for the control condition from the mean memory score for the violent media condition so that positive values meant that memory was better in the violent media condition and negative values meant that memory was worse in the violent media condition. What they found were Cohen's $d$ values ranging from a low of -1.66 (an extremely strong negative effect of violent media) to a high of +0.52 (a moderate positive effect of violent media). At first, this might seem inconclusive because, again, there are both negative and positive effects of violence on product memory. But now look at Figure 14.3, which shows the strength of all 31 effects. Here we see that only five of them are positive and four of those are quite close to zero. The vast majority are negative and the overall mean is -0.39. In other words, across these 31 studies and 3,907 participants—using a variety of violent media, product advertisements, and memory measures—there was a moderate tendency for people exposed to violent media to have poorer memory for the advertised products. The big picture comes into focus.

**FIGURE 14.3** Results of a Meta-Analysis on the Effect of Violent Media on Memory for Advertising

Effect sizes for 31 studies on the effect of violent media content on memory for advertising. The mean Cohen's *d* value (represented by the asterisk) is -0.39.

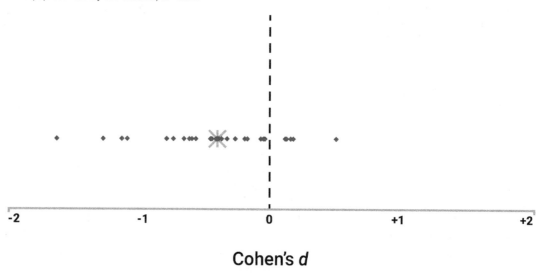

Cohen's *d*

Data based on Lull and Bushman (2014).

# Strengths and Weaknesses of Meta-Analysis

When a meta-analysis is well conceived and well executed, it can often provide a fairly definitive answer to the research question. The meta-analysis on sex differences in narcissism falls into this category. It was based on an extremely large number of studies—including a large number of unpublished ones—and nearly half a million participants. And the studies themselves used measures of narcissism that have been shown to be valid and reliable. Thus the conclusion that men are slightly higher in narcissism than women is one that we can be very confident about. And any new study that produces a different result (e.g., no sex difference) must be interpreted in the context of this overwhelming evidence to the contrary.

Meta-analysis can also identify areas that need further study. It can show, for example, that all the research on a particular question comes exclusively from studies on college students in the United States—suggesting that the question should be investigated with other kinds of samples in other other places.

Like all research methods, however, meta-analysis does have limitations that it is important to be aware of. First, it can only be done reliably when a sufficient number of primary studies have already been conducted. So it cannot be applied to brand new areas of research. Second, it does not necessarily get around the problem of publication bias. Even an extensive search for unpublished research may fail to turn up large numbers of studies that remain in researchers' file drawers. For this reason, the overall effect size from a meta-analysis might still be an overestimate. (There are, however, some ways to assess this possibility that are beyond the scope of this book.) Finally, if the studies that go into a meta-analysis are flawed in some consistent way (e.g., they use an unreliable measure), then of course the meta-analysis will reflect this same flaw.

## Key Takeaways

- Meta-analysis is a set of techniques for finding and statistically combining the results of all the research on a particular research question. It is a way to see the overall pattern in a large number of study results.
- The basic steps in a meta-analysis are identifying the research question, finding all the existing research that addresses that question (including unpublished research), extracting the effect size for each study, combining the effect sizes to find the overall effect size, and testing potential moderators of the effect size.
- A meta-analysis can be misleading if it is based on studies that all have the same flaw or if it based on a biased sample of studies. But a well conceptualized and well conducted meta-analysis probably comes as close as possible to providing the definitive answer to a research question.

## Exercise

1. Practice: Look up a published meta-analysis try to find the following information in it. A) The research question. B) The number of studies included in the meta-analysis and the total number of participants in those studies. C) The overall effect size across all the studies. D) Any statistically significant moderator variables.

# 14.3 Progress and the Promise of Open Science

## Learning Objectives

1. Explain what the open science movement is and list some of its goals.
2. Describe some important open science practices that are becoming more common in psychology.

When he was president of the American Psychological Association (APA), researcher Phillip Zimbardo (2004)[13] reminded us about many of the triumphs of psychological research, including reliable and valid psychological assessment, a better understanding of many psychological disorders and the development of effective treatments for them, insight into the power of positive reinforcement to change behavior, and an appreciation of the impact of psychological stress on many aspects of our daily lives. Today we could add several more items to Zimbardo's list, including improvements intraffic safety, computer design, police interview techniques, medical diagnosis, and public policydecision making.

At the same time, however, we have seen that there are some problems with the way psychological research has traditionally been conducted. The main issue is that the published research literature is biased toward novel and statistically significant results that are obtained in such a way that they have a good chance of being Type I errors. Even though such errors can be discovered by attempting to replicate those results, this rarely happens because there are few incentives for researchers to conduct replication studies. What can be done?

**open science**

A movement to make scientific practice more transparent to scientists and the general public. It includes practices such as preregistering studies, sharing raw data, and encouraging replications of previously published results.

**Open science** refers to a movement to make scientific practice more transparent to other scientists and to the general public. At the heart of this movement is the idea that researchers should share as much information as possible about their work—including their hypotheses, their research materials, their analyses, and even their raw data. Instead of reporting only the studies, conditions, dependent variables, and analyses that "worked," researchers should report *all* their studies, conditions, dependent variables, and analyses. They should also conduct more direct replications of their own and others' studies. The idea is that this kind of openness makes it easier for scientists to distinguish valid results from mere chance occurrences and therefore to converge more quickly on what is true.

Although the problems discussed in this chapter affect all the sciences, psychology has been on the leading edge of the reform movement. Psychologists Brian Nosek and Jeffrey Spies founded the nonprofit Center for Open Science (http://cos.io/) in 2013 to promote open practices throughout the sciences. Their Open Science Framework (http://osf.io/) is an online commons that provides numerous resources and tools to support scientists and scientific publishers in their efforts to be more open.

One change that has occurred as a result of this movement is that many journals have revised their standards for what researchers must report if their articles are to be published. *Psychological Science*, for example, now requires authors to justify their sample sizes, to reveal whether they added data after looking at the results, to explain how they decided to exclude data (and how much they excluded), and to report all dependent variables and conditions regardless of whether they "worked." The idea is that this kind of openness allows editors, reviewers, and readers to assess the results in light of all relevant information. Note also how this turns research practices that used to be common and even accepted (e.g., dropping dependent variables) into explicit violations of the journal's standards.

Another open science practice that is catching on is the **preregistration** of research studies before those studies have been conducted. To preregister a study, the researchers write a short description of it and provide details about exactly how they will conduct the study. They also list their hypotheses and exactly what data analyses they will do to test those hypotheses. Then they upload this information to one of several preregistration websites for this purpose. In psychology, the most common are AsPredicted (www.aspredicted.org) and the preregistration tool on the Open Science Framework (https://osf.io/registries/). This uploaded information is time stamped and cannot be changed. Note that this eliminates the problem of researcher degrees of freedom because the researchers have made all the important decisions *before* collecting the data. If the researchers submit their work for publication, they can provide a link to their preregistered description so that editors, reviewers, and eventually readers can verify that they have not engaged in *p*-hacking or other questionable research practices. Note that preregistration also helps combat the file drawer problem because there remains a permanent and publicly accessible record of the study even if the results turn out to be nonsignicant.

Some journals are taking preregistration a step further and making at least some publication decisions based entirely on preregistered descriptions. In other words, the journal editor and reviewers evaluate the research and decide whether or not to publish it before anyone knows the results. Publications that have been through this process are referred to as **preregistered reports**. The rationale for this approach is that if the researchers are asking a scientifically interesting and important question—and if the proposed methods are sound—then the results should be considered informative no matter what they turn out to be. This approach completely eliminates publication bias because it does not depend on whether the result was statistically significant.

In addition, some journals have begun setting aside some space specifically for replication studies. For example, the journal *Advances in Methods and Practices in Psychological Science* now encourages the submission of "registered replication reports," where several groups of researchers conduct their own replications of a published study based on a preregistered plan (much like in the Many Labs Replication Project). They then write a single article summarizing the results of all the replication attempts in the form of a meta-analysis.

## Open Science Badges

The Center for Open Science is a nonprofit organization that has led the way in promoting open science practices. (See their Open Science Framework at http://www.osf.io/.) One of these practices is the use of "badges"—icons that journals can use to indicate that a published article has met certain standards of openness. These include an *Open Data* badge (the data are publicly available), an *Open Materials* badge (the materials are openly available), and a *Preregistered* badge (the research was preregistered). Look for these badges in journals including the *Journal of Research in Personality*, *Law and Human Behavior*, *Psi Chi Journal of Psychological Research*, and *Psychological Science*.

**FIGURE 14.4**
Many journals now use badges like this one to indicate research that meets various standards of open science.

Source: Open Science Collaboration, 2018. "Badges to Acknowledge Open Practices." Open Science Framework. osf.io/tvyxz.

There is already evidence that the badges are having a positive impact on scientific practice. A study by Mallory Kidwell and her colleagues (2016) showed that the awarding of *Open Data* badges in the journal *Psychological Science* was followed by a dramatic increase in the number of articles that included open data.[14]

It seems clear that open science practices hold great promise for improving the quality of research in psychology and other fields. It remains to be seen, however, how widespread they will become.

## Key Takeaways

- Open science is a movement to make scientific practice more transparent to other scientists and the general public. It is a reaction to recent concerns about traditional scientific practices and the replicability of scientific results.
- Among the most common emerging open science practices are researchers preregistering their studies before conducting them, journals making publishing decisions based on the quality of the research question and method before the results are known (preregistered reports), and journals encouraging the submission of more replication studies.

## Exercises

1. Discussion: If you were a researcher, what concerns would you have about making your research materials and data publicly available online?

2. Discussion: If you were a journal editor, what percentage of your journal would you want to devote to studies of new research questions versus replications of previously published studies?

3. Practice: Go to AsPredicted (http://www.AsPredicted.org) and preregister a study that you are about to do. You can also click a box labeled "I am just trying things out" and preregister a fictional study to get a feel for the process.

# Endnotes

1. Wilkinson, L., & APA Task Force on Statistical Inference (1999). Statistical methods in psychology journals: Guidelines and explanations. *American Psychologist, 54*, 594-604.

2. Carter, T. J., Ferguson, M. J., & Hassin, R. R. (2011). A single exposure to the American flag shifts support toward Republicanism up to 8 months later. *Psychological Science, 22*, 1011-1018.

3. Rosenthal, R. (1979). The file drawer problem and tolerance for null results. *Psychological Bulletin, 86*, 638.

4. Simmons, J. P., Nelson, L. D., & Simonsohn, U. (2011). False-positive psychology: Undisclosed flexibility in data collection and analysis allows presenting anything as significant. *Psychological Science, 22*, 1359-1366.

5. Lindsay, D. S., Simons, D. J., & Lilienfeld, S. O. (2016). Preregistration 101. *APS Observer, 29*. Retrieved from http://www.psychologicalscience.org/observer/research-preregistration-101/.

6. Bargh, J. A., Chen, M., & Burrows, L. (1996). Automaticity of social behavior: Direct effects of trait construct and stereotype activation on action. *Journal of Personality and Social Psychology, 71*, 230-244.

7. Abbott, A. (2013). Disputed results a fresh blow for social psychology. *Nature, 497*, 16.

8. Open Science Collaboration (2015).

9. Klein, R. A., Ratliff, K. A., Vianello, M., Adams, R. B., Bahnik, S., Bernstein, M. J. ... Nosek, B. A. (2014). Investigating variation in replicability: A "Many Labs" replication project. *Social Psychology, 45*, 142-152.

10. Ioannidis, J. P. A. (2005). Why most published research findings are false. *PLOS Medicine, 2*, e124.

11. Grijalva, E., Newman, D. A., Tay, L., Donnellan, M. B., Harms, P. D., Robins, R. W., & Yan, T. (2015). Gender differences in narcissism: A meta-analytic review. *Psychological Bulletin, 141*, 261-310.

12. Smith, M. L., & Glass, G. V. (1977). Meta-analysis of psychotherapy outcome studies. *American Psychologist, 32*, 752-760.

13. Zimbardo, P. G. (2004). Does psychology make a significant difference in our lives? *American Psychologist, 59*, 339-351.

14. Kidwell, M. C., Lazarević, L. B., Baranski, E., Hardwicke, T. E., Piechowski, S., Falkenberg, L. S., ... & Errington, T. M. (2016). Badges to acknowledge open practices: a simple, low-cost, effective method for increasing transparency. *PLoS biology, 14*, e1002456.

# Index

CPSIA information can be obtained
at www.ICGtesting.com
Printed in the USA
LVHW061058100320
649504LV00007B/79